P9-DNH-736

# DOCUMENTS

## OF

## GESTALT

## PSYCHOLOGY

# DOCUMENTS
# OF
# GESTALT
# PSYCHOLOGY

EDITED BY

*Mary Henle*

UNIVERSITY OF CALIFORNIA PRESS
*Berkeley and Los Angeles : 1961*

University of California Press
Berkeley and Los Angeles
California
Cambridge University Press
London, England
© 1961 by
The Regents of the University of California
Library of Congress Catalog Card Number: 61-14554
Printed in the United States of America

*To Wolfgang Köhler*

# PREFACE

At the 1959 convention of the American Psychological Association, Wolfgang Köhler delivered a presidential address whose text serves as an introduction to the present volume. In his brief survey of "Gestalt Psychology Today," Professor Köhler, one of the founders of this movement, indicated certain differences in outlook and assumptions between Gestalt psychology and some other trends in American psychology. He also expressed confidence in the possibility of fruitful collaboration by representatives of the various approaches. Given this situation, it seems opportune to make available in a single volume a number of recent papers in which the principles and methods of Gestalt psychology are clearly expressed by a group of authors for whom this approach has been central.

The present volume is intended to supplement the fundamental texts of Gestalt psychology, for example, those by Köhler, Wertheimer, and Koffka. A forerunner of the present collection is *A Source Book of Gestalt Psychology,* edited by Willis D. Ellis, which contains abbreviated translations into English of a number of the early theoretical and experimental publications of Gestalt psychologists. The present book brings together more recent contributions by the founders of Gestalt psychology and by some of their immediate collaborators and students. With the exception of the essays by Wertheimer, which are not elsewhere easily accessible to the psychologist, most of these papers have been published since 1950. They thus illustrate the recent thinking and findings of the authors. They include work in the fields of social psychology, motivation, and art, in addition to new developments in the exploration of the cognitive processes, for which Gestalt psychology used to be best known.

The concepts of Gestalt psychology have been central for some workers in the field, have markedly influenced others, and have slightly tinged the work of hundreds more. Limitations of space have dictated the omission from the present volume of authors whose inclusion would have given a more rounded picture of the scope and influence of contemporary Gestalt psychology. Perhaps the most conspicuous omission is that of Kurt Lewin, whose work developed out of Gestalt psychology and whose approach and assumptions remained in many respects similar to those of Gestalt psychologists working in other fields. Lewin's recent papers are excluded because they have been collected elsewhere and are readily available in book form. For the same reason the work of Fritz Heider and of Lewin's students is not included.

In a sense this has become a volume of work from the New School for Social Research. As the reader will notice, all the senior authors whose work is included have had some connection with the New School, whose graduate psychology department was founded by Wertheimer in 1933 as part of the University in Exile. It must be mentioned, however, that the New School is presently the principal academic connection of only one of the authors, and that this volume by no means represents the varied points of view of all the psychologists at this institution. Still, the New School has in some sense provided a center for Gestalt psychology in America. This is, of course, not the first instance in the history of psychology in which one or a few universities have provided a home for a particular approach to our science.

This book was edited while the editor was a Fellow of the John Simon Guggenheim Memorial Foundation. It is a pleasure to call attention to an additional debt this book owes to the Foundation. Four of the studies in this collection were made while their authors were Guggenheim Fellows.

MARY HENLE

# CONTENTS

## PART IV.  SOCIAL PSYCHOLOGY AND MOTIVATION

## PART V.  PSYCHOLOGY OF EXPRESSION AND ART

*Wolfgang Köhler*

DARTMOUTH COLLEGE

# GESTALT

# PSYCHOLOGY

# TODAY

In 1949, the late Herbert Langfeld gave a lecture in Europe in which he described what appeared to him to be the major trends in American psychology. He also mentioned Gestalt psychology; but he added that the main observations, questions, and principles characteristic of this school had become part of every American psychologist's mental equipment. I was not so optimistic. And, in fact, the very next year attempts were made to explain the molar units in perception by processes which gradually connect neural elements. Soon afterwards, a theory of conditioning was developed, according to which more and more components of a stimulus object are gradually conditioned, and the course of the whole process can be explained in this fashion. Such theories may prove to be very useful, but one can hardly say that, at the time, their authors were greatly influenced by Gestalt psychology. It is for this and similar reasons that a new discussion of old questions seems to me indicated.

Reprinted with permission from the *American Psychologist,* Vol. 14, No. 12, December, 1959. This selection was the Address of the President of the American Psychological Association at its sixty-seventh annual convention in Cincinnati, Ohio, September 6, 1959.

I should like to begin with a few remarks about the history of Gestalt psychology—because not all chapters of this history are generally known. In the eighties of the past century, psychologists in Europe were greatly disturbed by von Ehrenfels' claim that thousands of percepts have characteristics which cannot be derived from the characteristics of their ultimate components, the so-called sensations. Chords and melodies in hearing, the shape characteristics of visual objects, the roughness or the smoothness of tactual impressions, and so forth, were used as examples. All these "Gestalt qualities" have one thing in common. When the physical stimuli in question are considerably changed, while their relations are kept constant, the Gestalt qualities remain about the same. But, at the time, it was generally assumed that the sensations involved are individually determined by their individual stimuli and must therefore change when these are greatly changed. How, then, could any characteristics of the perceptual situation remain constant under these conditions? Where did the Gestalt qualities come from? Ehrenfels' qualities are not fancy ingredients of this or that particular situation which we might safely ignore. Both positive and negative aesthetic characteristics of the world around us, not only of ornaments, paintings, sculptures, tunes, and so forth, but also of trees, landscapes, houses, cars—and other persons—belong to this class. That relations between the sexes largely depend on specimens of the same class needs hardly be emphasized. It is, therefore, not safe to deal with problems of psychology as though there were no such qualities. And yet, beginning with Ehrenfels himself, psychologists have not been able to explain their nature.

This holds also for the men who were later called Gestalt psychologists, including the present speaker. Wertheimer's ideas and investigations developed in a different direction. His thinking was also more radical than that of Ehrenfels. He did not ask: How are Gestalt qualities possible when, basically, the perceptual scene consists of separate elements? Rather, he objected to this premise, the thesis that the psychologist's thinking must begin with a consideration of such elements. From a subjective point of view, he felt, it may be tempting to assume that all perceptual situations consist of independent, very small components. For, on this assumption, we obtain a maximally clear picture of what lies behind the observed facts. But, how do we know that a subjective clarity of this kind agrees with the nature of what we have before us? Perhaps we pay for the subjective clearness of the customary picture by ignoring all processes, all functional interrelations, which may have operated before there is a perceptual scene and which thus influence the characteristics of this scene. Are we allowed to impose on perception an extreme simplicity which, objectively, it may not possess?

Wertheimer, we remember, began to reason in this fashion when experimenting not with perceptual situations which were stationary, and therefore comparatively silent, but with visual objects in motion when corresponding stimuli did not move. Such "apparent movements," we would now say, occur when several visual objects appear or disappear in certain temporal relations. Again in our present language, under these circumstances an interaction takes place which, for instance, makes a second object appear too near, or coincident with, a first object which is just disappearing, so that only when the first object, and therefore the interaction, really fades, the second object can move toward its normal position. If this is interaction, it does not, as such, occur on the perceptual scene. On this scene, we merely observe a movement. That movements of this kind do not correspond to real movements of the stimulus objects and must therefore be brought about by the sequence of the two objects, we can discover only by examining the physical situation. It follows that, if the seen movement is the perceptual result of an interaction, this interaction itself takes place outside the perceptual field. Thus, the apparent movement confirmed Wertheimer's more general suspicion: we cannot assume that the perceptual scene is an aggregate of unrelated elements because underlying processes are already functionally interrelated when that scene emerges and now exhibits corresponding effects.

Wertheimer did not offer a more specific physiological explanation. At the time, this would have been impossible. He next turned to the problem of whether the characteristics of stationary perceptual fields are also influenced by interactions. I need not repeat how he investigated the formation of molar perceptual units, and more particularly of groups of such objects. Patterns which he used for this purpose are now reproduced in many textbooks. They clearly demonstrate that it is *relations* among visual objects which decide what objects become group members, and what others do not, and where, therefore, one group separates itself from another. This fact strongly suggests that perceptual groups are established by interactions; and, since a naïve observer is merely aware of the result, the perceived groups, but not of their dependence upon particular relations, such interactions would again occur among the underlying processes rather than within the perceptual field.

Let me add a further remark about this early stage of the development. Surely, in those years, Gestalt psychologists were not satisfied with a quiet consideration of available facts. It seems that no major new trend in a science ever is. We were excited by what we found, and even more by the prospect of finding further revealing facts. Moreover, it was not only the stimulating newness of our enterprise which inspired us. There was also a great wave of relief—as though we were escaping from a prison. The prison was psychology as taught at the universities when we still were students. At the time, we had been shocked by the thesis that all psychological facts (not only those in perception) consist of unrelated inert atoms and that almost the only factors which combine these atoms and thus introduce action are associations formed under the influence of mere contiguity. What had disturbed us was the utter senselessness of this picture, and the implication that human life, apparently so colorful and so intensely dynamic, is actually a frightful bore. This was not true of our new picture, and we felt that further discoveries were bound to destroy what was left of the old picture. Soon further investigations, not all of them done by Gestalt psychologists, reinforced the new trend. Rubin called attention to the difference between figure and ground. David Katz found ample evidence for the role of Gestalt factors in the field of touch as well as in color vision, and so forth. Why so much interest just in perception? Simply because in no other part of psychology are facts so readily accessible to observation. It was the hope of everybody that, once some major functional principles had been revealed in this part of psychology, similar principles would prove to be relevant to other parts, such as memory, learning, thinking and motivation. In fact, Wertheimer and I undertook our early studies of intellectual processes precisely from this point of view; somewhat later, Kurt Lewin began his investigations of motivation which, in part, followed the same line; and we also applied the concept of *Gestaltung* or organization to memory, to learning, and to recall. With developments in America, Wertheimer's further analysis of thinking, Asch's and Heider's investigations in social psychology, our work on figural aftereffects, and eventually on currents of the brain, we are probably all familiar.

In the meantime, unexpected support had come from natural science. To mention only one point: Parts of molar perceptual units often have characteristics which they do not exhibit when separated from those units. Within a larger visual entity, a part may, for instance, be a corner of this entity, another part its contour or boundary, and so on. It now seems obvious; but nobody in psychology had seen it before: the same happens in any physical system that is pervaded by interactions. These interactions affect the parts of the system until, eventually, in a steady state, the characteristics of all parts are such that remaining interactions balance one another. Hence, if processes in the central nervous system follow the same rule, the dependence of local perceptual facts on conditions in larger entities could no longer be regarded as puzzling. Comparisons of this kind greatly encouraged the Gestalt psychologists.

In America, it may seem surprising that enthusiastic people such as the Gestalt psychologists were intensely interested in physics. Physics is generally assumed to be a particularly sober discipline. And yet, this happened to us most naturally. To be sure, our reasoning in physics involved no changes in the laws of physics, and no new assumptions in this field. Nevertheless, when we compared our psychological findings with the behavior of certain physical systems, some parts of natural science began to look different. When reading the formulae of the physicist, one may emphasize this or that aspect of their content. The particular aspect of the formulae in which the Gestalt psychologists became interested had, for decades, been given little attention. No mistake had ever been made in applications of the formulae, because what now fascinated us had all the time been present in their mathematical form. Hence, all calculations in physics had come out right. But it does make a difference whether you make explicit what a formula implies or merely use it as a reliable tool. We had, therefore, good reasons for being surprised by what we found; and we naturally felt elated when the new reading of the formulae told us that organization is as obvious in some parts of physics as it is in psychology.

Incidentally, others were no less interested in this "new reading" than we were. These other people were eminent physicists. Max Planck once told me that he expected our approach to clarify a difficult issue which had just arisen in quantum physics—if not the concept of the quantum itself. Several years later, Max Born, the great physicist who gave quantum mechanics its present form, made almost the same statement in one of his papers. And, only a few weeks ago, I read a paper in which Bridgman of Harvard interprets Heisenberg's famous principle in such terms that I am tempted to call him, Bridgman, a Gestalt physicist.

We will now return to psychology. More particularly, we will inspect the situation in which American psychology finds itself today. The spirit which we find here differs considerably from the one which characterized young Gestalt psychology. Let me try to formulate what members of this audience may have been thinking while I described that

European enterprise. "Enthusiasm?" they probably thought. "Feelings of relief when certain assumptions were found less dreary than those of earlier psychologists in Europe? But this is an admission that emotional factors and extrascientific values played a part in Gestalt psychology. We know about the often pernicious effects of the emotions in ordinary life. How, then, could emotions be permitted to influence scientific judgments and thus to disturb the objectivity of research? As we see it, the true spirit of science is a critical spirit. Our main obligation as scientists is that of avoiding mistakes. Hence our emphasis on strict method in experimentation and on equally strict procedures in the evaluation of results. The Gestalt psychologists seem to have been guilty of wishful thinking. Under the circumstances, were not some of their findings unreliable and some of their concepts vague?"

I will at once admit two facts. Almost from its beginning, American psychology has given more attention to questions of method and strict proof than Gestalt psychology did in those years. In this respect, American psychology was clearly superior. Secondly, sometimes the Gestalt psychologists did make mistakes. Not in all cases was the reliability of their findings up to American standards, and some concepts which they used were not immediately quite clear. I myself once used a certain concept in a somewhat misleading fashion. I had better explain this.

What is insight? In its strict sense, the term refers to the fact that, when we are aware of a relation, of any relation, this relation is not experienced as a fact by itself, but rather as something that follows from the characteristics of the objects under consideration. Now, when primates try to solve a problem, their behavior often shows that they are aware of a certain important relation. But when they now make use of this "insight," and thus solve their problem, should this achievement be called a *solution by insight?* No—it is by no means clear that it was also insight which made that particular relation *emerge.* In a given situation, we or a monkey may become aware of a great many relations. If, at a certain moment, we or a monkey attend to the right one, this may happen for several reasons, some entirely unrelated to insight. Consequently, it is misleading to call the whole process a "solution by insight." This will be particularly obvious when the solution of the problem is arbitrarily chosen by the experimenter. Take Harlow's excellent experiments in which primates are expected to choose the odd item in a group of objects. "Oddity" is a particular relational fact. Once a monkey attends to it, he will perceive it with insight. But why should he do so during his first trials? His first choices will be determined by one factor or another, until he happens to attend, once or repeatedly, to the oddity relation just when he chooses (or does not choose) the right object. Gradually, he will now attend to this particular relation in all trials; and he may do so even when entirely new objects are shown. Surely, such a process should not simply be called "learning by insight." If Harlow were to say that, under the circumstances, it is learning of one kind or another which gives the right relation and corresponding insight their chance to operate, I should at once agree. What, I believe, the monkeys do not learn is insight into which object in a given group is the odd one; but they must learn to pay attention to the oddity factor in the first place. I hope that this will clarify matters. They have not always been so clear to me.

When the solution of a problem is not arbitrarily chosen by the experimenter, but more directly related to the nature of the given situation, insight may play a more important role. But, even under these circumstances, it is not insight alone which brings about the solution. The mere fact that solutions often emerge to the subjects' own surprise is clear proof that it cannot be insight alone which is responsible for their origin.

But I intended to discuss some trends in American psychology. May I confess that I do not fully approve of all these trends?

First, I doubt whether it is advisable to regard caution and a critical spirit as *the* virtues of a scientist, as though little else counted. They are necessary in research, just as the brakes in our cars must be kept in order and their windshields clean. But it is not because of the brakes or of the windshields that we drive. Similarly, caution and a critical spirit are like tools. They ought to be kept ready during a scientific enterprise; however, the main business of a science is gaining more and more new knowledge. I wonder why great men in physics do not call caution and a critical spirit the most important characteristics of their behavior. They seem to regard the testing of brakes and the cleaning of windshields as mere precautions, but to look forward to the next trip as the business for which they have cars. Why is it only in psychology that we hear the slightly discouraging story of mere caution over and over again? Why are just psychologists so inclined to greet the announcement of a new fact (or a new working hypothesis) almost with scorn? This is caution that has gone sour and has almost become negativism— which, of course, is no less an emotional attitude than is enthusiasm. The enthusiasm of the early Gestalt psychologists was a virtue, because it led to new observations. But virtues, it has been said, tend to breed little accompanying vices. In their enthusiasm, the Gestalt psychologists were not always sufficiently careful.

In American psychology, it is rightly regarded as a virtue if a man feels great respect for method and for caution. But, if this virtue becomes too strong, it may bring forth a spirit of skepticism and thus prevent new work. Too many young psychologists, it seems to me, either work only against something done by others or merely vary slightly what others have done before; in other words, preoccupation with method may tend to limit the range of our research. We are, of course, after clear evidence. But not in all parts of psychology can evidence immediately be clear. In some, we cannot yet use our most exact methods. Where this happens, we hesitate to proceed. Experimentalists in particular tend to avoid work on new materials resistant to approved methods and to the immediate application of perfectly clear concepts. But concepts in a new field can only be clarified by work in this field. Should we limit our studies to areas already familiar from previous research? Obviously, this would mean a kind of conservatism in psychology. When I was his student, Max Planck repeated this warning over and over again in his lectures.

Our wish to use only perfect methods and clear concepts has led to methodological behaviorism. Human experience in the phenomenological sense cannot yet be treated with our most reliable methods; and, when dealing with it, we may be forced to form new concepts which, at first, will often be a bit vague. Most experimentalists, therefore, refrain from observing, or even from referring to, the phenomenal scene. And yet, this is the scene on which, so far as the actors are concerned, the drama of ordinary human living is being played all the time. If we never study this scene, but insist on methods and concepts developed in research "from the outside," our results are likely to look strange to those who intensely live "inside."

To be sure, in many respects, the graphs and tables obtained "from the outside" constitute a most satisfactory material; and, in animal psychology, we have no other material. But this material as such contains no direct evidence as to the processes by which it is brought about. In this respect it is a slightly defective, I am tempted to say, a meager, material. For it owes its particular clearness to the fact that the data from which the graphs and tables are derived are severely selected data. When subjects are told to say no more than "louder," "softer," and perhaps "equal" in certain experiments, or when we merely count how many items they recall in others, then we can surely apply precise statistical techniques to what they do. But, as a less attractive consequence, we never hear under these circumstances how they do the comparing in the first case, and what happens when they try to recall in the second case.

Are such questions now to be ignored? After all, not all phenomenal experiences are entirely vague; this Scheerer has rightly emphasized. And, if many are not yet accessible to quantitative procedures, what of it? One of the most fascinating disciplines, developmental physiology, the science investigating the growth of an organism from one cell, seldom uses quantitative techniques. And yet, nobody can deny that its merely qualitative description of morphogenesis has extraordinary scientific value. In new fields, not only quantitative data are relevant. As to the initial vagueness of concepts in a new field, I should like to add an historical remark. When the concept of energy was first introduced in physics, it was far from being a clear concept. For decades, its meaning could not be sharply distinguished from that of the term "force." And what did the physicists do? They worked and worked on it, until at last it did become perfectly clear. There is no other way of dealing with new, and therefore not yet perfect, concepts. Hence, if we refuse to study the phenomenal scene, because, here, few concepts are so far entirely clear, we thereby decide that this scene will never be investigated—at least not by us, the psychologists.

Now, I had better return to Gestalt psychology. Let me try to show you how Gestalt psychology tends to work today by discussing a more specific issue, an issue on which scores of American psychologists have worked for years. We shall thus be enabled to compare the way in which they approach this issue with the Gestalt psychologists' approach.

The issue in question refers to the concepts of conditioning and motivation. One school seems to regard conditioning as almost *the* process with which the psychologist has to deal. In a famous book with the general title *Principles of Behavior,* the late Clark Hull, then the most influential member of the school, actually dealt with little else—although he often used other terms. He felt that even such facts as thinking, insight, intentions, striving, and value would eventually be explained by a consistent investigation of the various forms of conditioning. We are all familiar with the basic concepts of his theory. Hence I will say only a few words about it. When conditions in an animal's tissue deviate from an optimal level, a state of need is said to exist in this tissue. Such needs produce, or simply are, drives—which means that they tend to cause actions in the nervous system, some more or less prescribed by inherited neural connections, others of a more random nature. Drives are also called motivations. None of these terms is to be understood in a phenomenological sense. They always refer to assumed states of the tissue. The main point is that, for biological reasons, states of need must, if possible, be reduced and that this may be achieved by certain responses of the organism to the given situation. In case first responses are of a random character, learning or conditioning will often select such responses as do reduce the needs in question. In a simple formulation, the well-known rule which governs such developments is as follows: when a response has repeatedly occurred in temporal contiguity with the neural effects of a certain stimulus, then this stimulus will tend to evoke the same response in the future—provided the response has caused a reduction of the need. I will not define such further concepts as habit strength, reaction potential, afferent stimulus interaction, reactive inhibition, and so forth, because they will play no role in my discussion.

But one term seems to me particularly important. Many recent, and important, investigations are concerned with so-called "learned drives," an expression which has, of course, this meaning: if a neutral stimulus is repeatedly followed by conditions which cause a primary state of drive such as pain, and the corresponding fear, then the fear with its usual effects on behavior will gradually become connected with that neutral stimulus, so that the stimulus alone now evokes the fear and its overt consequences. Certain drives are therefore said to be "learnable" in the sense that they can be attached to facts which, as such, are not related to the drive and hence would originally not evoke corresponding responses.

Some experiments in the field of conditioning in general are most interesting. I will only discuss the concepts used in the interpretation of this work and the conclusions which it is said to justify.

To begin with these conclusions: They refer to certain human experiences which, if the conclusions were justified, would have to be regarded as strange delusions. I mean our cognitive experiences. Suppose somebody discovers by accident that, every time he subtracts the square of a given integer from the square of the next integer in the series, the result is an odd number. A more learned friend now explains to him why this is a necessary rule, undoubtedly valid beyond any tests ever done by a person. The explanation refers to simple relations and to relations among relations—all readily understandable—and the final outcome is convincing. Now, is the understanding of the relations involved to be explained in terms of conditioning? Nothing in conditioning seems to give us access to the psychological fact which I just called understanding; and, since an understanding of relations is essential to all cognitive achievements, the same applies to the whole field.

Explanation of our intellectual life in terms of conditioning would simply mean: its reduction to the operations of an often most practical, but intrinsically blind, connection of mere facts. Promises that such an explanation will nevertheless be achieved cause in the present speaker a mild, incredulous horror. It is not the business of science to destroy evidence. Behaviorists would perhaps answer that arguments which refer to human thinking as an experience are irrelevant, because science is only concerned with facts observable from the outside, and therefore objective. This answer would hardly be acceptable. The behaviorist's own objective observations are invariably observations of facts in his perceptual field. No other form of objective observation has ever been discovered. Consequently, the behaviorist cannot, without giving more particular reasons, reject reference to other individual experiences merely because they are such experiences.

Thus we are justified in considering a further example of human experience. A need or drive, we are sometimes told, is a motivation. I do not entirely agree with this statement for the following reasons. A need or drive, we remember, is supposed to be a particular state in the tissue. There is no indication in Hull's writings that such a state "points beyond itself" toward any objects—although it may, of course, cause movements, or actions of glands. Now it is true that the same holds for certain needs as human experiences; because, when a need is felt, it does not always point toward an object, attainment of which would satisfy the need. At the time, no such object may be in sight; in fact, no such object may yet be known. But when the proper object appears, or becomes known, then the situation changes. For, now the subject feels attracted or (in certain instances) repelled by this object. In other words, an object may have characteristics which establish a dynamic relation between the subject and that object. According to common experience, it is this dynamic relation which makes the subject move toward, or away from, the object. We ought to use different terms for a mere need *per se* and the situation in which a subject is attracted or repelled by an object. Otherwise, the dynamic aspect of the latter situation might easily be ignored. I suggest that we reserve the term "motivation" for this dynamic situation. Here we are, of course, on familiar ground.

Motivation as just described was Kurt Lewin's main concern in psychology. He clearly recognized the part which certain characteristics of an object play in establishing the dynamic relation between this object and the subject. He called such characteristics of objects *Aufforderungscharaktere,* a term which then became "valences" in English.

So far as I know, there are no valences in objects, no attractions and no repulsions between objects and subjects in the behaviorist's vocabulary. I am afraid that, in this fashion, he misses a point not only important in human experience but also relevant to what he regards as true science.

How would a Gestalt psychologist handle motivation in the present sense? He would begin with the following psychological facts. I do not know up to what point Lewin would have accepted what I am now going to say. My facts are these: (a) In human experience, motivation is a dynamic vector, that is, a fact which has a direction and tends to cause a displacement in this direction. (b) Unless there are obstacles in the way, this direction coincides with an imaginary straight line drawn from the object to the subject. (c) The direction of the experienced vector is either that toward the object or away from it. In the first case, the vector tends to reduce the distance in question; in the second, to increase it. (d) The strength of both the need present in the subject and of the valence exhibited by the object can vary. Both in man and in animals it has been observed that, when the strength of the valence is low, this reduction can be compensated for by an increase of the need in the subject; and, conversely, that, when the need is lowered, an increase of the strength of the valence may compensate for this change.

When considering these simple statements, anybody familiar with the elements of physics will be reminded of the behavior of forces. (a) In physics, forces are dynamic vectors which tend to change the distance between one thing (or event) and another. (b) Unless there are obstacles in the way, a force operates along a straight line drawn from the first object (or event) to the other. (c) The direction in which a force operates is either that of an attraction or of a repulsion, of a reduction or of an increase of the given distance. (d) The formula by which the intensity of a force between two objects is given contains two terms which refer to the sizes of a decisive property (for instance, an electric charge) in one object and in the other. It is always the product of these two terms on which, according to the formula, the intensity of the force depends. Consequently, a reduction of the crucial term on one side can be compensated for by an increase of the term on the other side.

We have just seen that the behavior of vectors in motivational situations is the same as the behavior of forces in nature. Gestalt psychologists are, therefore, inclined to interpret motivation in terms of such forces or, rather, of forces which operate between certain perceptual processes and processes in another part of the brain, where a need may be physiologically represented. We have no time to discuss the question how cortical fields or forces would cause overt movements of the organism in the direction of these forces.

Now, not everybody likes the term "force." Its meaning, it has been said, has anthropomorphic connotations. But, in human psychology, we simply must use terms which—if I may use this expression—"sound human." If we refused to do so, we would not do justice to our subject matter which (to a high degree) is human experience. To be sure, in physics, Heinrich Hertz once tried to do without the concept "force." He actually wrote a treatise on mechanics in which he avoided this term. And what happened? He had to populate the physical world with unobservable masses, introduced only in order to make their hidden presence substitute for the much simpler action of forces. Ever since that time, physicists have happily returned to the old concept "force," and nobody has ever been harmed by the fact.

The present reasoning leads to a conclusion which distinguishes this reasoning from the treatment of motivation in the behaviorist's system. Clark Hull was a great admirer of science; but, to my knowledge, he hardly ever used the concepts characteristic of field physics. The fundamental distinction between physical facts which are scalars (that is, facts which have a magnitude but no direction) and vectors (which have both an intensity and a direction) played no decisive part in his theorizing. His main concepts were obviously meant to be scalars. There is no particular spatial direction in a habit strength, none in a reaction potential, and none even in what he called a drive state. Hence, the core of modern physics as developed by Faraday and Maxwell had no influence on his system. For this reason, and also because he refused to consider motivation as an experienced vector, he could not discover that the operations of motivation appear to be isomorphic with those of fields or forces in the brain.

But, if motivation is to be interpreted in this fashion, certain assumptions often made by behaviorists may no longer be acceptable. Take the concept of learned drives. As I understand this term, it means that learning can attach a drive state to a great variety of stimuli which, as such, are neutral facts. Now, so long as a drive is not regarded as a vector, this seems indeed quite possible. But, if the drive in Hull's sense is replaced by a motivational force which operates between a subject and some perceptual fact, no arbitrary connections of this kind can be established. For, now motivation becomes the experienced counterpart of a force in the brain, and this force depends entirely upon the relation between conditions in the subject and the characteristics of the perceived object. There can be no such force if the object is, and remains, a neutral object. Forces only operate between objects which have the right properties. Any example of a force in nature illustrates this fact.

How, then, are the observations to be explained which are now interpreted as a learning of drives? After all, some learning must be involved when an originally neutral object gradually begins to attract or repel a subject. From the present point of view, only one explanation is possible. Supposing that the subject's need does not vary, learning must change the characteristics of the object, and thus transform it into an adequate motivational object. One instance would be what Tolman calls a sign Gestalt; in other words, the neutral object would become the signal for the appearance of something else which is a proper motivational object. This expected object would now be the object of the motivation. Or also, when a neutral object is often accompanied by facts which are natural motivational objects, the characteristics of such facts may gradually "creep into" the very appearance of the formerly neutral object and thus make it a proper motivational object. Years ago, comparative psychologists in England stressed the importance of such processes, to which they gave the name "assimilation." They regarded assimilation as a particularly effective form of an association. And is it not true that, as a consequence of learning, a coffin *looks* forbidding or sinister? I also know somebody to whom a bottle covered with dust and just brought up from the cellar *looks* most attractive. As a further and particularly simple possibility, the subject might just learn more about the characteristics of the given object itself than he knew in the beginning; and the characteristics revealed by this learning might be such that now the same object fits a need. It seems to me that all these possibilities ought to be considered before we accept the thesis that motivations in the present sense can be attached to actually neutral objects. Incidentally, similar changes of objects may also be responsible for the developments which Gordon Allport once regarded as evidence of "functional autonomy."

You will ask me whether my suggestions lead to any consequences in actual research. Most surely, they do. But, since I have lived so long in America, and have therefore gradually become a most cautious scientist, I am now preparing myself for the study of motivation by investigating, first of all, the action of dynamic vectors in simpler fields, such as cognition and perception. It is a most interesting occupation to compare motivational action with dynamic events in those other parts of psychology. When you do so, everything looks different, not only in perception but also in certain forms of learning. Specific work? There is, and will be, more of it than I alone can possibly manage. Consequently, I need help. And where do I expect to find this help? I will tell you where.

The behaviorist's premises, we remember, lead to certain expectations and experiments. What I have just said invites us to proceed in another direction. I suggest that, in this situation, we forget about schools. The behaviorist is convinced that his functional concepts are those which we all ought to use. The Gestalt psychologist, who deals with a greater variety of both phenomenal and physical concepts, expects more from work based on such premises. Both parties feel that their procedures are scientifically sound. Why should we fight? Many experiments done by behaviorists seem to me to be very good experiments. May I now ask the behaviorists to regard the use of some phenomenal facts, and also of field physics, as perfectly permissible? If we were to agree on these points, we could, I am sure, do excellent work together. It would be an extraordinary experience—and good for psychology.

# PART I

# ESSAYS BY MAX WERTHEIMER

*Max Wertheimer*

LATE OF THE GRADUATE FACULTY,
NEW SCHOOL FOR SOCIAL RESEARCH

# ON TRUTH

Science is rooted in the will to truth. With the will to truth it stands or falls. Lower the standard even slightly and science becomes diseased at the core. Not only science, but man. The will to truth, pure and un-adulterated, is among the essential conditions of his existence; if the standard is compromised he easily becomes a kind of tragic caricature of himself.

The scientific situation with reference to the theory of truth is com-plicated at present. In the last decades logicians and epistemologists have worked intensively on its problems; many complications have emerged; some of them seemed to menace the whole inquiry. New ap-proaches have been made, much positive work has been done. In this paper I shall discuss only one aspect of the problems, and in the simplest way. What follows has to do with things that the natural man feels as self-evident; but the theory must envisage these things. Examples will be drawn from everyday life.

I begin with the classical definition of truth, a point of departure that lends itself to the simplest exposition of the subject, although what I have to say applies equally to many other approaches. According to the traditional definition it is propositions that are true and false. A statement or proposition is true which corresponds with its object, and

Reprinted with permission from *Social Research,* Vol. 1, No. 2, May, 1934.

vice versa a proposition is false if it fails to correspond with its object. Truth, so conceived, is a general quality of propositions. It is a question of the relationship between the proposition on the one hand and the object on the other.

Many new problems emerged in the criticism of this old formulation: for example, what, strictly, did the term "correspondence" mean, what could it mean? What is meant when we say a proposition should "correspond" with its object? Or when the question is raised as to whether reference to the object does not involve an illegitimate transition? There are many other fundamental questions that have led to new formulations.

But regardless of the necessity for changing the definition of truth in the sense of these objections and regardless of the great importance of these changes in some respects, the claim contained in the simple form of the old definitions is in itself important enough. Statistics, publications of one kind or another, do contain figures that are plainly false; in this respect there is lack of conscientiousness and worse. The standard is often lowered, especially in general statements in which whole realms of thought are disposed of on the basis of personal predispositions or of a few individual facts. What the old definition requires is straightforward fidelity to facts in the sense in which a proposition corresponds or fails to correspond with the facts.

But truth demands more.

If we consider the function of truth in life, in living thought and being, then the old definition is unsatisfactory. I will touch here only on one relatively simple point.

An example: a man hires another to steal something out of a desk; the theft is discovered; it has been established that the second man was seen near the house; the judge, who does not know their connection, asks the first man whether he took the article from the desk; the first man answers "No," gives his alibi, and is discharged. He did not take the article from the desk. His statement that he did not is true according to the definition. Nevertheless, he lied.

The difficulty need not necessarily invalidate the classical definition of truth. One could say that the difficulty was due to the way in which the suspect was questioned. The investigator should have asked, not "Did you take the article from the desk?" but "Are you guilty of stealing these valuables?" Why was the judge so stupid? The judge's stupidity is irrelevant. It has nothing to do with the fact that the man would have made an untrue statement, had he said that he did take it. In the old terminology, this is known as the false conclusion based on many questions. Or another explanation may be offered. One may point out that the word "taking" means not only the physical fact of taking but likewise its cause. There are two meanings of the word "take." For each of these meanings, the old definition of truth clearly establishes what is true and what is false.

But solutions of this kind tend to eliminate the problem instead of solving it. The issue is waived. The way to go about solving the problem, it would seem to me, is to attack it directly. The investigator's question to the suspect is not an isolated fact in a vacuum. It is an integral part of a well-defined situation in which the investigator, the suspect, and the theft form a characteristic whole. The detail that the suspect did not himself remove the valuables from the desk stands in an important and characteristic relation in the whole situation. Were the suspect really not guilty, had he nothing to do with the whole thing, then this detail would in the new whole have an entirely different function, a different significance, a different role.

The proposition, the statement, "I did not take it from the desk," corresponds with reality; but with a piecemeal reality, torn from its context, seen as a piece, blind as to its connections as a part in a related whole; or in another related whole in which the suspect appears innocent. The real truth must take account of any statement, and equally of its corresponding object, as parts of related wholes. A thing may be true in the piecemeal sense, and false, indeed a lie, as a part in its whole. We must distinguish the object as piece $|a|$, the object as part of its whole $\left|\dfrac{a}{abc}\right|$, the object as part of another whole $\left|\dfrac{a}{amn}\right|$.

For the time being let us indicate piecemeal truth and falsity by t and f; and by T and F what we have called the real truth, in which the statement and its object are considered as parts in their related wholes. The example that we have been discussing is of the form tF. For the function of truth and falsity, it is not a question only of the statement in itself (*an sich*), but of the statement S and the object O as parts of their wholes; S and O, in their roles, in their functions as parts of their wholes. The truth here does not consist only in the correspondence between the proposition and its crude, isolated object. If the object turns out to be a part in the pattern of a definite situation, then the proposition is really true when it corresponds not only with the part as such but with the role that it plays in the whole.

If each item in the situation were isolated from every other, if our world were in every instance nothing more than the sum of isolated facts, if we had to do only with "atomic facts," then the old definition of truth, the t and f, would be adequate. If, however, these facts or data exist, not in isolation but as parts of a whole, determined by their function in this whole, then it leads to blind and false conclusions to consider them as pieces. The whole plan of traditional logic, in all its rules and its general laws, is set up to deal with piecemeal content in a summation relation. And for this it is adequate.

Logistic (*Logistik*), the study of relational networks and of implicit definitions, provides the possibility, indeed the necessity, for seeing content as a part of its whole, but in a limited sense. It defines content by its place in the relational network, but the network is built up as a summation. (Cf. in logistic the new approaches to a structural theory of truth.) Logistic has failed hitherto to study the relationship between content as piece and content as part. In reality we frequently have the possibility of considering as pieces what are really parts of a system. Science for the most part indeed finds itself in this situation, at least in the early stages of a problem.

Before we proceed, let us consider briefly some other examples of this form. A newspaper writes: "We know now just what to expect from Minister X. Such are the steps he intends to take! At the banquet held on the twenty-seventh of this month, he declared himself against . . ." Indignant denial: "The truth is that Minister X was not even present at the banquet."

Any number of examples may be found in statistical material and in balance sheets. In the course of the last decades a whole technique of the form tF has been developed, the technique of doctoring balances, etc. This does not refer necessarily only to deliberately misleading figures. Simultaneous newspaper reports on the same facts in journals belonging to different political parties afford the psychologist and the logician a veritable treasure house of the various forms of tF.

Moreover it is not at all necessary to conceal any of the relevant details in order to arrive at blind or false statements in the sense of tF. All the data may be laid before the reader or hearer but in such a way as to deceive him by the technique of shifting the emphasis, displacing the center of gravity (*Umcentrierung*). An example of the simplest technique: during the war newspapers in some countries were compelled to give out reports in the exact words of the general staff. They achieved what they wanted by the use of heavy type for some parts, and it often happened that in this way entirely opposite impressions were produced.

I remember cases in which I received so strong an impression that the reports were different, that I could not believe they were the same until I had compared them word for word. (Cf. the old false conclusion by inflection.)

These were cases of the form tF. Instead of the two truth values t and f, we have schematically the four combinations tF, tT, fF, fT. That there are cases of tT and fF is clear. Are there also cases of fT, that is, false as pieces, true with respect to the whole, to reality? Yes: for example, an excellent caricature. It may be wrong in practically every detail and yet be a truer representation of its object than a photograph which is accurate in every detail. Other cases are anecdotes and stories about men, events and ages which are known to be inventions yet nevertheless hit the nail on the head. *Se non é vero, é ben trovato.* But of course it must be *ben trovato.*

Propositions of this type present an inherent danger, however. The danger is due to the fact that it is usually easier to prove the truth of an item in isolation than in its role in the whole. Indeed, many propositions for which the claim is made that they are true in relation to the whole, to the essence, are really false both in themselves and in relation to the whole. (Cf. the history of some scientific schemata.)

If, then, we are really to find out what is true and what is false, we must direct our attention to the role of any particular item in the whole of which it is a part.

This necessity has generated a number of problems that are as interesting as they are difficult. The basic problem here is the function of a part as a part of its whole. It is a central problem for the Gestalt theory. We may formulate it as follows. Facts occur in these ways: first, in isolation, as such, or as units in a sum; secondly, as parts of their wholes —and a part may figure in two or more different wholes. Often there is the possibility too of cutting off as a piece what should really figure as a part. What are the differences in these cases?

One may ask why we speak of two kinds of truth and not merely of two kinds of data. The answer is that the two kinds of truth may deal with the same data, but that one (T,F) goes to the heart of the matter while the other (t,f) may remain external—namely, when the set of facts is not merely a sum.

The approach that we have used, the formulation of a truth function T,F in relation to the old t,f, is not the only possible theoretical approach. The attempt can be made to do justice to objects by other approaches. The problems in question can only be pointed out, they cannot be dealt with even briefly here. But what is necessary is that the theory clearly envisage these objects. From whatever angle we approach the theory, concrete problems of research are generated in any serious attempt at a theoretical solution.

Remote as it may appear from logic as customarily defined and treated, we need a logic of objects. If there is any objection to calling it logic, the name is a matter of indifference. I believe that these questions rightly belong to logic; they are not questions merely of psychological fact but they raise issues in terms of correct, incorrect, adequate, true, false, logical, illogical.

Attempting to find a different approach, one may say that the truth function is not touched in all this, that in the burglary example, for instance, the difficulty is a matter simply of variously defined concepts. We need only to define carefully and to agree on definitions. Can any one suppose that all the difficulties consist solely in the failure to define clearly? We can readily see that the real problem is not solved; the question then is, in a given situation, in a given context, which definition is justified, correct, significant. In a context it is not a matter of indifference, of purely subjective appraisal which definition is to be chosen, which things are to be discussed. There are instances of misleading, inappropriate, inadequate definitions. And in the question here raised, of the logical formulation of definitions, we find again, if we look more closely, the problem of piece as opposed to part. Structurally this is entirely analogous to what was discussed above. (Cf. examples, pp. 26–27 below.)

Similar considerations hold for the problem of abstraction. There are logically bad, incorrect, misleading abstractions. All this is germane to the logical problems of the formulation of concepts.

The problem, to be sure, in a certain sense disappears if logic is to be nothing but the formal theory of deduction. In that case the question of an adequate formation of concepts that does justice to objects falls away, and the coördination of the model with reality becomes purely a matter of chance. There are similar problems, however, in a purely formal logic of implicit networks.

In traditional logic and in logistic the truth function t,f is fundamental. In some of the newest developments, logicians define all logical constants such as *not, and, or, following,* etc., by means of tables of truth functions. If we follow the method of multiplying truth functions, if we take T,F into consideration, very radical consequences follow.

The cases of tF and fT prove to be very complicated special cases. We soon see that the crux of the problem is the problem of the objective, content relationship between $|a|$ and $\left|{}^{a}_{abc}\right.$. When, how, in what are they different? Solutions prove to be too easy where the content of a part is held to be unaltered in cases of abstraction, or of the recurrence of similar pieces or sections in different wholes. Whether there is a difference and what that difference is—difference in role, in function, in dynamics, or actually in content itself—this is a task for research which leads to very concrete and formal problems.

If we put $|a|$ and $|b|$ in a real relationship as parts of a whole, then we have at all events not merely these two, each by itself as before, but we must consider the question of their alteration: $|a| + |b| \rightarrow \left|{}^{a}_{ab}\right. + \left|{}^{b}_{ab}\right.$. The same holds of the abstraction: in a real or a blind "abstraction," $\left[\left|{}^{a}_{ab}\right. + \left|{}^{b}_{ab}\right.\right] - \left|{}^{b}_{ab}\right.$ yields the result $\left|{}^{a}_{a'}\right., |a|$. This is already the case in relational networks: if a part is really taken from a system, then the remainder, implicitly defined, is substantially changed. And the same question is involved if we consider the relationship of $\left|{}^{a}_{abc}\right.$ and $\left|{}^{a}_{amn}\right.$.

The general science of logic demands the same rigorous exactitude as classical logic but classical logic represents a special case, like the Euclidean special case in geometry. For the most part it is adequate in those instances in which the inner functional content approaches zero.

A fundamental difficulty might be discerned in what follows. One might ask whether the truth values $|a|$ or $\left|{}^{a}_{a}\right.$ and $\left|{}^{a}_{ab}\right.$ should be distinguished, whether we should not likewise take into consideration the differences $\left|{}^{a}_{abc}\right.$ and $\left|{}^{a}_{abcd}\right.$ etc. Would not this lead to radical uncertainty? Until we had exhausted all the data, would we not be in permanent danger of a tT becoming transformed into a tF? And to exhaust all data is of course impossible.

There are actually instances of changes in truth values. If we look more closely we soon see that this is not a question of an objection but of a field of research. In the first place it by no means follows that the mere addition of indifferently assorted facts continues to affect the truth value at all points. All things are not interconnected in the same way; there are fields, there are questions, that are relatively self-enclosed. If to some object situations we continue to add new facts, we see that at a particular point the truth value actually no longer changes. And this has its own inner reasons. A Gestalt, a pattern, limits itself. Whereas in general the variation of a part demands the simultaneous variation of the other parts, this no longer follows, for example, when the variation takes place outside the boundaries and the field of the Gestalt. The question of establishing the boundaries of a Gestalt, as of a practical situation, is not a matter of choice but is subject to examination on grounds of being correct or incorrect, logical or illogical.

Moreover, if there are situations in which what we have here discussed is questionable, we should not permit our vision to be obscured for that reason. The cases of tF that actually occur are often entirely unequivocal.

I mention a special case. It happens that in a fight between two parties, the way out is found in this form: for each party his own point of view is immediately relevant; it seems impossible to bridge the differences in outlook; we have at first $\left|\begin{smallmatrix} a \\ ab \end{smallmatrix}\right.$ in the one case and $\left|\begin{smallmatrix} a \\ ac \end{smallmatrix}\right.$ in the other; the parties are starkly opposed. We find the solution $\left|\begin{smallmatrix} a \\ abc \end{smallmatrix}\right.$ the common solution that takes into account the viewpoints of both instead of doing violence to one by the other.

The form of this mode of solution touches questions of domination by the individual social and cultural milieu in the latest discussions on the theory of truth.

Here I should like to include a few more simple examples illustrative of the principal theoretical points.

1. Note these two musical motifs:

Corresponding to the motif at the left, assume the continuation in D flat major; at the right the continuation in D minor. Such a continuation is not absolutely necessary, however.

Someone may say that the first two tones and the first interval of the second motif are the same as in the first motif. That is true, for the piano. The musician replies that you have completely failed to understand. In the motif at the right it is a diminished fourth, the motif at the left a major third; the second tone at the left is the tonic, at the right the passing-note. And it would be false, illogical, if the second tone in the motif at the right were to be written as D flat. If we fail to hear the tones as different in these different combinations then we have understood absolutely nothing of what is involved in these motifs.[1] And actually the singer, the violinist, often intones quite differently in these two instances.

Here we have our example if we confine ourselves to the motif on the right and the listener takes the first two tones in isolation, really abstracts them, blindly unconscious as to the role, the function, they have in their whole (tF).

2. Take several members in a mathematical series. A formula is thought out; and it becomes evident then how the formula and the serial structure and the variability are entirely different if the further development of the series is taken into consideration. Or we have a mathematical series. We characterize it by a particular formula, blind as to which member it is of a family of curves.

3. Or the engineer discovers in his measurements that he has a straight line. Measurements taken in other subsections show that he is dealing not with a straight line but with the asymptote of a hyperbola.

Another step is indicated if we consider now in all its relevances the earlier remark following the tF examples. All the "data" may be given in sum, all the tones of a melody, all the members of a series—nothing omitted, accordingly, from the sum of the data. And yet nothing may have been grasped. What is really involved may not have been seen at all in these cases in which the sum of the data is present as the sum of individual pieces or fragments; and this in spite of the fact that all the single relations may also have been given in sum. In addition to the tF and tT, we have the t(?).

Someone makes a serious request, "Tell me the truth about this." The answer may contain many facts that are individually valid and can leave the questioner entirely ignorant. I have failed to understand, to grasp, if I know everything as a sum, if I have not grasped the inner connections of the whole, the inner determining principles, if the individual data are not present as parts, transparent, determined as parts. Here too we have to deal with concrete problems, with the problem of grasping what is really involved in the transition to what is understood from what is not understood. The same kind of understanding is necessary in order to make a reasonable prediction.

---

[1] Cf. examples in the *Z. Psychol.*, 1933, 129, 353 ff. [Reprinted in M. Wertheimer, *Productive Thinking,* enlarged edition (New York: Harper, 1959), pp. 260–265.—Ed.]

I should like briefly to indicate a second point here. The classical view, according to which truth and falsehood are qualities of propositions or assertions, seems to limit the meaning of truth and falsehood artificially. It is not only and primarily a question of what anyone says or states. Truth and falsity, indeed understanding, is not necessarily something purely intellectual, remote from feelings and attitudes. In many of the previous examples the most important thing is not the statement but the whole position, a man's attitude toward the thing itself. It is in the total conduct of men rather than in their statements that truth or falsehood lives, more in what a man does, in his real reaction to other men and to things, in his will to do them justice, to live at one with them. Here lies the inner connection between truth and justice. In the realm of behavior and action, the problem recurs as to the difference between piece and part.

Science is rooted in the will to truth.

If it is clear that science demands not only scrupulous fidelity to facts, however indispensable, but that it demands more—what we have here indicated by T; if decisions on this basis are reached with greater difficulty; if in certain scientific fields definite decisions are at present impossible for technical or for fundamental theoretical reasons; all these considerations cannot weaken the claims of truth. Indeed the responsibility of the scientist increases with his difficulties, the demand grows for unswerving determination in the search for truth, for that relationship to the things themselves that means to do them justice, and wills the truth untainted by wishes or commands.

Such is the real origin of the claims of science to free discussion: in the interests of safeguarding scrupulous fidelity to facts, in the attitude of every scientific worker toward his work, in his readiness for the most exacting proof of his theses. A conception is too easily influenced by will or by wish, too easily becomes instead of the object of research an idol, an end in itself. And even if we suppose that science should function in the service of life, we must beware lest the instrument corrupt itself. It is of no little importance to preserve in its purity the instrument that is the search for truth.

But the stake is not the instrument; it is man himself.

*Max Wertheimer*

LATE OF THE GRADUATE FACULTY,
NEW SCHOOL FOR SOCIAL RESEARCH

# SOME PROBLEMS

# IN THE THEORY

# OF ETHICS

The old conception of *homo sapiens* implies that some faculties, some abilities are important for man (although not always actually realized). Among these are the ability and tendency to understand, to gain insight; a feeling for truth, for justice, for good and evil, for sincerity. Connected with the realization of these abilities is the old conception of human dignity as an inner task of man. Only then is one a true man, if . . . , only then do we have a truly human society, if . . .

This conception of *homo sapiens* does not overlook human blindnesses and weaknesses, the differences between men and between situations. It does not ignore the fact that these faculties are often concealed and overgrown, that their development is sometimes hampered; that not every man is always a *homo sapiens,* that he may at times be his own tragic caricature; that there are often conditions and circumstances which interfere with their development or realization; that there are forces which often conceal these human qualities or counteract their development.

Reprinted with permission from *Social Research*, Vol. 2, No. 3, August, 1935.

Today we often encounter a thesis radically opposed to the concept of *homo sapiens*. This thesis maintains that it is simply wrong to speak of "man" in such a way, that "man" is only a pale abstraction, a fiction. It affirms that men, races, cultures are fundamentally different from one another in their conceptions and evaluations. To speak of *the* ethics is, according to this thesis, meaningless; we have only a variety of different systems of evaluations and these are mere historical facts changing with history. All values are fundamentally relative, changing with place and time. If we construct the systems of axioms for the ethics of various peoples and times, we have as a result simply a sum of different systems. Each system is only a fact like any other system. Many use this doctrine of the relativity of ethics today as a self-evident statement.

Manifold factors gave rise to this thesis. I will mention here only two relevant factors in the development of science. In recent decades, fortunately, there has been a wide development of special scientific investigations of the facts involved, investigations seeking to discover the numerous facts concerning our problems in ethnology, sociology and cultural history. With the assembling of the results, material for comparison is to some degree at hand. There have been reported very different moral concepts and evaluations. The conclusion was drawn by some that diversity as a fundamental principle has been established and that the old idea of unity is an empty fiction. Accordingly, this old idea is to be considered only as an historical fact determined by the conditions of time and place under which it was developed.

Formally, certain aspects of modern logic favored this development. Axioms now often appear only as propositions which are so chosen that the single data in a system may be deduced from them. Some formulate the problem as follows: The task of science can only be to state the single facts in a field and to seek, formally, general propositions which represent these facts. With the exception of logic and mathematics axioms have an arbitrary character. Opposites of one kind of axioms are always conceivable; differences in axioms cannot be settled except by arbitrary decision. Thus a system of evaluations of a certain social group may be represented by one system of axioms, the evaluations of another group by other axioms. "There is no way to prove, either by logical reasoning or by scientific demonstration of facts, which of two conflicting norms is more right than the other. The choice between two such norms must be an arbitrary one; all norms are facts with an absolutely equal claim to recognition." Thus we have different systems of ethical axioms representing simply different sets of facts, and that is all.

Thus one may formulate: Different axioms of evaluations, even if contradictory from one system to another, are equally sensible. You can get another ethics, equally sensible, if you reverse the evaluation signs in the axioms of one ethics, substituting plus for minus and minus for plus in the norms.

Certainly, this last statement is not true. Are there not common conditions in human societies, both on the technical and on the human side, limiting the possibilities? Are there not identities of conditions in human societies and in men?

But first of all, we want here to ask a formal question: is the direct inference from the statement of different (contradictory) facts of evaluations to the heterogeneity in axioms logically valid?

It is not. It would in a simple way be valid if the objective were here nothing more than a mere cataloguing of naked facts; if there were no differences in the meaning of contents, in the causation and determination of attitudes touching our problem; if all the facts were of equal theoretical rank; or if I consider the facts without further theoretical consideration, psychological or sociological, if I see them torn from their determining nexus and compare them as such. But facts of evaluations cannot be dealt with offhand as if they were of the same rank. There are, for example, critical psychological differences in the determination. I need only to mention suggestion, inertia, temporary blindness.

Consider a relatively simple example. It often happens that men in a psychological crowd situation take part ardently, and a short time later are unable to understand how they could have behaved so blindly. They did it under the blinding psychological conditions of the crowd situation. Their behavior was possible only because of a tremendous narrowing of the field of consciousness or a narrowing of the field of actual determining factors.

Is the transition from the one state to the other correctly described simply as a transition from one system of ethics to another? And have we then simply two contradictory systems of axioms of equal claim and rank? Is our problem satisfactorily settled with such a statement? Is the task of science here only to state the bare facts and to formulate generalizations, to state the different axioms? Do we not have to study how these different modes of behavior have been caused? And is it not possible in such cases that different conditions have led to different behavior and to different evaluations, although the principles of evaluation are identical? Temporary blindness to some of the factors involved can change the factual behavior under the identical ethical principles.

Such conditions as blindness are only special cases. Another type of case comes readily to mind. Because of a fallacy, a fallacious suggestion, because of a current theory, of a certain superstition, because of a custom or tradition the behavior or evaluation toward an A is formed in a certain way, for the reason that this A means a B for the person under these conditions. The result is an apparent contradiction between the evaluations of A in different groups, but does not mean necessarily a difference in the fundamental causal and determining evaluation of B. We have then a diversity, a relativity in the meaning of A but perhaps an identity in the determining principle B. And in a similar way different biological or sociological conditions often require, because of an identical basic need, different factual evaluations of an apparent content A, an A which is the same only when taken as an atomic fact but different in the role it plays in the whole situation.

The logical form may be illustrated in the simplest, baldest case. In one group there may be a positive evaluation, a positive response to the object A, in another group there is none. Now, I have to ask, what is the cause, what is the reason for this positive evaluation of the A in the first group? It may be, in the simplest case, a conditioned response. The A is thus evaluated because it is conditioned, connected with B, which is positively evaluated.[1] It may then be that we find in both groups the same fundamental positive evaluation of the B.

|  | Group I | | Group II | |
|---|---|---|---|---|
| *First step:* | | | | |
| Factual evaluations (conditioned responses) | A+ | | | |
| Conditioning | BA+ | | | |
| Sources (axioms, reflex) | B+ | | B+ | |
| *Second step:* | | | | |
| Factual evaluations | A+ | | A— | |
| Conditioning | BA+ | | DA— | |
| Sources | B+, | D— | D—, | B+ |
| *Third step:* | | | | |
| Factual evaluations | A+, | C— | C+, | A— |
| Conditioning | BA+, | DC— | BC+, | DA— |
| Sources | B+, | D— | B+, | D— |

---

[1] The response to A may be the "conditioned reflex," the response to B a "reflex."

The next step is that, in different whole situations, an A changes necessarily as part, in its role, in its function. This step transcends the purely summative constellations.[2]

If we try to look over the available factual material concerning the various evaluations so far as we know them on the basis of the present state of research, with consideration of the theoretical problems involved, there appears a mixture of different things. On the one hand, we have evaluations formed by varying meanings, varying traditional customs, usage, current theories, differences in the situation, etc., and in these there is a marked variety. These facts do not give directly the sources and principles of the evaluations in behavior. If we search for real principles, axioms, on the other hand, we find that the matter in most cases has not been sufficiently clarified; if we look for contradictory norms which would directly, clearly, unmistakably form a basis for contradictory axioms, there is little material at hand; if we look for contradictory differences in simple human relationships, in cases uncomplicated by misunderstandings, etc., in situations clearly concerned with open, friendly trustfulness, or scheming, cunning, selfish, petty deceitfulness, with wise understanding, sincere integrity, or reckless, egoistic, callous brutality or obvious, brutal injustice; then the facts seem to tend more strongly in the direction of fundamental identities.

Perhaps we can already trace the beginnings of a third stage in scientific development. In an earlier period, the first stage, ethnology used European concepts simply as universal and self-evident criteria. Then comparative research among different societies brought to light a wealth of diverse evaluations leading to the second stage: there seemed to be simply diversity, different ethical systems. Today the situation in ethnology seems to be advancing to a third stage. On the one hand, we have learned that in the determination of evaluations we must take into account so many biological and sociological, religious and historical complications, that we see that the inference from the single facts of evaluation to diversity of principles and axioms was too hasty; the apparent differences are not direct evidence for differences in the axioms. On the other hand, in clear cases of human relationships uncomplicated by "pejorisations" concerning truth and falsehood, justice and injustice, the facts tend more in the direction of fundamental identity than in the direction of contradictory norms.

---

[2] Cf. Max Wertheimer, On truth, *Soc. Res.,* 1934, 1. [This is the previous article in the present volume.—Ed.]

The problems of scientific ethics are very complicated. If the problems are to be studied scientifically we must try to distinguish the various problems involved and modestly proceed step by step in clearing up the field. We must study the differences in the causation, in the determination of factual values. We must also study differences in the logical structures in the facts of evaluation. I wish here to raise only a single problem of the many in this rich field, a point frequently overlooked in the present theories.

It is customary to speak of values indiscriminately as if they fitted into only one scheme. The usual scheme is the following: we have on the one hand an object, a content, and on the other hand the subjective feeling, the subjective judgment of value. To the object is only added an evaluation; this may be positive or negative; it is subjective in determination. Logically speaking, evaluations are determined externally to the object and are arbitrary with respect to the object.

For this scheme the following example may serve.

I call a food good because to me it tastes good, or because it is in fashion, because others call it good, because it is now considered aristocratic to prefer this food to other foods, etc.

This evaluation may be true for me, for another person not true. The evaluation depends on the relation to the subject, his subjective feeling which is entirely external to and arbitrary with respect to the object. The logical structure is: the object A *and* the added plus or minus evaluation.

We may compare with this example the following:

A judge convicts an obviously innocent person because the guilty person has bribed him, or because he hopes to achieve by this conviction a certain profit for himself or for his group. Or, a poor, hungry child has been given a piece of bread to eat; an adolescent rowdy comes along and grabs it to use it as a football.

If we try to understand such cases with the same formulation as we used in the earlier example, in terms of the arbitrary addition of a subjective evaluation to an object, then there is a lack of clarity, something does not jibe; the matter demands clarification, there seem to be various problems involved. Is the logical structure the same as in the case of tastes?

We have here an objective situation and a behavior, an action, and it is important first to sense, to see, to comprehend how this action actually stands in the situation. The most important question is not that of a subjective evaluation standing outside of an object, but the relations within the happening itself, how the action meets the requirements of the situation, the *zueinander* of the two, the relation between the situation and the action. The factual behavior may be determined without regard to the situation, blind to what it accomplishes in reality for the object. The behavior may do violence to the situation. The behavior may be determined so as to be appropriate to the structure of the situation, to accomplish what the situation requires. We have here various objective qualities, qualities concerned with the relationships *in* the situation. Whether a particular instance of real behavior is a case of the one or the other of these three classes is a matter for which my seeing or failing to see, my subjective evaluation, is irrelevant. Whether I evaluate it positively or negatively does not change by an iota the issue which quality of the three is present in the situation, what role the behavior really plays, what kind of part it is in the situation. This point must be understood first of all. If someone in a real situation fails to see it, and perhaps acts accordingly, then he has not a different ethics but he is blind to the main issue.

It is difficult for many theorists to see clearly this difference in the logical structure and to realize its relevance for the theory.

What is involved here in principle? In logic or mathematics there are decisive principles, such as, for example, the principle of contradiction. This is not an arbitrary subjective matter, it concerns the material and its relations.

But are there comparable principles for ethical questions, something which will naturally be entirely different in this different field? Many theorists deny it. We do not have such principles, they assert. Moreover, there seems no theoretical possibility for such principles because of the basic subjectivity of all values.

Perhaps the formulation of the problem was too narrow. Is it not possible that for certain problems of values there are principles which are identical with those in other fields, so that some principles in logical thinking would only represent a special case of a common principle? I will try to indicate an approach which may open the way to theoretical studies. It involves some radical changes in theoretical concepts but, on the other hand, it seems to formulate more directly something which has always been intended. I can sketch here only one side of the matter.

Someone in adding makes seven plus seven equal fifteen. This happens; such additions are real facts. And he says, I call it good because I love the number fifteen, or because I have set up the principle that in the addition of two whole numbers, the sum shall always be divisible by five, or, as may happen occasionally in the addition of a bill by a waiter, because I have a personal interest in the fifteen.

The determination of the fifteen is blind to the objects or in violation of that which is demanded by the structure of the objective situation. If I prefer the fifteen in this case, if I evaluate it positively, this is irrelevant to the fact that the fifteen is wrong.

What is the structure? The situation, "seven plus seven equals . . ." is a system with a lacuna, a gap (*eine Leerstelle*). It is possible to fill the gap in various ways. The one completion, fourteen, corresponds to the situation, fits in the gap, is what is structurally demanded in this system in this place, with its function in the whole. It does justice to the situation. Other completions, such as fifteen, do not fit. They are not the right ones. They are determined by caprice, in blindness or in violation of the function this gap has in the structure.

We have here the concepts of "system," of the "gap," of different kinds of "completion," of the demands of the situation, the "required-ness." [3]

The case is similar if a good mathematical curve has a gap, a place in which something is lacking. For the filling in of the gap, there are often, from the structure of the curve, determinations which indicate that the one completion is appropriate to the structure, is sensible, the right one; other completions are not. This is connected with the old concept of "inner necessity." And not only logical operations, conclusions, etc., but also happenings, doings, being, can be, in this sense, sensible or senseless, logical or illogical. [4]

We may formulate: given a situation, a system with a *Leerstelle,* whether a given completion (*Lueckenfüllung*) does justice to the structure, is the "right" one, is often determined by the structure of the system, of the situation. There are requirements, structurally determined; there are possible in pure cases unambiguous decisions as to which completion does justice to the situation, which does not, which violates the requirements and the situation. [5]

---

[3] These are quite complicated concepts; I may mention only that these concepts are connected with recent developments in mathematics, science, and Gestalt theory.

[4] This transcends in some respects the boundaries of the usual theory of traditional logic.

[5] Some fundamental principles of logical thinking are special cases of this principle. Thus you must not introduce a proposition blind to the conditions of the situation; it is not right to act blind to the structure or to other given data; in the law of contradiction, the filling in of a non-A is simply not permissible logically, if in the system a plus-A is already included. This is but the baldest special case of the general principle.

Now the case of the bribed judge is structurally similar to our first mathematical example. We have here again a system with a gap. If the judge convicts the obviously innocent man for reasons of personal interest or interests of his group, he may prefer this behavior subjectively but this does not alter the fact that his decision is unjust.

This case is very close to the traditional logic; but we can see the principle in other cases also. Here sits a hungry child; yonder a man, who is building a small house, and lacks a single brick. I have in one hand a piece of bread and in the other a brick. I give the hungry child the brick and take the soft bread to the man. Here we have two situations, two systems. The allotment is blind to the functions of the gap filling.[6]

These cases may serve to illustrate the principle in a preliminary fashion. Many further steps are naturally required (and with a single principle the task is not done). First a clarification of the terms "determination," "requiredness," etc., is necessary.[7]

A further step is involved when such a system with its gap is to be considered as only a part of a more inclusive system. If a gangster needs a revolver at a critical moment in order to carry out his particular task, then the gangster with his need is logically a part of the larger system of human society, in which he with his wishes is to be considered as a functional part. If there were always an infinite regress to ever larger wholes with subsequent changes in the determination, then the principle would be endangered in its application. But this is a point which cannot be settled with a simple generality but which presents a matter for research. It seems that in many cases there are not unlimited changes with enlargement of the whole, that often enlargement no longer changes the determination. And there are many cases in which a larger and more generally embracing field is common to conflicting fields.

However the matter may be, whatever the formulation of the further steps in the theoretical construction, and what place and rank the principle mentioned will have among other principles, it seems to be necessary to realize what is here involved.

I may mention that it has been customary to look upon logical thinking as an entirely intellectual field necessarily separated from feelings, attitudes, tendencies. The principle mentioned is not only static, to be

---

[6] Or it may be caused by scorn. There may be men who evaluate scorn positively, but this does not change the fact that the allotment does not do justice to the situation.

[7] I cannot deal with this here. I may only mention that the usual simple dichotomy of to be and ought to be has to be revised. "Determinations," "requirements" of such an order are objective qualities.

taken merely as a list of assertions about determinations, but touches on dynamics. Logical operations, logical proceedings have a great deal to do with feelings, attitudes, real behavior; they include them. Logical operations, as in the case of the thinking scientist, contain and demand such things as sincerity in doing, the will to do justice to the material.

We may add this further example. A young, idealistic party member is passionate in the negative evaluation of members of a certain race. It is not sufficient in such cases to give the formulation: in one system of evaluations, members of this race are positively evaluated, in another negatively. This young man perhaps behaves thus only because he has been brought to this state through suggestion, propaganda, through the wanton slander that this race is a poisonous snake. He does not really behave with respect to the A (members of this race) but to a B which he has been taught to identify with this race. The real problem here lies not only in the behavior of the young man, but in the enforcement of the blind identification. This involves a corollary to the principle mentioned. To take away by artifice the possibility of seeing the true situation, through the enforcement of blind judgments, of improper narrowing of the mental field, induction of blind centering, deprives man of the prerequisites for our problems.

The principle mentioned differs radically from many usual definitions of justice. Many traditional definitions use criteria which are strange, external to the essential centering of justice as viewed by this principle.[8]

I repeat, the formulated principle is no patent solution. It is rather a starting thesis for a field of research. This field demands not a simple solution but research and it seems necessary, as in each proper science, to start with the study of the most concrete, transparent examples. We have to start from "pure cases" in the scientific sense of this word. It happens that relativists argue against such examples; that they are not evidence against relativism "because they are too obvious." But this is a contradiction. In reality, the most obvious are the most needed at the outset of scientific studies. To be sure, most cases are much more complicated. The contents involved are very often not so easy to define as the seven in our mathematical example,[9] but that should not obscure our main issue.

There are many other problems I have not spoken of here. For instance, there are cases in which the situation at first does not contain the

---

[8] Compare such a statement as that the state creates law, with the statement that the state is an attempt to realize, to discover, to guarantee justice.

[9] Wertheimer, *op. cit.*

fact of a gap, where the gap is generated by an idea of man, by a new goal, etc. In such cases the goal is theoretically a part of the material of the situation and comes under the requirements of being the right one. To be sure, this brief remark does not solve this problem; another principle is involved here. I have also not dealt with the so-called cases of conflict, which for many theorists stand curiously enough in the foreground. They present complications. Some may believe that all applications to concrete human situations are so complicated that there is no possibility at all of using the principle mentioned. But there can be no doubt that at least there are, negatively, serious and brutal infringements which are perfectly unambiguous; and on the positive side there remains, in cases too complicated for an exhaustive answer, the possibility of proceeding according to the best knowledge (*nach bestem Wissen und Gewissen*); here the corollary mentioned plays an important role.

A difficulty can be seen in the fact that the problems of truth in logic itself are complicated. Whatever the answer may be, that modest sense of truth which declares fourteen to be the right answer in our mathematical example may suffice. It would be wonderful if all propagated or factual norms of values might be as adequate as this.

A few words about the psychological side of the problem. Are these "requirements," these "qualities" of justice and injustice, etc., psychological realities for man?

We have had very little real research work in this direction, but this much is clear, one cannot assume that men always feel or see these requirements vividly, and that they act accordingly. Sometimes one may have the impression that the real quality of man is not *homo sapiens* but rather *insipiens*. Whether these requirements are vivid and effective for a man depends on many factors, among them historical factors, conditions of his *Standort,* the state of his glands, etc. But we should not, as often happens, confuse such factors with what is meant by the requirements and confound conditions of evaluation from both fields. In the latest development of psychology some results seem to indicate that there are real psychological vectors tending in the direction of such requirements. In some experimental psychological investigations the results have indicated that the old principle is wrong which asserts that all acts of man are centered by the "ego" (striving for one-sided satisfaction of ego interests). Let us illustrate this by an analogy from the psychology of perception. It is not true that in perception the world is always centered around the individual. If I am standing in a special place in a room, then the walls are not out of line but I am out of line with the walls. The ego does not always determine the system of coördinates for the objects, but the ego often feels itself as a part oriented with respect to the system of coördinates of the objects. Similar facts were found in experiments on thinking and action. The vectors often arise in actual situations from the requirements of the situation, not from egocentric interests.

Many other psychological issues might be considered in this connection. I will mention only the following:

Important is the study of the "transitions" from, for example, the psychological state in a crowd situation to the "awakening" which occurs when these special conditions fall away. And there are also for most men moments in their lives when in a concrete situation they feel awakened, when they feel how narrow, blind, crooked they have been and acted, when their eyes are opened and they feel that their former behavior was possible only because something of their best, their finest, their most worthy was missing, that they had been robbed of it.

Further, there are experiences like the following. One knows a man who is an outstanding example of a certain caste, whose entire behavior expresses very definitely the evaluations of his caste. And in a serious moment the outer shell falls away, and from behind this exterior there now comes out a simple, good, somewhat immature man, for whom the seemingly serious attitudes which he had exhibited are in fact like strange, superficial clothing. There seem to be layers in men, and it is a question of fact what the inner layers of men really are. Concerning our problem there are opposing theses. I would believe that the optimistic thesis is the right one, however difficult, indeed however impossible it may be at times to penetrate to this layer.

Experience seems to indicate that the conditions often are not so difficult, if the situation is clear, transparent, simple and actual, and if there are not conditions of blindness, etc. Often it is surprising how intense are the reactions of men in simple human situations when faced with clear, actual injustice.

In any case the questions here cannot be decided simply by means of the statistics of the naked actions of men. There is required a study of the deeper connections and determinations. But even if the optimistic psychological thesis mentioned above should prove false, if it should be demonstrated that most men are blind or inimical in their inner nature to these requirements, would this mean a disproof of the principle? It would not. There would then be two races, the one for whom these requirements are vivid, the other which is blind or inimical to them. For there are good men, even if there be but few. But I believe that the pessimistic thesis is false.

We have dealt here with only a few issues from a rich and broad field. We may formulate as a result:

"Relativity" has an important place in the rich field of different "meanings," different biological, economic, cultural, sociological, historical conditions, etc., and it is important to study these facts as modern sociology, ethnology, and cultural history do, in order to achieve an understanding. But in order to get real axioms and to study the central ethical problems, it does not suffice to formulate axioms simply by generalization from the factual evaluations. There are needed studies of the causation, the determination, the structural conditions of the evaluations; there are needed psychological studies of the causation, the determination, the genetic development; there are needed studies of the logical structures in forms of evaluations.

I think that the modern methods of ethnology, sociology, and cultural history which have proved to possess great merit lead in themselves beyond a hasty, superficial relativism concerning the real ethical problems, in that they involve the study not only of the factual evaluations but also of their structural roles, their inner causation, their inner determination.

*Max Wertheimer*

LATE OF THE GRADUATE FACULTY,
NEW SCHOOL FOR SOCIAL RESEARCH

# ON THE CONCEPT

# OF DEMOCRACY

If one tries to understand scientifically what democracy is, one is confronted with this situation. On the one hand there seems to be simple agreement as to what is meant by democracy, as expressed in the usual definitions, including such characteristics as "government by the people," "majority rule," "freedom of speech," etc., etc. On the other hand if we look more closely, if we follow the way in which different men deal concretely with special problems of democracy, the trend, the direction of attitudes and arguments in actual political situations, in juridical decisions, and in scientific discussions, there seem to be big differences which often touch the very heart of the matter. Sometimes there are open contradictions: both parties to an argument insist they are advancing the real democratic claim; judges contradict each other as to what a certain democratic principle demands; criticisms of a scientific book on democracy assert that "the book is scientific, to be sure, but you see, what he is speaking of is not true democracy at all, he has not the right idea of democracy." Various factors are involved, factors that differ in

Reprinted from *Political and Economic Democracy*, edited by Max Ascoli and Fritz Lehmann. By permission of W. W. Norton & Company, Inc. Copyright 1937 by W. W. Norton & Company, Inc.

kind. Among them are certain logical-methodological problems, and it is with these latter that this discussion is concerned.

The usual method of stating what democracy is, is the old traditional one. Compare the object with other objects of the same class, compare democracy with other forms of government, find out the similarities and the differences, formulate them and you have characteristics, a number, an "and-sum" of items which differentiate it—*genus proximum, differentiae specificae*. This method of isolating special items in subtractive abstraction has its merits, seems often indeed to be *the* exact method, but it has its dangers. Such an item is likely to be used blindly, with no reference to the role it plays in the hierarchical logical structure; the view is one-sided, the mental horizon artificially narrowed. Such an enumeration of items is not enough. There is another method, which is to investigate the structural function of the items and the hierarchical structure of the whole idea. This method is certainly much more difficult. It is not so easy to decide such questions as it is to decide questions in subtractive abstraction, but it is necessary.

In order to illustrate the formal problems that must be met, let us consider some examples. These examples are given solely as illustrations for the formal problems; the truth or falsity of their material content will not concern us in this paper.

Comparing democracy with other forms of government we find, for example, that in democracy the people shall vote and that the will of the majority shall decide. This, we are told, is the democratic procedure. But if we look more closely we may see that if we take "majority rule" as an item for itself without regard to the function it has in democracy, we are blinding ourselves, and sometimes others, to what it means.

Various things must be taken into account, first that the vote is meant as a free vote, not a vote by threat or intimidation. This is not an accidental addition but is logically determining in the structure. Secondly, the voter must have access to as full and true information as possible, and there must be free and open discussion. Again, this is not simply an accidental addition. Thirdly, "Great issues cannot be resolved by counting noses, but only by an appeal to what is right and what is wrong," is a democratic statement. Majority without this tendency is not at all democratic in the sense of the "good old democrats."

These requirements involve others. Full information for the voter is one of the roots of the demand for free expression, which in this context has the function of a technical means to the centering end. As a means it is considered only the best available, not 100 per cent effective, which is interesting from the logical standpoint. Moreover, in genuine democracy free voting by personal decision is not meant simply as a means for the voter to protect his private interests, the profit interests of himself or his group. It is a means for preserving his rights—but his rights, not his private interests. The voter is envisaged as responsible for a decision that is right for the community, not simply for himself. There are times in which rights and private interests may coincide, but the idea as well as the reality of majority decisions between two profit-interest groups is a caricature of the idea and of the attitude of old democracy. Majority rule in a democracy also implies a characteristic attitude toward minorities. Simply to deny or to violate the rights of minorities, to blind oneself to their needs and their claims is not democratic. "We have the majority, so what?" is not a democratic attitude. An unjust decision against a minority because of majority-will is not democracy. Finally, a defeated minority has not simply to bow, to recognize a decision as right "because it is the will of the majority—the majority having spoken, the matter is settled." It *is* settled for the time being. But the minority has not simply to give in. If the minority is convinced that the decision was wrong or unjust, it becomes its duty to continue trying to clear the matter up, to find better arguments, a clearer presentation to help those of the majority to see the truth.

Against all this one may argue that the democratic way to decide *is* by majority, that of necessity the majority must eliminate aims and arguments of the minority, voting against minority needs, tendencies, and convictions. Since matters have to be settled and decisions have to be reached, decision by will of the majority is the democratic way. Here we reach a logically very interesting problem. Of course this is the democratic procedure. But this does not imply that the content of the majority principle is, taken in itself, a democratic principle. Some facts seem to show that it is nothing more than a technical means toward what is really wanted. Confronted with the necessity for a decision, the wise democrat will not feel very happy if the proper aims of a minority are brutally overridden by majority vote. In spite of seeing no better practical way, he does not like it. It is no real solution for him. In itself majority rule is by no means a democratic goal but only a technical means, only technically a solution, the best that is available but far from perfect. From the standpoint of logic it is not the *content* of the majority principle which is truly democratic, but only its *function* as the technical means to the real goal of more just decisions. It is not the will of the majority that is wanted but the better decision. (The vote has another source as well: the principle that man should not be subject to a ruler, but himself responsible.) In order to understand such an item as the majority principle we must not be satisfied with stating it by itself. We must go on to the role it plays in the hierarchical structure of the whole. Without this we fail to understand it at all.

One might add that the method of conciliation, in which one or more representatives of two conflicting parties try to reach a just decision in concrete discussions, although it does not count the noses of interested party groups, is a democratic idea.

What has been said has consequences in actual real proceedings. Men often act in the belief and the emphatic conviction that their way is the democratic way, but it is only superficially democratic because they are blind to functional meanings. In the meetings of democratic bodies a member may not uncommonly be heard to say: "Why should we discuss this matter at all? You are only a small minority. What the majority wishes is clear. Let us proceed in the democratic way, let us vote. And if you want to oppose calling for a vote on the measure now, we will follow the rules and vote first on closing discussion. If you want this formality, you can have it, but what's the use? You know we have the majority in both cases." Often this is blind or contemptuous misuse of what is really intended in democracy. Under the influence of a strong democratic wave, to take another example, some people demand quick introduction of the vote and speedy formation of a parliament. Others emphasize the prior need of real democratic preparation for the vote, the necessity for free propaganda to open the eyes of a people blinded by a mighty, one-sided press. The first ones have their way and emphasize that it is the true, democratic way. Finally during recent years some men have been blinded by the idea that as true democrats they had simply to bow to the will of the (alleged) majority.

Let us consider a second item which is interrelated with the first, as nearly all items are in the conception of democracy. There are discussions, arguments, claims, court decisions in which the principle of freedom of the press is used as an item in itself, or in a one-sided connection. There are instances in which the principle of freedom of the press is used simply as a special case of freedom of business enterprise, of the right of an individual to make profits. Combine it with the principle of free speech, free self-expression, and, if only these two are taken into account, the result may easily be emphatic assertion of the right not to be bothered, not to be interfered with, not to be blamed for building up a mighty chain of newspapers which by its business methods excludes the possibility of nearly all other information, which is a tool for arbitrary "self-expression," one-sided information, and one-sided influence, that may just happen to coincide with the selfish interests of oneself or one's group.

Certainly the principle of freedom of the press is very important in democracy, but its meaning is not meant to be restricted to consequences for the individual and individual rights. It also has the social function of providing the public with better information, if for no other reason than because information is indispensable to voting in the true sense. The underlying idea is that many will use self-expression because all have the right to it, that the result will be better information because numbers will help against bias, etc. Democracy requires that the people shall know what is important in order to vote justly. This is a vital function of freedom of the press, but it is very different from the meaning determined only by the two above mentioned principles of freedom of business enterprise combined with freedom of expression. In this context freedom is a means to an end.

(Historically the idea of freedom of the press is connected with liberalism's optimistic view of laissez faire. It may be that dissatisfaction with means for public information will bring about new policies directed toward providing avenues of self-expression for those popular groups that have hitherto been deprived of organs of their own.)

Many of the assertions that have been made may be questionable. Their truth or falsity is a matter for historical and other investigation. Here they are used simply as examples for the logical-methodological problem. Each example shows, I think, the big difference between taking a single item as an item in itself or in one-sided determination, and trying to understand it in its function in the whole structure. These questions must be asked: How are such items interrelated, how determined, how centered? What is their role and function, their functional position? Which items are central, which peripheral—is their content determined by other items, by which items, and how? We have to envisage them in their place in the hierarchical structure of the whole.

If we look at the different items by which democracy is usually defined as a sum, or better, if we look at the manifold of items included in democracy, there are at first two logical possibilities, viz., that all these items or some of them are in an "and-sum" with some interrelations, or that we have to deal with a hierarchical structure in which the items are to be conceived as parts in their relational place, in their function in this whole. This question is different from the question of the number and variety of historical sources, causes, etc. Certainly these are important, but to look for the various items that may be at work is a different problem from asking, "Is there an 'and-sum' or a structure?"

One might put as a possible question: "What is the heart of the matter? Is there a structural center?" Various hypotheses are possible. Scientifically they have to be chosen not arbitrarily or one-sidedly, but viewing the whole material in order to do justice to the manifold interrelations, in order to discover the structural center. Different hypothetical centers are to be studied and followed through the relational network, then compared for their merits. I will confine myself here to sketching only some of the steps in connection with one hypothesis to illustrate the structural problem.

If we look at the real beginnings of the great democracies—take for example the happenings in the United States and in France—the main point seems to be *not* opposition to the kingdom, to the king as king, but opposition to injustice, a wish to avoid injustices done by the king, both for oneself and the community, a wish not to be subjected to arbitrary, unjust commands of the ruler. As a hypothesis we may try to conceive as the center the wish to create and to assure a more just procedure, to get decisions and rulings that are not arbitrary but directed by reason and justice; which means that rule by oppression, violence, and trickery is opposed, that an open, honest way of procedure is sought. It appears then that the will to change the form of government is not at all primary.

It would be a logically secondary step toward better realization of the primary aim, inasmuch as kingdoms have the greater danger of arbitrary, unjust dealing, of dealing not determined by reason, justice, the common good. Moreover, in order that men unjustly dealt with, for example, may have the right to be heard, the possibility to appeal, to participate in decisions, the concept of government by the people, of parliament, is born. The principle of justice and reason as opposed to arbitrary dealing is not only chronologically earlier than the people-principle against the king-principle, it is likewise structurally primary, central in this hypothesis. In this structure items like government by the people, voting, majority rule, etc., etc., are to be conceived then as secondary items determined by the center and their content must be understood in the light of the centering idea—the vote, for example, as the enlightened vote of the people. This kind of vote, by reason of the central idea, requires again as means to the end, furnishing open information, permitting free speech, etc. Similarly with other items; the idea of division of powers is, for example, likewise logically determined by this central idea. Working this out in all the ramifications it becomes clear that most of the characteristics, most of the institutional ideas, of democracy are consistent if viewed in the light of the central idea of justice and reason, supplemented by faith in the people, the idea of *homo sapiens,* etc.

The problem of centering gives rise to such questions as these: What is the structural place of the decidedly important item of autonomy of the individual, participating in decisions, voting freely out of his convictions, the individual of the *contrat social?* It is possible to conceive this as another main point coördinate with the first we mentioned, as the centering idea instead of the first, or as secondary to it. They are somewhat different, at least in the emphasis. If we take as the center the "inborn rights of the individual" in the directions indicated we get a slightly different picture. I will say only briefly that studies of the interrelations of the two principles seem to show the principle of autonomy as structurally secondary, an outcome from the first principle in a special direction, just as the principle of equality, equality before the law, etc., seems a special outcome from the first principle.

Another problem arises as to the content of "liberty," of "noninterference" as understood by liberalism in its connection with the harmony theory of laissez faire. This idea has similar formal significance both in political and economic respects (cf. the Boltzmann principle in physics). Perhaps we really have an "and-sum" here. These ideas certainly include some features that are logically strange to the first principle, "arbitrary liberty," for example, noninterference with "arbitrary" freedom of enterprise, etc., but certainly there are likewise inner connections, features that come very near to the first principle of justice and reason. We cannot deal here explicitly with this complicated problem. I shall mention only one point, that the will to courageous truth, to objective reason, to just decisions, requires freedom of the man and of his mind, but this does not involve the harmony theory of laissez faire in enterprise, etc.

Irrespective of these and other features there appears to be a logical structure of democracy with a hierarchy of parts. It is striking to see how the different special items, the different points in the picture get their meaning in their place, in their role, in their function as parts in the picture along with the ethical and educational aims of democracy, the will to truth, to open-mindedness, to fair play, to honesty, etc. Viewed in this way the real essence of democracy seems to be not a form of government, a sum of institutions, etc., but a certain real attitude in life, behavior of a certain kind, not only in state matters but generally in relations between men. This attitude has some characteristic similarities to the role of the judge or the juror, rather than to the fighting of interests. The state is viewed not as a governing body, but as the guarantor of justice and reason which has not to create law but to fulfill it, to realize it by making the rules.

It seems necessary to work out such schemes clearly for the different part-items, their interrelations and their determinations as parts in the scheme, to try to test the conclusions as to the structural function of the items. There are methods for testing such hypotheses and for comparing different structural hypotheses. Structural theses, structural centers, are often blindly established. We often encounter statements and arguments determined simply by artificially narrowing the mental field, viewing parts as if they were in themselves the important thing. Certainly some court decisions, some political attitudes and arguments would run otherwise if they were not determined by viewing items one-sidedly, severed from their function in the whole.

Some theorists may ask the reasons for such investigations into the logical structure of these things. In their view they are all secondary things, "ideology," "rationalizations," "we should look for the real forces behind them." I will not discuss this view here. I will merely remark that they are certainly not only ideas; they live in the real attitudes and actions of men. Moreover in studying the "real forces behind" the ideas it seems equally necessary to see clearly what the ideas are and how they are structurally related. Finally, similar formal problems recur in the study of the forces themselves.

Another point must be added. The main point in our deliberation has been the difference between an item seen in itself or in one-sided determination and an item envisaged as part of the hierarchical structure, democracy. We have dealt with items within political democracy. The question is repeated when we envisage, as we must, the structure of democracy as a part functioning in the broader structure of the social field. Structurally democracy looks somewhat different as a part in various broader fields.

Suppose that our thesis is right in its main lines. Suppose that democracy is a hierarchical structure and that it has been realized to a certain extent. Now this political democracy is to be viewed not as a structure in itself but as a part in the social field, in the larger whole. Let me give some hints on this next step, simplified in order to show only the structural problem. Think of the frontier period. We may envisage it as a kind of social field in which the conditions of production, of economic life, of the possibilities for the individual, etc., resulted on the whole in rather good functioning, in mutuality, in a kind of equilibrium, if for no other reason than because of the wide-open possibilities for all men. Logically and structurally the conditions of life fitted well with the attitudes, aims, regulations of democracy. What we may call the "part-system" democracy, including laissez faire, fitted in well, supplied answers to the questions which arose, dealt with them in a satisfying way. Now think of an important change in the social field in which democracy is functioning as a part. Think of big changes in the economic "part-system," the development of big capitalistic forms, industrialization, masses of workers, depression, masses of unemployed, etc. Strains and stresses are born. The system democracy has to face new problems. Disequilibrium, strain, stresses in one part of the field, e.g., the economic, are not simply irrelevant for the "part-system" democracy. Problems of the whole—dynamics of the whole system—arise.

In the frontier period the Boltzmann principle functioned easily for the most part. Not only did the individual have his opportunities, the other fellow had his and it was consistent to feel that if you satisfied your private economic interests you were at the same time performing the best service for the common good. But when big changes take place in important parts of the field, it is no longer simple for the system of democracy to function as well as a part-system in the broader field. Tensions arise with regard to this "part-system." There are new problems. The old idea combined with the laissez faire principle cannot so easily overcome the difficulties and fit into the new field. Comparatively it was much easier to function unquestioned in the former field of the frontier period. Here the point is to envisage the functioning of a system as a part in a broader system, to study the systematic consequences that follow for the "part-system" from a changing of parts in the broader field.

After the change in the broad field, democracy continues to function, but under strain. The items in it get a somewhat different meaning structurally. Freedom of enterprise, freedom of contract, for example, mean something quite different under the new relations between employer and working masses. To put the extreme case, it is one thing to have freedom of enterprise and freedom of contract work in real mutual freedom, it is another to have them work as one-sided tools. The principle of noninterference if it does not result in real mutuality acquires a new meaning. A difference arises between a purely political democracy and a democracy which includes the now changed realities of life. Logically the content of some of the old items was not concerned with certain items of reality because these were functioning well, were giving mutual equilibrium. Now these old items are confronted with new realities which must be taken into account in order to re-establish the democratic principle. Holding rigidly to these items in their old meaning without facing the new conditions, without asking what is demanded in the light of the very principles of democracy, implies some blindness. There are dynamic systemic demands in the new situation which must be met so that democracy may again become a functioning part in the whole system of the social field.

With regard to this problem there are different attitudes which mean structurally different things. The first is: Wait, we have nothing to change; we have to hold to the old meanings rigidly; the weather will change, conditions will soon improve, the old meanings will again function with ease. The second is: We have to improve various items in order that the system may again work consistently with the demands of the inner meaning of democracy; "real democracy needs more than the old political and individual freedom," which is now only superficially freedom. The idea of social consciousness arises from a new meaning of the items within democracy. The third attitude is: Democracy is denied as not adequate. Some mean to suspend it temporarily in order to make possible real democracy after a time. Others deny the right of democracy to exist at all and set up utterly different principles. It would be better to have the proponents of these different attitudes look at the structural problem in a logically consistent and logically honest way instead of arbitrarily and artificially recentering and narrowing the logical field.

To summarize, stating and discussing items in subtractive abstraction is not enough. We have to consider their structural function. The methodological approach is not only to compare different forms of government by comparing items taken in subtractive abstraction, but to study the inner structure of the object and to view the system structurally in its functioning as a part in its field.

*Max Wertheimer*

LATE OF THE GRADUATE FACULTY,
NEW SCHOOL FOR SOCIAL RESEARCH

# A STORY

# OF THREE DAYS

I shall report what happened in the course of three days to a good man who, facing the world situation, longed for a clarification of the fundamentals of freedom.

He saw: ideological devaluation of freedom had spread; freedom in the humane meaning of the word was proclaimed false, outworn, useless; and the radiance of the old idea was often exploited for other ends. Some men seemed to have lost sight of it entirely, without realizing what they had lost. Confused by the complexity of actual situations many became uncertain, basically unclear with regard to the very concept of freedom, its meaning, value, actuality. Even men who loved freedom deeply often felt helpless in the face of actual arguments. So it was with our man; not that he felt uncertain in many or most of the concrete issues; but he felt impelled to reach a fundamental clarification. What at bottom is freedom? What does it require? Why is it so dear to me? He was a humble empiric, open-minded, thirsting for information.

Of course, those three days of his search were only a beginning for him. He touched only some of the issues involved, for it was by chance that he met just those men and read just those books. They represented only certain points of view and the discussions were by no means exhaustive, yet I think that what he experienced was in many respects characteristic, typical of some fundamental trends in actual thought.

Those were dramatic days for him, in which he became more and more bewildered, but at the end of those three days he felt that he had gained some clarification, that he now saw more clearly something that only his heart had told him before.

He sought out a sociologist who was immersed in studies of this very problem, and he asked his question. The sociologist was very kind. He told him about the investigations of modern sociology, about the history of societies, how ideas of freedom had developed in them and what freedom had meant to them; he told him how different were the ideas of freedom and the ways of realizing them, etc. Our man was fascinated by the richness of what he heard. He felt that here were men with an honest, sincere approach; these were serious studies, and he became more and more hopeful. "You are the right man," he said. "I am sure you feel as I do in the actual world situation," and he told him how he felt.

"I share your feelings," said the sociologist. "I too hold proudly and passionately to our traditional values."

"But why?" he was asked. "What is it that makes freedom so dear to you also, and what is freedom essentially?"

"I am at one with the traditions of our people," said the sociologist. "But if you ask me about the fundamentals, I must answer: It became more and more clear in our studies that the standards, the evaluations, the goals, that an individual has are shaped, determined, by the social group, the society of which he is a part. Different periods in history, different societies, different nations, have different views. Ethical standards are relative."

There was a long pause. After a time our man asked in a low tone: "Is that all? Should what these others assert be true? Are our ideas of freedom merely the historical standards of a certain time, now perhaps outworn? Are there no fundamental standards; are the requirements of freedom a fairy tale?"

"No fairy tale," said the sociologist, "but developed in and characteristic for certain historical, cultural, and social settings."

"And nothing more?" asked our man. "Is no decision possible among various systems? Are there no features that are basic in men with regard to questions of freedom, no requirements for men, as men should be? No features that are desirable, required in human society?"

"Here you are touching upon very difficult things," said the sociologist. "Some of my friends would say that the fight for freedom was always a fight against certain concrete restraints or compulsions and meant, necessarily, different things in different times. Society in its rules and institutions necessarily permits freedom, imposes restraints that with time change in different directions. There are no axioms which would allow me to speak of fundamental standards. To speak of 'the man' or 'the society' is only a pale abstraction."

Our man became more and more bewildered. "Was this," he said, "what your friends wrote and taught? And was this not one of the factors in the developments we now face, one of the factors that paved the way for political leaders proclaiming new and other national or racial ethics, willfully and efficiently?"

"Do not overestimate the role of the opinions of sociologists," said the sociologist quietly. "I told you that this is the position that most of my friends take. And certainly they were sincerely driven to these conclusions by their findings, which contain great factors in their favor. We cannot lightly dismiss them. I myself would not dismiss your questions with their answer. I feel that these are genuine questions; that as sociologists we must face not only diversities in various cultures but also must seek for fundamentals, for identities in the requirements of man and in the dynamics of society—in a doctrine of man and in a doctrine of society. There have been approaches in this direction. I feel as you do that in this context the problem of freedom will play a genuine role. But these are scientific Utopias, my friend; we are far from any real insight, far from even a real method of approach. There are some young sociologists who are groping in this direction and grappling with the problem.

"But if you ask for a definition of freedom, not in terms of the full reality of a specific society, which, of course, I should prefer to give you, then my answer would have to be: absence of restraints, of compulsions, of external hindrances from doing what one desires to do, and maybe I should add absence of imposed internal inhibitions. . . . Though I might say that such a definition certainly lacks concreteness."

Our man thanked the sociologist. He felt sad, puzzled, bewildered. He came home, sat down, and reached for one of the books he had ordered for his search. It was a novel by a famous writer of 1936. He was too disturbed to read thoroughly. A certain page caught his eye. He read, more and more excitedly, these sentences:

Anthony . . . turned over the pages of his latest notebook . . . he began to read.

"Acton wanted to write the History of Man in terms of a History of the Idea of Freedom. But you cannot write a History of the Idea of Freedom without at the same time writing a History of the Fact of Slavery. . . .

"Or rather of Slaveries. For, in his successive attempts to realize the Idea of Freedom, man is constantly changing one form of slavery for another. . . .

"Abolish slavery to nature. Another form of slavery instantly arises. Slavery to institutions. . . .

"All modern history is a History of the Idea of Freedom from Institutions. It is also the History of the Fact of Slavery to Institutions. . . .

"Institutions are changed in an attempt to realize the Idea of Freedom. To appreciate the fact of the new slavery takes a certain time. . . .

"The honeymoon may last for as much as twenty or thirty years. Then . . . it is perceived . . . that the new institutions are just as enslaving as the old. What is to be done? Change the new institutions for yet newer ones. . . . And so on—indefinitely, no doubt.

"In any given society the fact of freedom exists only for a very small number of individuals. . . . For them, institutions exist as a kind of solid framework on which they can perform whatever gymnastics they please. . . ."

Anthony shut his book, feeling that he couldn't read even one line more. Not that his words seemed any less true now than they had when he wrote them. In their own way and on their particular level they were true. Why then did it all seem utterly false and wrong?

"Utterly false and wrong," our man said passionately. How was it possible at all, he asked himself, for a man to formulate such assertions! What he had read seemed unbelievable. At the same time he felt strangely reminded of remarks he had encountered in the last years on one or another occasion, for which these unbelievable formulations seemed somehow fundamental. Now his longing for clarification changed into a passionate drive. I must, I must see through all this. Somehow it is a strange distortion—to view the facts in this way seems to press them into a blind and wrong direction. *What* is it that is wrong in the fundamentals of this picture?

He took up the next book. It was a book from the year 1928 by a famous psychoanalyst and dealt with culture. He read it through from beginning to end. Again and again he turned back to some basic formulations in it. There were some remarks of another character added here and there, but in the main those formulations seemed to him nakedly to express basic assumptions which led straight to those bewildering passages he had encountered in the novel.

. . . every culture must be built up on coercion and instinctual renunciation.
. . . abandoning coercion and [abandoning] the suppression of the instincts . . . would be the golden age, but it is questionable if such a state of affairs can ever be realized. . . . the psychical sphere of culture . . . frustration . . . prohibition . . . privation . . . the instinctual wishes that suffer under them are born anew with every child.

. . . Such instinctual wishes are those of incest, of cannibalism, and of murder.

. . . It is in accordance with the course of our development that external compulsion is gradually internalized.

. . . Every child presents to us the model of this transformation; it is only by that means that it becomes a moral and social being.

. . . Those people in whom it [the internalization of external compulsion] has taken place, from being foes of culture, become its supporters.

. . . [but] a majority of men obey the cultural prohibitions in question only under the pressure of external force, in fact only where the latter can assert itself and for as long as it is an object of fear. This also holds good for those so-called moral cultural demands.

. . . We have spoken of the hostility to culture, produced by the pressure it exercises and the instinctual renunciations that it demands. If one imagined its prohibitions removed, then one could choose any woman who took one's fancy as one's sexual object, one could kill without hesitation one's rival or whoever interfered with one in any other way, and one could seize what one wanted of another man's goods without asking his leave: how splendid, what a succession of delights life would be!

. . . [but] only one single person can be made unrestrictedly happy by abolishing thus the restrictions of culture, and that is a tyrant or dictator who has monopolized all the means of power. . . .

"Could this be true?" our man exclaimed. "Is this Man? Society? Freedom? Is freedom lack of restraint of 'instinctual impulsions,' external or internal? Is Man essentially so determined, impelled by fear of punishment or by habits, by internalized rules imposed on him by compulsion?"

"I must see a philosopher!"

He went next day to see a philosopher and asked, "Will you tell me please what freedom is, philosophically?"

The philosopher smiled. "This," he said, "is an old and famous topic of philosophy down through the centuries. If you like, I can give you the names of a great number of books which you can study—are you interested in the history of philosophy? There are a number of philosophers who still deal with these questions, but if you like, I can try to tell you briefly how the problem lies in modern philosophy as I see it, and, I may say, as it has been well established in modern philosophy.

"The concept of freedom, of free will, of free choice, played an important role in various religions and in various philosophies. It was wish-thinking. Modern developments in science and philosophy have shown that there are no free acts. Causality governs them or, as we formulate it, all actions take place under the principle of determination, are determined by their causes; there is no such thing as an action leaping into existence uncaused, and so what is going to happen, happens by necessity. It is mere blindness if men believe that they are free to act or to make decisions without realizing that their actions are the necessary outcome of forces which determine their choice.

"You might look into the modern textbooks of psychology. In most of them you will not even find mentioned such terms as free will, free decision, etc.

"There have been discussions about this principle of determinism. Some tried to save the old, outworn ideas by trying to defend a kind of psychological indeterminism. But there are few who would still hold these views to be defensible. There are some philosophers nowadays who believe that the newest developments in physics, viz., the uncertainty principle and statistics of probability, are again giving a foothold to indeterminism. But one should not misunderstand the meaning and role of these concepts in modern physics: they may make for some uncertainty or chance happenings but they give no basis for the existence of free will."

Our man lapsed into deep thought. "I think," he said, "I realize that important consequences are involved in this philosophical discovery of determinism. In looking, for example, at a man who has committed a crime, we should not forget to look for the causes which made him commit it. And we may find that his deed was due to factors which were beyond his control. We must try to understand his deed from the factors of causal necessity."

"Yes," answered the philosopher, "but don't forget that it is not only in cases in which you may discover an external force that compelled him, but also in cases in which it would have been said in olden times that he acted of his own free will, on his own decision, with nothing external to compel him. Such a description is utterly superficial. A man is determined even in these cases by the set of causal forces within him, by his desires, instincts, acquired habits."

"Is there not this important factor," asked our man humbly, "that man, after all, in a situation which calls for decision does not know of the forces that will determine him and, therefore, practically will have to choose, to decide? That everything is in fact determined may be of value to someone looking into the past, after the decision has been made, after the deed is done, but not before? And so the principle of determinism does not perhaps do away with the questions of free decision."

"There are some," said the philosopher, "who try to make use of this factor of past and future for our problem, again in connection with new developments in modern physics. But don't you see, this does not help—indeed this may be the very reason why man is deceived about himself, why he may appear to himself as free, which is nothing other than that he does not know how in his seemingly free decisions he is lawfully and by necessity determined by causes."

Our man felt uneasy about this answer, but, unable to clarify the issue, he proceeded with another question. "Aren't those ideas of determinism somewhat dangerous?" he asked. "I should guess that a man who really comes to believe in determinism and to act sincerely in accordance with this belief would not only change his philosophical opinions, but his very actions. He would become a fatalist, relieved of all troubles in facing a situation that calls for a decision . . . it will happen anyhow. . . ."

"True," said the philosopher with a sly twinkle. "But fortunately men believe in their will, and even if they are philosophically convinced of determinism, they will not make use of it in actual situations. On the other hand, you may see in your remark a profound confirmation of the very principle of determinism: even your belief or disbelief in the principle may be a determining factor."

Suddenly our man jumped up from his chair. "Now," he said excitedly, "permit me another question. If we state that all is determined, does this change anything in regard to the real problems of freedom (with the only possible exception of this problem of the realization of fatalism)? Suppose we attach to every deed, to every action, to every attitude, the quality, 'It is determined,' would not all real concrete problems of freedom remain just the same? The discussions between determinism and indeterminism do not touch the real problem, in fact they obscure it. Should the essence of free action be that it is in no way determined? Or if all actions are determined, that there are no free men?"

"Let us not mix up such practical problems with the philosophical issue," said the philosopher. Here from the fullness of his heart our man told the philosopher about his troubles, facing the world situation, about his meeting with the sociologist and about the formulas in the books he had read.

Said the philosopher, "Like you I am a lover of political freedom. Certainly there is the very important problem of how much the State should or should not restrain the freedom of individuals. These are questions with which the sociologists and men of political science may properly deal; but don't you see that the very foundation of all that you have told me about the sociologist and the formulations in the books *is* the modern discovery of determinism, of realizing it as basic in all these questions?"

Our man realized this and was more bewildered than before.

The next day he said to himself, This is what I have learned:

1. There is no freedom because all is determined, is the consequence of causes. Or,
2. Freedom is absence of external restraints, of compulsion, freedom to pursue whatever wish may come to one's mind. Or,
3. Because such wishes may be due to whatever standards may have been internalized on the basis of compulsion, freedom means to be able to follow those instinctual impulses without inhibitions.

Suddenly all he had heard in this context seemed to him utterly strange, narrow, inadequate; superficial, oversimplified, wrongly directed, blind to all the real problems of freedom, appropriate neither to the nature of man nor society, out of focus on both. He felt the desire to get away from all these terms and definitions, he wanted to face again the real situation, to restate the problem in full view of life.

He first thought of what the sociologist had told him and soon felt lost in the manifold features of history, its complexities, its diversities.

"First let me realize," he said passionately, "what I have seen with my own eyes. Have I not seen in my experience strong and indeed very characteristic cases of men, of children, who were free, who were unfree? What were the essentials? My experiences, of course, are no sufficient basis for statistical generalizations; nor do I wish to make any now. What I want is to grasp, to realize, what I have seen."

He recalled a number of cases. Then he said, "Sometimes one sees a man, and by the way he goes through life, by his attitudes, by his behavior in dealing with life situations one feels: this is a free man, he lives in an atmosphere of freedom. And so in observing children.

"On the other hand, one sees men or children, and feels strongly: in their behavior there is no freedom—there is no air of freedom in their world."

It is, he thought, not easy to put into words what one faces so vividly in these extreme cases. Let me think—what were these cases concretely?

The free man, he recalled, frank, open-minded, sincerely going ahead, facing the situation freely, looking for the right thing to do and so finding where to go.

The opposite—he first thought of children he had often seen—inhibited, pushed, or driven, acting by command or intimidation, one-track-minded, chained to certain ways of acting and of thinking, even in viewing situations—the very curves of their actions, of their movements, often showed these features, especially in meeting new situations. They often looked like sorry products of external influences or like slaves of any desire that might have come to their minds. Often they looked like robots, somehow crippled, robbed of essential abilities, narrow-minded, stiff, rigid, mechanical, their movements and postures often had the effect of puppets on strings. And grownups still more so. (Even slave drivers—he had seen such in our times—were they free? No, they belonged here.) Of course, many thus enslaved did not overtly behave timidly at all—just the opposite, brutal and overproud. But one sensed the same unfreedom, sometimes one saw what happened when they had to face a new situation in which their coat of armor was futile. . . .

And what experiences he had had in observing *transitions!*

If a child, if a man, having lived as that kind of slave, came to live in another social field in which there was the real air of freedom, what marvelous happenings had he not observed in such cases! Very similar indeed to regaining health after a long illness.

Suddenly the whole problem appeared to him to be no longer a problem of philosophical schools of whatever standards or evaluations, but a problem of hygiene—it seemed to require the biologist studying health conditions. This is a task of scientific investigation, he thought. But not in terms of those previous theses. What conditions, what institutions, make for the free? What for the unfree? And what price is paid in the change?

This, it was now clear to him, was not to be viewed piecemeal, in terms of a choice, of a wish, of an "instinctual impulsion," etc. One's whole attitude towards the world, towards the other fellow, towards one's group, towards one's own momentary wishes was involved. And suddenly those theses dealing only negatively with freedom appeared to him like saying that growth, that maturing, *is* absence of impediments to growth; that beauty *is* absence of ugliness; that good thinking *is* absence of mistakes; that genuine achievement is due to absence of inhibitions; that kindliness, or friendship, is nothing but absence of hostility; that justice is any legal rule imposed arbitrarily. "What we face," he said, "is not a problem to be dealt with in such a piecemeal, negative way."

After a while he found himself thinking of his experiences in certain specific situations in which there was clearly the one or the other kind of behavior. He recalled discussions. What differences! In the way a man faces a counterargument, faces new facts! There are men who face them freely, open-mindedly, frankly, dealing honestly with them, taking them duly into account. Others are not able to do so at all: they somehow remain blind, rigid; they stick to their axioms, unable to face the arguments, the facts; or, if they do, it is to avoid or to get rid of them by some means—they are incapable of looking them squarely in the face. They cannot deal with them as free men; they are narrowed and enslaved by their position.

For a moment he himself objected, Why are you connecting the issues of freedom with all these features? With questions of being blind or narrow-minded in contrast to facing situations with open eyes and dealing with them honestly? Yes, he decided, I must; these things are most closely and intimately correlated with the meaning and the facts of freedom.

How was it in history, in the times when people honestly fought for freedom? Those men fought against the arbitrary, willful acts of their governments, they fought for fair and honest dealing. To those men freedom was envisaged and endeared in these terms. Freedom was sought and longed for *not* in terms of being able to do whatever might come to one's mind, to act in as one-sided and as blind a way as one might wish, to be free to brutalize the other fellow willfully. Were not those praisers and lovers of freedom those very men who demanded enlightenment for everyone, who fought for just dealing in courts, and just laws?

Thinking of the three theses he had written down earlier, he felt as if the scales had fallen from his eyes. The real question was, what kind of attitude, what rules, what institutions make for the free, what for the unfree? The real problem is not as in thesis (1), which seemed to say that all determination, all causes and influences, are factors against freedom; the problem is which ones are? This is a matter of causes and consequences; some make for freedom in men, some for unfreedom!

"What nonsense!" he said. "If a man is blind, or sees things in a distorted way and you open his eyes, give him knowledge, make him see, you may thereby strongly influence him, change him, determine him, but are you thereby limiting his freedom?

"And do not men have a healthy desire not to be blind or blinded, at least in the long run? *Are* there not, thank God, some tendencies of this kind in men? And in the dynamics of society?"

Thinking of theses (2) and (3), he said to himself, There *is* something in formulating freedom as absence of restraint, of compulsion; a price is paid when spontaneity, genuineness, are impaired or destroyed. Yet the very term compulsion means willful, arbitrary force. And spontaneity, genuineness, are certainly not adequately viewed in terms of "whatever wish may come to one's mind" or in those "instinctual impulsions." What he had read about happiness was not happiness, was a crude caricature of happiness.

The assertions that "cultural institutions by necessity restrain, limit, freedom" now appeared to him astoundingly superficial. Is limiting freedom the essence of institutions for true education? of the roads that society constructs? Likewise of the development of law and of courts— if understood not in terms of any arbitrarily imposed law, but of making possible some degree of confidence in fair, just dealing? Is it not sheer piecemeal thinking to say "restraint is restraint," if a kidnapper restrains, imprisons, a child in order to extort ransom, and if another restrains the gangster from doing it in order to help the child? Is there not in the very birth of cruelty, of brutality, the factor of being blind, of being narrowed down?

And *are* there not tendencies in men and in children to be kind, to deal sincerely, justly with the other fellow? Are these nothing but "internalized rules on the basis of compulsion and of fear"? He thought of children whom he had seen grow—how little did this blind sweeping generalization apply to their kindness, to their desire for real grasp, to their horror in the face of an act of brute injustice.

"What is needed," he said, "is a sincere study of the tendencies, the vectors, their development in children, in men, in the dynamics of society, but not in terms of such rash definitions, or of those 'instinctual impulsions,' assumed in blind generalization. These are tasks for empirical study in the same way that problems of philosophy have become problems of modern science. Old theses, dependent on the philosophical school to which one adhered, should now be studied, discussed in scientific investigations. To be sure, superficial statistics will not help; these are deeper questions, involving the dynamics of men, of society. And if these fine tendencies are often weak, if their awakening, their growth, are often endangered, or if they are wholly overcome by other forces, does this justify constructing substitutes on the basis of their very opposites, or overlooking them, denying them entirely? There was some positive development in this direction. It needs help."

Marvelous tasks for investigations! he thought.

Then again he found himself thinking of the actual world situation. In full view of it, of the actual happenings, he reread the three theses he had written that morning. The whole line of approach appeared to him cruelly to miss the issue by focusing on "whatever wish may come to one's mind," and on those "instinctual impulsions." Was this the issue? (Probably it is just blind restraint that breeds and feeds such impulsions.)

Here are the basic issues, he felt, instead of in those three theses:

That human beings are exposed to injustice, to willfulness, to brutality; robbed of any hope of being treated with fairness, with kindness; that institutions are destroyed which had slowly developed, guaranteeing some justice, some fair dealing.

That men are forced to keep silent in the face of acts of injustice, with no possibility of helping the victims; forced even to help in performing those acts against their will and better knowledge.

Still more, that men, even children, by willfully distorted information become narrowed down, poisoned in their very souls, robbed of the preconditions of free judgment through being blinded, robbed of what in man and society is humane.

Now he felt more clearly why freedom was so dear to his heart.

What he had reached, he felt, was only a start. He saw that there are other problems to be faced; problems of the physical, economic constraints of men by hunger, dire lack of means of subsistence; problems of real coöperation (oh, what he had gone through were not problems of piecemeal individualism); problems of mutual justice between groups; problems of the individual called as a member of his group not only to coöperate in performing, but in facing and judging the very goals; etc. But in all these as in other urgent problems what he had gained did not seem useless. The task he felt was to face these problems also with the attitude of the free man, productively, sincerely; real help he felt would come only this way.

He was eagerly looking forward to the further steps.

Then he took his notebook and wrote down after the three theses:

"Logical remark. This is what I have gone through, logically: In these three theses freedom is viewed in a piecemeal way and defined as a thing in itself, cut off from its living role and function, basically merely negative. Freedom is (1) a condition in the social field, and a terribly important one. In viewing such a condition we should not view it as a thing in itself and so define it, but we should view it *in* its role, in its function, in its interactions, in its consequences for men and for society. Freedom is logically (2) not just a condition; what matters is how men are and how they develop, how society is and how it develops. Freedom is a Gestalt quality of attitude, of behavior, of a man's thinking, of his actions. (Think of the difference between the free and the unfree, the description of which was of course only a first approach to viewing the essentials.) Now logically freedom as condition (1) and freedom as Gestalt quality (2) must be viewed not as two pieces, but in their intimate interrelation. Freedom as condition is only one factor, but a very important one with regard to freedom as character quality. To put a man (or even a dog) in chains has consequences. Some men to be sure remain free in their hearts, even in chains, waiting for the moment to throw them off. But there are men whom chains enslave to the core. And here in the interaction between freedom as condition and freedom as character quality, one understands the real meaning of brute restraint and compulsion—the consequences for the victim and for the oppressor."

What matters is not a rash and elegant definition, but really facing the issues.

# PART II

# GENERAL THEORY

*Wolfgang Köhler*

DARTMOUTH COLLEGE

# PSYCHOLOGY

# AND EVOLUTION

In the psychology of human perception it is customary to distinguish between Empiristic and Nativistic interpretations of given facts. What do these terms mean? The answer seems obvious: an Empirist favors explanations of perceptual facts in terms of learning, while a Nativist prefers explanations in terms of inherited mechanisms which are located in the nervous system.[1] If there are any major difficulties in the Empirist's way of theorizing, such difficulties will not be discussed in these pages. Rather, I propose to analyze what is commonly supposed to be the Nativist's program; because the characterization of this program which I have just mentioned, and which would probably be regarded as

---

Reprinted with permission from *Acta Psychologica*, Vol. 7, Nos. 2–4, 1950.
[1] The term "Empirist" may sound unusual to English and American psychologists. But we need a special name for theorists who tend to give bewildering facts in perception an interpretation in terms of learning. The word "Empiricist" does not refer to such theorists. A philosopher of the Empiricist school might actually prefer Nativistic to Empiristic theories of perception; his principles do not compel him to prefer the latter. Again, philosophers who are Rationalists rather than Empiricists often reason in the Empiristic fashion when they deal with problems of perception. We should therefore confuse two different issues if we were to use the name "Empiricist" both when we mean a particular school in epistemology and when we talk of what I prefer to call the Empiristic trend in the explanation of perceptual facts.

adequate by many psychologists, seems to me to be most seriously misleading.

The main point is this. When referring to inherited particularities of the nervous system, we clearly mean *histological* facts, even if in a given case we may be unable to indicate precisely what these facts are. Thus, when it appears that a certain phenomenon in perception is not brought about by learning, we conclude that it is such histological conditions which are responsible for its occurrence. I should like to show that this inference is by no means generally justified. A phenomenon in perception which is unlearned need not, for this reason, depend upon the existence of special histological factors. Nativism is a dangerous term; it covers several theoretical possibilities. Unfortunately, we are for the most part aware only of the one toward which the expression "inherited" points. It is important that we know what other factors may be involved in unlearned function. For our issue is by no means restricted to a form of theorizing in perception. Even the intellectual life of man will easily be given a wrong interpretation if we do not realize that Nativistic theories tend to include a far too special premise.

At the present time, all biologists agree that, if a nervous system exhibits certain histological conditions, the cells of the species (and, in particulars, those of the individual) are ultimately responsible for the fact. It is the chromosomic equipment of the cells which has forced morphogenetic processes to establish those structures. The chromosomic equipment of a species, on the other hand, is assumed to be a product of evolution. Hence, if a theorist gives us a Nativistic explanation of certain phenomena, and if his theory is of the kind to which the name "Nativistic" commonly refers, he always assumes that, in the last analysis, those phenomena are made possible by particular achievements of evolution.

It seems to me that this procedure is incompatible with the very meaning of evolution. For the principle of evolution implies that all biological events, including the functions of the brain, have *some* characteristics on which evolution has never had any influence whatsoever.

In its most consistent form, the postulate of evolution maintains that once the behavior of the inanimate world is sufficiently known it must be possible to derive all biological facts from principles which hold for nonliving systems. At the present time, nobody can be forced to accept this radical postulate. I will nevertheless adopt it for my present purpose, because in this fashion my task will be greatly simplified. It follows, of course, that I cannot try to convince Vitalists or those who believe in Emergent Evolution. In a sense, this does not affect my argument. The error which I propose to discuss is often made by authors who regard the postulate as a necessary part of modern scientific thinking.

Evolution is commonly regarded as a principle of *change* or *development,* and this is also the natural meaning of the term. Nonetheless, the postulate which I have just mentioned is a postulate of *invariance.* It does not indicate what actually happens when organisms develop from inanimate systems, or when new species arise. Rather, it states that, however such changes may be brought about, the same principles as hold in physics and chemistry apply also to these transformations, and to the forms of life which thus originate. Of course, those who agree with this thesis will readily admit that present formulations of those principles may have to be modified when attempts are made to apply them to living systems. General formulations which excellently serve the physicist's purposes may not explicitly refer to situations which play a particularly important role in biology. In biological theory, principles of science may therefore have to be stated in a way to which the physicist is not accustomed. It goes without saying that reformulations of this kind are entirely compatible with the postulate of invariance in evolution.

When referring to principles, I have in mind such general propositions as the First and the Second Laws of Thermodynamics, but also the Law of Dynamic Direction, a law which is implied rather than explicitly formulated in physics.[2] But the postulate of invariance applies not only to general principles. It also demands that no forces and elementary processes occur in organisms which do not also occur in physics and chemistry. By forces I mean such vectors as electric and gravitational fields. Examples of elementary processes are electric currents and currents of diffusion. It does not, of course, follow from the postulate that all forces and elementary processes which are known in physics must also play a part in living systems. What is meant is merely that such forces and processes as are actually encountered in organisms invariably have counterparts in the inanimate world. It will be realized that all concepts to which the postulate of invariance refers, namely, general principles, forces, and elementary processes, are concerned with *action.* Obviously, as I am now using this word, it applies not only to events which involve changes but also to steady states.[3]

---

[2] Cf. W. Köhler, *The Place of Value in a World of Facts.* New York: Liveright, 1938, pp. 306 ff.

[3] I am aware of the fact that, in physics, the term action has also a much more technical meaning. In the present connection, we are not concerned with action in this sense.

If so much is supposed to have remained invariant in evolution, what can have varied while evolution took place? There must be factors in nature which can change irrespective of the fact that the general principles, the forces, and the elementary processes of all action remain the same. Any textbook of physics can tell us what these factors are. The same principles apply, the same forces operate, and the same processes occur under conditions which vary widely from one system to another. Take mechanics, the discipline which deals with the movements of objects. It is a form of action that objects in the neighborhood of our planet tend to approach its surface. But objects may either be free to follow the direction of the gravitational vector, or given conditions may restrict this freedom. When placed on an oblique plane which is rigid and solid, an object still approaches the earth, but it does so in the direction of the plane and more slowly, because the resistance of the plane eliminates the component of gravitation which would operate at right angles to the plane, and only the component parallel to the plane accelerates the object. Given conditions which exclude certain possibilities of action are called *constraints*. The mechanics of solid objects is not the only part of physics in which constraints modify action. If a gas is surrounded by the firm walls of a container, these walls are constraints. Many processes can occur in the gas, but all those are prevented from taking place which would involve a displacement of the walls, and thus the gas cannot expand as it would otherwise do. In hydrodynamics, a rigid tube in which a liquid is enclosed is obviously a constraint; in contact with the inner surface of the tube, the liquid can move only in the direction of the surface. It is perhaps not customary to use the same term in the case of electric phenomena; actually, however, when a nonconducting substance surrounds a material in which electric currents spread, this substance plays the part of a constraint.

No constraint in the sense in which we have just used the concept makes a positive contribution to the action upon which it is imposed. In this sense (although not in others) the role of such constraints is negative. They serve to exclude certain actions which would be possible if the constraints were not present. But while in this fashion some components of forces and of elementary processes are eliminated, the remaining components do not change their behavior. The laws which hold for forces and processes are formulated in general terms so that, when certain possibilities of action can no longer be realized, the same laws still apply to such actions as are not prevented by constraints. On an oblique plane, for instance, the component of gravitation which operates in the direction of the plane accelerates an object in precisely the same way as it would if the constraint were absent. The general principle which is here involved is the principle of the conservation of energy. On the oblique plane, increments of kinetic energy and losses of potential energy are smaller for a given period than they would be in the absence of the plane. Since both changes are of the same size, the principle holds in this situation just as it does in the case of free fall.[4] Similar considerations apply to the other instances of action under constraint which have been mentioned in the preceding paragraph.

We can now return to our discussion of evolution. While the general postulate of invariance in evolution claims that no essentially new kind of action appears in living systems, it imposes no limits upon the constraints which may develop when certain inanimate systems assume the characteristics of organisms, and when the various species acquire their distinguishing traits. In this respect, the postulate demands only that such constraints be established in a way which is compatible with the laws of physics and chemistry. In organisms, many different forms of action are, of course, combined (and mutually interrelated) which seldom occur together in the simpler systems commonly studied by physicists and chemists. Apart from this peculiarity of life, it can, according to our postulate, be *only* specific constraints by which the living world has been made possible. No examples of such constraints will here be needed, since most histological structures may be considered from this point of view. But, although the world of living creatures would not exist if evolution had not introduced these structures, action in the organisms can never be explained solely by the constraints to which it is subjected. Constraints alone, I repeat, never cause any action; they merely serve to modify actions which, as such, owe nothing to constraints. Thus, if our general postulate is accepted, any action in any organism involves the operation of factors which are entirely independent of evolution. We have seen that these factors are the forces and the elementary processes of nature, and such more general facts as are formulated in the principles of science.

Just as to any other biological processes, our reasoning must be applied to the cortical events on which the characteristics of mental facts depend. Generally speaking, cortical action is also modified by constraints, and to this extent evolution is partly responsible for the way in

---

[4] I am, of course, assuming that the influence of friction can be ignored. If this influence is not negligible, the energy balance of the system becomes more complicated, but the principle of the conservation of energy still remains valid,

which this action occurs. But, *qua* action, it can never be understood only in such terms. For all action is also a matter of processes which evolution has not affected, and which are now not affected by its products, the histological conditions found in nervous systems.

Since this argument may be too abstract to carry full conviction, I will give a simple example. It has recently been suggested that the processes underlying organized perception are steady electric currents which spread in the brain as a continuous medium. If this should prove to be true, the distribution of such currents would partly be determined by histological circumstances which evolution has established in the tissue. Quite irrespective of such special conditions, however, the currents would also follow the general laws which hold for any electric flow in any resisting medium, and cannot have been altered by evolution. If actually some other process plays the part which has just been ascribed to electric currents, our argument must be applied to this other action.

It will now be apparent why we cannot accept the statement that the explanation of all unlearned perceptual facts has to be given in terms of histological conditions. The statement cannot be entirely correct for any perceptual fact. It is only another form of the same mistake if all unlearned functions are attributed to achievements of evolution. For, quite apart from such achievements, unlearned functions are bound to exhibit certain characteristics which they share with actions in the inanimate world.

Although our argument is so simple that it may almost appear as banal, few discussions in which Nativistic explanations are being considered take account of the fact that when we deal with unlearned functions we must always distinguish between action and its constraints. All authors refer to histological conditions upon which such functions depend, and thus, indirectly, to evolution; but few seem to realize that any brain function whatsoever is also an example of actions which do not, as such, depend upon such conditions. One cannot play Hamlet without the Prince of Denmark; on our stage, however, we are consistently trying to do so.

The present issue is now becoming particularly important because the belief in the omnipotence of learning, which characterized an earlier period in the development of psychology, is rapidly beginning to weaken under the impact of evidence which points in the opposite direction. A few years ago, a Symposium on Heredity and Environment showed the change of trend in a most impressive fashion.[5] It seems, however, that

---

[5] Symposium on Heredity and Environment. *Psychol. Rev.*, 1947, 54, 297–352.

the factors involved in unlearned function which owe nothing to evolution, and can therefore hardly be called "inherited," were not explicitly discussed at this conference. We do tend to ignore these factors. In an excellent article on certain phenomena in human perception, a psychologist recently explained that these facts can be interpreted either in the Empiristic fashion or as consequences of the chromosomic equipment of man. Obviously, the chromosomic equipment of man cannot be made responsible for characteristics which action exhibits in inanimate systems as well as in organisms. I do not believe that the author is a Vitalist; most probably, he would accept our general postulate of invariance. Nevertheless, action and the principles which it follows were not mentioned in his paper. It is quite true that in the determination of all events which we study in human perception some inherited conditions and ultimately the constitution of our chromosomes must play a certain role. But they can do so only by influencing processes, the nature of which has not been altered in the least while evolution took its course, and while human chromosomes originated. Consequently, all facts in human perception have certain characteristics which are unrelated to the specific make-up of human cells. In this respect, only one point is open to debate. *To what degree* are constraints imposed upon physical actions when these actions occur in human brains?

Our distinction has to be made quite generally, not only when problems in perception are being considered. In fact, if the distinction is ignored in certain other parts of psychology, the consequences are actually much more important. In some cases, they may affect our very concept of man, and may thus have repercussions even in philosophy. In the early years of this century, a Naturalistic conception of man was strongly recommended by some philosophers. One topic to which they applied their program was human thinking. More specifically, they maintained that knowledge and the attempts to widen its scope are not primarily concerned with objective cognition. Rather thinking was to be regarded as a particular mechanism which evolution has developed in man, and which helps his species to survive. Now, human thinking which is objectively adequate can hardly fail to have useful consequences; but it does not follow that the usefulness of thinking in a particular environment is its most fundamental characteristic, and that its adequacy, when it is adequate, must be defined in terms of its usefulness. For again, although human thought may to a degree be influenced by special conditions which evolution has established, it is, first of all, a form of action. Consequently, the notion that only such conditions, i.e., histological factors, are responsible for the characteristics of thinking cannot possibly be defended. Thinking no less than perception must also follow principles which are unrelated to the particular circumstances of human life, to evolution, and to histological devices. I sometimes wonder what those philosophers meant by nature when they demanded that man be understood in Naturalistic terms. Surely, they ignored the most important of these terms.

In the meantime, their views have had an immense influence upon the intellectual and emotional climate of our historical period. Generally speaking, there is an optimistic trend in evolutionary reasoning. The changes which have occurred since life first appeared on this planet are commonly regarded as improvements. From this point of view, there is, of course, a great temptation to regard human thinking as the very greatest among all evolutionary achievements, and on this basis to feel more optimistic than ever. The Naturalists did not make this mistake. They realized, and sometimes apparently with a certain satisfaction, that in the evolutionary explanation of human thinking as a useful tool this thinking is actually devalued. There is general agreement among the biologists that of all imaginable devices which might have arisen in evolution those have become stable characteristics of a species which serve to make this species better adapted to its environment. Now, although in a way all adaptation implies improvement, it also has its less attractive phase. To the extent to which the various functions in animals and man are thus usefully conditioned, their value must be regarded as relative to the particular environment in which the adaptation has occurred. This is precisely what the Naturalists actually meant, or what their followers understood them to mean, when they said that human thinking is a product of evolution. When we now refer to "human nature," we use the expression with an unmistakable accent on the adjective. We seem to mean a quite particular part of nature, the one which is merely human, or human in a restrictive sense. This is the point at which evolutionary optimism has turned sour; at which evolution has become a powerful source of the relativistic defeatism from which our intellectual culture is suffering. And yet, if we follow the principle of invariance in evolution, there is no cause for this particular form of our ailment. When man is thinking, he invariably follows, at least in part, *some* principles of action which hold everywhere, and can therefore not be suspected of being merely relative to his particular environment. To be sure, he would not exist at all, if evolution had not occurred. At present, he would have little to think about if evolution had not given him sense organs, properly conducting nerve fibers, and many other particular devices. But even a modest nerve impulse which travels along one of those fibers obeys some general principles of action no less than the constraints to which it is subjected. Similarly, man's thinking must have some characteristics which are *not* in any sense determined by evolution and, for this reason, significant only in a relative sense.

In some instances, human thinking may be strongly affected by inherited conditions; in others, it may follow mainly general principles of action rather than such conditions. I have a suspicion that the latter alternative is often realized when human beings grasp relations between objects, and when they derive further relations from those which are given. If this were true, there would still remain unanswered questions as to the cognitive significance of such events. But whatever this significance might be, it would not be limited by the fact that it happens to be human beings in whom the events occur. Moreover, such processes would probably show a certain affinity to the facts which man observes in nature; because, as to certain fundamentals, he would find in such observations what he can also find in himself.

How would a human being be impressed by principles of action if he became aware of them as principles of his thinking? Factual generality, even if it is absolute, need not be related to such concepts as being valid or evident; but it might be so related in the present case. Man might find those principles necessary in the sense in which certain formal principles actually appear to us necessary when we think. Naturally, he would not feel that the recognition of such principles presupposes observation of any particular facts. Rather, their necessity would seem to him to have an a priori character. And yet, no subjectivism would follow, because, as I said before, for excellent reasons an a priori of this kind would tend to fit empirical evidence.

Possibilities such as these fairly obtrude themselves once the postulate of invariance in evolution has been understood and accepted. Even so, it remains to be seen whether principles of action in nature can really be recognized in the way in which human thinking proceeds. Obviously, if attempts in this direction should end in failure, the postulate of invariance could no longer be accepted in its radical form, and a Dualistic view of the world would become unavoidable.

*Mary Henle*

GRADUATE FACULTY, NEW SCHOOL FOR SOCIAL RESEARCH

# SOME PROBLEMS

# OF ECLECTICISM

Some ten years ago Woodworth, commenting on the situation in psychology as a whole, wrote: "Some may lean toward one school and some toward another, but on the whole the psychologists of the present time are proceeding on their way in the middle of the road . . ." (21, p. 254). He suggested that "If we could assemble all these psychologists [all the psychologists in the world] in a convention hall and ask the members of each school to stand and show themselves, a very large proportion of the entire group would remain seated" (21, pp. 254–255).

A similar position was taken by Boring at about the same time:

During the 1930's the *isms* pretty well dropped out of psychology. . . . The only reason for mentioning these four schools in this book is that the student hears about *behaviorism* and *Gestalt psychology* and has a right to be told what they are and that they are no longer important as schools. What was good in all the schools is now simply part of psychology (4, p. 11).

The eclectics, rising above the conflict of schools, hold that psychologists today are in happy agreement. It is their position that no real issues exist among the various points of view in psychology. For it is

Reprinted with permission from the *Psychological Review,* Vol. 64, No. 5, September, 1957.

only on the basis of such a belief that one is able to select from each approach, combining the theoretical contributions of all. As Woodworth presents the middle-of-the-road position:

Every school is good, though no one is good enough. . . . One points to one alluring prospect, another to another. . . . Their negative pronouncements we can discount while we accept their positive contributions to psychology as a whole (21, p. 255).

If eclecticism is as prevalent in contemporary psychology as the above statements suggest, it becomes important to examine its consequences for theory. It is the hypothesis of the present paper that the eclectics have, to a large extent, succeeded in reconciling differences only by obscuring theoretical issues. An alternative to this kind of eclecticism will be proposed.

We may begin with an examination of specific instances of eclectic reconciliations of differences. Examples of two kinds of eclecticism will be discussed, one having to do with reconciliations of positions which refer to the entire field of psychology—the attempt to resolve conflicts among "schools" or general points of view—and a more circumscribed eclecticism relating to particular psychological problems.

As an instance of the first kind, Woodworth [1] writes:

A broadly defined functional psychology starts with the question "What man *does*" and proceeds to the questions "How?" and "Why?" . . . So broadly defined . . . functional psychology scarcely deserves the name of a school because it would include so many psychologists who have not professed themselves. Now the question is whether our middle-of-the-roaders are not after all members of this broadly conceived functional school. . . . But if the middle-of-the-roaders are really functionalists, the question is then whether the same would not be true of all the schools. Are they not all functionalists at heart? (21, p. 255).

Commenting on such a functionalism, Boring wrote in 1950: "Woodworth believed that psychologists were more in agreement than their quarrels indicated, and he sought a system to which all could subscribe. He very nearly succeeded" (3, p. 565).

It is not likely to be denied that psychology today has a functionalist flavor. The interest in the adaptive value of psychological processes is everywhere apparent. Nor can there be much disagreement with a func-

---

[1] A number of the examples to be considered will be taken from Woodworth's writings because the present author regards him as one of the clearest of the eclectics and one of those whose theories are to be taken most seriously.

tionalism defined in terms of these three questions of Woodworth's. But it tells us very little about a psychologist to say that he is a functionalist in this sense. What we need to know are the kinds of answers which a particular psychology gives to these questions. These are the issues in contemporary psychology, and here it is that disagreements arise. What, for example, is the relation of re-inforcement, or of repetition, to learning? How does the learning process proceed? What is the nature of the fundamental human motives? How does the group exert its influence on the individual? It is the answers to such questions as these that divide psychologists. It would seem that Woodworth has succeeded in bringing all together only by obscuring such issues. If all are functionalists today, we still have the problem of examining the differences among the several varieties of functionalism.

The point may be made more specifically in connection with the same author's theory of the conditions of transfer of training, the doctrine of identical components (19), reformulated by Woodworth and Schlosberg (23) as a theory of "common factors." It is put forward to resolve the differences between those who hold that transfer is a function of the identical elements in two learning tasks, and those who maintain that it is a matter of the application of common principles or other whole properties to the two activities. Woodworth's view [2] is that anything concrete can be transferred—thus both identical elements and principles—since "any idea that can be recalled, or any attitude that can be reinstated is concrete enough to qualify. Perhaps anything that can be learned can be transferred" (19, p. 207). Again, "what is successfully transferred is usually something you can put your finger on—a principle, a good emotional attitude, a technique" (22, p. 582).

The controversy about the conditions of transfer is settled, in other words, by saying that *something* is carried over from one activity to the other. It is true that this is a formulation which covers most of the cases. But it lacks an advantage of both of the theories it displaces, namely the attempt to state the specific conditions of transfer. It would seem that the differences are resolved only at the expense of any specific theory in the area of the controversy. The theory covers all the cases only by telling us nothing specific about any of them.

To return to the more general kind of eclecticism, there exist today a number of efforts to reconcile the various significant theoretical posi-

---

[2] Since the earlier formulation (19) is the more explicit, and since the later (23) seems not to differ from it in principle, the former will be drawn upon here.

tions in psychology. A number of authors have attempted to resolve the differences between behavior theory and psychoanalysis, Gestalt psychology and psychoanalysis, behavior theory and Gestalt theory.[3] Several examples of this trend in contemporary psychology will be examined.

The problems seen above in Woodworth's formulations exist also in Abt's statements about basic agreements between psychoanalysis and Gestalt psychology with respect to the structure and development of the personality:

Freud's multiple-structured self is not essentially different conceptually from Lewin's division of the person into regions. The dynamic and economic interchanges that are postulated as occurring with respect to the id, ego and superego in psychoanalysis find parallel expression in Lewin's system of barriers and the classes of movements across them (1, pp. 38–39).

If Abt means that Lewin's *metatheory* is compatible with Freud's *theory* of personality structure, a case could be (but has not been) made for this position. But to equate Lewin's division of the personality into regions with Freud's topographical analysis of the person is to lose all the specific psychological insights of the latter and much of the metatheoretical contribution of the former. Lewin's inner-personal regions, if translated into Freudian terms, would undoubtedly fail to distinguish between id, ego, and superego; his motor-perceptual region includes some but not all of the functions of the Freudian ego.[4] Lewin is, indeed, largely unconcerned with the specific content of the personality, with the distinction between conscious and unconscious motivation, and with the historical development of the person; it is impossible to discuss Freud's topographical divisions apart from such considerations. Again, Lewin has not discussed the content and nature of the forces responsible for behavior; thus the parallel with Freud's statements about dynamics can be maintained only if one turns one's attention away from the specifics of Freud's successive instinct theories. It is indeed possible to find

---

[3] Not all of these discussions are eclectic, at least in the meaning used here. Some attempt to understand the contributions of one psychology in terms of the theory of another, rather than to resolve differences between them. Such work, for example *Personality and Psychotherapy* by John Dollard and Neal E. Miller, will not be considered here. It presents interesting problems of its own which deserve separate treatment.

[4] For example: "It is to a certain degree arbitrary where one draws the boundary between the motor-perceptual system and the inner regions, whether for instance one considers the understanding of speech as an event within the boundary zone or within the inner-personal systems" (16, p. 178).

parallels between Lewin's statements about the tendency of systems under tension to seek discharge and Freud's formulations about the pleasure principle; but to equate the two is to lose the specific character of both the pleasure and reality principles and to neglect Freud's theories about behavior which is independent of the pleasure principle (8).

A further illustration will be given of the tendency prevailing in contemporary psychology to reconcile the ideas of Freud and Lewin. Another author writes: "It is the thesis of this paper that a synthesis of the ideas of Lewin and Freud provides a basis for the beginnings of an integrated system of psychological theory . . ." (5, p. 206). More specifically, "We have already noted the structural parallelism between Freud's divisions of the personality and Lewin's psychical systems" (5, p. 222). This writer, it is true, limits the parallelism, remarking, "Freud has provided the living clay for the Lewinian scaffolding" (5, p. 228).[5] Still, closer examination suggests that essential differences between the "living clay" and the "scaffolding" have been neglected. For example, "one of these [defense mechanisms], projection, becomes the equivalent for Lewin's unreality" (5, p. 222). While there are, of course, important components of unreality in projections, the two concepts are by no means equivalent, if only because not all events on a level of unreality (for example, dreams, fantasies, vague hopes and wishes) can be described as projections, at least as Freud uses the term. Again, to put the Freudian unconscious "directly into Lewinian language" by saying that "there are sub-systems within the region of the self which are not in communication with each other" (5, p. 225) is to slip over the specific nature of unconscious processes in Freudian theory. Furthermore, if this is meant as an equation, it fails to do justice to the very important communications which do exist between conscious and unconscious systems. The point may be illustrated by the dream, which draws upon the person's waking experiences (e.g., experiences of the "dream day") and which is recalled by the waking individual.

Another instance of a premature reconciliation of Gestalt psychology and psychoanalysis may be taken from the work of Witkin *et al.* (18).[6] These authors point out:

---

[5] In this connection Bronfenbrenner comments on Lewin's neglect of the content of psychical systems: "This is indeed an unfortunate oversight" (5, p. 214). The thesis will be developed elsewhere that this is no oversight, but that Lewin undertook a different task.

[6] These remarks in no way detract from the excellence or the significance of these authors' study.

Although psychoanalytic theory, in its conception of primary and secondary processes, recognizes the relation between intellectual functioning and personality, it has not really been concerned with the nature of secondary processes. . . . Gestalt psychology, in contrast, has offered a well-developed theory of cognition, in which the role of the nature of reality in determining perceptual and thought processes has been emphasized. But . . . Gestalt theory has on the other hand neglected the role of personal factors in perception. By showing that a perceptual act cannot be understood without reference to *both* personal factors *and* the nature of reality, studies such as ours help to bridge the gap between Gestalt and psychoanalytic theory, and provide a basis for bringing together the main aspects of both into a single comprehensive theory of human psychological functioning (18, p. 481).

If, as I believe, the authors are correct in saying that "there is still lacking in psychoanalytic theory any specific account of cognition or of the nature of secondary process" (18, p. 481), and that Gestalt psychology has neglected personal factors in perception—these are precisely the reasons why studies such as theirs do *not* help to bridge the gap between the two theories. The gap can be bridged only by a true reconciliation of existing differences; and since these two approaches have been concerned, as the authors point out, with such different areas of psychology, it is difficult even to know where the essential differences lie. A systematic analysis of the assumptions of both psychologies, one concerned with implicit as well as explicit assumptions, would undoubtedly reveal both important differences and surprising compatibilities of the theories. But in the absence of such an analysis we cannot, without glossing over real differences, say that a particular finding helps to bring the two theories together. To do so, it would need to be shown (a) that the results demand a theory which reconciles actual differences between the two approaches; or (b) if the two psychologies are in agreement in the area in question (which would require demonstration), that the findings can be handled in terms which are compatible with both.

To say, in other words, that both personal factors and reality factors determine a perceptual effect is to pose a problem. It is to point out that we need a human psychology which will include both kinds of factors; but it is not to say that such a psychology will be compatible with Gestalt psychology or with psychoanalysis or both. To the present writer it seems more likely that a finding which cannot be handled adequately within the framework of either of these existing systems will demand, not a reconciliation of the two admittedly incomplete theories, but rather a new theory. This point will be discussed below.

A final example, which will show again how eclectic reconciliation of differences may be achieved at the expense of a specific theory in the area of the controversy, may be taken from Welch (17). This author has offered some fundamental propositions which he believes should be acceptable both to Gestalt psychology and to contemporary behaviorism. For example, "perceiving is the result of a stimulus compound producing effects upon the sense organs which establish brain traces similar to or in otherwise related to brain traces formerly established" (17, p. 181). Surely everyone will agree that present percepts are related to traces of past ones; where dispute exists it concerns the specific effects of past experience on perception. Welch has succeeded in reconciling the differences by omitting the specific area of controversy. Again, we are told:

In interacting with its environment, the organism changes in many ways. . . . [Among other changes] it may learn. Learning is the effect of a stimulus compound or stimulus compounds upon the nervous system of the organism and the responses which these evoke, that makes possible the establishment of new responses, as a result of such experiences (17, p. 187).

Many psychologists may, indeed, accept this as a rough definition of learning. But when one leaves this level of generality and raises the question of how this process is to be envisaged, this happy harmony disappears. Hilgard points out: "There are no laws of learning which can be taught with confidence" (12, p. 457). Likewise no one questions the fact that "behavior of any type is the result of the interaction of the organism and its environment" (17, p. 176). But what is the nature of this interaction? What are the roles of organism and environment? Here are questions on which different writers have taken divergent positions. (Cf. 11.) While no one will disagree that memorizing and generalizing (17, pp. 181, 182) occur, and while Welch's definitions might provoke little controversy as rough identifications of the phenomena in question, different theories exist about the nature of these processes.

It will be clear from the above discussion that the existence of facts which all psychologists accept is irrelevant to the problem of eclecticism. Likewise the circumstance that some developments in psychology have called attention to facts ignored by others has no bearing on the issue. The important questions are: How are these facts understood? What is their place in the over-all theoretical system? Even where agreement exists as to the facts, differences are current with respect to these questions.

In all the examples considered here, it would appear that differences have been reconciled and controversy eliminated at the price of obscuring the issues with which research is concerned in contemporary psychology.

Boring, years ago, pointed out the productive role of controversy in scientific research (2). Not only does the eclectic lose prematurely the advantages of controversy, he may to some extent give up the advantages of theory as well. The above discussion contains the suggestion that the eclectic at times renounces specific theory in the area of a controversy in order to reconcile differences. This statement will be qualified below. But now attention must be drawn to a consequence of the intimate relation between fact and theory.

There is a certain amount of fact that can be discovered in the absence of any theory. For example, time errors forced themselves to the attention of psychologists who were concerned with quite different problems. For the most part, however, problems for investigation arise out of the theories one holds. New facts are discovered in the course of research designed to test one's hypotheses. To the extent, therefore, that the eclectic gives up specific theory in the area of a controversy, he is handicapped in the discovery of new facts.

Closer examination will, however, often show implicit theories which may contradict the eclectic's avowed intention by placing him in a position on one side or the other of the (now only implicit) controversy. Woodworth, for example, deals with transfer in terms of *carrying over* something from one learning situation to another rather than in terms of *application* of what has been learned to the training tasks as well as to the new ones. That is, transfer is seen as occurring because knowledge acquired in the original training is carried over to the new activity; the new tasks, to the extent to which they are similar to the learned ones, are considered already partially learned. The alternative is ignored that what is learned is not tasks but principles or other whole properties; thus the training activity may merely provide examples of the use of the principle which can be applied equally to the new situation. Woodworth's theory is thus close to a theory of identical elements in this respect, opposing one derived from the study of learning by understanding (13, Chap. 5) and, indeed, unable to deal with many cases of such learning.[7] This consequence is particularly impressive since, as will be

---

[7] If a theory of common factors were correct, there should never be more than 100 per cent transfer, since two activities cannot have more than 100 per cent of their factors in common. Yet, as Katona has shown (13), cases

illustrated immediately below, Woodworth is by no means opposed to learning by understanding; it is another instance of the confusions which eclecticism breeds.

In another place Woodworth calls attention to the following controversy:

Among present-day theories of learning those which emphasize re-enforcement or the law of effect minimize the perceptual factor, often stigmatizing it as "mentalistic" and impossible to conceive in physical terms, while those which emphasize perceptual learning are apt to deny any direct importance to the factor of re-enforcement (20, p. 119).

In attempting to show that there is "no obvious incompatibility" of these two factors, he makes (explicit) assumptions about learning as a cognitive process [8] which would be likely to be unacceptable to many S-R theorists, and (both implicit and explicit) empiristic assumptions about perception [9] which many cognitive theorists might find equally unacceptable (assumptions, incidentally, which are not necessarily consistent with those about the learning process).[10]

---

exist in which performance on the test activity is superior to that on the training task.

It is of interest to note also that Woodworth's theory, while it succeeds in reconciling the differences, appears to lump together cases that do not belong together. There is evidence that transfer of specific data is different, in process as well as in the magnitude of the effect, from the application of principles derived from one set of data to new material. (Cf. 13.)

[8] For example: "As to connections, several may be established before the conditioning is complete, but the primary one connects the conditioned stimulus with the meaningful character it acquires as the first event in a regular sequence" (20, pp. 121–122). Also "In experiments that offer alternatives and demand a choice, what has to be learned is a distinction between stimulus-objects and not between motor responses. . . . What has to be learned is the difference between the two alleys" (20, p. 122).

[9] "When a new percept is in the making—when an obscure stimulus-complex is being deciphered, or when the meaning of a cue or sign is being discovered—an elementary two-phase process is observable. It is a trial-and-check, trial-and-check process. The trial phase is a tentative reading of the sign, a tentative decipherment of the puzzle, a tentative characterization of the object; and the check phase is an acceptance or rejection, a positive or negative reenforcement of the tentative perception" (20, p. 124).

Among the implicit assumptions seems to be the view that organization is not primary in perception, nor prior to the effects of learning; as well as the idea that there is no fruitful distinction to be made between perception and interpretation.

[10] As a final illustration, Welch states: "This distinction between elementary and higher forms of learning involves the distinction between a situation where the new elements are simple in nature, or simple in character and are simply

Several questions suggest themselves with respect to the theory implicit in eclectic solutions.

(a) A question worth examining is whether there is a tendency for such implicit theory to be too heavily weighted in the direction of traditional theory. As the above examples show, this need not always be the case; but it seems plausible to think that when theory is not explicit, and thus not examined, it draws upon doctrines prevailing both in psychology and in the culture in general rather than upon the newer and less widely accepted theoretical currents. In a similar connection Köhler has pointed to a certain conservatism in eclecticism:

. . . it has been said with approval that psychology now tends to be eclectic. Again, we have been told that in psychology we had better stay in the middle of the road. I cannot agree with these prescriptions because, if they were followed, psychologists would have to look first of all backward. In an eclectic attitude, they would be too much concerned with ideas which are already available; and, in attempting to find the middle of the road in psychology, they would have to give too much attention to the tracks along which others have moved before them. Such attitudes could perhaps be recommended if, in research, security were an important issue. Actually there is no place for it in this field. In research, we have to look forward, and to take risks (15, p. 136).

(b) Another question which arises in connection with the theory underlying eclectic solutions is the following: since such theory is often implicit, and thus unexpressed and unexamined, is it adequate to lead to the discovery of new facts? For example, since the idea of "carrying over" (i.e., as opposed to that of "application") is only implicit in Woodworth's theory of identical components, it seems unlikely that it would be subjected to test. Or again, the implicit elementarism in Welch's statement about learning (cf. footnote 10) is unlikely to be tested, since the author's main focus is on other aspects of the statement.

Also worth looking into in connection with the theory implicit in eclectic solutions are the questions of its adequacy for ordering the facts and its susceptibility to proof or disproof. For example, to say that "something" is transferred is too unspecific a statement of the conditions of transfer to test empirically. Any finding of transfer seems to confirm

---

integrated, and a situation where the new elements are complex and integrated in a complex manner" (17, p. 188). This statement implies an elementaristic view of the learning process—learning being envisaged as the integration of elements—which would be far from acceptable to all the psychologists Welch is trying to reconcile.

it, and there is no result which could disprove it. Again, it has been suggested above that the theory implicit in a given eclecticism is not always
internally consistent. This is a question which deserves examination in
connection with particular eclectic psychologies.

We may summarize the discussion so far by saying that eclectics have
to a large extent succeeded in resolving conflicts in psychology by ignoring differences and obscuring the issues. Some reasons for dissatisfaction with such solutions have been indicated.[11] Is there no alternative? It seems to the present writer that reconciliations can be reached
in psychology only by focusing on the existing differences, examining
them, and carrying on research to settle issues. If this is eclecticism, it
is eclecticism after the fact rather than the prevailing eclecticism before
the fact. And it is clear that it will not be a matter of reconciling existing
theories. Since competing theories on any particular issue in psychology
today—or competing psychological systems—each tend to be plausible
and to be supported by evidence, it is unlikely that any one will win a
clear victory over the others. Yet none can offer a fully satisfactory explanation—or else the controversy would not exist. Controversies do
not exist in science with regard to processes which are fully understood.
Thus the task seems to be one of arriving at new, more comprehensive
theories of the processes in question.

An example should make this clear. It seems safe to say that theories
of forgetting arising out of experimental psychology have found no adequate place for the facts of repression. Nor have the psychoanalysts succeeded (or tried) to bring these facts into relation with a general theory

---

[11] It is of interest to note that eclecticism seems to have presented similar
problems in other fields of knowledge in their comparative youth. I quote an
observation on the medical science of a century ago: "And as the rules derived from fundamental truths seemed to come into unsolvable contradiction
with the experiences and the sanctioned standards of practice, there sprang up
under the name 'eclectic' the representatives of sober elucidation, of the *juste
milieu*, of the medium of the extremes. The breach between theory and practice, which they feared, was avoided or postponed if theory gave up the pre-
tension to penetrate into particulars and if practice agreed that, because of its
youthful immaturity, it should be excluded from counsel, and progress in
silence and in hope. The conflict was settled and peace was achieved, not by
the reconciliation of the parties, but by separating them. The so-called im-
partial examination of the facts should lead only to a middle road between
them. [The eclectics] thought they had principles and avoided their application; they proclaimed themselves free and in practice clung to the consequences
of old dogmas. They practiced tolerance not because they included the truth
of each dogma, but because a chasm existed between theory and life, beyond
which theory didn't matter" (9, p. 9).

of memory and forgetting. Can the two kinds of theories be brought together? It seems to me that the most fruitful starting point is not the attempt to reconcile existing theories. Actually, useful theories of repression do not exist. (Cf. 6 for a similar point, more generally stated.) It is hardly sufficient to say:

Repression proceeds from the ego, which possibly at the command of the superego, does not wish to be a party to an instinct cathexis originating in the id. Through repression the ego accomplishes the exclusion from consciousness of the idea which was the carrier of the unwelcome impulse (7, p. 19).

This statement contains no hypothesis about the processes involved, about how repression can possibly be brought about. Thus there seems to be no point to attempt to reconcile the theories of experimental psychology and of psychoanalysis on repression; neither has an effective theory in this area. What we need is to look into the processes themselves, in the light of what we know about forgetting in general (cf. 10). Can affective processes act, for example, to produce a failure of the Höffding function, i.e., that selective interaction between present process and memory trace which is the basis of recognition and the first step in the process of recall? (Cf. 14, pp. 126 ff.) Under what conditions can emotional and motivational processes introduce interferences? Answers to such questions might lead not only to a hypothesis about the nature of repression, but might also introduce considerable modification into our present theories of the nature of forgetting in general.

The eclectics are, of course, right in maintaining that where a genuine controversy exists in psychology, and where evidence seems to support both sides, there is likely to be some truth to both positions. But they solve their problem too soon. Existing theories cannot be made more comprehensive by adding divergent ones together. They can be broadened to include all the relevant evidence only by looking more deeply into the phenomena with which they are concerned; and this means arriving at new theories.

At this point the parallel between productive solutions of theoretical problems and of personal problems becomes striking. In connection with the reconciliation of opposites within the personality, C. G. Jung points out that conflicts are never resolved on their own level. They are outgrown. Only on a higher level can you see both sides.

SUMMARY

Examples have been presented to show that eclectics tend to resolve conflicts in psychology by glossing over real differences and obscuring the issues. Such solutions achieve harmony at the price of specific theory in the area of the controversy, and thus sacrifice fruitfulness in the discovery of new fact. Closer examination often reveals implicit theories underlying such solutions, but unexpressed and unexamined theory can hardly be expected to equal explicit hypotheses either in fruitfulness or in adequacy in dealing with known facts.

It is here suggested that differences need to be resolved in psychology not by denying them and attempting to combine existing theories, but by focusing on the differences and using them to get a better view of the relevant phenomena. We will achieve more comprehensive theories not by combining existing ones but by understanding better the processes in question.

REFERENCES

1. Abt, L. E. A theory of projective psychology. In L. E. Abt and L. Bellak (Eds.), *Projective psychology.* New York: Knopf, 1950.
2. Boring, E. G. The psychology of controversy. *Psychol. Rev.,* 1929, 36, 97–121.
3. Boring, E. G. *A history of experimental psychology* (2nd ed.). New York: Appleton-Century-Crofts, 1950.
4. Boring, E. G. The nature of psychology. In E. G. Boring, H. S. Langfeld, and H. P. Weld (Eds.), *Foundations of psychology.* New York: Wiley, 1948.
5. Bronfenbrenner, U. Toward an integrated theory of personality. In R. R. Blake and G. V. Ramsey (Eds.), *Perception, an approach to personality.* New York: Ronald Press, 1951.
6. Bruner, J. S. Freud and the image of man. *Amer. Psychologist,* 1956, 11, 463–466.
7. Freud, S. *The problem of anxiety.* New York: Norton, 1936.
8. Freud, S. *Beyond the pleasure principle.* London: Hogarth Press and the Institute of Psycho-Analysis, 1950.
9. Henle, J. *Handbuch der rationellen Pathologie.* Erster Band (2nd ed.). Braunschweig: F. Vieweg u. Sohn, 1846.
10. Henle, Mary. Some effects of motivational processes on cognition. *Psychol. Rev.,* 1955, 62, 423–432. [See pp. 172–186 of the present book.]

11. Henle, Mary. On field forces. *J. Psychol.,* 1957, 43, 239–249. [See pp. 286–297 of the present book.]
12. Hilgard, E. R. *Theories of learning* (2nd ed.). New York: Appleton-Century-Crofts, 1956.
13. Katona, G. *Organizing and memorizing.* New York: Columbia University Press, 1940.
14. Köhler, W. *Dynamics in psychology.* New York: Liveright, 1940.
15. Köhler, W. The scientists and their new environment. In W. R. Crawford (Ed.), *The cultural migration.* Philadelphia: University of Pennsylvania Press, 1953.
16. Lewin, K. *Principles of topological psychology.* New York: McGraw-Hill, 1936.
17. Welch, L. An integration of some fundamental principles of modern behaviorism and Gestalt psychology. *J. gen. Psychol.,* 1948, 39, 175–190.
18. Witkin, H. A., Lewis, H. B., Hertzman, M., Machover, K., Meissner, P. B., and Wapner, S. *Personality through perception.* New York: Harper, 1954.
19. Woodworth, R. S. *Experimental psychology.* New York: Holt, 1938.
20. Woodworth, R. S. Reenforcement of perception. *Amer. J. Psychol.,* 1947, 60, 119–124.
21. Woodworth, R. S. *Contemporary schools of psychology* (Rev. ed.). New York: Ronald Press, 1948.
22. Woodworth, R. S., and Marquis, D. G. *Psychology* (5th ed.). New York: Holt, 1947.
23. Woodworth, R. S., and Schlosberg, H. *Experimental psychology* (Rev. ed.). New York: Holt, 1954.

*Rudolf Arnheim*

SARAH LAWRENCE COLLEGE

# GESTALTEN—

# YESTERDAY AND TODAY

Written on the occasion of the 100th anniversary
of the birth of Christian von Ehrenfels (June 20, 1959)

The remarkable essay "On Gestalt Qualities" (6), published in 1890 by the Austrian philosopher Christian von Ehrenfels when he was in his early thirties, has fallen on fertile ground. It has given a name to one of the most characteristic schools of scientific thought in our time and thereby established its existence formally. It is responsible for the word "Gestalt" having acquired citizenship in the English language; and even the term "Ehrenfels qualities" is encountered here and there in the American psychological literature as a term designating Gestalt properties.

But Ehrenfels did more than baptize the new movement. With great discernment he immediately posed, or at least alluded to, many of the questions that the Gestalt problem raises in the minds of thoughtful theorists even today.

We are accustomed to considering Ehrenfels' approach as transi-

Reprinted with permission from *Gestalthaftes Sehen,* edited by Ferdinand Weinhandl. Darmstadt: Wissenschaftliche Buchgesellschaft, 1960. Translated by the author.

tional: boldly and accurately he showed that the traditional "atomistic" method of science was unsatisfactory; but in order to go beyond the mere summation of elements he added a further, hypothetical element, intended as an explanatory device. Described in this fashion, the theory sounds quaint (9, p. 10). It seems to put new wine into an old bottle. We have learned in the meantime that the Gestalt springs from the organization of the parts themselves, not from a quality added to the parts. We do not say: the whole is "more" than the sum of the parts; we prefer to assert that the whole is "something else" than the sum of its parts. But does this not mean distorting the true situation in our own way?

Ehrenfels' Gestalt qualities were not simply a "gimmick," introduced because an explanation was needed. He was an observer rather than a sophist. When he examined an integrated whole, for example, a painting, he found indeed an over-all composition, but also a collection of parts, which could be perceived one by one and were each distinguished by an independent character of their own. To be sure, when he isolated a patch of color or a shape it changed its character. However, seen in context, a part was not simply "something else"; rather, more often than not, it clearly resembled the isolated piece. The element did not simply disappear in the whole. It underwent changes, lawfully dependent on the interaction of whole-structure and part-structure. We are used to comparing various Gestalt contexts with each other. But isolation, too, is a Gestalt context after all, and indeed a particularly illuminating one. And therefore, although to assert that the whole "adds" something new to the parts is to speak imprecisely and uncautiously, such a formulation points to a neglected aspect of the Gestalt problem.

It is true that Ehrenfels, inevitably perhaps, thought of visual units as the direct counterparts of the retinal stimuli, thus arriving at a set of hypothetical elements which he confused with the actually observed parts of a perceptual whole. What he called the "foundation" of his Gestalt qualities was the sum of the "sensations." Today it is evident that the often quite self-contained parts of a perceptual whole are not unaffected by that whole but, on the contrary, created by it or at least tolerated as sub-wholes, which are thoroughly different from the raw material of elements. In this sense, progress has been made. If, however, we define Ehrenfels' "foundation" in our own way as the sum of the actually perceived, genuine parts and if consequently we ask the question of how the whole is constituted of these parts, we can derive from his concept a fruitful approach even today.

The so-called constancy hypothesis (4, p. 86) led psychologists astray, not so much because it assumed a point-by-point relationship between each act of consciousness and the corresponding process in the nervous system, but because the physiological equivalents selected for the purpose were the additive stimuli in the sense organ rather than the field processes that organize the stimulus material in the projection centers of the brain. Owing to this coupling of the "sensations" with the activities of the peripheral sensory organ, Ehrenfels and his contemporaries assumed without question that one could speak of perception only as long as there was a direct response to a stimulus, whereas memory and the forecasting imagination had to take care of what preceded and followed the immediate present. This meant that the experience of listening to a melody or viewing an object in motion was assumed to be composed of dissimilar elements, namely, direct percepts and indirect "representations." Such a notion surely contradicts introspective evidence, which suggests no such distinction. Do we see a dancer "arrive out of the future and jump through the present into the past?" (2, p. 306). Even in this matter, however, Ehrenfels was farsighted enough to remark that when Ernst Mach, unconcerned with such theoretical scruples, talked about the direct perception of a sound-Gestalt, "he obviously was speaking of perception in a sense that differed from the ordinary."

In the course of time, theory has caught up with observation by recognizing the projection centers in the brain as the probable physiological equivalent of the perceptual field. In the brain field, the temporal succession of past, present, and future is translated into spatial relationships, i.e., some sort of chain of traces, corresponding to sounds or phases of perceived motion. To such a chain of traces further "links" attach themselves seamlessly as soon as new percepts are transmitted to the brain. To what extent these links fuse in unified wholes does not depend on whether they derive from perception directly or only indirectly, but depends—as Ehrenfels recognized intuitively—upon the Gestalt structure of the sequence. "In the case of perceiving a walking person," he says,

we can indicate, with some precision, the range within which we clearly apprehend the Gestalt quality of the percept, in this case, the visually perceived motion. We are convinced that we *see* the most recent phase of the action— the latest step, in the case of medium-fast walking—whereas the earlier steps convey the quite different experience of being merely *remembered*.

This "illusion," as he calls it, "is likely to come about because memory preserves the full continuum of all the positions of the leg only for the latest step so that the corresponding temporal Gestalt quality can be fully visualized, whereas there remains of the preceding one nothing but an incomplete impression" (6, pp. 270–271). In our present-day language this means that the range of the psychological present is determined by the strength and boundary of the Gestalt context. A passage of music, for example, which is conceived by the listener as an indivisible unity, appears to be "in the present."

Strictly speaking, anybody who assumes that the sensory experience of a sequence of sounds is based on perception only for the short moment of the actual present but otherwise on memory, ought to make the same assertion for the visual field, since objects are perceived by successive scanning if they are at all extensive. Ehrenfels, however, maintains that for spatial Gestalten the situation is much simpler because "all the parts of the complex on which the Gestalt is based are given simultaneously" (6, p. 253). Evidently he has in mind the phenomenal difference between the succession of what is heard and the simultaneity—or better, timelessness—of what is seen. The question of how this difference comes about would seem to us not at all easy to answer since both kinds of process derive physiologically from temporal successions of stimulations. Quite in general, psychologists are coming to realize more and more that perception is not primarily an effect of sustained sensory stimulation. On the contrary, perception seems to record essentially the changes in stimulation. Even in the peripheral sense organ any persistence of a stimulus seems to cause a weakening of the response. In fact, Grey Walter in his studies of brain waves has recently suggested that the terminal phase of the sensory process might be the kind of scanning motion we know from cathode rays and that the $\alpha$-rhythm of the EEG may reflect such a "searching for pattern" (7, pp. 108 ff.). The fact that our eyesight presents the things of our world in timeless immobility, in spite of the dynamic origin of vision, may find its explanation in the nature of the stimulus material. Also the cortical center of vision uses its spatial dimension for the purpose of discerning the locations of stimuli, whereas in hearing the same dimension is used to distinguish pitch.

Essentially Ehrenfels thought of a Gestalt as a synthesis brought about when physiological processes make direct contact with each other. He held that, for reasons not yet known, spatial cohabitation in the brain produced a "new" psychical entity with properties still to be determined. Psychology was unable to move beyond this step, decisive though it was, until a Gestalt was understood to be the result of a concretely describable whole-structure, which determines the place and function of the parts constituting it. Only this further insight mobilized experimental research. It showed, for example, that a Gestalt, in order to come about, does not require the presence of all parts but only that of the skeleton of factors which determine the total structure. The "effort" often needed to produce a perceptual Gestalt had been observed by Ehrenfels and explained by the need to supply missing elements of the "foundation"; nowadays we are more inclined to believe that the "effort" is needed when a conglomeration of parts is slow to resolve itself in a comprehensive whole (2, p. 49, Fig. 44).

Nevertheless, Ehrenfels recognized the fundamental problem of structural organization when he raised the question of "why there emerge from that infinite crowd of elements the particular Gestalten that seem primordial and, as it were, privileged" (6, p. 288). Wertheimer has treated this problem thoroughly in what he used to call his "dot paper" (8), which starts out with an answer to the question: What are the rules according to which elements combine? Intuitively Ehrenfels anticipated a principle that might be called complementary to Wertheimer's "factor of similarity" (8, p. 309) by pointing out that a white square on a dark ground is discerned because it "detaches itself from its surroundings by different coloration"—a factor of dissimilarity, in other words, which appears as a useful supplement to the concept of "grouping," particularly if we remember William James's briskly formulated rule: "The law is that all things fuse that *can* fuse, and nothing separates except what must" (3, Vol. I, p. 488).

Our philosophical predecessor is at his most modern when he explains that Gestalt qualities submit to abstraction. What he has in mind is not only the strict identity of structure, which can serve as a common denominator for all transpositions. He also points out that, for instance, a common rhythm may be the basis of comparison for Gestalt patterns otherwise different from each other. Most important, he suggests that abstractions occur not only in the traditional way on the basis of common elements but because of a similarity in the total phenomenon, the style or habitude "which often resists tenaciously any attempt at an analysis based on the identity of single components" (6, p. 279). He does not tell us how to go about such classification according to structural types; but then, up to this day, nobody else has dealt concretely with this problem of abstraction based on structural similarities, fundamental though it is for the Gestalt approach to scientific method.

Incidentally, Ehrenfels extends his observations on structural similarities even to the question "whether Gestalt qualities belonging to different and apparently incommensurable realms of perception—for example, a crescendo or the growing stronger of the light at dawn or the mounting of suspense—might not possess a direct similarity, which would go beyond the mere identity of common traits (such as in this case the time) and yet be inherent in the phenomena themselves" (6, pp. 279–280). He describes here the principle of isomorphism, i.e., the structural similarity of processes in different media. Today, the Gestalt psychology of expression and of the body-mind problem is founded on this principle (5, p. 61; 4, pp. 56 ff.; 2, pp. 363 ff.).

By pointing out that Gestalt qualities are subject to abstraction Ehrenfels provided, at the same time and apparently without realizing it, the "counterweight to the individualistic tendencies" of which he speaks in the last paragraph of his paper. More recently, Gestalt theory has indeed been claimed as an ally for the idiographic (*geisteswissenschaftlich*) view, according to which the uniqueness of the individual whole excludes any kind of lawful generalization (1, p. 16)—a misunderstanding that, we discover, can be refuted by reference to the very "prime source."

Ehrenfels touches the most sensitive spot of Gestalt theory when he discusses a question likely to be raised in response to his approach. If there is to be assumed an infinitely large number of mutual influences among the parts or combinations of parts, would not "an unending complication of our mental life" be the consequence? His most striking counterargument is: But if we look at the facts, we do find that each part is clearly given to us as to its own nature and function in the whole (6, pp. 256–257)! This observation is certainly correct. It means to us that the nervous system fulfills indeed the seemingly superhuman task of having all the innumerable interactions among parts or complexes of parts take place in such a way as to make the result appear with precision in each part and at each structural level of the whole. The miracle is made possible by the fact that it takes place in perception. This means it is accomplished by a physiological field process in which the forces constituting the field organize themselves automatically in the direction of a minimum of over-all tension.

Well and good; but what happens when the reasoning intellect undertakes to trace such accomplishment? It seems safe to assume that conceptual thinking is not a field process but consists in the tying of relations among items. Therefore if we attempted even in the simplest example to describe the multitude of interactions and to explain why a given part appears at its place in the whole in that particular fashion rather than another, our interpretation, like meshes thrown over a statue, could offer a relational network of any desired density but never the Gestalt process itself.

If this is true we may have to think of the Gestalt as a limiting case, a scientific objective which conceptual thinking approaches asymptotically but which—because of its own nature—it can never reach. Perhaps we are faced here with one of the ineluctable differences between perceiving (*Anschaulichkeit*) and conceptual reasoning (*Begrifflichkeit*). Granted that in the practice of research it makes all the difference whether we describe the object of an investigation as the sum of independent parts and relations or whether, with our mind intent upon the whole, we select for our description the relations closest to the total structure we perceive. In principle, however, we should have to realize that conceptual reasoning, given its phenomenal as well as its physiological character, is doomed to atomicity.

Once this is admitted, must we say that this limitation means the tragic foundering of science? Or shall we remember with some serenity that it is precisely in the nature of science to trace some of the significant lines of force in what we call reality, not however to duplicate this reality itself in all its complexity? This is a question which the psychologist may have to hand back to the philosopher for further treatment.

REFERENCES

1. Allport, G. W. *Personality*. New York: Holt, 1937.
2. Arnheim, R. *Art and visual perception: a psychology of the creative eye.* Berkeley and Los Angeles: University of California Press, 1957.
3. James, W. *The principles of psychology*. New York: Dover, 1950.
4. Koffka, K. *Principles of Gestalt psychology*. New York: Harcourt, Brace, 1935.
5. Köhler, W. *Gestalt psychology*. New York: Liveright, 1947.
6. Von Ehrenfels, C. Ueber 'Gestaltqualitäten.' *Vierteljahrsschr. f. wiss. Philos.,* 1890, 14, 249–292. [Reprinted in Ferdinand Weinhandl (Ed.), *Gestalthaftes Sehen*. Darmstadt: Wissensch. Buchges., 1960.]
7. Walter, W. G. *The living brain*. New York: Norton, 1953.
8. Wertheimer, M. Untersuchungen zur Lehre von der Gestalt. II. *Psych. Forsch.,* 1923, 4, 301–350.
9. Wertheimer, M. *Ueber Gestalttheorie*. Sonderdrucke des Symposion, Heft 1. Erlangen: Philos. Akad., 1925.

*Wolfgang Köhler*

DARTMOUTH COLLEGE

# THE PRESENT

# SITUATION IN

# BRAIN PHYSIOLOGY

During the past ten years, I have worked in physiological psychology. This term refers to a rapidly growing number of problems and procedures. Most firmly established is the interest in questions of localization. Excellent investigations have shown how loss of function in one part of the brain or another affects behavioral achievements. Equally interesting are the results of tests in which the brain is either locally stimulated or, as a whole, subjected to electric shocks. We are especially impressed by the discovery that stimulation of certain parts of the brain seems to be equivalent to an award and that of other parts to a punishment. Attempts to influence behavior by chemical action have so far not had equally satisfactory results. For, while the changes in question are often strong, it is still difficult to describe them in precise terms. But so great is the interest which the medical profession takes in such experiments that present shortcomings of the chemical approach will probably be overcome within the next few decades. Efforts to relate the chemical characteristics of individual brains to behavior are just beginning to yield promising findings.

Reprinted with permission from the *American Psychologist,* Vol. 13, No. 4, April, 1958.

While there can be no objection to these endeavors as such, physiological psychology should also be concerned with problems to which such investigations rarely refer. First of all, what exactly happens in the brain when certain psychological events take place? Even if we knew in detail what areas of the tissue are involved in particular achievements, we would still not be able to answer that question. Let me mention a simple example. To my knowledge, neither birds nor fishes have a visual cortex; and yet, the pattern vision of certain birds and fishes resembles that of the primates who have a visual cortex. Consequently, a given kind of process may occur in different locations; and, if this is true, we have to deal with a functional problem which studies of localization alone cannot solve. My own work in physiological psychology refers to functional questions in this sense.

I do not believe that this part of our task can be entirely left to the neurophysiologists. For, much as I admire their actual achievements, we disagree on one major issue. At the present time, no evidence as to the nature of brain function can compare with our own, that is, the psychologists' evidence, and most of this the physiologists quietly ignore. They obviously do so in the conviction that the main principles of peripheral nervous function are also those of central function. Hence, since they know the former processes extremely well, they do not seem to expect that, when studying the brain, they might sooner or later need our help.

But the most important process of the peripheral nervous system is the nerve impulse. If brain function, too, consisted mainly of such impulses, then hosts of psychological facts could never be understood in physiological terms. Nerve impulses are particularly lonely events. While they travel along their fibers, each is almost, if not entirely, unrelated to the others. The principal characteristic of most psychological situations, on the other hand, is interrelation of their parts. Some such relations may be established by impulses which travel in transverse neurons from one place in the brain to another. But in many instances this explanation does not work because the interactions in question depend upon the specific nature of the various interacting facts. Nerve impulses which seem to be always events of the same kind can hardly represent the specific characteristics of one local fact at the place of another. Psychologists will also hesitate to admit that such different phenomena as perception with all its modes, memory, learning, attending to, feeling, thinking, and planning can all be derived from such a monotonous principle of action.

I do not, of course, deny that impulses travel in axons of the brain just as they do in peripheral fibers. I merely suspect that, in addition, there are other forms of brain action and that, from the point of view of psychology, such other actions are no less important than the impulses. Hypotheses about these further processes can be developed only by those who are familiar with certain parts of physics, with neurophysiology, and with the basic facts of psychology. I do not suggest that we return to what was once called brain speculation.

In recent years, my collaborators and I have formulated such an hypothesis and have then tried to verify it in physiological experiments (10–18). The psychological fact from which we started was the segregation of molar units or things in visual fields. It seemed to us a plausible assumption that, when the brightness of a certain area differs from that of its environment, this area will be pervaded and surrounded by an electric current. The current inside and the current outside would flow in opposite directions. Functionally, therefore, a sharp discontinuity would be established at the boundary of the area.

A few years later, Wallach and I began to study the distorting effects which prolonged inspection of a visual object has upon this object itself and upon test objects afterwards shown in about the same region (17). I need not describe how we soon found ourselves in the good company of Gibson, who had discovered similar effects in other instances (6). Our own experiments showed that the observed distortions follow a general rule. Test objects recede from the regions in which the previously inspected objects, and particularly their contours, have been seen —as though an obstruction had been established in these regions. Not only our own observations but also those of Gibson could be derived from this rule.

It was, of course, our next question whether such phenomena can be explained in terms of known physiological facts. Does any process cause obstructions in the nervous system? There is such a process. When a current flows through cells of the nervous system, it affects their surfaces. Where it enters the cells, it raises the local impedance and thus blocks its own way. Where it leaves the cells, the opposite happens. But since, after a short while, the former effect becomes stronger, the final result is an obstruction. Thus the current is weakened, and its distribution in the tissue changes. When it is interrupted, the affected tissue remains in its altered condition for considerable periods. Test currents which are now conducted through this region will, therefore, also deviate from their normal course. They will be weakened where the im-

46523

pedance has been raised, and their intensity will grow in less affected parts. Hence, the current as a whole will recede from the affected region just as, in a figural aftereffect, a test object recedes from the area previously occupied by an inspection object.

Our assumption that activated parts of the visual cortex are sources of electric currents can, therefore, also explain the figural aftereffects. Are we right in saying that the displacement of test objects in figural aftereffects and the deflection of test currents in the neighborhood of obstructed tissue are remarkably similar facts? I once had an opportunity to demonstrate aftereffects to a well-known physiologist who was not yet acquainted with these phenomena. After several observations, he turned to me and said with a smile: "Nice demonstrations of electrotonus, aren't they?" Electrotonus is an old name for the obstructions which currents establish in the nervous system.

When electrotonus was first discovered, it was caused by currents conducted through the tissue from the outside. Since, in our theory, this condition is supposed to be established by currents which issue from active parts of the tissue itself, we now had to demonstrate that there are such currents. This proved to be a difficult enterprise, but eventually we succeeded (12–18). At the present time, numerous records of visual and auditory currents are available. They were taken from intact human heads and from the exposed projection areas of cats. Occasionally, visual currents have also been registered from the brains of monkeys. I wish to thank Held, O'Connell, Neff, Wegener, Pribram, and Rosenblith for their invaluable collaboration.

Our findings agree with known facts of cortical localization and may therefore be regarded as reliable. The electrotonic action of the registered currents is also obvious. Continuation of the flow in given parts of the tissue soon reduces its intensity. So far, therefore, our factual evidence agrees with our expectations, and our theory of figural aftereffects seems now to rest on fairly firm ground.

Figural aftereffects are merely deviations from what we call normal perception. An explanation of these effects in physiological terms must therefore include statements about the processes underlying perception in general. Actually, our suggestion that cortical currents play an important part in normal visual perception preceded our work on figural aftereffects. This thesis, however, has not been generally accepted, partly because it seems to be at odds with certain experimental findings.

Lashley and his collaborators (19) laid strips of gold foil on the visual cortex of one monkey and thrust thin wedges of the same material into the occipital lobes of another. It was assumed that these measures would greatly distort the distribution of visual currents. When postoperational tests showed no disturbance of the animals' vision, the authors concluded that perceptual organization cannot be related to such currents.

I do not believe that this conclusion is justified. Strips of gold foil attached to the surface of the brain can cause no major disturbance of cortical currents because the electromotive forces involved operate at right angles to those metallic conductors. Under these circumstances, only an exceedingly small part of the flow will be deflected into the very thin strips and, since this part, too, must return to the other side of the source, it cannot follow them for more than a very short stretch. Wedges of gold foil thrust into the cortex will at first cause a stronger disturbance; but the very fact that now a highly concentrated flow must pass through these wedges will establish abnormally high electrotonic obstructions in the tissue around their tips, and soon the conductors may practically be sealed up.

Sperry, Miner, and Myers (22), who worked with cats, took several steps to distort the cortical currents. In one experiment, they inserted tantalum wires into the visual cortex. In some animals, the tissue was sliced by vertical cuts in various directions; in others, small plates of an insulating material were pushed into the visual region. Extraordinarily difficult discriminations between visual patterns which the cats had previously learned to perform were, on the whole, not very greatly disturbed by these radical measures.

I have difficulties in understanding this finding. It seems to me incompatible not only with my own views but also with generally accepted neurological evidence. For, autopsies revealed that, in several instances, the visual projection system including the geniculate bodies had been very severely damaged. Even during the initial training, the discriminations which the cats had to perform must have taxed their abilities to the utmost. How could their achievements remain similarly precise when much of the tissue necessary for vision had been destroyed? It is to be hoped that these experiments will soon be repeated. The authors realize that any material which is frequently used in animal experiments will gradually acquire particular characteristics which may serve as extraneous cues; but their statements in this respect do not answer one question: With very few exceptions, they always used the same pattern, an equilateral triangle, as the positive object, while up to 40 modifications of this triangle served as negative objects. Were correspondingly numerous copies of the positive object presented during the training and the final tests?

No comments on our work have so far been made by the neurophysiologists. I suspect that they do not like its general trend. Cortical currents or fields differ from the more popular nerve impulses in three respects. In the first place, they do not follow the all-or-none principle which holds for the impulses. The currents are graded processes; the degree to which their cortical sources are activated, and therefore also their own intensity, varies from one instance to another. Physiologists will hardly raise objections on this particular ground because they are quite familiar with graded events in the nervous system. Such events are known to occur at the surface of axons and also at synapses.

Secondly, unlike the nerve impulses and the electric rhythms of cortical cells, the currents shown in our records have not the form of short-lived waves; rather, they are quasi-steady states. But again, such states occur quite regularly at synapses and have been recorded in numerous physiological investigations. I will presently return to these studies.

A third difference between cortical currents and nerve impulses refers less to certain facts than to the interpretation of these facts. While the currents spread freely in the tissue as a continuous medium, nerve impulses follow prescribed linear conductors, the nerve fibers. But no physiologist will deny that many electric states of cells and fibers have fields which also spread beyond their sources. The field of nerve impulses has been measured at considerable distances from the active fibers (20). The alpha-rhythm of cortical cells can be registered from intact human heads only because this rhythm establishes corresponding currents not only in the cortex but also in the skull and the scalp. Or take the evoked potentials which announce the first arrival of afferent impulses in the projection areas of the brain. It has been shown that these potentials, too, can be recorded from the intact head. Physiologists accept these facts, but they do not seem to regard them as very important. The reason is obvious and has once been clearly formulated by Adrian (2). To the extent to which neural processes are located in or on histological elements, their behavior in the tissue is prescribed by the arrangement of these elements; and, since this arrangement appears to be most orderly and practical, the distribution of corresponding functions will be equally precise and practical. On the other hand, the currents which spread around the active elements are not subjected to such restrictions. Hence, it is often assumed that, if they do not cause confusion and disorder, their influence on the tissue and on other processes must be negligible.

Every now and then, a physiologist discovers facts which cannot be reconciled with this interpretation of neural action. The fields of activated elements do influence processes in other elements. For instance, under certain conditions the cat's spinal cord exhibits a regular rhythm. Bremer (4) has demonstrated that this activity is synchronized from one end of the cord to the other. The author himself remarks that the rhythm spreads with a speed far beyond the speed of ordinary neural transmission and that the interaction involved must therefore be mediated by electric fields of the active cells. To prove that this is true, he even made a sharp cut through the cord which left its two parts unconnected by histological elements, that is, connected only by physical contact. Afterwards, the rhythms on one side and the other of the cut were just as nicely synchronized as they had been before. Similar observations made by Gerard and Libet (5) in their work on the frog's brain are, of course, generally known. It follows that neural interactions can be maintained quite independently of messages which travel along fibers.

Even more important is another function of neural fields. In 1938, Barron and Matthews (3) published a most important paper on the steady potentials which impulses establish at dorsal and ventral synapses in the spinal cords of frogs and cats. They realized that such potentials must be sources of equally steady currents, and they also discovered that these currents have a remarkable effect upon the cells through which they pass. As soon as their intensity has reached a certain threshold value, they throw these cells into rhythmic action, which is then, in the form of impulses, propagated along the axons of the cells. To my knowledge, all records of ventral synaptic potentials and their currents show this effect. Consequently, while occasionally transmission at a synapse may be a direct effect of the impulses which arrive in presynaptic fibers, this transmission is for the most part mediated by synaptic currents. Under the circumstances, one can no longer maintain that the currents of the nervous system are mere epiphenomena.

Steady potentials of neural structures have been demonstrated by several physiologists. Adrian (1) has shown that the electric response of a beetle's optic ganglion is a steady state or current. Quite recently, Goldring and O'Leary (7, 8) have registered steady currents from the visual cortex of the rabbit and have thus confirmed our own findings. There seems to be little doubt as to the origin of cortical currents. The steady spinal currents discovered by Barron and Matthews issue from activated spinal synapses. Most probably, the sources of perceptual currents are activated synapses in the cortex.

Let me add a few remarks about problems in my field which ought to be solved next. First of all, figural aftereffects have been demonstrated not only in the frontal plane but also in the third dimension. Years ago, Gibson (6) discovered such effects in kinesthesis, and we studied further examples in this modality. In addition, figural aftereffects occur in passive touch, and most probably also in hearing. Even certain inhibitions which tend to impede learning may partly be caused by what we have called "satiation." It has not yet been possible to apply our physiological assumptions to all these phenomena. The reason is simply that nobody knows the physiological facts which underlie visual depth, kinesthesis, and learning. Naturally, we cannot tell how electrotonus affects these processes until their nature as such has been revealed. Thus, we have three new tasks which follow from the study of figural aftereffects.

As though this were not enough, there is another problem to be solved in this field. Ever since Gibson's first discovery, it has been known that, under certain conditions, figural aftereffects are not prevented by eye movements of the subject. Again, when many objects of a given kind slowly move across the visual field while the subject fixates a mark, the moving pattern still causes a figural aftereffect, and this effect corresponds to the shape of the moving objects. During Ivo Kohler's well-known experiments (9), the subjects could also move their eyes as they wished; and yet, the resulting specific adaptations had much in common with figural aftereffects. Now, if the obstructions established under such conditions were all localized at exactly the same neural level, the statistical result would be a homogeneous layer of satiation which could cause no specific aftereffects. It seems to follow that the location of obstructions which arise at different times cannot be precisely the same— in other words, that time is spatially represented in the brain just as it is in the geological strata on the surface of the earth. This may seem to be a bold hypothesis; but it is the only assumption which can explain such remarkable facts. Incidentally, there is also no other explanation for certain facts in memory. Memory traces, too, remain individual entities; although, statistically speaking, they must be established everywhere and would therefore form a homogeneous layer of affected tissue if their location in detail did not depend upon the time of their origin. As a further task, we must therefore try to discover how the temporal dimension is represented in the tissue.

These are fairly formidable problems. Another task which is again related to the figural aftereffects does not look quite so forbidding. I mentioned that the term electrotonus is commonly used as a name for the obstructions caused by currents. Actually, as we have seen, currents affect the surfaces of cells in two ways: they establish an obstruction only where they enter cells, and they lower the local impedance where they leave them. The more precise name for the former change is anelectrotonus, and the latter is called catelectrotonus. Strictly speaking, therefore, our theory of figural aftereffects is mainly concerned with anelectrotonic action.

But are we allowed to make use of this particular action alone and simply to ignore that cortical currents must also establish catelectrotonic changes? Under the conditions which give rise to figural aftereffects we can safely do so, because under these conditions the anelectrotonic changes are particularly strong. There are, however, situations in which the catelectrotonic effects ought to be stronger, and where this happens the flow of currents will be facilitated rather than impeded. As a consequence, tissue in the catelectrotonic state must attract test currents and, if these currents are those of perceptual objects, these objects must appear displaced *toward* the tissue in question.

Physiological evidence permits us to predict under what circumstances currents and objects will be attracted by certain places in their neighborhood. Best conditions will be those in which perceptual objects just appear or disappear, and also those in which one object appears while the other is just disappearing. On the other hand, when perception begins to be stable, catelectrotonic attraction will soon be overcome by anelectrotonic repulsion. We all know perceptual facts which only arise under the conditions favorable to catelectrotonic effects. I am referring to the various forms of apparent movement. But certain achievements of memory may also be related to catelectrotonic facilitation. At the present time, our studies are mainly concerned with these two issues.

REFERENCES

1. Adrian, E. D. Synchronized reactions in the optic ganglion of *Dytiscus*. *J. Physiol.*, 1937, 91, 66–89.
2. Adrian, E. D. General principles of nervous activity. *Brain*, 1947, 70, 1–17.
3. Barron, D. H., and Matthews, B. H. C. The interpretation of potential changes in the spinal cord. *J. Physiol.*, 1938, 92, 276–321.

4. Bremer, F. *Some problems in neurophysiology.* London: Athlone Press, 1953.

5. Gerard, R. W., and Libet, B. The control of normal and "convulsive" brain potentials. *Amer. J. Psychiat.,* 1940, 96, 1125–1153.

6. Gibson, J. J. Adaptation, after-effect and contrast in the perception of curved lines. *J. exp. Psychol.,* 1933, 16, 1–31.

7. Goldring, S., and O'Leary, J. L. Experimentally derived correlates between ECG and steady cortical potential. *J. Neurophysiol.,* 1951, 14, 275–288.

8. Goldring, S., and O'Leary, J. L. Summation of certain enduring sequelae of cortical activation in the rabbit. *EEG clin. Neurophysiol.,* 1951, 3, 329–340.

9. Kohler, Ivo. *Über Aufbau und Wandlungen der Wahrnehmungswelt.* Vienna: Rohrer, 1951.

10. Köhler, W. *The place of value in a world of facts.* New York: Liveright, 1938.

11. Köhler, W. *Dynamics in psychology.* New York: Liveright, 1940.

12. Köhler, W. Relational determination in perception. In L. A. Jeffress (Ed.), *Cerebral mechanisms in behavior.* New York: Wiley, 1951. Pp. 200–243.

13. Köhler, W., and Held, R. The cortical correlate of pattern vision. *Science,* 1949, 110, 414–419.

14. Köhler, W., Held, R., and O'Connell, D. N. An investigation of cortical currents. *Proc. Amer. phil. Soc.,* 1952, 96, 290–330.

15. Köhler, W., Neff, W. D., and Wegener, J. Currents of the auditory cortex in the cat. *J. cell. comp. Physiol.,* 1955, 45, Suppl. 1, 1–24.

16. Köhler, W., and O'Connell, D. N. Currents of the visual cortex in the cat. *J. cell. comp. Physiol.,* 1957, 49, Suppl. 2, 1–43.

17. Köhler, W., and Wallach, H. Figural after-effects: An investigation of visual processes. *Proc. Amer. phil. Soc.,* 1944, 88, 269–357.

18. Köhler, W., and Wegener, J. Currents of the human auditory cortex. *J. cell. comp. Physiol.,* 1955, 45, Suppl. 1, 25–54.

19. Lashley, K. S., Chow, K. L., and Semmes, J. An examination of the electric field theory of cerebral integration. *Psychol. Rev.,* 1951, 58, 123–136.

20. Lorente de Nó, R. *A study of nerve physiology.* New York: Rockefeller Institute, 1947.

21. Sperry, R. W., and Miner, N. Pattern perception following insertion of mica plates into visual cortex. *J. comp. physiol. Psychol.,* 1955, 48, 463–469.

22. Sperry, R. W., Miner, N., and Myers, R. E. Visual pattern perception following subpial slicing and tantalum wire implantations in the visual cortex. *J. comp. physiol. Psychol.,* 1955, 48, 50–58.

# PART III

# COGNITIVE PROCESSES

*Hans Wallach*

SWARTHMORE COLLEGE

# BRIGHTNESS CONSTANCY

# AND THE NATURE

# OF ACHROMATIC COLORS

PART I

The problem of brightness constancy arises through the following circumstances. The amount of light which is reflected by an opaque object
and which stimulates the eye depends not only upon the color of the
object but just as much upon the amount of light which falls on the object, that is upon the illumination in which the object is seen. When in
spite of this, the seen colors are in agreement with the object colors,
when a given object appears to have the same color in various illuminations, we speak of brightness constancy.

The majority of investigators who aim at all at functional explanations understand this problem to mean: How is illumination registered
and in what way is it taken into account so that the experienced colors
remain constant when the illumination is varied? In this version the
problem is a difficult one at the outset, for illumination is never directly
or independently given but is represented in stimulation only inasmuch

Reprinted with permission from the *Journal of Experimental Psychology,* Vol.
38, No. 3, June, 1948.

as it affects the amount of light which is reflected by the objects. To be sure, we perceive illumination as well as surface color; a spot of light here, a shadow there, a brightly lighted region near the window or the dim light of dusk on everything. But the fact remains that both variables, object color and objective illumination, affect the eye through the same medium, the varying amount of reflected light. If the seen illumination were found to be in agreement with the objective illumination, in principle the same problem would arise which we face regarding the surface colors. There is only one stimulus variable to represent two objective variables each of which seems to have its counterpart in experience. Under these circumstances investigation has largely consisted in the study of factors by which illumination could be recognized and in the demonstration of their effectiveness in bringing about constancy.

The following observations suggested a radically different approach to the writer. They concern some variations of an experiment by A. Gelb which demonstrated brightness constancy in a most impressive way. Gelb's experiment [1] is most conveniently performed by opening the door of a dimly lighted room and by suspending in the frame a piece of black paper. This paper is illuminated by a strong projection lantern which stands on the floor or on a low table and is tilted upwards so that the part of its beam which is not intercepted by the black paper passes through the open door onto the ceiling of the adjacent room where it is invisible to the observer. In the light of the strong lantern the paper may look white instead of black. When a white piece of paper is held up in front of the black paper so that it too reflects the strong light of the lantern, the black paper assumes a black color. According to the usual interpretation it looks first white because no cues for the special strong illumination are available when this illumination affects only one visible surface. With the introduction of the white paper into the beam a special brilliant illumination becomes visible and constancy is restored: the two papers are perceived with their real color.

The arrangement of Gelb's experiment lends itself to a still more impressive demonstration. When the black paper is presented alone, reducing the intensity of the lantern light by small steps to zero causes the perceived color of the paper to vary all the way from white through gray to black. Every change in illumination is accompanied by a corresponding change in the perceived color. However, when a larger white paper

---

[1] Described in W. D. Ellis, *A source book of Gestalt psychology*. New York: Harcourt, Brace, 1939, p. 207.

is fastened behind the black paper so that the latter is seen surrounded by white, the same changes in illumination do not at all affect the seen colors, which remain white and black throughout. Paired in this way the colors are immune to changes in illumination and remain "constant." It is rather a change in the perceived illumination which now accompanies the change in the objective illumination.

The question arises: what determines the color with which the black paper is seen at a given intensity of the lantern light when the paper is presented alone? Do we deal in this situation with an absolute relation between the intensity of the light which stimulates a portion of the retina and the resulting perceived color? In considering this question we have to remember that there is another variable in the situation, the dim general illumination of the room. When this is varied it becomes immediately clear that this general illumination also affects the color of the black paper. When, with a high intensity of the lantern light, the general illumination is raised, the color of the black paper changes from white to gray, and this in spite of the fact that the paper too now reflects light of a somewhat higher intensity than before. Only *relatively,* that is in relation to the light which comes from other surfaces, has the light reflected by the black paper become less intense.

Such dependence of the perceived color on the *relative* intensity of the perceived light should be demonstrable in a much simpler form, and this is the case.

In a dark room a white screen is illuminated by the light of two slide projectors. In one of the projectors an opaque card with a circular hole of ½ in. diameter is inserted, and the bright image of the hole is focused on the screen. The slide for the other projector consists of a blank glass covered with an opaque card with a circular hole of 1 in. diameter and with a ½ in. cardboard disk which is pasted concentrically into the hole. Focused on the screen this slide produces a bright ring. The two projectors are so adjusted that this ring surrounds the image of the ½ in. hole so that the edge of the latter coincides with the inner edge of the ring. The light intensity of the projectors can be changed by running them on variable transformers or by letting their beams pass through episcotisters.

We have then on the screen a circular region (disk) and surrounding it a ring-shaped region which reflect light intensities that can be separately controlled. When the intensity of the disk is kept constant and that of the ring is widely varied, the color of the disk may change all the way from white to dark gray. The disk looks dark gray when the light reflected from the ring is of high intensity, and it becomes white when the brightness of the ring is greatly lowered. When the light intensity of the disk is varied and that of the ring is kept constant, the color of the disk, of course, undergoes similar changes. Again it is quite clear that the color which appears in one region, namely in that of the disk, depends on the relation of the light intensity of this region to that of its surroundings. This is true also of the ring. It can be shown in corresponding fashion that its color depends on the relation of the intensity of the ring to that of the disk.

When the ring is altogether omitted so that the disk is seen in completely dark surroundings, it ceases to look white or gray and assumes instead a luminous appearance similar to that of the moon at dusk. Lowering the intensity of the disk greatly does not change this mode of appearance, provided the rest of the room is really dark; the disk looks merely dimmer. The same observation can be made with the ring when it is presented without the disk, or with both the ring and the disk when they are placed far from each other on the screen. Opaque colors which deserve to be called white or gray, in other words "surface colors," will make their appearance only when two regions of different light intensity are in contact with each other, for instance when the ring surrounds the disk or when two oblongs have the longer edges as their common border.

The importance of a close contact for the emergence of surface colors becomes strikingly clear in the following observation. The intensity of the disk is adjusted to be one-quarter that of the ring, which makes the color of the disk a medium gray. An opaque object is moved from the side into the beam of the lantern which projects the ring so that part of it is blotted out by the shadow of that object. When this happens the gray color disappears almost simultaneously from that part of the disk which is adjacent to the shadow. It looks as if the dense gray there were dissolving, leaving the screen transparent to let a light behind it shine through. Brought about in this fashion, the change from surface color to a luminous appearance is quite impressive. That side of the disk which is still well surrounded by a brighter ring continues to show the gray color, and between it and the luminous side the disk shows a steady gradient in the density of the gray.

These observations make it clear that, at least under these conditions, surface colors occur in our experience when regions of different light intensity are in contact with each other and that the particular surface colors which come about depend on the relation of these light intensities. They are apparently the product of nervous processes of limited scope, for close spatial contact between the regions of different light intensity is required for their emergence. Moreover, the degree to which surface color is present in a certain region depends on the intimacy of the contact between this region and its partner. This is easily demonstrated by the following observations.

No matter what the brightness relation between ring and disk be, the ring will always show a less dense surface color and have more of a luminous appearance than the disk. This becomes quite clear when two pairs of such regions are presented for comparison which are so chosen that the intensity of the ring in one pair equals that of the disk in the other one, and vice versa. Even the region of lower light intensity in each pair, which is perceived as a gray, has a more luminous appearance where it occurs in the ring than where it occurs in the disk. The most obvious explanation for this difference in the mode of appearance is that the disk is more under the influence of the ring than vice versa, inasmuch as the disk is completely surrounded by the ring, whereas the ring is in contact with the disk only on one side. This explanation agrees well with the observation reported earlier that the elimination of part of the ring rendered that part of the disk more luminous which was then no longer enclosed by a region of different light intensity.

This influence under which surface colors emerge is clearly a mutual one. Though less so, the ring does display surface color. There is a great difference in the mode of appearance between a ring which surrounds, for instance, an area of higher intensity and an equal ring presented in an otherwise dark field. Whereas the latter looks merely luminous, the former shows in addition to some luminosity a distinct gray.

The mutual influence on which the emergence of surface colors depends must also account for the fact that the particular colors which come about depend on the relation of the stimulating light intensities. It is probably best conceived of as some kind of interaction which takes place as part of the nervous process which underlies color perception.

It will be remembered that the dependence of the perceived colors on the relative intensities of the stimulating light was also evident in the variations of Gelb's experiment which were first reported. It remains to be added that the transition from surface color to a luminous mode of appearance can be demonstrated with Gelb's setup in the following way. At first the special illumination of the black paper and the general illumination of the room are so adjusted that the black paper looks white. When now the general illumination is further reduced, the paper becomes more and more luminous, and it ceases altogether to look white when the rest of the room is completely dark. Luminosity of the paper can also be produced by excluding the general illumination from its immediate neighborhood. By such measures a rather luminous gray, not unlike that appearing in the ring, may also be achieved. Thus it is not only in projected rings and disks that luminosity appears as an alternative to surface colors when adequate differences in intensity are lacking or when the contact between those regions is diminished. Clearly discernible segregated objects, as for instance a suspended piece of black paper, function in the same fashion.

PART II

So far, we have become acquainted with the way in which surface colors come into existence and with the manner in which they depend on the stimulus situation. They depend on the relation of stimulus intensities on the retina which are so located with regard to each other that the subsequent nervous processes interact. Now the question arises what bearing this has on the problem of brightness constancy.

In order to answer this question, some clarification of the nature of brightness constancy is needed. One may say that brightness constancy prevails when a perceived color is in agreement with the corresponding object color. Object color is a persistent physical characteristic of a surface, the property to reflect a certain proportion of the light which falls on that surface. For instance, a surface which looks black under constancy conditions reflects about 4 per cent of the illuminating light, and a white one about 80 per cent. This property, called reflectance, is not conveyed to the eye as such. It is rather represented to the eye by light of a given intensity. This fact constitutes the problem of brightness constancy, for the intensity of the reflected light depends to the same degree on the color of the reflecting surface as on the strength of the illumination. If in our environment illumination were always and everywhere the same, the fact that our visual sense is not directly affected by reflectances but only by the reflected light intensities would not raise a problem in perception, for the reflected light could represent the object colors unequivocally. But illumination varies widely, even between different parts of the same visual field, and often very different light intensities come to represent the same reflectance to the eye and, in constancy, produce the same color in the observer's experience. When, for instance, a medium gray which reflects 20 per cent of the illuminating light is presented once in an illumination of an intensity 100 and again under light of an intensity 300, the intensities of the reflected light are 20 and 60, respectively; if complete constancy prevails, both stimulus intensities lead to perception of the same medium gray. Similarly the white background on which the gray samples are shown will reflect light of the intensity 80 in the weaker illumination and of the intensity 240 where it is in the stronger illumination, and the two differently illuminated parts of the background will probably both be judged as white. At first glance no orderly connection between stimulus intensity and perceived color seems to exist.

There is, however, one feature in the stimulus situation which remains the same when the illumination is varied. The intensity of the light reflected by the gray in the weaker illumination (20) stands in a ratio of 1 : 4 to that reflected by the white in the weaker illumination (80), and the same ratio exists between the intensities reflected by the gray and the white in the stronger illumination (60 and 240). It is easy to see that in the case of any given set of object colors the *ratios* of the intensities of the reflected light remain the same for any change in illumination which affects all of them.[2] Thus, if the perceived colors were to depend on the *ratios* of the intensities of the reflected lights, they would remain unchanged when a given set of object colors were presented in changed illumination, and constancy would be assured. A medium gray may serve again as an example. Although it affects the eye with different light intensities when the illumination is changed, it would be perceived as the same color because the ratio of the intensity that it reflects to the intensity of the light reflected by the surrounding white would remain the same, for a change in illumination affects the latter in the same proportion.

At this point we have to consider the observations reported in Part I. They suggested that the perceived surface colors depend on the relation, not yet quantitatively defined, of the light intensities in interacting regions. But we now find that constancy would result, if our visual perception functioned in such a fashion that the perceived colors depended on the *ratios* of the intensities of the reflected light.

Thus, we merely have to make the assumption that the relation on which surface colors depend is one of simple proportionality to give the observations of Part I a direct bearing on the problem of brightness constancy. If this assumption were correct brightness constancy would find

---

[2] This is a simple consequence of the fact already mentioned that object colors reflect a constant *fraction* of the illumination.

its explanation in the very process by which surface colors come about.

This assumption can be tested by simple experiments. If it is correct, the particular colors which are perceived in a pair of ring and disk should depend on the ratio of the intensities of the two regions, and only on that ratio. In other words, no matter what the absolute intensities of ring and disk may be, the same colors should be seen in the case of any pair of intensities which happen to stand in the same ratio to each other. This is, in close approximation, the case, as the following report of quantitative experiments [3] shows.

Two pairs of ring and disk were used, in order to permit simultaneous comparison. The intensity of each of these four regions could be varied independently.

Four identical projection lanterns equipped with 500-watt bulbs were used for this purpose. They were arranged in two groups, and each group produced on the screen a pair of ring and disk as described in Part I. They were all so adjusted that they gave their respective regions the same light intensity. This was done in the following way. First a pair of ring and disk was formed with one lantern from group I and one from group II, and the intensity of one of them was varied until the contour between the ring and the disk disappeared because of brightness equality. Then these two lanterns were restored to their respective groups and similar adjustments were made within each group by varying the light intensities of the not yet equated lanterns.

The intensity variations required by the experiments were brought about with the help of episcotisters through which the lantern beams had to pass before reaching the screen. This technique has the advantage that the episcotister apertures are a direct measure of the relative intensities in the various regions.

Measurements were made by the method of limits. Ring and disk of one pair and the ring of the other pair were kept at constant intensities, and the intensity of the remaining disk was varied in suitable steps until the S judged the colors of the two disks as equal.

In the first experiment one of the rings was given the full illumination of its lantern and the disk inside it received half of the intensity, for its light beam passed through an episcotister of 180 degrees aperture. The light for the ring of the other pair was cut down to one-eighth of full intensity by passing it through an episcotister of 45 degrees aperture.

---

[3] These experiments were performed by the students of various seminars in perception and classes in experimental psychology at Swarthmore College under the author's supervision.

The aperture for the disk of the latter pair was varied in steps of two degrees. The following are the means of one upper and one lower limit for each of five Ss: 24, 26, 24, 23, 24 degrees with a total mean of 24.2 degrees. This result means that, on the average, a light intensity in a disk corresponding to an episcotister aperture of 24.2 degrees when it is surrounded by a ring of an intensity of 45 degrees aperture brings about in the S's experience the same gray as does a disk of an intensity of 180 degrees aperture inside a ring of an intensity of 360 degrees aperture. There is only a small deviation from the value of 22.5 degrees which with 45 degrees forms the same ratio as does 180 degrees with 360 degrees. Comparing the grays in the two disks was not difficult for the Ss. The great difference in absolute intensity between the two pairs of ring and disk (8 : 1) made the less intense pair look much dimmer, but that did not affect the distinctness of the disks' color. However, it made the rings look very different; though both were white, the more intense one was by far more luminous. This latter observation, which was also made in most of the following experiments, seems to be important, for it corresponds to a fact which can be observed in real constancy situations. When identical sets of object colors are placed in different illuminations and appear approximately the same, the set in the stronger objective illumination is often also *seen* to be more strongly illuminated. Perceived illumination and the different degree of luminous appearance which was frequently observed in our experiments seem, functionally speaking, to be closely related experiences.

In another experiment a disk of 90 degrees intensity was shown in a ring of 360 degrees intensity. This combination, which forms an intensity ratio of 4 : 1, brings about a much darker gray in the disk. In the other pair, the disk whose intensity was varied was surrounded by a ring of 180 degrees intensity. The proportionate value for the disk is here 45 degrees. The averages of two upper and two lower limits for each of four Ss were 46, 52, 45, 44 degrees with a mean of 47 degrees.

In the following experiment the disk of the brighter pair was varied and a ratio of 3 : 1 between ring and disk was used. In the darker pair, the ring had an intensity of 180 degrees and the disk one of 60 degrees, and the variable disk was surrounded by a ring of 360 degrees intensity. Five upper and five lower limits were determined for each of three Ss. The means were 113, 115, 121 degrees. The proportionate value is here 120 degrees.

It will be noted that so far all deviations from the proportionate values were in one direction. They all imply that, where they occur, a disk of proportionate intensity in the dimmer pair looks darker than the disk in the pair of higher intensity; viz., in the first two experiments the disk in the less intense pair had to be given a slightly higher than proportionate intensity to give a color match and in the last experiment the disk in the more intense pair had to be made objectively darker. Thus, although these deviations are small, they deserve our attention. Experiments with an improved technique were made to find out how significant they are.

To facilitate measuring a variable episcotister [4] was used for the determination of the limits. This device permits changing the aperture by definite amounts while it is spinning. Only when the Ss had given a judgment of equality was the episcotister stopped and its angle measured with a protractor.

It has been described above how the intensities of the four lanterns were equated at the outset of the experiments. These equations are likely to contain subliminal errors which could affect our measurements. In the experiments which follow the episcotisters were interchanged between the groups of lanterns after half the number of limits had been determined for a given S, so that the group which during the first half of an experiment produced the brighter pair of ring and disk were made to produce the dimmer pair during the second half, and vice versa. Thus any error in the original lantern adjustment which would affect the measurements during the first half of the experiment in one direction would in the second half affect it in the opposite direction. In this manner such an error will appear in the scatter of the limit values but will not affect their mean.

The first experiment (1) done with this improved technique was one with a small difference between the brighter and the dimmer pair. The former had a ring of 360 degrees intensity and a disk of 180 degrees, and the other pair had a variable disk in a ring of 180 degrees. Four Ss took part in the experiment. For each one four upper and four lower limits were determined. Table 1 presents the means of these limits. The proportionate value is here 90 degrees. It will be noted that the small deviations from this value are in a direction opposite to those previously reported, for they would imply that a disk of proportionate intensity in the dimmer pair is perceived as a slightly lighter gray than the disk in the more intense pair.

---

[4] Designed and built by R. Gerbrands, Emerson Hall, Cambridge, Mass.

## TABLE 1

EPISCOTISTER SETTINGS IN DEGREES FOR DISK WITHIN RING OF
180 DEGREES IN COMPARISON WITH DISK OF 180 DEGREES
WITHIN RING OF 360 DEGREES

| Subjects | Ad. | McN. | Ba. | Cl. | |
|---|---|---|---|---|---|
| Upper limit | 88 | 86 | 85.5 | 90 | |
| Lower limit | 84 | 84 | 79.5 | 84.5 | |
| Mean | 86 | 85 | 82 | 86 | Grand mean: 85 |

## TABLE 2

EPISCOTISTER SETTINGS IN DEGREES FOR DISK WITHIN RING OF
90 DEGREES IN COMPARISON WITH DISK OF 240 DEGREES
WITHIN RING OF 360 DEGREES

| Subjects | Mo. | Cr. | Ke. | Cy. | |
|---|---|---|---|---|---|
| Upper limit | 61 | 62 | 73 | 74 | |
| Lower limit | 62 | 64 | 68 | 67 | |
| Mean | 61.5 | 63 | 70.5 | 70.5 | Grand mean: 66.4 |

This is not so with the results of the following experiment (2), in which a still lighter gray was produced and in which the intensity of the dimmer ring was only one-quarter of that of the brighter one. In the dimmer pair the ring had an intensity of 90 degrees and the disk was variable, while in the brighter pair the ring had 360 degrees and the disk 240 degrees of light. The results are given in Table 2. With the Ss Mo. and Cr., 10 upper and 10 lower limits were determined, with Ke. and Cy. only six. Individual differences are larger in this experiment. For two of the Ss there was a marked deviation from the proportionate value of 60 degrees, which implied that for them a disk of 60 degrees intensity in the dimmer pair showed a slightly darker gray than the disk in the brighter pair.

Ten Ss were employed in an experiment (3) in which the variable disk was surrounded by a ring of 360 degrees of light and the dimmer pair consisted of a ring of 90 degrees and a disk of 30 degrees intensity. Six upper and lower limits were determined for each S, except for Ss Mo. and Cr., who again supplied 10 pairs of limits each. The average of the

TABLE 3

EPISCOTISTER SETTINGS IN DEGREES FOR DISK WITHIN RING OF
360 DEGREES IN COMPARISON WITH DISK OF 30 DEGREES
WITHIN RING OF 90 DEGREES

| Subjects | Ca. | Ga. | Hs. | Ht. | Lu. | Ro. | Mo. | Cr. | Ke. | Cy. | |
|---|---|---|---|---|---|---|---|---|---|---|---|
| Upper limit | 104.5 | 91 | 117.5 | 116.5 | 113 | 130 | 128 | 107.5 | 105 | 113 | |
| Lower limit | 92.5 | 91 | 99.5 | 98.5 | 103 | 112 | 100 | 103 | 97 | 95 | |
| Mean | 98.5 | 91 | 108.5 | 107.5 | 108 | 121 | 114 | 105 | 101 | 104 | Grand mean: 106 |

individual means as shown in Table 3 was 106 degrees, a clear deviation
from the proportionate value of 120 degrees. It implies that the gray
in the disk of low intensity looks somewhat darker than a disk of proportionate value in the brighter pair.

The direction of the deviations from proportionate values encountered in the last two experiments was such that they could be regarded
as the effect of a slight influence of the absolute stimulus intensities on
the color process which otherwise could be conceived as functioning
according to a proportional law. The question arose whether these deviations reflected intrinsic properties of the color process or whether they
were introduced by incidental experimental conditions. An answer cannot yet be given and must be left to further detailed investigation. However, an experiment which was performed with this question in mind
will be reported below, because it will add the data of still another combination of intensities.

It was suspected that the presence of the brighter pair of ring and
disk in the visual field when the gray in the disk of the dimmer pair developed was responsible for the fact that this gray looked a trifle too
dark. If the high intensities of the brighter pair had an influence across
the spatial interval on the colors which emerged in the dimmer pair,
this is what should have happened. Such an influence can be avoided
by presenting the pairs successively. This was done in the following
experiment (4). The intensities in the brighter pair were 360 and 180
degrees, the ring in the dimmer pair was 90 degrees and the disk was
varied. Table 4 shows for four Ss the means of four upper and four
lower limits. Ordinarily, with an intensity ratio of 4 : 1 between the
rings the deviation under discussion was to be expected. It did not appear. The slight deviation from the proportionate value of 45 degrees
was in the opposite direction.

In another experiment, however, successive presentation failed to eliminate completely the deviation under discussion. Experiment 3 was repeated with three further Ss who did the experiment twice, once with successive and once with simultaneous presentation. The limits listed in Table 5 are the averages of four determinations each. Although successive presentation reduces the deviation from the proportionate value of 120 degrees, it does not eliminate it.

### TABLE 4

EPISCOTISTER SETTINGS IN DEGREES FOR DISK WITHIN RING OF
90 DEGREES IN COMPARISON WITH DISK OF 180 DEGREES
WITHIN RING OF 360 DEGREES

| Subjects | Ad. | McN. | Ba. | Cl. | |
|---|---|---|---|---|---|
| Upper limit | 43 | 42 | 41 | 44 | |
| Lower limit | 41 | 40 | 42 | 44 | |
| Mean | 42 | 41 | 41.5 | 44 | Grand mean: 42 |

### TABLE 5

EPISCOTISTER SETTINGS IN DEGREES FOR DISK WITHIN RING OF
360 DEGREES IN COMPARISON WITH DISK OF 30 DEGREES
WITHIN RING OF 90 DEGREES

| Subjects | Cl. | | He. | | Be. | |
|---|---|---|---|---|---|---|
| Presen-tation | Simul-taneous | Succes-sive | Simul-taneous | Succes-sive | Simul-taneous | Succes-sive |
| Upper limit | 110.5 | 121 | 99 | 108.5 | 104 | 112 |
| Lower limit | 99.5 | 99 | 97.5 | 99 | 94 | 104 |
| Mean | 105 | 110 | 98 | 104 | 99 | 108 |

These deviations from proportionate values appear rather insignificant when one compares them with the remaining effect of the proportional law. For example, in experiment 3, which showed the largest deviation, a disk of an intensity of 30 degrees aperture had on the average the same color as one of an intensity of 106 degrees aperture, that is, an intensity 3.5 times as high. The deviation from the proportionate value of 120 degrees amounts only to 12 per cent.

It should be mentioned at this point that such experiments can also be done with a less elaborate setup. Two color mixers and one projection lantern suffice for a crude demonstration of the proportional law. With the help of a large color wheel of black and white disks and a small one fastened on top of it to the same mixer one can obtain a ring-shaped and a circular region in which the intensities of the reflected light can be varied independently. On one mixer, e.g., the large wheel can be set to show a sector of 90 degrees white and the small one a sector of 45 degrees white. To the other mixer are fastened a small wheel with a white sector of 180 degrees and a large wheel of 360 degrees white. When the mixers spin in general room illumination, one sees a dark gray disk surrounded by a medium gray ring on one mixer and a light gray disk in a white ring on the other one. However, when the mixers are placed in separate, strictly local illumination they look quite different. That illumination can be provided by a lantern equipped with an opaque slide which has two circular holes a good distance apart. It projects two narrow beams of light of equal intensity. When the mixers are placed each in one of the beams at such a distance from the projector that their wheels are covered by the light almost to the outer rim and the rest of the room is entirely dark, both color mixers show a white ring and a light gray disk much alike in color. The reason for this change is easy to understand. Under local illumination the two color mixers provide exactly the same pattern of stimulus intensities as the setup in experiment 4, and thus the same colors develop as in that experiment. In general illumination, on the other hand, the pairs of ring and disk are surrounded by regions of other intensity, e.g., the light reflected by the wall of the room, which coöperate in determining the colors which come about in the pairs. If, for instance, light reflected by a white wall forms the stimulus intensity of the surrounding region, that intensity stands to the intensity of the dimmer ring in a ratio of 4 : 1, and in this relation the ring should assume a medium gray color, as indeed it did.

It was explained above how the assumption that the achromatic colors depend on the ratios of the pertinent stimulus intensities accounts for brightness constancy. On that occasion complete constancy was shown to follow from this assumption. However, complete constancy has hardly ever been demonstrated experimentally. An object color presented in reduced illumination usually looks somewhat darker than another sample of that color in full illumination, though not as much darker as the difference of the reflected light intensities would warrant if there were no constancy. Yet complete constancy would follow from a direct application of the proportional law. Deviations from proportionality which occurred in our experiments are by far too small to account for the usual lag in constancy. The difficulty resolves itself when it is realized that the proportional law cannot be applied so simply to this situation. Here the two pairs of regions, the sample and its background in full illumination and the other sample with background in reduced illumination, are not as completely separated from each other as the corresponding regions in our experiments, for the regions of different illumination are in contact with each other, and the brighter one can have an influence on the dimmer one. In other words, we have here a case where three or more regions of different intensity interact. Such processes have not yet been sufficiently investigated, and no report can be made at this time. It seems, however, quite likely that a full investigation will furnish the rules for the prediction of the lag in constancy in individual experiments.

This report may so far have given the impression that, apart from the small deviations discussed, the proportional law permits prediction of color equations if the pertinent stimulus intensities are known. However, this is so only with important qualifications. To a certain extent also the geometrical arrangement of the regions of different intensity has an influence on what colors come about in these regions. Some brief experiments which permit a first appraisal of the importance of these conditions will be reported below.

In the measuring experiments so far reported the width of the ring was ⅝ of the diameter of the disk so that the area of the ring was four times as large as the area of the disk. A reduction of the width of the ring to ¼ of the diameter of the disk so that its area was about the same as that of the disk did not affect the color in the disk as the following experiment shows, in which the colors in two disks were compared which were surrounded by rings of different width. Both rings were given the same intensity of 120 degrees aperture; the disk in the narrow ring had an intensity of 15 degrees and appeared as a very dark gray; the disk in the ring of standard width was variable. The mean of two upper and two lower limits for a single S was also 15 degrees. A number of other observers were satisfied with that equation.

The width of the narrow ring was further reduced so that it amounted to only 1/16 of the diameter of the disk. The same constant intensities as in the last experiment were used. The averages of two upper and two lower limits for each of two Ss were 37 and 37 degrees. This result means that a disk of 15 degrees intensity inside the very narrow ring looked as light as a disk of 37 degrees intensity inside a ring of standard width. The outcome of this experiment was so striking that we repeated it with another combination of intensities. The intensity of the two rings remained the same, but the disk in the very narrow ring had an intensity of 60 degrees. Again a higher intensity was needed for an equation in the disk inside the standard ring. The averages of two upper and two lower limits for the same two Ss were 87 and 86 degrees. However, with this intensity ratio of 120 : 60, which produces a light gray, the effect of making the ring very narrow was not so great. It amounted only to 45 per cent, whereas in the case of a ratio of 120 : 15 which normally produces a very dark gray the disk in the standard ring had to be made 145 per cent more intense. On the whole it looks as if the very narrow ring which has only one-quarter of the area of the disk cannot make the disk color as dark as does a ring of sufficient width.

As just reported, no difference in the effect of a ring which has about the same area as the disk and of one which has four times the area of the disk has been found. Two further measurements were made with a much wider ring. Its width was 1.5 the diameter of the disk and its area 15 times that of the disk. In one experiment the intensity ratio between the wide ring and its disk was again 120 : 15. In the disk of the standard pair the averages of four upper and four lower limits for the two Ss were 17 and 16 degrees. When a ratio of 120 : 60 was used, averages for two pairs of limits were 66 and 63 degrees. The deviations from 15 and 60 degrees respectively are probably incidental. At any rate, they are not in the direction which would indicate an enhancement in the effectiveness of the ring with increased width. It seems that, once the ring has an area equal to that of the disk, any further increase in its width does not affect the resulting color of the disk.

It was reported in Part I that a ring looks more luminous than a disk of the same intensity in another pair in which the intensities of ring and disk are the same as in the first pair but interchanged. The question arises whether such a reversal of intensities also causes a color difference in the regions of equal intensity. Two pairs of disk and ring in which the area of the ring was the same as that of the disk were presented and lights were so arranged that in one pair the lower intensity was in the ring and in the other pair in the disk. The two higher intensities in the two pairs amounted both to 360 degrees, the ring of lower intensity was kept at 45 degrees, and the disk of lower intensity was variable. Measurements were made with four Ss. The means of three upper and three lower limits were 54, 71, 83, 86 degrees. These figures indicate that for the same intensity ratio the lower intensity appears as a lighter gray when it is given in the ring than when it is given in the disk. A rather dark gray results from a ratio of 360 : 45 degrees. In the case of smaller ratios which give rise to lighter grays the differences in color which result when the intensities of ring and disk are interchanged are very much smaller. For an intensity ratio of 2 : 1 only a difference in luminosity can be discerned.

SUMMARY

It was found that opaque achromatic surface colors are perceived when light of different intensity stimulates adjacent areas on the retina. The achromatic color which is seen in a particular region must be regarded as the result of stimulation received from that region *and* of stimulation from neighboring regions. Although these colors are qualities which are perceived in a given region, they are products of an interaction process, which depends on difference in stimulation in at least two areas. In the absence of a suitable difference in stimulation a color of an entirely different mode of appearance is seen. A single bright region in an otherwise dark field, for instance, looks luminous instead of white, and reducing the light intensity in that region fails to make it look gray; it continues to appear luminous and merely becomes dimmer.

The first steps were taken to investigate quantitatively the rules of this dependence in the simplest case, that of two regions of different intensities of stimulation where one region surrounds the other. The colors which come about under these circumstances depend in close approximation on the *ratios* of the intensities involved and seem independent of the absolute intensity of local stimulation. The region of higher intensity will assume the color white and that of lower intensity will show a gray (or a black) which depends on the intensity ratio of the two regions. The greater the difference in intensity the darker will be the gray which appears in the region of the lower intensity.

It can be shown that a dependence of perceived colors on the ratios of stimulus intensities accounts for the constancy of achromatic colors under varying illumination. Complete constancy would follow from this rule of interaction of two intensities. The fact that measurements of brightness constancy rarely give results which denote complete constancy presents no difficulty for this explanation. These experiments involve interaction between more than two regions of different stimulus intensity.

*Hans Wallach and D. N. O'Connell*

SWARTHMORE COLLEGE

# THE KINETIC

# DEPTH EFFECT

The problem of how three-dimensional form is perceived in spite of the fact that pertinent stimulation consists only in two-dimensional retinal images has been only partly solved.[1] Much is known about the impressive effectiveness of binocular disparity. However, the excellent perception of three-dimensional form in monocular vision has remained essentially unexplained.

It has been proposed that some patterns of stimulation on the retina give rise to three-dimensional experiences, because visual processes differ in the spontaneous organization that results from certain properties of the retinal pattern. Rules of organization are supposed to exist according to which most retinal projections of three-dimensional forms happen to produce three-dimensional percepts and most retinal images of flat forms lead to flat forms in experience also. This view has been held mainly by Gestalt psychologists.

Another approach to this problem maintains that the projected stimulus patterns are interpreted on the basis of previous experience, either

Reprinted with permission from the *Journal of Experimental Psychology,* Vol. 45, No. 4, April, 1953.

[1] Most of the work reported in this paper was done while the senior author was holder of a John Simon Guggenheim Memorial Fellowship.

visual or kinesthetic. However, such empiricistic assumptions do not explain much, unless it is made clear how those previous experiences come about whose influence is supposed to account for the current perception. Kinesthetic form perception itself presents far more complex problems than does three-dimensionality in vision, and recourse to kinesthesis appears at present quite futile. Retinal disparity can of course account for that previous visual experience insofar as Ss with binocular vision are concerned. Whether in the absence of binocular vision, e.g., in congenitally monocular Ss, head movement parallax can fully play the role of binocular parallax appears doubtful. It seems that all we have left to account for an original experience of three-dimensional form in monocular Ss is the assumption that certain patterns of retinal stimulation will naturally produce experience of solid form. However, once it is assumed that perception of three-dimensional form can follow directly from retinal stimulation because of spontaneous organization of visual processes alone, there is no point in postulating an influence of past experience.

Unfortunately it appears that no one has succeeded in formulating rules of spontaneous organization adequate to predict which pattern of retinal stimulation will lead to perceived flat figures and which one will produce three-dimensional forms. We have made a vain attempt of our own and have become convinced that the three-dimensional forms perceived in perspective drawings, photographs, etc., are indeed a matter of previous experience.[2] In this situation the search for a visual process which can account for an original perception of three-dimensional form in monocular vision becomes imperative. Such a process will be described in this paper.

When one moves about, the retinal image of solid objects lying to the side of one's path not only expands but also distorts, because the objects are seen successively from different directions. More specifically, a retinal image distorts under these conditions as if the corresponding object were rotated through a certain angle in front of the eye of a stationary observer.

This fact suggests a simple technique for the investigation of the perceptual results of these distortions. An object is placed between a punctiform light source and a translucent screen and is rotated or turned back

---

[2] Evidence supporting this point of view will be reported in a subsequent paper. [Hans Wallach, D. N. O'Connell, and Ulric Neisser, The memory effect of visual perception of three-dimensional form. *J. exp. Psychol.*, 1953, 45, 360–368.—Ed.]

and forth. Its shadow is observed from the other side of the screen. The shadow-casting object is placed as close to the screen as possible, whereas the distance between the light source and the object is made large. Owing to this arrangement isometric projection is closely approximated. The shadows of a great number of three-dimensional forms, solid or wire-edged, will be perceived as three-dimensional under these circumstances. The shadows of some forms will look three-dimensional *only* in such a moving presentation; that is, in none of the positions through which such a form passes during rotation will it cast a stationary shadow which looks three-dimensional. With such forms one can study this effect in isolation. It will be referred to by the term "kinetic depth effect." It is important because it answers our problem: It appears that the kinetic depth effect can cause a genuine perception of three-dimensional form in a monocular S whenever he moves and keeps looking at an object which does not lie directly in his path.

Similar setups have been used before by Miles (3) and Metzger (2). Miles presented to Ss the shadow of a two-bladed fan wheel in rotation, the shaft of which was parallel to the screen on which the shadow was formed. His Ss reported a large number of different motion patterns, most of them involving depth, but no attempt was made to find out whether the object that was seen in motion was a good representation of the fan wheel whose shadow was presented. Metzger also was not primarily concerned with the perception of three-dimensional form which such a setup can yield. In fact, he investigated with great thoroughness the effects of a very special kind of arrangement which is not favorable to the emergence of stable three-dimensional forms. He had arrangements of vertical rods rotate about a vertical axis and showed their shadows in a low oblong aperture which hid the ends of the rod shadows from view. As in Miles's experiment the motion patterns seen by a given S during an extended period of inspection were very changeable. Moreover, naïve Ss mostly differ among each other as to whether the first movement process which they perceive is in three dimensions or takes place in a plane. Suggestion has a strong influence, in the course of longer observation as well as initially. We shall see below that the patterns of line shadows which Metzger presented to his Ss do not contain the condition essential for the kinetic depth effect.

The depth observed in Lissajous figures (1, 4) is the result of complex effects and will be discussed in a later paper.

EXPERIMENTS TO DEFINE CONDITIONS OF KINETIC
DEPTH PERCEPTION

*Experiment 1. Rotation of solids.* One of the figures which we presented to many Ss was a solid block in the shape of a roof with sloping gables, as shown in Fig. 1*A*. This was rotated continually about its longest axis. Figures 1*B* and 1*C* show two of the forms of the shadow

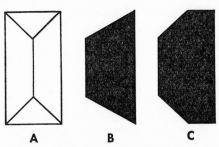

A      B      C

FIG. 1. Solid form (*A*) used in experiment 1, and two samples (*B*, *C*) of its shadows.

during rotation. When any one of the three figures is shown stationary to a naïve S, it is described as a two-dimensional figure. When the solid is slowly rotated so that the shadow undergoes continuous deformation, S sees a three-dimensional solid in rotation. The direction of the seen rotation may or may not coincide with that of the object behind the screen, and this is in agreement with the conditions of stimulation which give no clue of the object's real direction of rotation. Which one of the two directions of rotation is seen seems entirely a matter of chance, and with prolonged observation S usually experiences a number of spontaneous reversals of the direction of rotation. Occasionally an S sees for long periods reversals after each rotation of 180 degrees.

In experiments like this the impression of three-dimensional form is so natural that many Ss who are not psychologists are not astonished by their observations. They correctly assume that behind the screen is just such an object as they see. Only after reversals of the direction of rotation have occurred do they begin to wonder.

Where the kinetic depth effect takes place, a rigid three-dimensional form in rotation is seen instead of the distorted two-dimensional figure given on the shadow screen. The distorting two-dimensional shape may occasionally be *seen* after prolonged exposure of the same kinetic presentation, or when one looks from a sharply oblique direction at the screen. The S's experience of a continuously flowing form seems to him abnormal or unusual, although this is exactly what is given on the retina.

The essential difference between this two-dimensional experience and the three-dimensional form which is usually seen seems to be that the latter is unchanging and rigid instead of ever changing and flowing. The changes in the shape of the retinal image are accounted for by a perceived rotation of the three-dimensional object, whereas in the two-dimensional process the seen movement distorts the form itself. As far as we can see, the distortions of the perceived two-dimensional form agree closely with the changes of the retinal image. But the perceived three-dimensional form is not determined merely by what is presented on the retina at a given moment. A single one of the projections of the shadow-casting object which make up the changing shapes of the shadow does not look three-dimensional. Only the sequence of changing shapes gives rise to the seen three-dimensional form. In other words, a single projection causes a three-dimensional form to be seen only because it was preceded by a number of other projections. By itself, it simply does not convey enough data about the three-dimensional form which it represents. The seen three-dimensional form is richer in structure than any single projection and it is built up in a temporally extended process. The individual retinal image determines only which aspect of the turning three-dimensional form appears to be given at the moment. Thus, perceptual experience far surpasses what one should expect of a process determined by momentary stimulation and seems to a higher degree a product of the immediate past than of stimulation occurring at a given moment.

*Experiment 2. Partial rotation of wire figures.* Experiments of the kind just reported differ in two ways from the realistic situations in which the kinetic depth effect occurs. In the first place, a shadow-casting object is put through a complete rotation and produces a pattern of distortion on the screen which corresponds to that obtained when under natural viewing conditions an S moves completely around an object, which is hardly ever done. In the second place, in the shadow of a solid object an edge of the three-dimensional form is visible only for a comparatively short period, namely as long as it forms a contour of the shadow, whereas in the realistic situation it usually can also be seen when it passes across the front of the figure. We therefore performed quantitative experiments with wire figures which of course show all edges continuously, and had them turn back and forth through an angle of only 42 degrees.

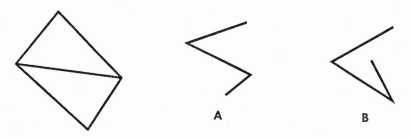

FIG. 2. The wire "parallelo-gram" used in experiment 2.

FIG. 3. The wire "helix" used in experiment 2 (*A*) and its appearance from the top (*B*).

Figures 2 and 3 each show projections of two of the wire figures used. The figure represented in Fig. 2 can best be described as a parallelogram containing one diagonal, which was bent along this diagonal so that the planes of the upper and the lower half formed an angle of 110 degrees with each other. The other figure (Fig. 3*A*) consisted of a piece of wire twice bent to form part of what might be described as a triangular helix. Figure 3*B* shows a view from the top. These figures were turned back and forth through an angle of 42 degrees at a rate of one cycle per 1.5 sec. and their deforming shadows were shown to individual Ss one at a time for as many periods of 10 sec. as were necessary to obtain a clear report. After each 10-sec. exposure, S was asked for a report.

In the case of the parallelogram (Fig. 2) all of 50 Ss sooner or later during the exposure periods reported seeing a three-dimensional figure turning back and forth apparently very much like the wire figure behind the screen, except that it sometimes appeared to S in its inverted form. In the case of the "helix" 48 of the same 50 Ss reported a three-dimensional form like the wire figure and 2 Ss saw a flat zigzag line which distorted before their eyes, a process which corresponds to the changing pattern of stimulation. Evidence that the three-dimensional forms which were perceived were due to the kinetic depth effect and that none of the projections represented in the deforming shadow by itself would have been seen as three-dimensional was obtained in the following way. To a new group of 22 Ss five such projections of each figure were presented individually in random order. They were the projections of the two extreme positions at which the figures stopped and started to turn the other way and of three intervening positions chosen to be at about 10 degrees of rotation apart. None of these stationary projections looked three-dimensional to any one of the 22 Ss. Positions intermediate between the ones presented resembled them so closely that it seems impossible that they would lead to a radically different perceived form.

Often the turning wire figures were seen three-dimensionally immediately upon presentation. Of 16 Ss for whom time records were taken, 11 reported the "parallelogram" in the correct three-dimensional shape after the first 10-sec. exposure period. In the case of the "helix" only 4 of 16 Ss reported its shape correctly after the first exposure. The reason for this difference is yet to be investigated.

Once it has occurred, the three-dimensional impression is so strong that one cannot voluntarily see the two-dimensional figure which is given on the screen. It has been mentioned that the perceived three-dimensional figure may resemble the inverted form of the wire figure rather than that figure itself. This is to be expected, inasmuch as a three-dimensional figure and its inverted form have identical projections, such that a given projection is always a representation of both, a figure and its inverted form. The added fact that with prolonged observation of the distorting shadow the perceived three-dimensional figure may spontaneously invert in Necker cubelike fashion is also a consequence.

*Experiment 3. Rotation of a truncated cylinder.* A systematic investigation of the kinetic depth effect resulting from rotation of a solid was attempted in the following manner.

A cylinder which is rotated about its axis casts a shadow which does not change in any way, but any cut that is taken off the cylinder and which is not at right angles to its axis produces a characteristic deformation of its shadow. A large number of wooden cylinders, about as high as wide, were made and cuts were varied systematically. The solid forms which were produced in this fashion were shown in complete rotation to Ss who had no previous experience with our studies.

The results can be summarized in the following way: (a) Shadows whose only deformation consists in an expansion and contraction in one dimension will look flat; a dark figure is seen which periodically becomes wider and narrower. An example is the shadow of a rectangular block which is rotated about an axis parallel to a set of edges. (b) Shadows which display contour lines that change their direction and their length will appear as turning solid forms. The roof-shaped figure described above (experiment 1) is an example; the shadow contour produced by an edge of a gable tilts and changes its length simultaneously (compare Fig. 1*B* and 1*C*). (c) Curved contours which are deformed without displaying a form feature which identifies a specific point along the curve are seen as distorting, often even if for some reason the shadow is seen as a three-dimensional form. This peculiarity is in disagreement with our description of the kinetic depth effect and has delayed our work for years. It is now clear that the perceived distortions of deforming curved contours are not related to the kinetic depth effect at all. They will be dealt with in a later paper.[3]

*Experiment 4. Rotation of straight rods.* When it became clearly recognized that shadows which display contour lines that change their direction and length will appear as turning solid forms, we checked whether this would also apply to single lines. Will a detached line which changes its direction on the screen and its length at the same time display a kinetic depth effect, i.e., will it appear to tilt into depth in such a way as to account for its shortening? The following experiments show that this is the case.

When a rod is fastened to the end of a vertical shaft at an angle of, say, 45 degrees and is rotated about this shaft, the shadow which it produces tips from side to side. From a tilt of 45 degrees toward the left, the shadow rights itself and goes through the vertical into a tilt of 45 degrees toward the right and back through the same positions. At the same time it shortens and lengthens periodically. Its end points move on horizontal lines across the screen. This process is invariably seen as a motion in three dimensions, as nearly as one can tell exactly like the real movement of the rod behind the screen, a rotation describing a conical surface about a vertical axis.

This setup lends itself to a variation which is interesting because the three-dimensional motion which is perceived is a different one from that which the rod behind the screen undergoes. The shaft on which the rod turns is tilted toward or away from the screen by 15 or 20 degrees. This changes the pattern of expansion and contraction of the rod shadow completely; its end points now move on elliptic paths on the screen. Only rarely does the rod motion seem to describe a circular cone like the real movement of the rod behind the screen. In most cases a movement is seen in which the movement component of tilting toward or away from S is much smaller than the lateral movement component such that the surface described is that of an elliptic cone. Whereas the real rod goes in one rotation from a tilt toward S into a tilt away from

---

[3] Hans Wallach, Alexander Weisz, and Pauline Austin Adams, Circles and derived figures in rotation. *Amer. J. Psychol.,* 1956, 69, 48–59.—Ed.

him, the perceived motion of the rod is restricted either to a changing forward tilt or to a changing tilt away from S. Either one of these two different movements can of course be perceived because, like a three-dimensional figure and its inverted form, they would if they were objectively given produce the same projection.

It seems that what distinguishes in these experiments perceived movement from the two-dimensional process which is given on the screen and therefore on the retina is the fact that the perceived rod is seen with a constant length. Tilting into depth is seen instead of shortening. Inasmuch as the rod as a whole must anyway be seen to move, this tilting motion is only a modification of a necessary process and not an added change, which is what a perceived stretching and shrinking would amount to. Thus, a tendency to see one motion instead of the two simultaneous movements of the two-dimensional process (a tipping from side to side, and a stretching and shrinking) may be held responsible for the depth effect. Another possibility would be a selective principle according to which a line of constant length is seen rather than a changing one. No decision between these two possibilities can be made on the basis of our present results.

*Experiment 5. Rotation of T and △ figures.* It is important to realize that a shadow line must undergo both a displacement and a lengthening or shortening in order to produce a kinetic depth effect. Both these changes must be given together. A change in length alone is not sufficient to produce a reliable kinetic depth effect. This is shown in the following experiment.

A piece of $\frac{1}{16}$-in. wire 4 in. long was fastened at right angles to a vertical shaft of the same diameter so that the two formed a figure of T shape. When this form was turned back and forth about the vertical shaft through an angle of 42 degrees, the shadow of the horizontal wire formed a line of 105-mm. length which periodically contracted to a length of 75 mm. and expanded again. We presented it with a rate of one period per 1.5 sec. for 10 sec. to 24 Ss.

Eighteen of 24 Ss saw a line in the plane of the screen expanding and contracting and only 6 Ss perceived the line turning in the third dimension. Had the horizontal wire been in an oblique position with respect to the axis of rotation so that its shadow had shown a displacement in addition to the change in length, the kinetic depth effect would have been obtained with the majority of the Ss, as the experiment with the oblique rod would predict.

Because of its importance we had the experiment with the T figure repeated by another E and obtained the same result: Of 40 Ss, 30 saw the horizontal line expand and contract in the plane of the screen and 10 saw it turn.

These results must be compared with those of a different wire figure which does produce a kinetic depth effect under identical conditions. Comparable data come from a shadow presentation of an equilateral triangle. Its sides consisted of wires 5 in. in length, and one of them was tilted by 15 degrees against the horizontal. When this figure was turned back and forth, the shadow of one of its sides changed from a slope of 45 degrees to one of 57 degrees and thus presented conditions favorable to the kinetic depth effect. Of 20 Ss who observed the triangle for 10 sec., 17 reported a turning in depth and only 3 expansion and contraction. (With such a plane figure the kinetic depth effect consists, of course, in the perception of a plane figure that turns into depth.) This score is to be compared with that for the T figure where only one-third of the Ss saw a turning. The difference is reliable at the .001 level of confidence.

Still, the 6 and 10 Ss who saw the T figure turning in depth need be accounted for, if our claim is correct that they are not the outcome of a genuine kinetic depth effect. Here the following result is significant. When the T figure was presented *following* the presentation of the triangle, 15 out of the 17 Ss who saw the triangle turn saw the T figure turn also. (Three Ss who saw the triangle expand and contract reported the same for the T figure.) In other words, when a figure that Ss saw turning preceded the presentation of the T figure, a large majority of Ss saw it turning also. This shows a strong influence of a previous perception on the manner in which the T figure is seen, for only one-third of the Ss saw the T figure turning when it was given as a first presentation. This difference is significant at the .05 level of confidence. We suggest that in the case of these latter Ss some such influence of a previous experience, though a more remote one, has been at work also.

We are inclined to conclude that a line which changes in length but is not displaced at the same time does not give rise to the kinetic depth effect. This agrees well with the already reported finding that a solid shadow which expands and contracts only in one dimension will not show the kinetic depth effect either.

THE ACCURACY OF KINETIC DEPTH PERCEPTION

When we described the kinetic depth effect in complex figures, we stated that the change in the retinal image is accounted for in perception by a rotation of a three-dimensional form. This implies, of course, that a *real* form which is like the perceived one would in rotation produce a sequence of retinal images very similar to that actually given, or, in other words, that the perceived form resembles closely the shadow-casting object. That this is the case has been confirmed by many Ss to whom the shadow-casting object was directly shown immediately following the kinetic presentation.

For more stringent confirmation several methods were used: In the case of the "helix" (Fig. 3), Ss were asked to bend a piece of wire into the shape of the figure which they saw turning on the screen. Only Ss who reported seeing a three-dimensional form turning back and forth were given this test. Of 29 Ss, 13 made good reproductions, 12 fair ones, and only 4 Ss made poor reproductions. Eleven of the 12 Ss whose reproductions were fair were later asked to make another reproduction while they looked *directly* at the turning wire figure. Of these only 7 were able to make good reproductions and 4 made only fair ones under these conditions. Altogether there were 8 Ss who could make only fair reproductions when they viewed the figure directly.

In the case of the parallelogram (Fig. 2), the accuracy of perception by virtue of the kinetic depth effect was checked by showing S four similar wire figures and asking him to pick out the one that matched best the form he saw turning on the screen. As mentioned earlier, the bend in the shadow-casting figure amounted to an angle of 110 degrees between the planes of the two triangles which made up this figure. This angle is, of course, characteristic of its three-dimensional form. If this angle were 180 degrees, the wire figure would be plane. In our four models the bend amounted to angles of 95, 110, 125, and 140 degrees, respectively. The one with the 110-degree angle was an exact copy of the shadow-casting figure; the other three models had the same height as the standard and were made to produce projections on the frontal plane which were identical with the projection of the standard. The four models were inserted in a wooden block and handed to S. The choices of 30 Ss who had previously reported seeing the three-dimensional figure were 8, 17, 4, and 1 for the 95, 110, 125, and 140-degree figure, respectively. Only one S found it impossible to make a choice. It is unfortunate that we did not include one more model with a still sharper angle, but even so the data give a rough idea of the accuracy of the perception of three-dimensional form which is based on the kinetic depth effect.[4]

*Experiment 6. Rotation of luminous rod.* Another attempt to obtain a measure of the accuracy with which depth perception functions by virtue of the kinetic depth effect was made employing a straight line which rotated in an oblique plane. When a line is turned in a frontal-parallel plane about its midpoint, the end points of its retinal projection move on a circle. However, when it rotates in an oblique plane, its retinal image changes in length as it turns, and its end points move on an elliptic path. Therefore, when in the dark a luminous line is rotated in a frontal-parallel plane about its midpoint and is exposed from behind an elliptic aperture, its retinal projection will be the same as that of a line which turns in an oblique plane, for the aperture causes the line to be visible with the same changes in length. If the motion of the line that rotates in an oblique plane can be correctly perceived with the help of the kinetic depth effect alone, then the line rotating behind an elliptic aperture should also appear to rotate in an oblique plane, because the two lines produce identical stimulation so far as the kinetic depth effect is concerned. Other cues for depth perception as, for instance, retinal disparity, would give rise to experienced rotation in an oblique plane only in the first case. Thus when the rotating line behind the aperture is presented to a naïve S and he perceives it turning in a properly oblique plane, one can be sure that this is due to the kinetic depth effect. By this procedure, as by the use of the shadow screen, the effect can be studied in isolation; other cues for depth perception would tend only to prevent the line from turning in an oblique plane.

A ½-in. lucite rod, approximately 23 in. long, served as light source for the luminous line. Its ends were flat and finely ground to admit a maximum of light. They were inserted in metal caps which contained hidden flashlight bulbs and also served as mountings. The light from these bulbs made the lucite rod appear to glow evenly over its whole length. The rod was inserted in a U-shaped sheet-metal trough of proper length and attached by the mountings. A bushing was fastened to the back of the trough at its midpoint and attached to the horizontal slow shaft of a reduction gear motor, so that the lucite rod could be turned

---

[4] It should be noted that a turning by 42 degrees produces only a moderate distortion of the shadow. Its width, which is most strongly affected, suffers a reduction of only 27 per cent.

in a vertical plane. The trough and rod were covered by a long strip of cardboard into which was cut an aperture 22 in. long and ⅛ in. wide. Through this aperture part of the rod's surface was visible. In front of this apparatus was a frame to which cardboards with different elliptic apertures could be attached parallel to the plane of rotation of the rod. Three different elliptic apertures were used. They were 40 cm. long and 35 cm. wide, 39.5 cm. long and 28.9 cm. wide, and 40 cm. long and 20.6 cm. wide, respectively. They produced projections of the turning luminous rod identical with the projections produced by a luminous line that turns in a plane forming an angle of 29, 46, and 59 degrees, respectively, with the plane of the aperture. They were attached with the large axis of the elliptic opening in vertical position.

The S was seated in front of this apparatus at a distance of 9 ft. He had before him a small table covered with a light gray cardboard. A metal rod was joined at right angles to a shaft which was fastened vertically to the table, so that the rod could be swung around in a plane parallel to the table top about an inch above it. A degree scale was marked out on the cardboard by which the position of the rod could be read. With the help of the rod, S could indicate the position of the plane in which the luminous line seemed to turn. A darkroom amber bulb illuminated this arrangement in such a way that S could see the rod but not the scale markings and that the remainder of the room was completely dark. After each setting of the rod E asked S to close his eyes and then read the scale with a flashlight.

During testing E asked S to look at the luminous line before him and close one eye, and that eye was covered. The luminous line which, when presented in the appropriate elliptic aperture, produced the projection of a 46-degree tilt was set into clockwise rotation at a rate of one revolution in 10 sec. When S reported that it turned in an oblique plane, he was asked to turn the measuring rod before him into a position parallel with that of the luminous line in rotation. This was repeated with the 59-degree and the 29-degree apertures, and thereafter the three apertures were used twice more in random order for the purpose of practice. Neither in this practice period nor later during the experimental trials was S told whether his settings were correct or not correct. No time limit was set on the presentation of the revolving line and S made his setting when he felt ready. After a rest period of 3 or 4 min. the experimental series began. It consisted of nine presentations; that is, each one of the three apertures was presented three times in random order.

The means and SD's of the 15 means of the three measurements for each of the three degrees of tilt were 14.9 (SD = 6.6), 44.0 (SD = 3.4), and 59.8 (SD = 4.4) for the 29, 46, and 59-degree tilt, respectively. There was *no* overlap between the means of the settings by individual Ss from one tilt to another, and there was *no* overlap between the individual settings which a given S made for the three tilts.

Where projections of tilts of 46 degrees and of 59 degrees were presented, the averages for all Ss came close to the expected values. However, in the case of the 29-degree tilt, the average of 14.9 deviates significantly from this value; only one individual setting out of 45 is as high as, or exceeds 29 degrees.

Why this is so is not clear. However, it should be pointed out that the change in length which a line turning with a 29-degree tilt undergoes amounts only to 12.5 per cent, and one of 14.9-degree tilt (the value of the average) only to 3.4 per cent. In other words, a tilt of 14.9 degrees produces a change in length that is very likely below the limen. Yet, that does not necessarily mean that those Ss who gave settings of 15 degrees or lower did not receive effective stimulation for a tilt. Whereas the small angles of tilt (due to the negligible change of the cosine function in this range of values) probably do not lead to a change in length sufficient to produce a kinetic depth effect, settings of such low values do not indicate that no tilt was perceived when these settings were made. In experience, a tilt of 15 degrees is of distinct significance, and objectively conditions of stimulation of 29 degrees were given.

It would have been important to find out whether these results can be improved by making the luminous line wider. To make it wider would have the advantage that the contraction of the line would be given by a change in its proportions, that is, in figural terms, rather than by a change in its absolute length. Improved results would indicate that change in proportions is effective in producing the kinetic depth effect. Unfortunately, this variation could not be done with the present setup, because a wider line would have shown up the intersections with the elliptic aperture by their changing obliqueness. A more expensive manner of presentation would be needed.

OTHER FACTORS IN KINETIC DEPTH PERCEPTION

*Experiment 7. The effect of angle constancy.* Such a variation of the experiment might have contributed to the solution of the following problem. It has been reported that shadows of solid blocks will produce the kinetic depth effect only if they have contours which are displaced and change their length simultaneously. Should we assume then that the presence of such contours solely accounts for the kinetic depth effect in complex forms, imparting their depth to the whole figure, or do complex forms produce such an effect in their own right? Just as we have considered the possibility that a line is seen to move into the third dimension to account for the given change of its retinal image while it is perceived with constant length, we might assume a tendency to see in general rigid, unchanging forms instead of the given distorting shapes. For the present this question must remain unanswered.

However, a question which can be considered a part of the question just raised was actually put to a test. Most shadows of turning figures do not only display contours which are displaced and change their length; their angles also change. Is there a separate tendency for angles to remain constant which produces kinetic depth effects?

To answer this question we used a figure which consisted of three rods all meeting in one point under angles of 110 degrees and forming a wire-edged representation of an obtuse corner (Fig. 4). When this figure was turned back and forth through an angle of 42 degrees and its shadow was shown to 56 Ss who before had seen its stationary shadow as two-dimensional, 53 Ss reported seeing a rigid obtuse corner. In this presentation two of the three dark lines forming the shadow not only were displaced but also underwent considerable changes in length.

FIG. 4. The figure used in experiment 7.

Entirely different results were obtained when the length of the shadow lines was made indefinite. To achieve this, the shadow screen was covered with a cardboard with a circular aperture where the shadow of the corner figure fell on the screen. The size of the aperture was so chosen that the ends of the shadow lines were always hidden from S. Thus, only movement of the corner point, angular displacements of each of the three lines, and changes of the angles which they formed with each other were visible. As the corner point shifted sideways, one of the lines seemed to move farther under the aperture edge and another one seemed to pull out from under it, and the length of all three of them seemed indefinite.

All 22 Ss employed in this experiment reported seeing a flat figure which distorted. Had the kinetic depth effect occurred, the Ss would have seen instead a rigid three-dimensional form with constant angles. However, no such effect was observed where changes in the length of the lines which constituted the figure were not given, because that length was indefinite. We may conclude that a displacement of lines which is linked only with a change of angles does not give rise to the kinetic depth effect; displacement of lines and change in their length is needed. The question remains unanswered whether length must be understood only in absolute terms, or whether change in proportion has an effect of its own.

*Experiment 8. Variation of distances between objects.* Not only are the retinal images of solid objects deformed when one moves about; the same is true to various degrees of the projection of the whole environment. That the objects which make up the environment are seen arranged in three-dimensional space and with unchanging distances between each other may also result from a kinetic depth effect. Just as some of the contours of solid objects produce appropriately changing retinal projections when the objects are seen from different angles, the projections of many of the intervals between objects change their length and their direction when one moves about. That this has the effect of producing visual depth can be demonstrated with the shadows of an arrangement of several objects on a rotating platform.

We used spheres supported by thin vertical rods because the shadow of a sphere in rotation does not change its shape and will therefore not produce a kinetic depth effect of its own. Four spheres of $1\frac{3}{16}$-in. diameter were arranged at the corners of a square concentric with the platform. The four rods were all of different height so that all the intervals between the shadows of the spheres were periodically oblique when the platform turned, and changed length and direction simultaneously. The lower part of the screen was covered so that the shadow of the turntable itself was hidden. The arrangement was turned at a rate of one revolution in 5 sec. and was exposed to individual Ss for 20 sec.

Under these circumstances all 30 Ss who took part reported the spheres to move in three dimensions. Twenty-four Ss saw the spheres in a rigid spatial arrangement which turned about its center just like the actual arrangement behind the screen. The others saw them move in open single file in snakelike fashion into depth. In this latter motion only the shorter intervals between spheres are rigidly maintained, and each sphere changes direction of rotation with each excursion; but there can be no doubt that this is an incomplete form of a kinetic depth effect. It should be mentioned that 15 of the 30 Ss had no other experience with these shadow experiments except for another experiment with the spheres which will be reported below. It is apparent that the kinetic depth effect will readily yield a perception of a rigid spatial arrangement of unconnected objects.

*Experiment 9. Variation of distances between objects.* The arrangement of experiment 8 offers still another opportunity to check on our finding that a line must change both in length and in direction in order to produce a kinetic depth effect. From our experiments with solid blocks and with the T figure we concluded that a shadow which merely expands and contracts in one dimension will not give rise to the effect. Here we set out to show that the same is true for intervals between objects; we modified the experiment with the spheres to correspond to these experiments.

All the rods were given the same height so that the spheres were aligned on a horizontal line and the intervals between the shadows changed in length only. This arrangement was shown to the same 30 Ss and under exactly the same conditions that prevailed in experiment 8, but was presented prior to it. The fact that the T figure proved so susceptible to the influence of previous perceptions made this sequence advisable. The experiment with the luminous rod which has been reported at length was done with the same Ss in between the two experiments with spheres.

As in the case of the T figure, only a minority of the Ss now saw movement in three dimensions, namely 10 out of 30. The difference between this result and that of experiment 8 is reliable at the .03 level of confidence. Of the 15 naïve Ss, 12 saw the shadows move back and forth in the plane of the screen, 1 S reported movement in three dimensions, and 2 saw in the beginning of the observation period the plane and later the three-dimensional version. For the other group of 15 Ss who had observed the shadows of some wire figures before, the numbers were: 8 flat, 2 three-dimensional, and 5 first flat and later three-dimensional. When these results are compared with those of the previous experiment where imaginary lines connecting sphere shadows changed both in length and in direction, it becomes again apparent that these are essential conditions for the kinetic depth effect and that a mere expanding and contracting of retinal distances is insufficient.

This is the reason for our view that Metzger's work (2) is not directly concerned with the kinetic depth effect. He exposed shadows of arrangements of vertical rods whose changing patterns presented Ss with rectangular intervals which changed in width only. No other deformations were visible, because no marks were distinguishable along the shadow lines, and the latter ended only at the edges of the aperture in which they were given. As with the aligned spheres, no reliable depth effects are produced spontaneously in naïve Ss with such an arrangement. Whether Metzger's work contributes to an understanding of the kinetic depth effect remains to be seen when more of the nature of the effect is known.

*Experiment 10. Effect of set.* In our experiments, the kinetic depth effect results in two perceptual characteristics: (a) a turning in the depth dimension, and (b) three-dimensionality of form. However, when the effect is observed under realistic conditions, namely when by moving about one obtains a changing retinal projection for a stationary solid object, no turning is perceived. The reason for this is that the object remains in unaltered relation to its environment with respect to which S perceives himself moving. Thus, only three-dimensionality and rigidity of form, seen instead of the deforming two-dimensional pattern which is given on the retina, are here the overt manifestations of the kinetic depth effect.

The fact that under realistic conditions the object remains in unaltered relation to its environment needs some consideration, because this is not so in our experiments. There the deforming shadow of the object denotes a turning while the environment, that is, the screen on which the shadow is shown, remains stationary. Under realistic conditions, on the other hand, both the object and its environment are given retinally with deformations which denote a turning in relation to S. The kinetic depth effect transforms the deforming retinal projection of the environment into a three-dimensional structure, and once this has happened, the perception of the object as a three-dimensional form is probably facilitated. That such a facilitation is likely to take place is indicated by experimental results which show a strong influence of preceding exposures on the readiness with which the kinetic depth effect occurs.

The following results may serve as an example. When the "helix" (Fig. 3) was shown following the presentation of one or two figures which readily show the kinetic depth effect, all of 18 Ss saw it as three-dimensional during the first 10-sec. exposure. This is to be compared with results in experiment 2 according to which only 4 out of 16 naïve Ss gave a clear report of three-dimensional form for this figure after the first 10-sec. exposure.

The question of how this influence is exerted must remain open. It is conceivable that it consists merely in a set to see a turning in the depth dimension. However that may be, the influence is a strong one.

If such an influence is effective between succeeding exposures of different figures as shown, it should be expected to work also within a given visual field. Under realistic conditions, once the environment of a given object is perceived as a rigid spatial structure which changes its orientation with respect to the moving S, such an influence should facilitate a kinetic depth effect for the object. There are several reasons why the environment should easily be seen in this fashion. To mention only one: the environment will usually contain familiar features which would cause the facilitating influence of previous experience with similar situations to operate. Thus we have good reason to believe that the kinetic depth effect takes place more readily under realistic conditions than it does in our shadow-screen experiments.

SUMMARY

When a three-dimensional form, solid or wire-edged, is turned behind a translucent screen and its shadow on the screen is observed, the shadow will appear as a rule as a three-dimensional rigid object which turns, quite similar to the physical object behind the screen. This happens notwithstanding the fact that S actually looks at a plane figure which is being deformed.

One condition seems to be essential for the occurrence of this effect: the shadow must display contours or lines which change their length and their direction simultaneously. If this condition is not fulfilled, a plane distorting figure like the one on the screen is perceived unless an influence of previous perception operates.

This effect is believed to operate widely under ordinary circumstances. When one moves about, objects near one's path are successively seen from different angles, and this change in orientation of the object to S is the same as occurs when the object is turned by an equivalent angle. Thus, the object's retinal projection undergoes the same deformation as do shadows in our experiments, and the same perceptual processes should result.

REFERENCES

1. Fisichelli, V. R. Effect of rotational axis and dimensional variations on the reversals of apparent movement in Lissajous figures. *Amer. J. Psychol.,* 1946, 59, 669–675.
2. Metzger, W. Tiefenerscheinungen in optischen Bewegungsfeldern. *Psychol. Forsch.,* 1934, 20, 195–260.
3. Miles, W. R. Movement interpretation of the silhouette of a revolving fan. *Amer. J. Psychol.,* 1931, 43, 392–405.
4. Philip, B. R., and Fisichelli, V. R. Effect of speed of rotation and complexity of pattern on the reversals of apparent movement in Lissajous figures. *Amer. J. Psychol.,* 1945, 58, 530–539.

*Wolfgang Köhler and Pauline Austin Adams*

DARTMOUTH COLLEGE

# PERCEPTION

# AND ATTENTION

### ARTICULATION AND ATTENTION

In a recent paper on perceptual organization and learning, the senior author was led to the following conclusions: (1) In many situations, learning is at least as much a matter of perceptual *articulation* as of large-scale organization. (2) Large-scale organizations exert a strong pressure upon their material, which operates against articulation of this material. The larger organizations are likely to prevail, and to prevent learning, unless objective conditions for articulation are particularly favorable. To a degree, the pressure of a large-scale organization can, however, be overcome by Os who intend to learn and, for this purpose, introduce or support the required articulation. (3) It follows from (2) that the threshold for articulation within larger organizations must be high. The threshold is probably lower, but still fairly high, when Os inspect the material in an attitude which facilitates the articulation.[1]

These conclusions refer to the perceptual phase of learning. It should

Reprinted from the *American Journal of Psychology*, Vol. 71, No. 3, September, 1958.

[1] Wolfgang Köhler, Perceptual organization and learning. *Amer. J. Psychol.*, 1958, 71, 311–315.

therefore be possible to verify them in perceptual situations in which learning plays hardly any part. To our knowledge, there have so far been only two investigations which are concerned with the present issue, an older study by Krechevsky [2] and more recent experiments done by Krech and Calvin.[3] In both cases, results have been striking, and in line with the present conclusions.

Since Wertheimer's work on visual grouping, patterns such as that shown in Fig. 1 have often been used for demonstrating perceptual organization.[4] Actually, the fact that in such patterns certain rows of dots form horizontal (or vertical) lines is a demonstration of articulation; for the complete patterns are seen as large units which have the shapes of squares, and, when the horizontal (or vertical) lines are formed, they remain parts of the larger organization. This has already been emphasized by Krech and Calvin, who used such patterns in their experiments. These investigators did not measure the threshold for articulation in Wertheimer's patterns; nevertheless, their results clearly prove that this threshold must be very high indeed; for when distances between the dots in one direction were very much greater than in the other, not a few Os remained entirely unaware of the fact, and did not see the corresponding articulation even when the patterns were shown many times in succession.

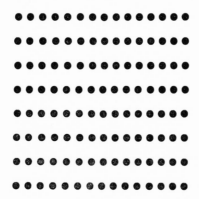

FIG. 1. An example of articulation.

[2] I. Krechevsky, An experimental investigation of the principle of proximity in the visual perception of the rat. *J. exp. Psychol.,* 1938, 22, 497–523.

[3] David Krech and A. D. Calvin, Levels of perceptual organization and cognition. *J. abnorm. soc. Psychol.,* 1953, 48, 394–400.

[4] Max Wertheimer, Untersuchungen zur Lehre von der Gestalt. *Psychol. Forsch.,* 1923, 4, 301–350.

One might be inclined to object that this fact was only caused by the short time during which the patterns were seen; namely, 0.06 sec. This objection would not be justified. The threshold for articulation in such patterns is also very high when exposure times are much longer. We have recently shown this in very simple experiments in which the patterns were seen for one or several seconds. To obtain an estimate of the threshold for articulation, we varied the ratio of the distances in the vertical and horizontal dimensions. Some observations were made when Os were concentrating on a "cover task" which was meant to deflect attention from the patterns; in others, they were expressly asked to attend to the patterns as such. In our first tests, we used the former procedure.

The patterns consisted of black circles with the diameter ⅛ in., which were attached to squares of white cardboard (7 in. square). In one direction (either vertical or horizontal) the distance between the circles remained constant; namely, $1\frac{2}{16}$ in. In the other direction, it was reduced in small steps from $1\frac{2}{16}$ to $\frac{4}{16}$ in. To protect the patterns against the effects of repeated handling, they were covered with cellophane. The contrast between the circles and their background was not appreciably affected by this procedure.

The patterns were used as backgrounds for cardboard figures of much smaller size, and Os were instructed to indicate whether they liked, or disliked, each figure by removing it in one direction or the opposite. The figures did not seriously disturb perception of the patterns. Moreover, the patterns alone remained before the Os between the removal of one figure and the presentation of the next.

During the choices of a given O, of which there were six in succession, the background pattern was not changed. Only four of the available patterns had to be used in the present tests. Each served as background in tests with 5 Os; no O saw more than one pattern.

Immediately after O's six judgments, E removed the pattern, and asked him to describe the background on which the figures had been seen. The statements obtained under these conditions varied little. Sometimes the circles were said to have been evenly spaced; more often, to have been arranged in vertical and horizontal rows. Clearly distinguished from such descriptions were those which referred only to horizontal (or only to vertical) rows. Since actual articulation in one dimension goes with suppression of corresponding relations in the other dimension, only statements of the latter kind can be regarded as evidence that articulation has occurred.

In one-half of our tests, distances in the vertical direction were varied from one group of Os to another; in the other half, the variations occurred in the horizontal direction. Students of Bryn Mawr and Swarthmore Colleges served as Os in the former case; and of Stanford University in the latter.

In our tests with the cover task, results from 20 Os were as follows: With the distance in the horizontal (or vertical) direction constant ($^{12}/_{16}$ in.), and with the distance in the vertical (or horizontal) direction reduced to

$$^{7}/_{16} \qquad ^{6}/_{16} \qquad ^{5}/_{16} \qquad ^{4}/_{16} \text{ in.,}$$

articulation in the vertical direction occurred

$$0 \qquad 1 \qquad 2 \qquad 4 \text{ times}$$

and in the horizontal direction

$$0 \qquad 0 \qquad 1 \qquad 4 \text{ times}$$

Since every O was tested with only one ratio of the distances, these results are independent of any particular "set." The threshold for articulation which the present numbers indicate can, of course, be regarded as a threshold only when differences among the individuals in the various groups are ignored. On the other hand, the agreement between the two sequences of numbers suggests that, under the conditions of our tests and with comparable Os, most individual thresholds would lie between $^{5}/_{16}$ and $^{4}/_{16}$ in. The probable threshold in this sense is extremely high. Suppose that, on the average, the threshold lies at $^{9}/_{32}$ in. The difference between this distance and the constant distance in the other direction amounts to about 60 per cent of this greater distance.

In the next group of tests, Os were shown patterns of the same type, with the instruction to describe each immediately after its presentation. There was now no cover task. Under these conditions, perception was obviously "attentional." We have not yet tried to introduce more specific attitudes than mere attention to the patterns. Obviously, during intentional *learning,* the operations of Os often go far beyond this simplest condition.

The Os (10 in number) were students of Bryn Mawr and Swarthmore. All saw the complete series of patterns in its regular sequence, beginning with the situation in which distances in the two directions were the same ($^{12}/_{16}$ in.). Patterns in which distances in the vertical or in the horizontal direction were shorter were shown in alternation. All patterns were exposed for 1 sec. Since articulation in the two directions seemed to occur at the same ratio of the distances, results for both situations are here combined. Out of 10 cases, they are as follows:

| Distance (in inches): | $12\frac{2}{16}$ | $10\frac{0}{16}$ | $\frac{9}{16}$ | $\frac{8}{16}$ | $\frac{7}{16}$ | $\frac{6}{16}$ | $\frac{5}{16}$ |
|---|---|---|---|---|---|---|---|
| Number of articulations: | 0 | 0 | 1 | 2 | 8 | 9 | 10 |

These numbers are cumulative: once O had seen a pattern as articulated, he also reported articulation in the following patterns, in which conditions for it were further improved. For the group as a whole, the threshold may now be said to lie between $\frac{8}{16}$ and $\frac{7}{16}$ in., that is, at a difference between the two distances which is distinctly smaller than it was when Os were occupied with a cover task. On the assumption that it lies at $15\frac{5}{32}$ in., it amounts to approximately 37 per cent of the larger distance. Hence, the attentional attitude has considerably lowered the threshold, although the threshold still remains very high. Articulation does not often occur until distances in one direction are reduced by more than one-third.

Since it seemed possible that a 1-sec. exposure was too short for articulation to occur easily, the experiments were repeated at Stanford University under the same conditions, excepting that now the patterns were shown for 3 sec. There were again 10 Os. The results were as follows:

| Distance (in inches): | $12\frac{2}{16}$ | $10\frac{0}{16}$ | $\frac{9}{16}$ | $\frac{8}{16}$ | $\frac{7}{16}$ | $\frac{6}{16}$ | $\frac{5}{16}$ |
|---|---|---|---|---|---|---|---|
| Number of articulations: | 0 | 0 | 0 | 2 | 8 | 9 | 10 |

There is hardly any difference between these results and those obtained with the shorter exposure times. We may therefore trust the results of both tests. They confirm the results of Krech and Calvin. In such patterns the threshold for articulation is far greater than more familiar spatial thresholds.

Krech and Calvin have demonstrated that the ease with which articulation occurs in different persons is not related to their visual acuity. The size of the threshold for our groups may be regarded as proof of the same fact. Not one out of our 20 Os showed evidence of articulation when the distances in the two directions were $12\frac{2}{16}$ and $10\frac{0}{16}$, that is, when the difference amounted to $\frac{1}{8}$, or 20 per cent of the smaller distance. Most people can compare visual distances as such far more accurately. In this respect, we find a very simple observation particularly impressive. When confronted with one of our patterns which, in spite of a considerable difference between the two distances, does not appear to us articulated, we have no difficulty in singling out three circles which together form a right triangle, and in ignoring the surrounding circles.[5] The great difference between the vertical and horizontal sides of the triangle is perfectly obvious under these conditions; and yet, when the triangle is allowed to disappear again in the total pattern, the same objective difference is once more quite unable to bring about articulation.

The conclusion that the suppression of articulation is caused by organizational rather than by more elementary visual factors is also supported by the following fact. In the sequence in which the various patterns were shown, a next reduction of the distance-ratio occurred just as often first in the horizontal as in the vertical dimension. Results did not indicate that articulation occurred more easily in the horizontal dimension, although the vertical-horizontal illusion might have been expected to operate in this direction. Apparently, it had no appreciable effect on the outcome of our tests. The illusion is, however, present when a right triangle is singled out. When this is done with a pattern in which objective distances are the same in both dimensions, the vertical distance is clearly greater.

While, under the conditions of our observations, articulation is suppressed within surprisingly wide limits, it is, of course, no longer suppressed under more extreme conditions.[6] Even when the patterns are seen only incidentally, as they were in our first tests, articulated organization becomes perfectly natural with very great differences between the distances in the two dimensions. After all, in the first tests, 8 out of 10 Os did report articulation when distances in one direction were three times as great as those in the other. In the same connection, it must be remembered that, if in such patterns vertical (or horizontal) lines are formed only against strong resistance, the same patterns have smaller parts which are seen as such all the time; namely, the dots or circles. Conditions for their survival as separate entities are, of course, so favorable that they are not appreciably affected by their inclusion in the total patterns—or, under conditions of articulation, in vertical or horizontal lines.[7]

---

[5] This is a much easier task than that of articulating the whole pattern to form vertical (or horizontal) lines.

[6] Krech and Calvin, *op. cit.,* 399.

[7] Even the articulation with which our tests are concerned seems to occur

The sequence in which the patterns were shown under conditions of attentional perception may have caused a certain set in favor of non-articulated organization. The threshold found in these tests may, therefore, be higher than it would have been under other conditions. If this is true, our results do not show the articulating effect of attention in its full size, but we doubt whether, in the present situation, the threshold is greatly increased in this fashion. When we inspect a pattern which only a few of our Os see as articulated, it generally does not appear as articulated to ourselves, and then a strong effort to introduce the "right" articulation seldom produces more than temporary articulation in restricted regions of the pattern.[8]

We agree with Krech and Calvin on all facts, but not with some of their remarks about Gestalt psychology. In the first place, their own observations and ours can hardly be said to mean that, under certain conditions, the principles of Gestalt psychology do not hold. Surely, Gestalt psychologists have never maintained that differential proximity always wins, even when organizational factors which operate in another direction are extremely powerful. Is it an objection to the law of gravitation that airplanes may rise from the ground, and stay in the air for hours? Secondly, on the basis of their findings, the authors object to statements that the effects of proximity are "immediately" perceived. When, many years ago, Gestalt psychologists made statements of this kind, they used the term "immediate" in protest against the view that organization is merely a matter of learning which has gradually transformed so-called sensations into objects and groups. The term was not meant to deny that it takes organization a certain (very short) time to complete its work. On the contrary, certain phenomena such as the $\gamma$-movement were always regarded as evidence for precisely

---

more easily under certain conditions. Occasionally, we have observed that a pattern, which is not seen as articulated when shown in large size, begins to show articulation when, under otherwise identical conditions, its size is greatly reduced.

[8] Articulation of larger patterns can be produced by distinctive similarity of some parts as well as by differential proximity. Consequently, the questions which have arisen in the latter case must also be asked in the former: (1) What is the threshold for articulation when differential similarity is the decisive factor? (2) Does attention affect this threshold just as it affects articulation by proximity? So far we have done only preliminary tests when attention was deflected by a cover task. On a middle-gray background, alternating rows of dark-gray and white circles were shown when distances in both directions were the same. Only 2 out of 15 Os gave evidence of having seen the pattern as articulated when describing it after completion of the cover task. In future tests, the brightness difference between the circles will have to be varied.

this fact. In the same connection, the authors state more specifically that even simple perceptual structures are products of a rapid development which proceeds from the more homogeneous to the more differentiated. This again is a view with which Gestalt psychologists are quite familiar. In fact, in an article in which he discussed perceptual grouping, Wertheimer expressed exactly the same view a long time ago.

The tendency of larger organizations to prevent the emergence of more particular structures is not restricted to patterns of dots. In further tests, we used patterns of another kind which have also been introduced by Wertheimer. Letters and words tend to disappear as particular entities with their familiar characteristics when their mirror images are added, as in Fig. 2. Few people who see this pattern are spontaneously aware of the fact that its upper half is the word *men*. In camouflage of this type, it is mainly the tendency of organization to form closed entities which so changes some characteristics of parts that they are not spontaneously recognized. For instance, when seen in the pattern as a whole, the lines of the letter *m* and those of its mirror image become mere boundaries of area between them which now assume the figural character described by Rubin. When shown alone, the lines of the letter have no such function; they are then merely *linear* phenomena. Within the larger pattern, however, the word and its letters tend to lose their familiar characteristics, and are therefore seldom spontaneously recognized. The principle which is here involved differs from the one which operates in Wertheimer's dot-patterns; and yet, as to the relation between larger organizations and particular parts of them, the two situations resemble each other so much that we expected analogous tests to give similar results also with the present pattern.

FIG. 2. A word and its mirror image.

As used in our observations, the pattern had a horizontal length of 18 cm., and a height of 3 cm. We varied the distance between the upper and the lower halves of the pattern from 0–3.5 cm. in steps of 0.5 cm.[9]

---

[9] Dr. Mary Henle once did experiments of this kind which have not been published. She found that the larger organization tends to prevail even when the word and its mirror image were clearly separated in space.

Preliminary tests made us suspect that, when Os are first shown the pattern without separation, and then the various versions with gradually growing separations, the effect of set tends to prevent awareness and recognition of the word, even when separations are very great. Tests for the various distances were, therefore, made with separate Os, 5 for each separation. Our Os were again students of Bryn Mawr and Swarthmore Colleges.

In a first procedure, perception of the patterns was incidental. Horizontal lines of approximately equal length were shown, one 1.8 cm. above and the other the same distance below the pattern and, as a cover task, Os had to compare their lengths. The time of exposure was always 1.5 sec. After six comparisons, the pattern was removed, and O was asked what he had seen between the lines. In the reports, certain terms such as "leaves," "hearts," and "wavy lines" occurred very often. The word "men" was mentioned only when the patterns with very great separations were shown, and even then only by a few Os.

The results from 40 Os, 5 at every separation, were as follows:

| Separation (in cm.): | 0.0 | 0.5 | 1.0 | 1.5 | 2.0 | 2.5 | 3.0 | 3.5 |
|---|---|---|---|---|---|---|---|---|
| Times "men" observed: | 0 | 0 | 0 | 0 | 1 | 0 | 2 | 1 |

Only 4 of 40 Os discovered that a well-known word was shown to them, although in several groups the separation between this word and its mirror image was large—even at separations of 3.0 and 3.5 cm. only 3 of 10 Os perceived the word.

We next performed tests under conditions of attentional perception. Objective conditions remained the same, including the time of presentation. The horizontal lines were also left in their places. Again, 5 Os were tested with a given separation. Before the pattern was shown, the Os were instructed to describe its appearance as soon as it had been removed by E. The horizontal lines were not mentioned in the instructions.

The results with 40 Os, 5 at every separation, were:

| Separation (in cm.): | 0.0 | 0.5 | 1.0 | 1.5 | 2.0 | 2.5 | 3.0 | 3.5 |
|---|---|---|---|---|---|---|---|---|
| Times "men" reported: | 0 | 1 | 2 | 3 | 4 | 4 | 5 | 5 |

It is remarkable that, even when Os attend to the patterns before them, separations such as 0.5 and 1 cm. do not regularly permit recognition of the word. No more than 3 of 10 Os are aware of its presence under these conditions, and only when the distance grows to 3 cm. is the word seen by all. Since no set operated against its emergence, we can only conclude that, with some Os, the word is still strongly affected by the larger organization when the separating distance amounts to about 2 cm. On the other hand, the difference between the present results and those found under conditions of incidental perception is also very great. When confronted with the same patterns, 24 (rather than 4) Os altogether have now recognized the word.

There is no doubt that our Os were aware of the distance between the two halves of the pattern. We often asked them to make drawings in connection with their descriptions. For the most part, these drawings consisted of two separate figures, even when the Os had not recognized the word; but, just under these circumstances, the figures showed little resemblance to the word or its mirror image. The drawings were generally too regular.

## SATIATION AND ATTENTION

The conclusions drawn from certain learning experiments have been confirmed in the preceding tests. We now turn to the question why attention operates against the tendency of larger organizations to suppress more articulated perception. In trying to answer this question, we must briefly refer to certain principles of natural science. More particularly, we must consider the fact that, when open systems receive energy from the outside, processes in their interiors are intensified, and tend to become more differentiated. It is our suggestion that the effect of attention on visual patterns is a special instance of this fact.

Suppose that, in a closed system, inert velocities are immediately destroyed by friction. Such a system pays for any transformations in its interior by a reduction of the energy available for such work. When this energy has been reduced to a minimum, the system is either in a state of equilibrium or in a steady state. Several physicists have called attention to the fact that, in such states, the distribution of materials and processes within the system is maximally homogeneous or symmetrical. The reason for this fact is, of course, that the energies which the system spends in transforming itself are closely related to differences, inhomogeneities, and asymmetries of materials and processes. The very simplest example is that of a closed system in which only one particular transformation is possible to begin with, which is brought about by one difference of potential (in the more general sense of this term). In this special case, the difference of potential is gradually lowered to a minimum, and the corresponding process of transformation weakened.

The present rule applies only to closed systems *as wholes*. Very often, developments in parts of such systems occur in the opposite, the "upward," direction. This is entirely in line with the general rule so long as the local increase of energy is accompanied by greater decreases elsewhere in the system, as it actually always is. Under such circumstances, the part in which developments occur in the direction of growing energy is a special instance of an "open" system. In such a part of the whole (or closed) system, energy and the intensity of processes can grow because other parts of the system play the role of sources from which that particular section can borrow energy. When the energy within an open system of this kind grows, existing differences and inhomogeneities in its interior will be enhanced, and may develop to maximal size. In extremely simple cases, an open system in this sense will again be capable of only one transformation. This transformation (and the supporting difference of potential) will now be intensified until a highest value is reached.[10]

The most obvious examples of open systems are the organisms. They maintain (or even increase) the energy in their interior by absorbing energy from their environment. If the parts of the environment which thus serve as sources are included, we have, of course, again closed systems, of which the organisms are open parts. In organisms, too, the absorption of energy from the outside has the effect of giving processes the upward direction, or of keeping them at high levels of energy.

What has just been said about organisms applies also to some of their parts, for instance, to the visual projection areas of the human brain. Quite apart from the energy inherent in afferent impulses, the visual cortex may, or may not, receive energy from other parts of the brain. The former condition seems to be realized when a person takes interest in his visual field. For, under these circumstances, the segregation of objects in the field is sharpened, differences between various parts of the field are enhanced, and so forth. These changes have again the well-known direction of developments within open systems to which energy is transferred from the outside.

---

[10] Some recent statements about open systems give the impression that the meaning of this term is not always clearly understood. Authors who believe that open systems are mysterious entities to which the laws of physics do not apply are making a serious mistake. To be sure, the behavior of some open systems is fascinating; but there is no evidence that this behavior follows principles which are at odds with those of the physicists. It is, however, true that physics has so far given attention only to a few examples of open systems, and that, as a consequence, the relation between the behavior of *some* such systems and the principles of physics has never been explicitly formulated.

It need not be the visual field as a whole which is so affected. What we call "visual attention" may be directed toward particular parts of the visual scene. It thus relates other (as yet unknown) parts of the nervous system to such particular visual objects; and, in doing so, it also seems to increase the energy level of the processes in question; for local differences are again intensified, and the clearness of local structures is enhanced.

Our tests with Wertheimer's dot patterns may serve as examples of such effects of attention inasmuch as, under conditions of incidental perception, these patterns tended to appear as homogeneous distributions while, under the influence of attention, the differences between the distances in the two directions became much more effective, and articulation appeared where none had been seen before. Attention had a similar effect upon the combination of a word with its mirror image. As long as perception of this pattern was incidental, the word as a visual entity remained submerged in the total structure in spite of considerable distances between the two parts. Attention changed this situation in the direction of a more specific organization, in which the word could show its known characteristics, and thus be recognized. Hence, attention operates in the direction of differentiation, and is in this respect comparable to events in physics which transfer energy to an open system from the outside.

If we are right in assuming that, under conditions of attentional perception, the energy of the visual processes in question is increased, it should be possible to demonstrate this fact in psychological experiments. When complicated situations are involved, such a demonstration may be difficult. But in some open physical systems only one process will be intensified under such circumstances. It therefore seemed advisable to perform the necessary psychological tests under similarly simple conditions.

According to a theory developed by Köhler and Wallach, the cortical counterpart of a segregated visual object is pervaded and surrounded by an electric current.[11] This current will be weaker or stronger depending upon the difference between the brightness inside and outside; but soon the flow will always be weakened by its own electrotonic (or satiating) effect upon the tissue, whatever its initial intensity may have been.

We have just assumed that, when attention is concentrated on an

---

[11] Wolfgang Köhler and Hans Wallach, Figural after-effects. *Proc. Amer. philos. Soc.,* 1944, 88, 269–357.

object, the underlying cortical process (which, according to Köhler and Wallach, is the current of the object) will be intensified, and that, as a consequence, the object will stand out more clearly; but this intensification of the current will also accelerate its electrotonic action. As a result, satiation in the crucial area will soon be stronger, and corresponding figural aftereffects will be greater than those caused by a comparison object to which O does not attend. Köhler and Emery have made observations which demonstrate this fact.[12] An object gradually shrinks (by "self-satiation") when it occupies a given place for some time. Now, when two equal objects are shown on the left and the right side of a fixation point, attention may be concentrated on one or the other. When this is done, the object to which O attends soon appears smaller. If now attention is shifted to the other object, *this* object will, after a while, appear smaller, and so forth. Since this phenomenon confirms the present reasoning, we decided to do the following tests.[13]

Our first tests referred to the influence of visual attention upon a well-known figural aftereffect in the third dimension of visual space. When an object on one side of a fixation point has been seen for some time, a test (T-) object shown in front of the former object is displaced toward O; it appears nearer than a comparison object which is presented on the other side of the fixation mark in a symmetrical location and in the same objective plane. If attention really intensifies satiation, its influence should be demonstrable in a situation in which two equal and symmetrically placed satiation (I-) objects are shown first, and then two equal T-objects which have strictly corresponding locations in front of the two I-objects. In such an objectively balanced arrangement, the concentration of attention on one or the other I-object during

---

12 Wolfgang Köhler and D. A. Emery, Figural after-effects in the third dimension of visual space. *Amer. J. Psychol.*, 1947, 60, 159–201.

13 It is by no means easy to make observations in which attention must be shifted from one object to another while O fixates a mark between them. Visual attention has sometimes been compared with the use of a flashlight which can be turned one way or the other as its owner wishes. This comparison is seriously misleading. Once attention is concentrated on one more or less peripheral object, this vector cannot be transferred at will to an object in another peripheral location. For a considerable period, it refuses to move from its first target to the new one, even when O makes every effort to bring about the change. Visual attention seems to be a far more earthy fact than we have realized in the past. From a practical point of view, it follows that, when the effects of attention on visual objects are to be studied, Os cannot be expected to shift the vector from one object to another whenever they are asked to do so. In our experiments, no such instruction was ever given.

the satiation period should have the effect of displacing the corresponding T-object farther toward O.

The experimental arrangement which we used has been described by Köhler and Emery.[14] The I-objects were light gray squares (1.5 in. on a side). They were shown at a distance of 10.5 ft. from O, who fixated a mark 3 in. in front of their plane for 45 sec. Two T-squares (2 in. sq.) then appeared 3 in. in front of the fixation mark, and O now compared their locations in the third dimension. Some Os were instructed to concentrate on the left I-object and others on the right I-object during the satiation period.

Since the distance between the squares and the fixation mark was small (about 1.2 in.), concentration of attention only on one square proved practically impossible. It seems that, in such a situation, the width of the region to which O attends cannot be reduced *ad libitum*. We therefore instructed our Os to concentrate on the fixation mark and one of the squares *as a pair of objects*. This is a much easier task. The Os also were asked not to judge immediately, because many figural aftereffects tend to grow to some extent while the T-objects are perceived. In the present experiments, this phenomenon was particularly striking. Our Os were mostly students of Swarthmore College who did not know the purpose of the tests. Of 19 altogether, 7 were instructed to concentrate on the right object, and the remaining 12 on the left I-object. All were tested twice. Before the tests, depth discrimination when attention was concentrated on the fixation mark alone had been examined in all cases. Accuracy had always been found so high that actual measurement of thresholds would have been difficult with our apparatus.

The results of our tests are shown in Table1, in which *plus* refers to judgments in the expected direction; *zero,* to the absence of any asymmetry in the location of the T-objects; and *minus,* to judgments in the opposite direction. "Right" and "left" mean the two directions of attention, and the numbers indicate how many Os gave judgments belonging to the three categories. The last column gives the *p*-values found in a sign test, ignoring the *zero*-cases. Altogether, 31 judgments out of 38 agree with expectation, 4 disagree, and in 3 instances no difference has been observed. The number of Os tested with attention concentrated on the left side is greater, because it proved advisable to increase their number when the observed effect seemed weaker on this side. The data

---

[14] Köhler and Emery, *op. cit.,* 180.

TABLE 1

THE EFFECT OF ATTENTION ON SATIATION: VISUAL TESTS

| Direction | Test | + | 0 | − | p |
|-----------|------|---|---|---|---|
| Right | first | 6 | 1 | 0 | 0.016 |
| | second | 7 | 0 | 0 | 0.008 |
| Left | first | 9 | 1 | 2 | 0.032 |
| | second | 9 | 1 | 2 | 0.032 |

of Table 1 suggest such an asymmetry. This phenomenon may be related to observations mentioned by Hebb.[15] A more specific relation may exist to asymmetries in visual perception which Gaffron has described.[16] Our tests have not been repeated in a situation in which T-objects are displaced backward. The present form of the tests must be regarded as more conclusive.[17]

We felt that the present results were in need of confirmation. It also seemed advisable to study the same problem in a different situation, for instance, when the aftereffect which attention might, or might not, intensify occurs in another sense modality. Further tests were, therefore, done with the figural aftereffect in kinesthesis, in which satiation changes the width of a T-object. Is this effect also enhanced on one side

---

[15] D. O. Hebb, *Organization of behavior.* New York: Wiley, 1949, p. 49.

[16] Mercedes Gaffron, Right and left in pictures. *Art Quart.*, 1950, 311–331.

[17] Köhler and Emery, *op. cit.*, 179. Dorothy Dinnerstein and the senior author once did experiments in which the effect of self-satiation upon objects shown before or behind the plane of the fixation mark was tested. A square was presented either behind or in front of the fixation mark, and either on the right or the left side of this mark. After a satiation period, the location of the satiated square was compared with that of another square which now appeared on the other side of the fixation mark, and in the same objective plane. In all observations of this kind, the affected square was found to appear nearer the plane of the fixation mark, irrespective of its objective location behind or in front of this plane. We have recently repeated these tests with 6 Os. Without exception, their judgments confirmed this rule. The rule suggests that, under conditions of self-satiation, the depth of three-dimensional visual structures is gradually reduced. One can easily demonstrate that this is true by presenting in a stereoscope two slightly disparate projections of a three-dimensional object to the two eyes, which are given the proper directions by means of fixation marks on one side of the two projections. After a satiation period, two further disparate projections, identical with the former, are added on the other side of the marks so that the three-dimensional appearance of the old and the new visual objects can be directly compared. It is then found that in the satiated object the third dimension is strikingly reduced; it looks much flatter than the new object.

(in one hand) when, in an otherwise symmetrical situation, O's attention is concentrated on this side? It is not known whether attending to kinesthetic facts is basically the same process as concentrating on a visual object; but, on the assumption that it is, we performed the following tests.

The experimental arrangement which we used has been described by Köhler and Dinnerstein.[18] In a first experiment, two equal I-objects, 2.5 in. wide, were presented to the two hands for a period of 45 sec. The T-object which O then felt with one hand was 1.5 in. wide. With the other hand, he had to find a place on a scale, which appeared to have the same width as the T-object. In a second experiment, the width of the I-object was 1 in., that of the T-object again 1.5 in. Thus, the aftereffects established in the two experiments, and therefore also corresponding differential effects produced by one-sided concentration of attention, would lie in opposite directions. Moreover, in both experiments, concentration on the side where later the T-object is presented would have one, and concentration on the other side, the opposite effect on the measurements.

The scale was always placed on O's right side. O was blindfolded. Since subjective equality need not coincide with objective equality,[19] the first two measures were made without preceding satiation. In one measurement, O's right hand was placed on the scale three steps below the point of objective equality (POE); in the other, three steps above this point. The actual sequence was one for one-half of the Os and the opposite for the other half. The mean point of subjective equality (PSE) for all 42 Os was $+0.93$ of one step on the scale. This value differs significantly from the POE ($p < 0.01$). The width touched with the right hand was underestimated by 28 Os, overestimated by 9, and judged equal by 5. Our results in this respect agree with those of other investigators.[20] Only a few of our Os were left-handed. The average PSE for the Os who concentrated, in the following tests, on the left or the right side did not differ significantly from each other. The differen-

[18] Wolfgang Köhler and Dorothy Dinnerstein, Figural after-effects in kinesthesis. *Miscellanea Psychologica Albert Michotte,* Louvain: Institut Superieur de Philosophie, 1947, 199.

[19] Michael Wertheimer, Constant errors in the measurement of figural aftereffects. *Amer. J. Psychol.,* 1954, 67, 543–546.

[20] G. S. Klein and David Krech, Cortical conductivity in the brain injured. *J. Personal.,* 1952, 21, 118–148; A. McPherson and Samuel Renfrew, Asymmetry of perception of size between the right and left hands in normal subjects. *Quart. J. exp. Psychol.,* 1953, 5, 66–74; Michael Wertheimer, *op. cit.,* 543–546.

tial aftereffects measured after satiation were, for each O, related to his PSE as a zero.

Before satiation began, the Os were instructed to concentrate on the impressions in one hand. As a pretext they were told that their results would be compared with those of other Os who, during the same tests, would learn some material by heart.

Table 2 gives the numbers of Os whose judgments had the expected direction ($+$), of those who showed no differential effect ($0$), and of those whose judgments were at odds with our expectation ($-$). Out

TABLE 2

The Effect of Attention on Satiation: Kinesthetic Tests

| Experiment | Direction | $+$ | $0$ | $-$ | $p$ |
|:---:|:---:|:---:|:---:|:---:|:---:|
| 1 | right | 10 | 1 | 0 | 0.001 |
|  | left | 10 | 1 | 0 | 0.001 |
| 2 | right | 8 | 2 | 0 | 0.004 |
|  | left | 7 | 3 | 0 | 0.008 |

of 42 cases altogether, 35 judgments agree with our hypothesis, no judgment had the opposite direction, and in the remaining 7 instances no direction was indicated. The $p$-values are derived from a sign test in which *zero*-cases were not included. There seems to be no doubt that our assumption is verified. The decision is less satisfactory in experiment 2 than in experiment 1. Such a difference would have to be expected if, in experiment 2 the relation between the widths of the I- and the T-object was less favorably chosen.

Since, actually, the judgments of our Os had the form of quantitative deviations from their PSEs, we can add a further table (Table 3) which

TABLE 3

The Effect of Attention on Satiation: Further
Kinesthetic Data

| Experiment | Direction | Mean | $SE_m$ | $p$ |
|:---:|:---:|:---:|:---:|:---:|
|  | right | $+1.27$ | .22 | $<0.01$ |
| 1 | left | $-1.14$ | .21 | $<0.01$ |
|  | right | $-1.10$ | .39 | $<0.01$ |
| 2 | left | $+1.15$ | .39 | $<0.01$ |

refers to such quantities, the means of the results of the individual Os in each group, rather than to mere directions of judgment. Under $SE_m$, the standard errors of the means are given. The unit in which results are here measured is one step on the scale ($\frac{1}{12}$ in.).

Table 3 confirms the results shown in Table 2. When, in such experiments, attention is concentrated on the kinesthetic impression in one hand, it intensifies the corresponding satiation.

SUMMARY

(1) In certain patterns introduced by Wertheimer, approximate thresholds for articulation have been determined under conditions of incidental and attentional perception. The thresholds are always very high, but clearly lower when perception is attentional. The same result was found when a word was shown at varying distances from its mirror image. Under conditions of attentional perception, the word as such is seen and recognized at much shorter distances from its mirror image.

(2) Attention intensifies the process which underlies the perception of an object. Under such circumstances, satiation is accelerated, and corresponding figural aftereffects are enhanced. Figural aftereffects both in the third dimension of visual space and in kinesthesis show this influence of attention.

*Hans Wallach*

SWARTHMORE COLLEGE

# SOME CONSIDERATIONS

# CONCERNING THE RELATION

# BETWEEN PERCEPTION

# AND COGNITION

I look around in a familiar environment and find that nearly every object has meaning.[1] This meaning I experience as an objective fact, and I perceive it out there in the thing. A hammer looks like something with which to drive a nail into a wall or something with which to smash a vase. I have the impression that I perceive these meanings in the object even while I realize that they do not come to me through my eyes at the moment of perceiving them but must be furnished by a memory function, for they were given by previous experience with the object.

I suspect that this discrepancy between experience and function is responsible for some of the vagueness of conception in this part of psychology. The remedy seems to be to acknowledge it explicitly: The meaning which the hammer has for me is, *functionally* speaking, the effect of past commerce with that object, but it is experienced as being

Reprinted with permission from the *Journal of Personality*, Vol. 18, No. 1, September, 1949.

[1] This paper was written while the author was a John Simon Guggenheim Memorial Fellow.

seen in the object of equal status with color and form. We have here the effect of a recall process in which recall is not experienced as such. Instead the contribution of memory appears as part of a percept.

There is no reason why this recall process should be essentially different from other recall processes as, for instance, recognition and recall by association. As Köhler, reviving an old argument of Höffding's, has pointed out (5; 3, pp. 126–144), any recall which is occasioned by a perceptual experience involves a process in which such an experience brings into function a memory trace of a similar experience of the past. This is true also where the subject recalls an associated content. When I pass a man on the street whom I have met before, I may, for instance, recall his name. This recall presupposes an association between a visual trace, say of the man's face, and a trace of his name. But the association alone does not explain recall of the name on this occasion. Face and name left associated traces when I was introduced to the man in the past. When I meet the man again, he is, of course, on the whole the same physical object, and I may immediately experience him as the same person I met before; but *functionally* speaking there are two separate psychological events involved, the perception of the face on the occasion of the first meeting and a present perceptual process of the "same" face. The former is now represented by a memory trace, and it is this trace which provides the access to the trace of the name. Yet it is one of many traces of faces which I might recognize, and so the question arises how the appropriate one is brought into function. As Köhler has argued, the only possible answer is that the similarity between the original process of seeing the face, now represented by its trace, and the present process is responsible for the proper selection of this trace. Recall by association, then, consists of two steps: A process of recall by similarity by which the present perceptual process makes contact with the trace of a similar process of the past, and secondly, recall of a content associated with this trace.

The necessity for such an assumption is not avoided by thinking in terms of responses instead of associated contents. One speaks of the same stimulus when the same combination of physical processes affects the sense organs of the subject or, more loosely, when these combinations appear to the experimenter as the same. Yet, when the same stimulus occurs repeatedly to produce a particular response, we deal, of course, with different, initially unconnected psychological events, and they must in some fashion manifest their identity in the nervous system of the subject before that particular response can be aroused.

In a relatively small number of cases the assumption might possibly be made that afferent processes produced by different stimuli will arrive at different places in the nervous system and manifest the identity of the respective stimuli by their locale. But where the stimulus is characterized only by its spatially or temporally extended pattern as, for instance, in the case of visual forms, of speech sounds, and of noises, this assumption cannot be made. Similarity between the processes produced by different occurrences of the "same" stimulus must account for its identification.

Recall by similarity may occur without recall of an associated content, namely, in pure recognition where it merely produces a feeling of familiarity.

The same process of recall by similarity must be involved when meaning is perceived, unless a set is operating. No matter what the nature of meaning may be, as long as a meaning content was acquired in the past it is necessary to postulate the same sequence of recall processes in order to explain how meaning comes to appear in perceptual experience: first, a step of recall by similarity between the sensorily determined perceptual process and a trace complex with which the meaning content is connected, and secondly, the coming into function of the connected meaning. Since in a familiar environment most perceptual objects appear meaningful, such recall processes must readily take place all the time, and because they do, their mediation usually goes unrecognized.

I have just used the term trace complex, because often what appears as a familiar or meaningful object has occurred in the past not only once but at several different times. Frequently a number of these occurrences have contributed in different ways to the meaning content. When recall takes place, the total meaning seems to be given. This indicates that the recall process established contact, not with a trace of any one of these occurrences, but with a trace complex which represents features of a number of them. In short, the various occurrences must have previously become connected so that they could contribute to the total meaning content and later, in a recall process, function together. These connections are themselves the effects of recall processes which took place in the past, when at the second occurrence of the object contact was made with the trace of the first one, and later, when the third occurrence brought into function the trace complex of the first two, and so on. In this fashion, recall by similarity accounts for a cognitive product of temporally separated events and, in many cases, makes learning by repetition possible.

Often the function of a memory trace which participates in a perceptual process is not merely to add its content to the sensorily determined qualities of color and shape. It may change the organization of the primary process by imposing a different internal grouping as in the case of the Street figures.[2] Or new perceptual qualities may emerge after a trace reference has been established, as, for instance, physiognomic qualities. They are seen only when the primary form pattern has been recognized as a face. But when that has happened, the seen physiognomic qualities depend mainly on the sensory conditions.

Yet no matter how intimate and varied in function the interplay of a primary process and an aroused trace may be, it must be preceded by a process of trace selection. Where no set is operating, this selection process consists of recall by similarity and is therefore initiated by the primary perceptual process and highly dependent on its characteristics. The selection process must be distinguished from the interplay between trace and primary process, for it is prerequisite for this interplay.

The intervening of this selection process before a pertinent memory trace can influence a perceptual process introduces an element of fortuity into experiments on the effect of central factors on perception, or, rather, what amounts to fortuity from the viewpoint of such studies. We are all aware of the difficulties which the incomplete knowledge of the subject's past means for experimentation and its evaluation. But even if we had a complete inventory of the subject's previous experience, we would not be much better off because it would still be to a degree fortuitous whether a psychologically pertinent trace content actually comes to participate in the present process. Köhler and Restorff have demonstrated that whether or not an experience of the past through recall by similarity gains an influence on a present process depends on the content and structure of the time interval between that experience and the present (1; 5; 3, pp. 126–144). Frequency and recency of the mental event which the pertinent trace represents undoubtedly also play a role in whether or not contact is made with the trace (1, 5). Therefore, where trace selection is left to spontaneous recall, the influence of a need or of another central factor on perception is not altogether a dynamic matter. This must be borne in mind when quantitative

---

[2] See R. F. Street, A Gestalt completion test. *Teachers Coll. Contrib. to Educ.*, 1931, No. 481.—Ed.

results are interpreted. They represent not only the strength of the central factor in the perceptual process but also the probability of the occurrence of the contact with the pertinent trace.

This last consideration presupposes, of course, that, as in the case of meaning, central factors gain whatever influence they may have on perception through mediation of a more or less specific memory trace. This is certainly true of values which with few exceptions are themselves mediated by meaning. This is also true of needs. On the whole, particularly in a mentally healthy individual, a need becomes operative only in specific situations. A given situation must be recognized as belonging to a certain kind which is specific for the operation of a particular need. It is even true of drives when they are aroused by their drive objects. Except for the relatively rare cases where cathexis of a novel drive object occurs in the perceptual situation, the capacity of an object or situation to arouse a drive was acquired in the past, and this product of previous cathexis is brought into function through a recognition process.

That the arousal of a pertinent memory trace must precede the influence of central factors on perception is particularly important where these factors are supposed to affect recognition, as in the case of tachistoscopic studies (6). It seems very likely that the arousal of a pertinent trace amounts to recognition. But the assumption that values and needs affect recognition seems to contradict this simple conception. For these central factors which supposedly have an influence on whether or not recognition occurs come into play through the arousal of pertinent traces. This makes no sense if recognition is equivalent to trace arousal. A solution to this dilemma will have to be found in a closer analysis of the psychological processes which go on in such experiments.

Up to the present the main interest of the studies on the influence of central factors on perception has been in demonstrating such effects. Such demonstrations show to what extent the organization of perceptual processes can be influenced by contents and conditions of central origin. But this is not the only way in which studies of this kind may contribute to the investigation of perceptual functions. They may be helpful in answering the following question: To what stage of organization must a visual process develop before it can arouse a memory trace? Since, in the absence of a "set," central factors gain an influence only *after* pertinent traces have been aroused, properly designed experiments which attempt to produce such an influence may be a way to answer this question.

I should like to clarify this question briefly: A number of perceptual functions besides the strictly sensory processes have to take effect to bring about visual percepts as we experience them. They are, to name only those which are of interest in this context, the interaction process on which the formation of dense surface colors depends, organization due to grouping factors, and the formation of "figure and ground." The question is whether they must also take effect before a pertinent memory trace can be aroused.

The answer to this question has certainly to be affirmative insofar as the colors of the achromatic scale are concerned. The gray color seen in a certain region of the visual field depends on the relation of the intensity of stimulation received from this region and the stimulus intensity of the surrounding region (9). An interaction between the local processes must be responsible for the gray color. A light gray can be changed into a dark gray either by lowering the stimulus intensity in the region in which the gray is seen or by raising the intensity in the surroundings. The end results of these changes cannot be told apart, although in one case stimulation in the gray region changes and in the other it does not. This shows that no sensory process which corresponds to the intensity of local stimulation has trace representation; only the product of the interaction process plays a role in recognition.

The evidence concerning grouping pertains only to line figures. Demonstrations of Köhler's (4) and the work of Gottschaldt (2) have made it clear that figures with which the subject is well acquainted will not be spontaneously recognized when lines are added which prevent these figures from appearing as separate units. I think it is easy to rule out the possibility that the comprehensive figure which comes about through such addition prevents recognition of the "hidden" figure by initiating its own recall process in competition with the "hidden" figure. Rather, "hidden" figures fail to be recognized because they do not appear as separate units and are therefore unable to make trace contacts. Since in the case of line figures the formation of units is ruled by grouping principles, organization due to grouping factors should precede trace arousal. There is certainly need for direct evidence to support this reasoning.

The evidence concerning "figure and ground" is at present contradictory. The essence of the distinction of figure and ground is that only the area designated as figure has form. Rubin has demonstrated that an area will be recognized by its shape only if it is seen as figure (7). This means that the sensory pattern must first be organized in terms of figure and ground, before the figure areas establish contact with specific memory traces.

This seems to be irreconcilable with the result of the brilliant experiment of Shafer and Murphy (8). It demonstrated an influence of previous reward and punishment on the perception of figure and ground in an ambiguous design. An outline circle was divided by an irregular vertical line of such a shape that each half of the circle could be seen as a profile of a face of half-moon shape. Prior to the test in which two such ambiguous figures were used each half-moon shape was presented singly, and each presentation was always accompanied by a reward or a punishment. In the test, the previously rewarded half-moon shapes were predominantly recognized, that is, seen as figure.

There can be no doubt that in this experiment the aftereffect of previous reward and punishment was connected with the traces of the forms of the training series and could become effective only through the arousal of these traces. Thus, figure-ground distribution is influenced by factors which can only come into play *after* the pertinent trace has been aroused. This seems to contradict the conclusion drawn from Rubin's result that formation of figure and ground must precede trace arousal.

This contradiction disappears only when one takes into account that Rubin worked with solid figures, that is, pattern where the contour between figure and ground is formed by the borderline between different colors, whereas Shafer and Murphy used outline figures. The black line on white which here forms the contour between figure and ground also has form in its own right and can therefore make trace contact. A repetition of Shafer and Murphy's experiment with solid figures would really go to the heart of the matter. My hunch is that it would fail to demonstrate any influence of reward and punishment on figure-ground distribution.

I have recently become impressed with the extent to which memory traces participate in simple perceptual processes. They not only impart meaning or impose grouping as previously mentioned; they also seem to be responsible for the perception of three-dimensional form where perceptual conditions for primary organization in depth are absent or weak.

In this situation the full answer to the question, at what stage of perceptual organization pertinent traces can be aroused, seems to be very much needed. As matters stand I would say that the interaction process on which the formation of dense surfaces depends, the formation of figure and ground, and in some cases, organization due to the grouping factors must develop before traces can be aroused through similarity of form. That such processes must occur before traces can be aroused may possibly be one of the reasons for the great stability of simple perceptual processes and the high degree of independence from other psychological functions which they exhibit. One may say that, up to a certain point, the development of percepts is protected against interference by central factors, because the developing percepts are inaccessible before trace contact has been made.

REFERENCES

1. Bartel, H. Ueber die Abhängigkeit spontaner Reproduktionen von Feldbedingungen. *Psychol. Forsch.,* 1937, 22, 1–25.
2. Gottschaldt, K. Ueber den Einfluss der Erfahrung auf die Wahrnehmung von Figuren. I. *Psychol. Forsch.,* 1926, 8, 261–317.
3. Köhler, W. *Dynamics in psychology.* New York: Liveright, 1940.
4. Köhler, W. *Gestalt psychology.* (Rev. ed.) New York: Liveright, 1947. Chap. VI.
5. Köhler, W., and von Restorff, H. Zur Theorie der Reproduktion. *Psychol. Forsch.,* 1935, 21, 56–112.
6. Postman, L., Bruner, J. S., and McGinnies, E. Personal values as selective factors in perception. *J. abnorm. soc. Psychol.,* 1948, 43, 142–154.
7. Rubin, E. *Visuell wahrgenommene Figuren.* Copenhagen: Gyldendal, 1921.
8. Shafer, R., and Murphy, G. The role of autism in a visual figure-ground relationship. *J. exp. Psychol.,* 1943, 32, 335–343.
9. Wallach, H. Brightness constancy and the nature of achromatic colors. *J. exp. Psychol.,* 1948, 38, 310–324. [See pp. 109–125 of the present book.]

*Mary Henle*

GRADUATE FACULTY, NEW SCHOOL FOR SOCIAL RESEARCH

# SOME EFFECTS OF

# MOTIVATIONAL PROCESSES

# ON COGNITION

Work on the influence of needs and attitudes on perception and other cognitive processes has proceeded with insufficient analysis of the problem. It is the purpose of the present paper to outline a number of possible effects of motivational processes on cognitive ones.[1] The influences to be described are regarded neither as established nor as exhaustive, but are offered as hypotheses for future research.

Frequently it seems to be tacitly assumed that the mere presence of a need or attitude is sufficient to account for an observed effect. The task of research has become, therefore, one of relating the presence or absence of particular motivational conditions to quantitative variations in performance on cognitive tasks. The point of view to be presented here is, rather, that the finding of such a correlation only opens up a problem: that of understanding *how* motivation influences cognition (cf. 44; also 6, p. 139).

Reprinted with permission from the *Psychological Review*, Vol. 62, No. 6, November, 1955.

[1] This paper is part of a project undertaken when the writer was a Fellow of the John Simon Guggenheim Memorial Foundation.

The point may be illustrated by reference to the question of the effect of attitudes on recall of controversial material. There is some evidence to indicate that we remember material we agree with better than apparently equivalent material with which we disagree (e.g., 14, 32). That we agree with certain points is no explanation of their superiority in recall. But if we take this finding as a point of departure, it is indeed possible to find plausible reasons why material we agree with should be favored in memory. These are, of course, only hypotheses which require independent testing. (a) It may be suggested that an attitude functions as context for related material (cf. 5, p. 582). Presented data are understood in relation to the subject's existing attitudinal structure. Items which are in harmony with the attitude find their place in the structure in a simpler and more direct manner than does opposing material. There seems to be little doubt—although it needs to be demonstrated for material comparable to that used in the studies on recall of controversial material—that structured material is better recalled than unrelated items (24). The superior recall of items we agree with might follow, then, from the advantage of structured over unstructured data in memory. (b) Material we agree with may be better recalled because it is better understood than material which opposes our own attitude. Material which is understood is known to fare better in memory than that which we do not understand (24). A point we agree with is not, of course, better understood just *because* we agree with it, but because we have thought about it, have placed it in context, etc. Nor are data that confirm our attitudes always better understood; an insult may be very well understood. (c) Facts and arguments we agree with may have an advantage in memory over opposing ones when they are, to start with, more familiar. (d) Material we agree with may be received in a more friendly manner, while that with which we disagree may be rejected at the outset, regarded as nonsense, etc. The former condition is, very likely, the more favorable for recall. Other things being equal, material to which we have given attention is favored in memory. (e) Intention to recall, a factor known to be important for memory, may operate to favor items with which we agree.[2] We may try to remember certain points because we wish to refer to

---

[2] We are not concerned here with the problem of how intention operates in memory. It should be pointed out, however, that the intention does not impose itself on recall, but seems to act by altering other known conditions of recall. The problem of the influence of intentions on cognitive processes may be of the same order as the problem here under consideration.

them again, to use them in argument, because they are flattering to us, etc.

Repression will not be discussed in the present connection because, even if it operates in the experiments under consideration, there would seem to be no way of knowing that it does. It would be necessary to have detailed knowledge of the repressions of individual subjects in order to guess what new data might be repressed by association with them. It is, in addition, highly unlikely that the experiments which deal with the recall of controversial material have set up the conditions necessary to produce repression.

While there is evidence that makes the above hypotheses seem plausible, it is also becoming recognized that there are conditions under which material which opposes our attitudes is favored in recall (cf. 2, 4). We may begin to define these conditions too. (a) We may remember something that disturbs us precisely because it does not fit into our schema. It might be that when an attitudinal structure is ripe for change, such disturbing, contradictory material is favored, while the organizing effects of attitudes enhance recall of confirming material at other times. (b) Points we disagree with may stand out, in contrast to repeated evidence for something we believe. It is known that such outstandingness can favor recall. The fact that outstanding items within a system are favored does not, of course, contradict the statement made earlier that structured data are more likely than unorganized ones to be well recalled. (c) We may remember something in order to refute it, to accuse somebody of it, in some way to cope with it, etc. Intention to recall, in the service of some other need, may also favor the opposing material.

Finally, certain attitudes may operate to produce about equal recall of material we agree with and of that with which we disagree—for example, an objective attitude, a desire to be fair, to hear both sides of the case, a wish to recall as much as possible so as to do well in the recall test, etc. (2).

It is clear from the variety of hypotheses presented above that it is necessary to have detailed information about a particular subject's understanding of, and attitude toward, the presented material if we are to attempt any predictions about the kind of material which will be favored in recall. It will also be clear that the really interesting problems about motivational factors in recall are not confined to the favoring of some particular kind of material, but concern also the qualitative dimensions of the individual subject's pattern of recall, involving the kinds of processes suggested here. It may even be that the individual's pattern of recall of personally relevant material is so distinctive that, in the hands of a skilled clinician, it may yield projective data which agree well with personal information derived from interview and projective methods.[3]

The above hypotheses, it will be noted, seek the effects of attitudes on remembering *in terms of factors known to favor or inhibit recall*. They introduce no new determinants, but are largely statements of ways in which attitudes might alter the structural conditions of recall.

By contrast, much of the interest of current research in this field has been to find distortions of cognitive processes by needs and attitudes. Such distortions undoubtedly occur, although their frequency under normal conditions may be questioned. But it is here suggested that the influence of motivational processes on cognitive ones is not limited to distortions, and that such effects are not necessarily the ones most likely to give us an understanding of the processes involved. Rather, as has been pointed out elsewhere (22), a possibly more fruitful starting point for research would seem to be to look for changes by motivational processes *in accordance with* the nature of the material on which they act.[4] The present paper will seek to describe ways in which needs and attitudes may alter cognitive processes in a manner that does not violate the presented structure.

As is implied in the above remarks, it is maintained here that motivational processes may influence, but do not produce, cognitive organization. A vector (e.g., a need, expectation, intention, or attitude) or a trace system can influence a perceived form or another memory trace only if the latter already exists. The problem, as Wallach (52) has pointed out, is to determine the stage of organization to which a visual process must develop before central factors can influence it.[5]

To see motivational processes as operating through the presented

---

[3] I am indebted to Florence R. Miale for a preliminary demonstration of this kind.

Alper and Korchin (4, p. 35) make a similar suggestion: ". . . selective recall may well function here as it does in the so-called projective tests: the subject reacts to the material selectively in terms of his needs and tension-systems, the products of his recall being themselves projections of these needs and tension-systems." These authors fail, however, to follow up their suggestion with detailed comparisons of recall and personality data of individual subjects.

[4] The theoretical consequences of taking distortions as the paradigm of the influence of needs and attitudes on cognition have been shown elsewhere (22).

[5] The present writer fails to see how the assumption of *unbewusster Schluss* (e.g., 9) solves this problem. In order to initiate processes of inference or recall, perceptual data must already be organized. We cannot make inferences about an object until we can perceive it; the inferences thus do not account for, but presuppose, the perception.

structure is not, however, to deny the influence of needs and attitudes on cognition. In a recent paper, Postman (38) seems to reduce such influences to others which are not themselves motivational, viz., set and past experience. Certainly the latter processes have important influences on cognitive ones, and motivation *may* act on cognition through them. Furthermore, they seem to cut across a number of the other influences of needs and attitudes; but it will be maintained in the paragraphs that follow that they by no means fully account for the effects in question.

We are not concerned here with imagination, wishing, etc., which for present purposes may be considered to be very largely determined by motivational factors.[6] Rather, the present discussion is limited to some of the interactions which occur between motivational and structural determinants of cognition.

The following hypotheses are offered as possible modes of influence of needs and attitudes on cognitive processes. They may guide, but they do not, of course, take the place of concrete analysis of particular problems. Some of these hypotheses are already to be found in the literature. Others seem to derive some support from existing studies, even though these were not specifically designed to test them. In the case of still other hypotheses, the task of testing them remains for the future.

1. A need or attitude may operate as a vector, pointing in one direction rather than another. It is sometimes possible, under the influence of a need or attitude, to find an item which would otherwise be unnoticed in the perceptual field. This is easy to demonstrate with camouflaged items. Likewise a recall vector may bring things to mind that do not occur spontaneously. (Of course the search refers to memory traces established in the past. The vector, to be effective, must have something to point to; aroused traces, supplying this, enable the vector to be effective. Here, as in other effects to be discussed below, the attitude or need operates in coöperation with the individual's past experience.)

It is likely that effects of pointing may be demonstrated with other vectors besides simple search vectors in perception and memory. It

---

[6] This is probably an oversimplification. It would be worth knowing to what extent even these processes are limited by our knowledge, experience, and assumptions—both conscious and unconscious—about ourselves and about reality.

seems that, under the influence of a need or attitude, we are attuned to events to which we would not otherwise be sensitive. Under the pressure of an unresolved need, we find things to be angry or worried or hurt about.

This hypothesis seems to be essentially the same as earlier views of Bruner and Postman and others (e.g., 9, 42) on selective sensitization to valued or needed aspects of the environment. In later writings these authors seem to regard this process as a function of expectancies or "hypotheses" only. Postman, for example, states that "There is little evidence for direct sensitizing effects of motivational conditions on perception" (38, p. 99). It is here suggested that this function needs to be re-examined with respect to motivational states.

Some experimental work on the relation of recognition thresholds to motivational states seems to be relevant. If these studies have indeed demonstrated a lowering of threshold for need-related material that cannot be accounted for by differential frequency or the operation of specific expectancies, a process of pointing may be operating. For example, Postman and Brown (39) have shown that experiences of success attune the individual to tachistoscopically presented goal words (e.g., "succeed"), while after failure the subject is relatively more sensitive to deprivation words (e.g., "obstacle," "failure"). A possible interpretation of this finding is that the persisting mood attunes the individual to material congruent with it. McClelland and Liberman (34) report comparable results for individuals differing in the strength of their need for achievement. For example, subjects (Ss) with a strong need for achievement, recognized goal and instrumental words relating to achievement (e.g., "success," "achieve") faster than those whose need was weak. Two studies on the influence of hunger on perceptual sensitivity to need-related material seem also to be relevant. Lazarus, Yousem, and Arenberg (31) report that recognition thresholds for photographs of food objects declined with increasing hours of food deprivation (within limits set by the habitual eating cycle), and Wispé and Drambarean (54) found that need-related words were recognized more rapidly than neutral ones under conditions of food and water deprivation, but not when Ss were satisfied.

These experiments need to be repeated under conditions where possible sets for need-related items are not allowed to develop during the experimental series. For example, the relative sensitivity to the *first* need-related item in the series should be studied (cf. 28). If the findings should be confirmed under these conditions, they would suggest the operation of the kind of sensitization to need-related material here described as pointing.

2. Closely related to pointing may be the organizing effects of needs and attitudes. Within certain limits we can voluntarily influence organizations in the perceptual field, grouping together items which would not spontaneously go together. Likewise in recall, interaction between a process and a trace which would not occur spontaneously may take place under the influence of a vector (27). In the case of other cognitive processes, the same organizing effects of needs suggest themselves. It is a fact of common observation that when a strong need or interest is aroused, the facts of experience organize themselves around it. When I am working on a scientific problem, for example, everything I read appears to bear on the issues with which I am concerned. It seems that under the influence of an aroused need we perceive similarities not otherwise noticeable. These vectors, I repeat, operate in conjunction with the individual's knowledge and previous experience. But here, as in the cases that follow, it is insufficient to refer to past experience alone.

3. The perception of other relations is likewise influenced by needs and attitudes. It has been suggested that under the influence of an aroused need, the psychological field may be restructured so that learning occurs (1). For example, an object previously seen as unrelated to a goal may come to be perceived as the means to attaining it, one event may acquire the meaning of a signal for another, etc.

4. An aroused need or attitude may act on cognition by selection among the various possibilities presented. This hypothesis has frequently appeared in the literature. It has not, however, customarily been separated from sensitization or pointing, as discussed above (e.g., 9, 42).

The following example, among the many possible, illustrates the selective effect of an attitude in cognition. If two individuals who hold opposed attitudes are presented with a given fact, they do not necessarily perceive the same fact, but each may select for it a different meaning out of several possibilities it presents. As Asch puts it (5, p. 584): "One can observe much adroitness in the manipulation of meanings in the interests of an undisturbed outlook." Selective effects of needs and attitudes are most familiar from the projective methods. In the Rorschach, for instance, a variety of interpretations may be given to a similarly perceived portion of a blot; consider, for example, the variety of actions attributed by different individuals to the animals in the side details in Card VIII. Examples of this kind could be multiplied.

The experimental literature provides comparable examples. Sanford (46, 47) and Levine, Chein, and Murphy (33) found that hungry subjects gave more food responses in the interpretation of incomplete or ambiguous pictures than did satisfied ones, and that the effect increased (within limits) as hunger increased. (The effect of the need cannot, however, be separated from possible selective effects of a food set, in the experiment of Levine, Chein, and Murphy.) There appears to be a selection of need-relevant interpretations from among the many meanings the ambiguous material could be given.

5. The need or attitude may supply context. Since the context may influence decisively the manner in which an item is experienced, it follows that a given item may be differently viewed in accordance with the need or attitude aroused. This effect of attitudes was illustrated above in the case of a problem of memory. Needs may be expected to have comparable effects, since they function typically in need-object organizations or "sentiments."

6. One particular effect of the fact that needs and attitudes function as temporally extended organizations deserves special mention: memory traces relevant to these organizations may be aroused. Past experience has important effects on cognitive processes, of which the more relevant in the present connection may be such effects as the contributing of meanings, the establishing of norms or adaptation levels (20), and the rendering commonplace of some item of experience so that it is overlooked or its significance lessened in the cognitive field. Past experience likewise facilitates perception under conditions of reduced stimulation (37, 21, 23, 49, 50; but cf. also 17, 29). It probably acts also as a selective factor, favoring certain possibilities among those which are structurally given (e.g., 13, 53).

These effects of past experience have been demonstrated in cognitive situations having little bearing on subjects' needs and attitudes. The work on the role of past experience needs to be extended to other cognitive situations which have motivational relevance.

7. A need may arouse an expectation, which is known to have certain effects on cognitive processes. For example, Titchener long ago formulated a principle of prior entry. "The stimulus for which we are predisposed requires less time than a like stimulus, for which we are unprepared, to produce its full conscious effect" (51, p. 251). The sensitizing, organizing, and selective effects of sets have been mentioned above. Bruner has suggested that the function of expectancies

"is to re-order the availability of traces" (7, p. 307; cf. previous hypothesis). A number of recent experiments have dealt with the effects of sets on cognitive processes and the conditions under which they operate (e.g., 41, 10, 11). It is clearly important to distinguish between direct effects of motivational processes on cognition and their indirect effects through the arousal of expectations, which frequently have similar consequences (cf. 38).

Postman and Crutchfield (43) have recently discussed the arousal of expectations by a state of need. These authors presented incomplete words for completion, varying the intensity of hunger of their Ss and the degree of selective set for food responses. They found the effects of set in determining food responses to be larger than those of differing intensities of hunger; the relationship between the latter and frequency of food responses depended largely on S's expectation for such responses. They conclude (p. 217): "*Intensity of need is one of the variables which modify the operation of such general principles of cognition as selective 'set' within limits defined by the characteristics of the stimulus-materials.*"

8. Needs or attitudes may make us unwilling to ask certain questions, discourage the desire to understand, keep us from considering relevant evidence or from seeing the relevance of presented evidence. They may narrow the mental field (1, 5), with significant consequences for cognition. Much current work has been concerned with such influences (e.g., the effects of prejudice, the clouding of judgment by strong emotion). These effects are not, at the outset, to be dismissed as entirely automatic evasions. Reasons are frequently used in these instances to give them at least the appearance of sense. The cognitive processes involved need to be understood.

9. Needs or attitudes, in a manner closely related to the last-mentioned effect, may cause us to overlook differences, to fail to make distinctions, just as in the perceptual field a great contrast may make us fail to see a lesser one. For example, several years ago the writer heard a debate on a perceptual problem held before a group which was bitterly opposed to the use of the experimental method in psychology. The audience seemed not to know that a debate was going on, but attacked both speakers alike for dissecting their human subject matter. They saw no important difference between the two positions presented. Common experience suggests similar phenomena in the realm of social and political attitudes. To a conservative person everything left of center

may seem to be radical, while the more radical individual may regard everything right of center as reactionary. The range over which fine distinctions can be made appears to be shortened.

10. A possible effect of needs and attitudes is a specific disturbance of recognition and recall. Some evidence suggests that individuals who are shown, by independent methods, to differ in the extent to which given experimental material is disturbing to them, show corresponding differences in their recognition thresholds for such material (15, 16, 30). If these findings are confirmed, and if alternative explanations (e.g., differential readiness to report) can be eliminated, a disturbance of the recognition of certain kinds of threatening material suggests itself. Again, the facts of repression, insofar as this mechanism involves forgetting, raise a similar problem.

How might such a disturbance of recognition and recall operate? The phenomena of repression suggest that it is not a matter of destruction of memory traces; for repressed material to express itself in dreams, symptoms, and other forms requires that the corresponding traces be intact. The disturbance seems, rather, to concern that interaction between process and trace, based on their similarity, which underlies recognition and is the first step in the process of recall by association. (For a discussion of the selective influence of similarity in recognition and recall, cf. Köhler, 26, pp. 126 ff.)

It is very tentatively suggested, then, that a vector may operate to prevent that interaction between a present process and a memory trace which is necessary for recognition and recall.

11. Needs and attitudes may act on the physiognomic properties of experience. Consider, for example, the change which can sometimes be noted in a person's appearance for us with the change from acquaintance to friendship. That the change is not a matter of familiarity alone is suggested by the fact that such physiognomic changes seem to be much less pronounced when increasing acquaintance is not accompanied by friendship. It is true that the friend looks upon us with a more kindly eye than the mere acquaintance, may be happier and more relaxed with us, etc., so that some of the perceived change is accounted for by actual changes in his appearance. It is worth considering, however, whether changes in the person's physiognomic properties—changes which transcend differences in mood—may not be, in part, a function of the attitudes and sentiments we have for him.

It might be that, if Murray (35) has demonstrated a genuine influence of fear on judgments of maliciousness, it is of the nature of an effect on physiognomic properties. (Other interpretations, however, are possible.)

12. Needs or attitudes may animate, enliven, activate, or give outstanding position to relevant parts of the cognitive field. These effects, in turn, have certain consequences for cognition.[7] In a very real sense the significant person stands out in a group. The effects of outstanding position in perception, memory, and thinking are well known. As another example, the possibility is suggested that Zeigarnik's main result—the favoring of incomplete over completed tasks in recall (55)—may be accounted for if it can be assumed that need tension may in some way make a trace more lively or more active and thus increase its availability. Gilchrist and Nesberg (18) have reported an experiment which suggests an interpretation in these terms. Hungry and thirsty subjects were asked to match the illuminance of just previously projected pictures of need-relevant objects. Increasing need gave rise to increasingly bright matches. In the case of thirsty subjects, the error dropped to its starting level immediately after drinking. If such a result should be confirmed, it could be viewed as an instance of the enlivening effect of need in immediate memory.

13. A strong need or interest leads us to exert efforts in its service. These may show themselves in increased efficiency in cognitive tasks, while a relaxation of effort reduces efficiency. In the case of excessive effort there may be a disruption of performance. A number of studies seem to permit interpretation in these terms rather than in terms of actual perceptual change.

Bruner and Postman (8) found that when Ss were given electric shock during a task, they judged the size of a disk which figured in the task as accurately as control Ss; but when the shock was removed, their size judgments increased. Since magnification in size is here equivalent to increased inaccuracy, it is suggested that this effect is not a matter of "post-tension expansion" in perception, but of relaxation of efforts in a judging task. In another study (40) the same authors found that Ss

---

[7] This hypothesis does not depend upon a principle of "prior entry" (9, p. 96). It sounds like some of Bruner and Postman's statements about perceptual "accentuation" (e.g., 9, p. 100). In practice, however, these authors have used accentuation only to mean increase in perceived size. As such, it comes under the heading of perceptual distortions, which are not being discussed here. In the present writer's opinion, accentuation of perceived size has, in any case, not been demonstrated as a function of value, with autochthonous factors properly controlled (cf. 2, 12, 19, 25, 36).

who had been harassed and badgered during an impossible perceptual task showed higher recognition thresholds in another perceptual situation than control Ss, as well as premature and frequently nonsensical prerecognition hypotheses. It seems plausible to regard these findings as indications of disruption of test performance as a result of the actually reported excessive efforts of the experimental Ss. Rosen (45), on the other hand, found that Ss who were able to avoid an electric shock by correct perception had lower recognition thresholds for nonsense syllables than members of a control group who did not receive shock. Here it would seem that added, but not excessive, effort increased efficiency of test performance.

Other reports suggest comparable effects of attitudes in perception and memory. Allport and Kramer (3) found that anti-Semitic individuals were able to identify photographs of Jewish and non-Jewish faces more accurately than Ss free of prejudice. The result is attributed to the greater importance of racial identity to prejudiced persons. Similarly Seeleman (48) found that different attitudes led to different degrees of effort and attention to an exposure series, with consequent differences of performance in a recognition test. Thus individuals with favorable attitudes toward the Negro correctly recognized more Negro photographs than did anti-Negro Ss.

Such differences in performance are, of course, to be distinguished from actual cognitive change under the influence of a need or attitude.[8]

SUMMARY

This paper has been concerned with the question of how needs and attitudes influence cognitive processes. The attempt has been made to describe ways in which motivational processes alter cognitive ones in accordance with the nature of the material on which they act. It was suggested that needs and attitudes may act by pointing or sensitizing, organizing and reorganizing, selecting, supplying context, arousing relevant memory traces, arousing expectations, discouraging the desire to understand, obscuring differences, disturbing the recognition process, altering the physiognomic properties of experience, and animating or enlivening aspects of experience. In addition, strength of motivation

---

[8] Postman (38) has discussed other motivational influences on performance in perceptual experiments, including the matter of selective reporting, which is a serious problem for all attempts to study possible differences in the perception of emotional and neutral material.

may influence performance on perceptual or other cognitive tasks without producing actual cognitive change.

REFERENCES

1. Adams, D. K. A restatement of the problem of learning. *Brit. J. Psychol.,* 1931, 22, 150–178.
2. Adelman, C., *et al.* An investigation of the influence of needs and attitudes on perception and memory. Unpublished research, New School for Social Research, 1951.
3. Allport, G. W., and Kramer, B. M. Some roots of prejudice. *J. Psychol.,* 1946, 22, 9–39.
4. Alper, Thelma G., and Korchin, S. J. Memory for socially relevant material. *J. abnorm. soc. Psychol.,* 1952, 47, 25–37.
5. Asch, S. E. *Social psychology.* New York: Prentice-Hall, 1952.
6. Bruner, J. S. Personality dynamics and the process of perceiving. In R. R. Blake and G. V. Ramsey (Eds.), *Perception: an approach to personality.* New York: Ronald, 1951.
7. Bruner, J. S. One kind of perception: a reply to Professor Luchins. *Psychol. Rev.,* 1951, 58, 306–312.
8. Bruner, J. S., and Postman, L. Tension and tension release as organizing factors in perception. *J. Pers.,* 1947, 15, 300–308.
9. Bruner, J. S., and Postman, L. An approach to social perception. In W. Dennis (Ed.), *Current trends in social psychology.* Pittsburgh: University of Pittsburgh Press, 1948.
10. Bruner, J. S., and Postman, L. On the perception of incongruity: a paradigm. *J. Pers.,* 1949, 18, 206–223.
11. Bruner, J. S., Postman, L., and Rodrigues, J. Expectation and the perception of color. *Amer. J. Psychol.,* 1951, 64, 216–227.
12. Carter, L., and Schooler, K. Value, need, and other factors in perception. *Psychol. Rev.,* 1949, 56, 200–207.
13. Djang, S. The role of past experience in the visual apprehension of masked forms. *J. exp. Psychol.,* 1937, 20, 29–59.
14. Edwards, A. L. Political frames of reference as a factor influencing recognition. *J. abnorm. soc. Psychol.,* 1941, 36, 34–50.
15. Eriksen, C. W. Perceptual defense as a function of unacceptable needs. *J. abnorm. soc. Psychol.,* 1951, 46, 557–564.
16. Eriksen, C. W. Defense against ego-threat in memory and perception. *J. abnorm. soc. Psychol.,* 1952, 47, 230–235.
17. Eriksen, C. W. The case for perceptual defense. *Psychol. Rev.,* 1954, 61, 175–182.
18. Gilchrist, J. C., and Nesberg, L. S. Need and perceptual change in need-related objects. *J. exp. Psychol.,* 1952, 44, 369–376.
19. Golden, S. An experimental investigation into some factors that determine the perception of size. Unpublished master's thesis, New School for Social Research, 1950.

20. Helson, H. Adaptation-level as a basis for a quantitative theory of frames of reference. *Psychol. Rev.,* 1948, 55, 297–313.
21. Henle, Mary. An experimental investigation of past experience as a determinant of visual form perception. *J. exp. Psychol.,* 1942, 30, 1–22.
22. Henle, Mary, and Michael, M. The influence of attitudes on syllogistic reasoning. *J. soc. Psychol.,* 1956, 44, 115–127.
23. Howes, D. H., and Solomon, R. L. Visual duration threshold as a function of word-probability. *J. exp. Psychol.,* 1951, 41, 401–410.
24. Katona, G. *Organizing and memorizing.* New York: Columbia University Press, 1940.
25. Klein, G., Schlesinger, H., and Meister, D. The effect of personal values on perception: an experimental critique. *Psychol. Rev.,* 1951, 58, 96–112.
26. Köhler, W. *Dynamics in psychology.* New York: Liveright, 1940.
27. Köhler, W., and von Restorff, H. Zur Theorie der Reproduktion. *Psychol. Forsch.,* 1935, 21, 56–112.
28. Lacy, O. W., Lewinger, N., and Adamson, J. F. Foreknowledge as a factor affecting perceptual defense and alertness. *J. exp. Psychol.,* 1953, 45, 169–174.
29. Lazarus, R. S. Is there a mechanism of perceptual defense? A reply to Postman, Bronson, and Gropper. *J. abnorm. soc. Psychol.,* 1954, 49, 396–398.
30. Lazarus, R. S., Eriksen, C. W., and Fonda, C. P. Personality dynamics and auditory perceptual recognition. *J. Pers.,* 1951, 19, 471–482.
31. Lazarus, R. S., Yousem, H., and Arenberg, D. Hunger and perception. *J. Pers.,* 1953, 21, 312–328.
32. Levine, J. M., and Murphy, G. The learning and forgetting of controversial material. *J. abnorm. soc. Psychol.,* 1943, 38, 507–517.
33. Levine, R., Chein, I., and Murphy, G. The relation of the intensity of a need to the amount of perceptual distortion: a preliminary report. *J. Psychol.,* 1942, 13, 283–293.
34. McClelland, D., and Liberman, A. The effect of need for achievement on recognition of need-related words. *J. Pers.,* 1949, 18, 236–251.
35. Murray, H. A. The effect of fear upon estimates of the maliciousness of other personalities. *J. soc. Psychol.,* 1933, 4, 310–329.
36. Norton, E. N. Is symbolic value an organizing factor in perception? Unpublished master's thesis, New School for Social Research, 1950.
37. Ortner, A. Nachweis der Retentionsstörung beim Erkennen. *Psychol. Forsch.,* 1937, 22, 59–88.
38. Postman, L. The experimental analysis of motivational factors in perception. In *Current theory and research in motivation.* Lincoln: University of Nebraska Press, 1953.
39. Postman, L., and Brown, D. Perceptual consequences of success and failure. *J. abnorm. soc. Psychol.,* 1952, 47, 213–221.
40. Postman, L., and Bruner, J. S. Perception under stress. *Psychol. Rev.,* 1948, 55, 314–323.

41. Postman, L., and Bruner, J. S. Multiplicity of set as a determinant of perceptual behavior. *J. exp. Psychol.,* 1949, 39, 369–377.
42. Postman, L., Bruner, J. S., and McGinnies, E. Personal values as selective factors in perception. *J. abnorm. soc. Psychol.,* 1948, 43, 142–154.
43. Postman, L., and Crutchfield, R. S. The interaction of need, set and stimulus-structure in a cognitive task. *Amer. J. Psychol.,* 1952, 65, 196–217.
44. Prentice, W. C. H. "Functionalism" in perception. *Psychol. Rev.,* 1956, 63, 29–38.
45. Rosen, A. C. Change in perceptual threshold as a protective function of the organism. *J. Pers.,* 1954, 23, 182–194.
46. Sanford, R. N. The effects of abstinence from food upon imaginal processes: a preliminary experiment. *J. Psychol.,* 1936, 2, 129–136.
47. Sanford, R. N. The effects of abstinence from food upon imaginal processes: a further experiment. *J. Psychol.,* 1937, 3, 145–159.
48. Seeleman, V. The influence of attitude upon the remembering of pictorial material. *Arch. Psychol.,* 1940, No. 258.
49. Solomon, R. L., and Howes, D. H. Word frequency, personal values, and visual duration thresholds. *Psychol. Rev.,* 1951, 58, 256–270.
50. Solomon, R. L., and Postman, L. Frequency of usage as a determinant of recognition thresholds for words. *J. exp. Psychol.,* 1952, 43, 195–201.
51. Titchener, E. B. *Lectures on the elementary psychology of feeling and attention.* New York: Macmillan, 1908.
52. Wallach, H. Some considerations concerning the relation between perception and cognition. *J. Pers.,* 1949, 18, 6–13. [See pp. 164–171 of the present book.]
53. Wallach, H., O'Connell, D. N., and Neisser, U. The memory effect of visual perception of three-dimensional form. *J. exp. Psychol.,* 1953, 45, 360–368.
54. Wispé, L. G., and Drambarean, N. C. Physiological need, word frequency, and visual duration thresholds. *J. exp. Psychol.,* 1953, 46, 25–31.
55. Zeigarnik, B. Das Behalten erledigter und unerledigter Handlungen. *Psychol. Forsch.,* 1927, 9, 1–85.

*Solomon E. Asch*

SWARTHMORE COLLEGE

# PERCEPTUAL

# CONDITIONS

# OF ASSOCIATION

The study of the formation of associations has followed a highly uniform pattern whose special character has escaped notice. The prevailing mode of investigation possesses a one-sidedness that obscures a fundamental question concerning the nature of associations.

The observation from which we begin is that the study of associations has been restricted to associations *between units*. The terms entering into association have been, virtually without exception, distinct and independent units. Of the various relations that may obtain between terms, only one has been selected for analysis; the consequence is that our knowledge of associative processes rests almost entirely on a limited, and perhaps not representative, set of conditions. We propose to extend the study of associations to certain hitherto neglected relations, and in particular to inquire into the role of the unit relation in association.

There is an important theoretical reason for this partiality of investigation, which may serve to introduce the present discussion. The

Based upon S. E. Asch, J. Ceraso, and W. Heimer, "Perceptual Conditions of Association," *Psychological Monographs*, Vol. 74, 1960.

problem of association came into prominence during the modern period as part of a more comprehensive doctrine, whose account of psychological functioning started with a theory of sense data. The British empirical philosophers, who were most responsible for this development, described the original contents of mental life as discrete, irreducible sensations, each aroused by a given physical energy acting on a particular sense organ. Given this starting point, a process was needed to bind or join the elements, in order to account for the formation of sequences in experience corresponding to the regularities of objective events. Further, theorists in this tradition proposed to derive all psychological functions other than sensory—from perception to thinking and imagination—from associative combinations. Thus association was made responsible for order in mental life. (Behaviorism adopted these assumptions without substantial change. The conditioning of responses was the formal counterpart to the "association of ideas.")

This starting point prescribed the identification of associations and the interpretation of the underlying process. If the units of mental life are discrete and irreducible, the achievement of association is to join what is initially entirely unrelated. Thus virtually by definition, the formation of associations early became synonymous with the association of one unit with another discrete unit. The experimental movement has adhered to this orientation with remarkable strictness up to the present. Although investigation has only rarely worked with elementary stimuli, it has not deviated from the paradigm that pairs heterogeneous, and as far as possible, unrelated units. The paradigm has served as the basic, general case, to which other conditions and effects must be reduced. This is, we believe, the reason that investigation has concentrated on "empty," rote associations, limited to the relation of contiguity.[1]

There are other relations equally deserving of study. The most challenging are those that obtain between terms belonging to the same unit. As a rule, units are not homogeneous, but possess distinct parts or aspects. When one perceives or recalls such a unit, one is perceiving or recalling a definite order and relation among the parts or aspects. If so, all questions concerning associations between units have their formal

---

[1] The reason generally advanced for the study of rote associations is a technical one, namely that they exclude unobservable effects of past experience. This argument conceals the decisive point. The need to control past experience restricts the content of terms, but it does not necessarily prescribe the relations between them.

counterpart when one turns to the internal relations of a unit. The latter have not been the object of investigation; students have made the customary assumption that the constitution of units is precisely the problem of association, that units are the products of associations between units. We considered that the similarities and differences between these important conditions is a problem of consequence. Accordingly, we proceeded to compare the forming of connections between terms when the relations between them were systematically varied, and in particular when they differed with respect to unity. We asked, first, whether association follows the same course in these instances, and second, whether they are the same or distinct in process.

The general procedure was that of the classical association experiment. The stimuli were visual forms. The terms to be associated were, as far as possible, constant in all experimental variations; the latter differed mainly in the relations between the terms. All the data to be described were obtained with one-trial learning.

THE CONSTITUTIVE RELATION

For the first step we selected stimuli bound by the *constitutive* relation (see Fig. 1, column 1). Each stimulus of this series is a particular visual form whose contour is delineated by another, smaller form that is identically repeated. We will refer to the over-all stimulus as the *form,* and to the constituents of the contour as *modes*. In view of their phenomenal character, we will call the percepts of this series *unitary*. To anticipate the procedure briefly, the stimuli will be shown to subjects who will subsequently be tested for recall of coherence between form and mode, the latter corresponding to the *a* and *b* terms of the standard association experiment.

For purposes of comparison we need a parallel condition corresponding to the conventional association experiment. This series (see Fig. 1, columns 2 and 3) consisted of pairs of terms—a figure in continuous contour, and to the right of it a linear array of identical forms. The left and right terms are identical in content with the forms and modes of the constitutive or unitary series. Since the terms are clearly heterogeneous, we will call this series *non-unitary*. In this manner we constructed two sets of stimuli composed of the same contents but differing in relation. We are concerned to compare the mastery of the two series under the same conditions of learning and recall.

Let us briefly describe the differences and similarities between the series. In the non-unitary series the members of each pair are discrete and heterogeneous; each is a perceptual unit, and they stand in the relation of contiguity. The unitary series has the following properties: (1) Form and mode are in a relation of dependence; the modes are the constituents of the contour. (2) The spatial distribution of the modes gives the over-all form. The modes contribute to the form by virtue of their properties as points, not through their own form-character. (3) Form and mode are identical in locus. Finally, the paired terms are equally heterogeneous or dual in both series.

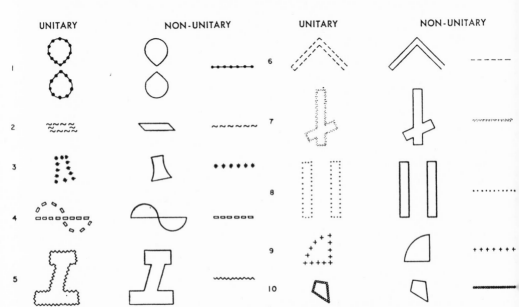

Fig. 1. Unitary and nonunitary series.

Except where otherwise noted, the general procedure employed in the experiments to be described was as follows. The stimuli of each series were shown, to comparable groups of subjects, singly and in succession. The conditions of learning and recall were identical in both groups. Experimentation was done individually. Each member of the series was exposed for 4 seconds. The instructions were to inspect each stimulus (or pair) so as to be able subsequently to reproduce as many as possible. Thus learning was intentional, and under "free recall" instructions. A test of recall came after 3 minutes. The subjects were men and women undergraduate students.

*Experiment 1.* Following the learning procedure just described, there came a test of free recall. The subjects were provided with blank booklets, and were requested to reproduce each stimulus (or pair), one to a page, as completely as they could, but to reproduce in part when necessary. These reproductions were scored first for recall of content alone, or of the forms and modes regardless of whether they were correctly joined. Second, we scored the frequencies of correct and incorrect pairings, and of recalls of one term alone. (For a detailed account of the procedure and scoring, see reference 1, p. 6.)

The principal finding (see Table 1, experiment 1) is that the two conditions were substantially alike in recall of content, but differed markedly and significantly in joint recall. The unitary series produced a higher level of accurate pairing and a lower level of inaccurate pairing than the non-unitary series.

*Experiments 2 and 3.* These results were fully confirmed under conditions of aided recall, when at the time of test the subject was provided with either the form (in continuous contour) or the modes (in linear array) and requested to reproduce the other. Again recall of content was much the same in the two series, but the unitary series was distinctly superior in accuracy of paired recall (although the stimuli initiating recall differed perceptibly from those of the unitary series but were identical with those of the non-unitary series). See Table 1, experiments 2 and 3.

*Experiment 4.* A further variation was done in which the forms and modes of experiment 1 were paired randomly in a new way. The conditions of learning and recall were those of experiment 1. The results were substantially those of experiment 1.

These effects persisted in full force when the conditions of learning and recall were varied widely. The results were substantially the same when the conditions of learning were *incidental,* and when the final test was that of *matching* or of *recognition.* The latter findings establish that the advantage of unity persisted when the burden of recall was reduced, and tell us that the experimental effect refers to the *formation* of functional connections.

THE FIGURE-GROUND RELATION

*Experiment 5.* We proceeded next to the study of another stimulus relation between terms—that of figure and ground. This fundamental

## TABLE 1
### RECALL UNDER UNITARY AND NON-UNITARY CONDITIONS
#### (IN PERCENTAGES)

| Experimental Condition | Unitary Series * | | | | | | Non-Unitary Series | | | | | |
| --- | --- | --- | --- | --- | --- | --- | --- | --- | --- | --- | --- | --- |
| | N | 1 Correctly Paired Recall | 2 Incorrectly Paired Recall | 3 Recall of Form Alone | 4 Recall of Mode Alone | 5 Mean of Total Recall | N | 1 Correctly Paired Recall | 2 Incorrectly Paired Recall | 3 Recall of Form Alone | 4 Recall of Mode Alone | 5 Mean of Total Recall |
| Constitutive Relation: † | | | | | | | | | | | | |
| Experiment 1 | 24 | 76.2% | 7.4% | 11.9% | 4.5% | 10.2 | 24 | 49.2% | 31.4% | 8.1% | 11.4% | 9.8 |
| Experiment 2 | 12 | 77.8 | 22.2 | | | 5.3 | 12 | 40.7 | 59.3 | | | 4.9 |
| Experiment 3 | 12 | 74.6 | 25.4 | | | 4.9 | 12 | 48.5 | 51.5 | | | 5.5 |
| Experiment 4 | 24 | 65.5 | 13.8 | 16.8 | 3.9 | 9.7 | 24 | 38.1 | 33.8 | 9.9 | 18.2 | 9.6 |
| Figure-Ground Relation: | | | | | | | | | | | | |
| Experiment 5 | | | | | | | 24 | 37.1 | 25.7 | 20.5 | 16.7 | 8.8 |
| Relation of Inclusion: | | | | | | | | | | | | |
| Experiment 6 | 24 | 67.2 | 13.6 | 9.6 | 9.6 | 5.2 | 24 | 27.5 | 26.2 | 30.3 | 15.2 | 3.3 |

\* Columns 1 to 4 represent percentage values. These were computed by dividing the score in each of the four categories by total recall. Column 5 gives the absolute mean of total recall.

† Experiments 2 and 3 employed the test of aided recall. For Experiment 2 the test went from form to mode, and in the reverse direction for Experiment 3. With this procedure all recalls fall either into Column 1 or 2. The mean of total recall under these conditions is, understandably, approximately one-half of the means in the other constitutive conditions.

192

perceptual relation has not been brought into connection with the associative problem, mainly because most students have divorced the issues in the two regions.

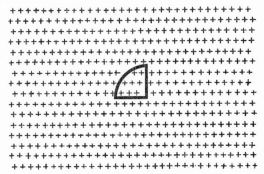

FIG. 2. A sample stimulus for the figure-ground condition.

Figure 2 illustrates the relation. Each member of the series consisted of a form in continuous contour, located on a ground of smaller forms identical with the modes of the earlier series. The modes did not overlap with the contour. All other conditions of learning and recall were those of experiment 1.

Recall of content was somewhat but not significantly lower than in experiment 1, but coherence of recall was significantly poorer than in the unitary series, and insignificantly different from the non-unitary series (see Table 1, experiment 5). The result is in accordance with general evidence that the figure-ground relation is a segregating condition.

Considered as a perceptual situation, the traditional association experiment (here represented by the non-unitary series of experiment 1) consists of paired heterogeneous figures on a single ground. The associative similarity between the latter and the figure-ground condition indicates that their segregating properties are approximately equal. We consider this an illustration of the relevance of perceptual data to issues in the psychology of association.

THE RELATION OF INCLUSION

*Experiment 6.* A further relation we studied was that of inclusion. The series consisted of forms drawn in continuous contour, the inner area being filled with the previously paired modes (see Fig. 3). Again the modes were drawn so as not to touch the contour. Learning was intentional and the test that of free recall.

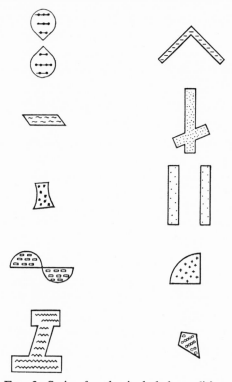

FIG. 3. Series for the included condition.

Recall of content was similar to the preceding conditions, but recall of the connections between the terms was almost exactly intermediate between the levels of the unitary and non-unitary series. Further examination showed, however, that this was not an intermediate condition. Despite the standard procedure followed in constructing it, the series was not uniform: some stimuli produced high levels of pairing, in contrast to others that were far more resistant to pairing. Inspection suggested that the inner forms of some stimuli cohered with the contour to establish a *surface,* but that the inner forms of other stimuli remained simply an aggregation of small units enclosed by a contour line. To check on this possibility, six judges who had no knowledge of the problem were asked to rank the stimuli in terms of "how well" the contour and the included material went together. There was substantial agreement among the judges; on the basis of the mean rankings the series was divided into two halves, which we will call "unitary" and "non-unitary."

The two categories of stimuli produced strikingly different results: those judged "unitary" were far superior in pairing, and also in absolute recall. Further, accuracy of pairing of the "unitary" subset was similar to that of the unitary series of experiment 1, while the "non-unitary" subset resembled the non-unitary series of experiment 1 (see Table 1, experiments 1 and 6).

It is instructive to apply this analysis to the figure-ground series, since the latter too contained forms that enclosed other forms. The results fail to reveal the slightest trace of a difference between the subsets, when the division is based on the judgments obtained in the inclusion series. When the modes extended beyond the contour into the surrounding area, they lost their specific relation to the contour. The figure-ground relation functioned throughout as a segregating condition, unlike the relation of inclusion.

Marked and consistent differences of coherence were found when the perceptual relations between terms were varied. The relations in question are describable geometrical properties. In addition, the results grouped the several sets of relations in two categories, which differed with respect to unity. The sources of the property of unity are diverse, but the effects upon coherence were quite stable. Unitary percepts were consistently superior in coherence; in this investigation unity was represented by the constitutive relation, and by the relation of inclusion when it permitted surface formation. Non-unitary percepts were considerably more resistant to joining; they were represented here by the relation of contiguity between heterogeneous terms, the relation of figure and ground, and the relation of inclusion when it did not permit surface formation. The criterion of unity is phenomenal; it is a reliable criterion and one obtained independently of the results. The conclusion we reach is that *coherence between terms is a function of the unit relation.* This conclusion is based on data from only one modality, the visual, and on a few properties within that modality; it will therefore need to be verified over a wider range. It seems justified, however, to propose that if we can specify the relative unity of two percepts, we can predict their relative coherence.

ALTERNATIVE INTERPRETATIONS

Before one can consider this conclusion as secure, it is necessary to examine alternative interpretations and certain possible sources of error.

The rationale of this study required that the several experimental conditions should be identical except for the property that was varied. This was the reason for the attempt to maintain the constancy of terms while varying the relation between them. But a change of relation might have introduced unintended modifications that could be responsible for the observed effects.

1. The preceding comparisons require that the respective stimulus conditions should be equally perceptible or discriminable, or that differences in this respect should not favor the conditions that are superior in coherence. Accordingly, we repeated experiment 1 (with the unitary and non-unitary series, respectively) without change of conditions except for the final test. The latter called for the recognition of the individual forms and modes, when these were interspersed with others that had not been part of the learning series. Thus we took recognition as an index of perceptibility. The forms of both series were equally recognizable, but the non-unitary series was superior in recognition of modes. Since the non-unitary series was far poorer in coherence, the main finding cannot be attributed to recognition differences.

2. The non-unitary series may have been more homogeneous and therefore more susceptible to intraserial interference than the apparently more differentiated unitary series. To check on this possibility experiment 1 was again repeated, but was now preceded by familiarization with the individual forms and modes. We reasoned that familiarization should reduce and equalize subsequent internal interference in the two series, and thus reduce the experimental effect. Although the procedure of familiarization was highly effective, the difference of coherence was not reduced; indeed, it became more substantial.

3. We need also ask whether the unitary and non-unitary conditions differed in amount of information to be mastered. The relevant answer is that the respective stimulus conditions were remarkably similar in recall of content, differing only in coherence. The procedure of familiarization described above points to the same conclusion.

4. The relations here studied differed with respect to the spatial proximity between terms; examination shows that proximity cannot

account for the findings. Identical relations of proximity (in experiment 6) produced the most different effects, while conditions differing in proximity (experiments 1 and 5) were quite similar associatively. In this investigation proximity was effective only as it mediated the property of unity.

These alternatives, and certain others not here discussed, fail to account for the findings. We conclude that coherence is dependent on unity, not on conditions only secondarily dependent on unity.

PERCEPTION AND ASSOCIATION

Traditionally there has existed a sharp separation between perceptual and associative investigation. When the principal function assigned to association was the joining of unrelated contents, it followed that the observation of data was one kind of event, and their association another. This was the reason that an association was initially conceptualized as the establishment of a pathway between excitations, which was independent of the contents joined. This divorce has persisted substantially to the present day. Students do not question that perceptual conditions decide what will be observed and associated, but they insist that the associative operations have their own exclusive character. This is the cornerstone of what we may call the associationistic theory of associations: it denies a direct effect of perceptual conditions on association.

It is precisely this account that Gestalt theory challenges. The classic formulation of Köhler (1929, 1941) proposes that association is the aftereffect of organization in immediate experience, not an event added to it. Traces preserve the organization of earlier events; and the principles pertaining to each are intimately related, often the same. The principal consequence of this position is that conditions favoring organization in experience favor trace organization, and therefore coherence of recall.

This investigation provides convincing evidence that perceptual relations *directly* determine the formation of associations. It thus supports the theory of Köhler and raises a question about a postulate of associationistic theory. At the same time, neither of the principal theories of association have concerned themselves closely with the particular problem under discussion, with the difference between coherence within a unit and the coherence of one unit with another. A concern with this problem raises a new question to which we now turn.

UNITARY AND NON-UNITARY COHERENCE

It would be entirely consistent with the evidence here reported to conclude that there is *one* process of coherence, or that the unitary and
non-unitary conditions differ in associativeness, but the conclusion
does not follow with necessity. To be sure, the obtained differences
were throughout quantitative, and this may appear to support a continuum interpretation; but the argument is not logically decisive, in
addition to which the presence of quantitative differences alone may
reflect limitations of procedure. We ask: Is the coherence established
within units and between units referable to a single process, or are they
distinct in process?

An answer cannot be found within the frame of current thinking and
evidence; to put the question is to realize how pragmatic is the prevailing characterization of an association. We need to ask in what
respects processes of coherence might differ. The following comments
are necessarily tentative.

One hint toward a solution comes from the following finding reported in this investigation. The occurrence of associative errors—or
the mispairing of terms—was remarkably low in unitary series (see
Table 1). The relevant data are those that do not force choices upon
subjects; therefore free recall results are the most pertinent. Under free
recall test conditions the majority of subjects did not mispair at all,
and there were only rare instances of others mispairing more than once.
(There are also reasons for questioning whether the latter were au-
thentic associative errors; see reference 1, pp. 37–39.) A further finding goes in the same direction. When subjects separately reproduced,
in free recall, the two terms belonging to a given unitary stimulus,
eventually they almost always paired them correctly; this was definitely
not the case with non-unitary terms.

These observations raise an unexpected question: Do unitary percepts produce *invariable* coherence? Or, do the terms of a unit persist
—and disappear—jointly? If this were the case, we would have a more
thoroughgoing difference between stimulus conditions than those previously described (although one that is still logically compatible with
a single-process interpretation). The question is also of interest aside
from its theoretical implications. It is of consequence to know whether
invariable coherence is a fact, and if so, what the responsible stimulus
conditions are. (It should be noted that invariable coherence is only

superficially similar to the older idea of "indissoluble" associations, which was based on the operation of frequency.)

The question cannot be answered at this time. (For a discussion of the evidence necessary for a decision, see reference 1, p. 37.) But it suggests a more concrete way of characterizing the difference between unitary and non-unitary (or between non-associative and associative) coherence. Briefly, the recall of an association between heterogeneous units often requires two steps: a step of recognition (of one of the terms), followed by associative recall proper, or the transition to the other term. The recall of a unit may collapse these steps into one; that is, recognition of one of the terms may produce an unfailing transition to the other term.

The traditional study of associations has limited observation to the coherence established between units, neglecting relations internal to units. Employing the technique of the association experiment, we varied systematically the perceptual relations between the parts of a stimulus distribution. The relations studied were those of constitution or composition, of figure and ground, of inclusion, and of contiguity between heterogeneous units. The relations were either phenomenally unitary or non-unitary.

The capacity to recall jointly the parts or aspects of a stimulus distribution was markedly and significantly superior when these belonged to the same phenomenal unit. Errors were regularly more frequent when the terms belonged to distinct units. These findings persisted as the conditions of learning and recall varied widely. The evidence is convincing that the effect occurs at the time of primary experience. We conclude that there is a direct relation between perceptual unity and coherence.

The question was considered whether unitary and non-unitary coherence differs in process, or whether we may have to distinguish between associative coherence and a coherence that is non-associative.

This investigation, which demonstrates a direct effect of organizational conditions on coherence, questions the traditional divorce between the regions of association and perception. This separation has rested on a doctrine of psychological elements that preceded the study of perception, and that has become untenable in the light of Gestalt investigations. In this sense the present inquiry provides convincing evidence for the theory of associations formulated by Köhler. It also demonstrates that to take the relations between terms into account in the study of associations is both necessary and fruitful. The procedure here adopted permits an independent and objective characterization of stimulus properties, to which data at the level of recall can be systematically related. Indeed, it is perhaps not too much to hope that perceptual data may be a source of solutions to some questions in the theory of association.

The present investigation raises a host of questions that require further study. (1) The range of relations here considered is far from inclusive. In particular, they are distinct from the grouping principles of Wertheimer, nor do they include the part-whole relation.[2] (2) The psychological constitution of *objects* may be a function of their unit character. Traditionally the formation of an object has been considered as the product of associations between sense data that were distinct units. We need to ask what the consequences are of the fact that the data in question refer to the same object. (3) The issues here considered cannot be restricted to perceptual organization; their relevance may extend to organizational processes generally. To give one illustration, the relation of meaning may be an instance of conceptual unit formation; the contribution of meaning, which has been frequently confirmed, may be a function of the unit relation.[3]

REFERENCES

1. Asch, S. E., Ceraso, J., and Heimer, W. Perceptual conditions of association. *Psychol. Monogr.,* 1960, 74, No. 3.
2. Kaswan, J. Association of nonsense-figures as a function of fittingness and intention to learn, *Amer. J. Psychol.,* 1957, 70, 447–450.
3. Köhler, W. *Gestalt psychology.* New York: Liveright, 1929.
4. Köhler, W. On the nature of association. *Proc. Amer. phil. Soc.,* 1941, 84, 489–502.
5. Prentice, W. C. H., and Asch, S. E. Paired association with related and unrelated pairs of nonsense-figures. *Amer. J. Psychol.,* 1958, 71, 247–254.

---

[2] A pronounced facilitating effect of relations of fittingness on coherence in recall was demonstrated by Prentice and Asch (1958); see also Kaswan (1957).

A recent investigation (unpublished) of Asch and Ceraso has demonstrated a similar effect of perceptual unity when it is based on the part-whole relation.

[3] For a recent investigation of the role of meaning in association, see W. Epstein, I. Rock, and C. B. Zuckerman, Meaning and familiarity in associative learning, *Psychological Monographs,* 1960, Vol. 74, No. 491.

PART IV

SOCIAL PSYCHOLOGY

AND MOTIVATION

*Wolfgang Köhler*

DARTMOUTH COLLEGE

# PSYCHOLOGICAL REMARKS

# ON SOME QUESTIONS

# OF ANTHROPOLOGY

In his investigation of primitive mentality Lévy-Bruhl is led to the conclusion that in primitive man mental operations are essentially different from those with which we are familiar. "Les représentations collectives," all the notions with which, during childhood and adolescence, an individual is imbued by the surrounding group, are "mystiques" in the case of primitive tribes. Where we apply the laws of logic "la mentalité prélogique" applies "la loi de participation." The author seems to conclude that in many cases the anthropologist's attempt really to understand and to explain primitive behavior will necessarily end in failure. We even have difficulties in defining the term "mystique." Again, who can formulate clearly what is implied in the "loi de participation"? Still, when we find that one more primitive belief or custom is mystical and that it follows the law of participation, this is, according to the French sociologist, perhaps all that we can do about the case in question.

Often, I am afraid, Lévy-Bruhl's skepticism is justified in practice,

Reprinted with permission from the *American Journal of Psychology*, Vol. 50 (Golden Jubilee Volume), 1937.

though perhaps not for the reasons which he indicates. The origin of some tribal beliefs and institutions may be so complicated historically that there simply is no unitary sense in the phenomena themselves. To that extent, of course, we cannot fully "understand" their nature, whether or not primitive mentality differs essentially from our own. Besides, several primitive cultures are known only from reports in which the white observer's preconceived notions seem to be hopelessly intermingled with the ethnological material as such. Not a few of these cultures disintegrate quickly, if they have not actually disappeared. Since the opportunity for more objective investigation is gone, in such cases the available data themselves will remain ambiguous. Much of their obscurity may be due to serious misunderstandings rather than to an alleged impermeable nature of primitive mentality.

Though some anthropologists do not like to admit it, psychological principles play an important role in the interpretation of anthropological facts. Theoretical difficulties may, therefore, arise quite as easily from inadequate psychological notions as from the strange ways of primitive mentality. As Lévy-Bruhl has pointed out, the psychology which Tylor and his school applied to anthropological problems can hardly be regarded as an adequate tool in this field. In the meantime, however, psychology has again changed a great deal. Perhaps some of the facts in anthropology which, to the French author, seem to be outside the white man's understanding will prove more approachable if we apply to them recently developed psychological ideas. In the following pages a modest and hesitant attempt will be made in this direction. It must be hesitant because, for the two reasons given in the last paragraph, we should not try to find more psychological sense in our material than it can be expected really to contain. Our attempt must be modest since no outsider can hope to have a sufficient survey of anthropological data for a more comprehensive interpretation of primitive cultures. It ought to be modest in another sense, too, because some of the ideas which I shall bring forward have, at least implicitly, been used before by experts. I should be pleased, however, if psychologists would give some attention to the following discussion. In our desire to be thoroughly exact, we are in the present phase of psychology apt to concentrate our efforts on a few special problems. In consequence of this we begin to lose sight of most questions for which the social sciences expect answers from psychology. If we do not answer because our outlook is too narrow, discontent, of which there are some signs already, will doubtless grow steadily. It may be that the following discussion will satisfy neither psychologists nor anthropologists. In this case it might still have some value, if it induces other psychologists to do better work in the same field.

Many examples may be given in which the behavior of primitive man certainly looks incomprehensible at first. May I select two at random?

Moffat reports from South Africa that once a woman came to him in order to get the medicine which he had prepared for her sick husband. When he made it clear to her that half of the potion should be taken at once and the rest several hours later, she asked whether it would not be possible to drink all of it at once. Upon his assent the woman suddenly swallowed the medicine herself. To the missionary's protest she answered by asking whether it would not cure her husband if she drank the medicine.[1] Many Africans, it is true, like to take our drugs because of their "power." It would, however, hardly be fair to assume that this factor suffices as an explanation. Anthropology knows of too many cases in which what we might call medical treatment or measures of hygiene apply to the family group almost as much as to an individual member upon whom our physicians would concentrate their efforts. Neither is it satisfactory to say that among primitives the individual is less a separate entity than in our society; or that, for them, the individual's boundaries are not the same as for us. Both statements may be true. But in such matters our own point of view seems to us so obvious and necessary that we fail to understand on what basis other views could ever develop.

I have the following report from a missionary who is working in East Africa. While sleeping in his hut a man dreams that he is in another village and that there he commits a crime which, according to the convictions of the tribe, deserves death punishment. Frightened, he tells his people about the dream. Unfortunately something of the kind really happens in that other village and approximately at the same time. The man is indicted, he confesses and is killed, although he was miles away from that other village when the crime was committed. Such things will occur less often the more European officials and European schools begin to influence the natives, but my informant, a perfectly calm and sober man, told me that he has direct knowledge of more such cases. Primitive mentality does move in strange ways; it does not seem to mind

---

[1] R. Moffat, *Missionary labours and scenes in Southern Africa*. London: J. Snow, 1842, pp. 591 f.

contradiction. According to our thinking the man could not be in another village while he was sleeping in his hut. This is exactly, however, what the natives believe and what the poor victim of such logic apparently believes himself.

( I have gradually become convinced that in many such cases our difficulties are due to a special coördinate system of our own no less than to peculiarities of primitive mentality.) In a way scientifically trained people of our time may be particularly unfit for the understanding of less intellectual cultures. What are the objective facts of nature? What is the best access to objective knowledge in this sense? What influences on the other hand are apt to hamper our progress in this field? Since the seventeenth century such questions have gradually introduced a definite set of values which is now so dominant that far beyond the circle of scientists proper the outlook of civilized people is thoroughly governed by these particular ideals. A sober attitude towards a real world is instilled in children of our civilization by the words and actions of their parents. Long ago the most basic convictions of scientific culture lost the character of theoretically formulated sentences. Gradually they have become aspects of the world as we *perceive* it; the world *looks* today what our forefathers learned to say about it; we act and we speak accordingly. In this form the consequences of a few centuries of science are present in the remotest corners of the civilized world.

The ideals which I mentioned, the special interest which they represent, and the particular aspect which they have given to the world, are doubtless very apt to further quick progress of natural science and practical behavior in contact with reality. I wonder whether to some degree they do not disturb the advance of anthropology. Physicists have gradually separated their real world from the realm of mere percepts. In doing this they have also learned to distinguish between phenomena which tell the truth about the real world and others which are illusory. On this basis percepts and their traits are good or valueless according to this distinction. Similarly, properties of percepts which are easily understood in their relation to physical stimulation will be readily accepted in sense physiology. Whatever does not fit into this scheme will be neglected and despised because of its "subjective" nature. Under the influence of scientific culture the very appearance of the world around us is being transformed. It will not only be "intellectualized." Such characteristics of the world will become less conspicuous, they will gradually recede into the background, for which the physicist and the sense physiologist have definitely no use. Those aspects on the other hand are made outstanding which we regard as representatives of reality.

For natural science, I repeat, this development may mean strict progress. I shall not deny that the modern aspect of the world around us agrees better with our picture of physical reality than older views did. But I insist upon the fact that before the era of scientific culture the perceptual world could not have looked as it appears to us now. Psychologically speaking our view of the "given" world is the product of complicated historical processes. Judged from a merely psychological standpoint and without any reference to physical reality, this aspect of the world is therefore no more genuine than any previous appearance of man's perceived environment. To some extent even more "natural" traits of perception will be found where science has not exerted its modifying influence. They would be most prominent in the primitive's world.

Their study, however, is difficult. The psychologist no less than other people has learned to see the world through the eyeglasses of natural science. What he beholds in this manner seems to him so obvious, he is so little aware of his eyeglasses, that any other view will appear to him as a distortion of the genuine aspect of the world. If primitives have such another view, their mystical thinking will be made responsible for it. They have changed the genuine appearance of the world which is, of course, originally the same everywhere and identical with our own view.

It seems to me that the opposite judgment would be at least as correct. Primitive perception, to be sure, contains a great deal of intellectual elaboration. It is improbable, however, that such influences should ever have been more systematic and intense than have been the effects of scientific learning in our own case. It would therefore be of great advantage if, in studying the appearance which the world has for primitives, we could overcome the tendency to use our own view as a norm. Anthropologists have generally been at pains to follow this principle. More might be done, however, if even in the application of psychological thought to primitive perception the white man's customary outlook were recognized as a disturbing factor. Recently we learned that a definite type of scientific analysis had nearly made us unable to apprehend most common sides of perception and of mental life in general. We shall try to apply this lesson to anthropological questions.

Almost 50 years ago von Ehrenfels pointed out that percepts have properties which cannot be derived from so-called sensations. A sensation has a good physiological standing. It is the phenomenal correlate of a well-defined stimulus. The properties of percepts which von Ehrenfels had in mind seem, however, to occur only where groups of stimuli coöperate in causing one phenomenal datum. The stimuli in question may be spatially or temporally distributed. Correspondingly, von Ehrenfels' qualities are the attributes of percepts which extend through areas in space or through stretches of time. They are not popular in sense physiology, which likes to study the reactions of single receptor cells to single stimuli. Properties which are characteristic of larger entities—and only of these—will evidently not fit into this scheme. A well-known example is the "major" or the "minor" character of a melody or of a chord. No single tone has minor character, whereas it is an essential trait of many tunes and chords. Although quite familiar to musicians, among psychologists such traits of auditory percepts had never before found the attention which they deserve. After what has been said above we need not discuss the reasons for such aloofness.

It would not be difficult to show that all percepts have such qualities. When things are called "tall" or "bulky," persons "slender" or "stout," movements "clumsy" or "graceful," reference is made to definite von Ehrenfels qualities. When we describe events as "sudden" or "smooth," "jerky" or "continuous," we refer to the same class. Esthetically they are doubtless of paramount importance, but they are hardly less so, I think, in biological contexts. The color of the hair, the pitch of the voice may have much to do with the strong impression which specific persons of one sex make upon specific persons of the other. Still, properties of shape, of gesture, and of general movement are generally found to be at least as dangerous—and these are von Ehrenfels qualities.

In a certain sense such qualities of percepts are "subjective." As we perceive them they are functions of nervous processes; but this is true of all properties of all percepts. They seem more "subjective" than "green" or "blue" because no simple physical stimuli are responsible for their occurrence. It may be doubted whether, despite this serious disadvantage, they are not often particularly important as witnesses of objective reality.[2] Beyond any doubt they appear quite as much as properties of the world around us as, for instance, colors and smells. Phenomenally, they are *objective.*

---

[2] W. Köhler, *Gestalt psychology*. New York: Liveright, 1929, pp. 174 ff.

If I am present when two cars crash at a crossing, and if then I speak about the "vehement" or "violent" impact of one upon the other, one might say that in this description I attribute to what I see traits which are borrowed from my own muscular or other subjective experiences. My answer would be that this is not the point which we are discussing at present. Whether the explanation by "empathy" is right or wrong, we have to distinguish between the functional genesis of phenomenal characters and their phenomenal appearance and localization as such. Supposing even that von Ehrenfels qualities like "vehement" have a subjective origin, from a descriptive point of view they are therefore no less objectively localized, are no less aspects of events themselves. Clumsy dancing looks clumsy there, outside, in a man or woman whom I see moving before me. It is again Fred Astaire, not I, who performs unheard-of von Ehrenfels qualities in dancing; it is on the screen that I perceive them, not in my muscles. If genetically I should be responsible for all this, I am at least in simple experience unaware of my authorship. After all, it is a theory, not an observed fact, that such traits of percepts are always due to subjective sources. For unsophisticated perception vast numbers of von Ehrenfels qualities appear precisely where colors and other attributes appear with which customary thinking is better acquainted: in and on things, persons and events. It follows that the less sophisticated people are, the more will they accept such properties of percepts at their face value.

Primitives are, of course, naïve realists. They cannot possibly distinguish between "mere percepts" and independent physical realities. A thing-percept is for them the very prototype of reality, although they believe in further realities besides. In fact, percepts are for them— as for children—so real that they would hesitate to accept the name, if they could clearly understand its meaning. Why should they call a tree a "percept"? There simply *is* a tree before them to which, it is true, more or less attention may be given. That this tree which we call a percept remains unaltered in its place even when nobody is present who might have the percept, this is, for a naïve view of the world, the most natural thing. When before us, the tree certainly shows no striking symptoms of depending upon any subjects for its existence. One has to be far ahead in physics, physiology, or philosophy before anything like a problem can be discovered in this connection.

It is again well known that without such sophistication no doubt will ever arise about the independent reality of all the sensory qualities which the tree or any other object may possess. We have seen, however, that the von Ehrenfels qualities of percepts are localized in and on these percepts. Primitives have no physics, no physiology, and no epistemology which could throw any shadow of suspicion upon these qualities. Consequently their naïve realism will apply to such characteristics of the world as it applies to any others. For them, things and events will have these properties independently and objectively. Thus their environment will have many aspects to which they attribute full objective value, while our scientific civilization denies such value and accordingly tends to impoverish our perception.

Many of these qualities are distinctly *dynamic*. What is "sudden" may, with increasing intensity, become "startling," "frightening" and "threatening." Such terms imply the subject's emotional reaction. But they also imply that in certain events or things there is a perceptual basis for the reaction. Here, as so often, much phenomenological truth is contained in language.

Not always is the "threatening" a high degree of the "sudden." While climbing once in the Alps I beheld, on stepping cautiously around a corner of the rocks, a big dark cloud which moved slowly and silently towards me along the slope. Nothing could look more sinister and more threatening. Genetically this might have been a case of empathy; but for my awareness the menace was certainly in the cloud. I could perhaps persuade myself that a cloud as such is an indifferent percept. If, however, I had been a primitive, no reason whatsoever could have given me such sober consolation. The threatening character of the cloud itself would have remained just as "objective" as its ugly dark color. Similarly the ocean itself is "wild" in a gale; and a mountain which appears high above the other tops in strange illumination is itself "majestic" or "forbidding." Primitives have no science of physics in our sense of the word, but those opinions about the world which they develop instead will necessarily differ widely from our own views. If the expression is admissible, it must be a curious "physics" in which the menacing character of a cloud, the wildness of a gale, the majesty of a mountain percept have at least the same rank and objectivity as, with us, measured distances, velocities, and weights. It is in the nature of such "physics" that it can never be a calm and critical survey of facts as our science likes to be. The primitive's reality is apt to be too exciting for sober appreciation, since not only its effect on the subject, but also its own appearance is so often emotional. Awe and respect are more likely to characterize the primitive's attitude in such matters than is a spirit of critical investigation. Whatever else may follow, from this starting point ways may even lead to religion.

In passing, a remark should be made on an old philosophical controversy. David Hume denies that any of our "impressions" contain the quality of power or force. His opinion can only be held so long as, in a quiet environment, we discuss phenomenological questions *in abstracto*. At his writing desk the philosopher is apt to see the world as static and tranquil. It is, however, the sailor in a small ocean-going vessel, the airplane pilot, the tramp left to his own resources in any weather, who can tell us best whether there are any experiences of power, force, or dynamic traits in general. For us it is, of course, another question whether such dynamic traits of experience have any physical counterparts; but on the level of naïve realism this question has no sense. Here the objective world exhibits forces directly and not at all infrequently.

Not all dynamic qualities of things are startling. There is "heaviness" in a middle-sized stone, "hardness" in the same object, "elasticity"— not as a property defined by the physicists but as a perceived quality— in a young tree which my arm bends. Everyday physics of the layman deals with such properties of things as he is directly aware of them. This is true in Central Africa, but also in civilized countries, whenever people do not actually use the more sophisticated concepts of physical science—which is of course only done by a few. Regularly and with many objects this procedure is quite safe, because in many respects such simple von Ehrenfels qualities correspond fairly well with certain concepts of physics. So long as this is the case nobody objects and nobody would speak of mystical ideas.

Now and again, however, the situation acquires a slightly different character; namely, where the dynamic side of things and events grows beyond our feeling of control. Instead of a young sapling a primitive may have bent an older and stronger tree. If he had any physics, he would look upon the situation with some knowledge of objective danger, otherwise with a sober and calm mind—but he has no physics in our meaning of the word. Instead, there is now in the tree a perceived power beyond the limits of what the man is able to handle safely. He will respect such power. It may be actually frightening when suddenly the tall stem breaks its bonds and jumps fiercely up into space. There is an awe-inspiring quality in the thing, just as there is in the sudden rush of high wind which often precedes a thunderstorm, or in the lightning which accompanies it.

Even when enhanced beyond the common and concentrated to fearful intensity, such characteristics will for naïve realism still remain objective properties of things and events themselves. There is no reason why primitive man should not behave correspondingly. From the more trivial power qualities a nearly continuous series will extend for him through more striking cases to those where he is overwhelmed by fear. It is only natural that in his environment nothing should appear to him more important and impressive than unusual power in this sense, particularly since he knows so little of its rules and whims.

Here, it seems to me, we have the perceptual foundation of what some Melanesians call "mana," the Crow Indians of North America "maxpé," and some tribes in West Africa "njomm." [3] Mana at least is a notion in which the thinking of widely differing peoples seems to agree. When Codrington first mentioned it, it appeared as a rather enigmatic term. If the phenomenological side of psychology had then been further developed the notion would have seemed less puzzling. In earlier phases of anthropology, before mana became better known, the notion was probably often misunderstood to mean a deity, a spirit, or a soul in things. Though it seems possible that on a certain level the concept of a soul develops as a special case of the general class mana, this term and its synonyms cannot originally and generally have had the special meaning of our word "soul." Tribes in many parts of the world find mana in certain things and events; but among these tribes there are some in which not even the human person himself has a soul comparable in meaning with the soul of Christian doctrine or Descartes' philosophy.[4] Few factors in our civilization make the anthropologist's work so difficult as our popularized mind-body dualism.

I should also hesitate to interpret mana as though it meant "supernatural." Where a thing, a person or an event has mana it remains for primitive man on the same general level of existence as other parts of his environment, although it is more conspicuous by its peculiar appearance or inherent power. Using our word "supernatural" in this connection we are apt to lose sight of those obvious phenomenal facts upon which, if I am right, the notion of mana is ultimately founded. To some extent all things may have their mana. Innocent enough as simple

---

[3] R. H. Lowie, *Primitive religion.* New York: Boni and Liveright, 1924, pp. 75 f.

[4] D. Westermann, *Die Kpelle: Ein Negerstamm in Liberia.* Göttingen: Vandenhoeck, 1921, pp. 174 ff.

heaviness of a stone, it may still be the same in principle where its intensity or particular behavior arouses respect and fear.

I mentioned above that in ordinary life our own treatment of many things refers to their power qualities as we perceive them naïvely. This attitude, however, is rather strictly limited by the scientific atmosphere in which we live. We have learned that most mana is merely a "subjective" phenomenon. No such restraint disturbs the naïve realism of primitive man. He remains consistent in handling things according to their inherent dynamic qualities. Consequently some of his activities will seem to us quite natural and sober, others altogether strange because they are contrary to the lessons of science. Here we begin to speak about *mystical* thinking and about *magic*. Westermann, however, denies that for the Kpelle themselves there is any sharp dividing line between "normal" activities and everyday magic. This may not apply to the Indians of North America; but among Africanists the same opinion seems to win more and more adherents. Take the special case of medical practices. "The word *musamo* . . . connotes . . . not only various medicinal remedies proper, but also, and much more, many things whose power we should call magical. The difficulty is to separate the two. From the native point of view there is no difference." [5] When the African takes a hearty meal and thereby "fills himself with power," we are not surprised. If he is convinced, however, that by eating the meat of a courageous animal he will himself acquire more courage, we speak about superstition. As a matter of fact, we have no evidence that for the native there is any essential difference between these cases.

With this example, it is true, we have touched upon a new aspect of power qualities. Even where for us their functional subjectivity seems altogether obvious, people without any science will still remain naïve realists. For an object to have mana it is by no means necessary that its peculiar characteristic appear under all circumstances. The *new* thing, an event which does not usually happen, is for this extraneous reason apt to be mana. Certainly, the unexpected looks different; it has its peculiar appearance even for us; surprise, as other emotions, has its phenomenally objective counterpart. But we subtract easily from "the real facts" what, for our critical attitude, reveals its subjective genesis so easily. Not so the native. Objects may have for him the very highest degrees of mana which are for us as trivial as possible. He does not yet

<hr>

[5] E. W. Smith and A. M. Dale, *The Ila-speaking peoples of Northern Rhodesia.* London: Macmillan, I, 1920, p. 222.

realize clearly that the "striking" in the new thing is due to its newness only. Strangeness is a property of the thing itself; awe is the consequence, and action will be taken corespondingly.

On the other hand, if an object has once exhibited power, such experience has an aftereffect. It will look its power or have the flavor of it, even under conditions where, without such previous experience, nobody would find its mana aspect very impressive. If in our own psychology we had no examples of "sign Gestalt," as Tolman calls it, we could hardly understand much primitive behavior. It is this principle which imbues thousands of objects with power which for the neutral observer may seem quite incapable of having any particular mana. When the courageous animal has been killed, its meat certainly does not look courageous to those who do not know from what it has been taken. But as the living animal will be regarded as courageous even at times when it is peacefully at rest, so its meat will still contain the valuable power. We add skeptically: for those whose apprehension of the object is distorted under the influence of previous experience. Yet the natives are not so sophisticated. So long as naïve realism is quite undisturbed the effect of previous experience prevails, while little attention is given to its psychological history. After all, it can happen here. The place where yesterday a cruel murder was committed would have today a strange look for most of us, even if no visible trace of the crime were left; many would feel uneasy in such a locality, and few would choose it as their living place.

For the native, mana qualities not only *exist* in his environment; they also have definite forms of *behavior*. At least one of these is easily understood, if only we begin with examples where our own judgment agrees with that of primitive man. What is a smell? Very few people, those who have studied this special part of sense physiology, can give a clear answer. On the level of naïve realism, on which to some degree we all remain in everyday life, a smell is a quality that tends to spread from one object and one place to others, as though it had the properties of an intangible light liquid. We do not put kerosene near butter or bread, lest the kerosene smell penetrate into the food. With onions the same precaution has to be taken, although here it is another quality which spreads to surrounding objects.

Smell is by no means the only entity that shows this behavior. From a fire the quality of heat migrates in all directions. The rain, the fog, and the thunderstorm spread from one place to the other. Most important of all, many a sickness creeps through the community from hut to hut; and an uncanny change which has just come over one man is soon discernible in others. Qualities of all kinds seem thus to travel through space, even though we cannot trace their ways in every detail. Should we object to this description of facts? One hundred years ago heat was an unweighable stuff even in orthodox physics; and its behavior was akin to that of smells and of infectious diseases. In a more general formulation: Qualities are transmitted from one object to another; and for primitive thinking such *transmission* seems to be the basic form of *causation*.

The same idea lingers still in our thought. It may also be entitled to more attention than it receives in modern epistemology. Even now our theorists are under the spell of David Hume's powerful work. Transmission of qualities has no place in our positivistic concept of causality. For our present purpose this concept may be sufficiently characterized as follows: An object has the property x, while in the same object and in its immediate environment we have the conditions a, b, c. . . . When a, b, c . . . change into $a^1$, $b^1$, $c^1$ . . . , instead of x the object assumes the property y. It is, since Hume, customary to say that no internal relation connects the nature of the change $x \rightarrow y$ with the nature of the change a, b, c . . . $\rightarrow a^1$, $b^1$, $c^1$. . . . Facts of coexistence and of sequence are *mere* facts, which means that *a priori* any datum might coexist with or follow any other. In principle, we do not get more out of nature than incomprehensible rules.

One sees at once that between this idea of causation and causation by transmission there is a striking difference. According to the positivistic notion, no matter how long we consider causes, we can never derive from this inspection any prediction as to the nature of the effect. Contrariwise, if causation is transmission of an identical quality, state, or entity from one locality, it follows necessarily that the effect, the appearance of that entity in the second place, must be similar to the cause which is the same entity as it appeared in its first place. *Causa aequat effectum.*

It seems appropriate at this point to say one more word about a famous period in the history of European philosophy. Why should Descartes' school be so uneasy about the idea that mind and body interact? The reason seems to be simple. In his time causation was still widely conceived of as transmission of some quality from one thing to another. This primitive but rather plausible idea had much power on the best minds as late as 1650. Two incomparable substances, they say, cannot influence each other. A modern positivist might ask: Where is the difficulty? But for the older view the problem is doubtless serious. If mind and body are really incomparable substances, nothing can be transmitted from one to the other. Otherwise the second would, by the fact of transmission, become similar to the first, which is impossible, since they are supposed to be incomparable forever. Thus neither can exert an influence upon the other. "Influence" is just the right word. No other term could express more characteristically what causation normally meant before the concept was so utterly changed by Hume.

Primitive people could point to many examples in which observation agrees well with the concept of causation by transmission. Effects are so often similar to causes that modern epistemology would do well to give the fact at least some attention. Take any of the cases which I have mentioned above. What is first in one place soon appears as something similar in the neighborhood. Some qualities do travel like thin fluids. But primitive man never formulates a definite notion of causality. It is probably not by a great number of confirming experiences that he is induced implicitly to favor just this particular notion. Rather its intrinsic plausibility seems to make it dominant—so dominant in fact that where the primitive is definitely wrong the white man's appeal to contradictory experience is generally of no avail.

Very often the primitive *is* wrong. Unacquainted with any of our critical procedures he extends his naïve realism to all possible qualities of things. Quite as uncritically he applies to all these qualities his unformulated principle of causation by transmission. We accept some of the qualities and neglect many in our practical behavior; for we are trained by science. We are not very clear about causality; but our tacit acknowledgment of causation by transmission is definitely checked, again by the scientific attitude of our culture. Superadded criticism distinguishes our view of the world from that of primitive man, not mental traits of his which we could not understand at all. Once more: It seems a misconception to say that in some domains primitive man acts soberly, as we do, while in others he relies on peculiar mystical practices which constitute the sphere of magic. So long as no scientific criticism is possible the practices of magic are probably as natural as any activities of which we approve. Both spring from the same sources: naïve realism and causation by transmission.

The fundamental rule of magic follows from these premises. If you wish to produce a definite effect in an object or in a person, you have to bring near him or, better, into him such things as are conspicuous by the quality in question. When we are cold we approach the fire or take a hot drink. This is not regarded as magic. Apply the principle generally and civilized people will say that you perform magical practices. The primitive's child is slow in acquiring speech. The child's tongue lacks the necessary agility. Where do the parents find agility? In the lizard's tongue. Consequently the child will be fed lizard's tongues. The white critic might say that agility is not like calories which can really be transmitted from one object to another. Why not? The strange power of fire can thus be transmitted. We light a match, hold it near the cigarette, and at once the burning quality is transferred to the cigarette. For people who have no science there is no essential difference between one case and the other. Among the Thonga in southeast Africa a mother who has not enough milk for her baby will eat euphorbia plants. These contain the necessary milkiness.[6] Without any chemistry people will rely on perceptual characteristics as they are directly given. Among the Spaniards of Tenerife, men who are losing their hair will eat the hairy stems of certain plants. The "hairiness" of these will make the hair grow. Primitive mentality need certainly not be essentially different from our own in order to develop such ideas. It has only to remain naïve and, in its basic primitive conceptions, thoroughly consistent.

Where power qualities are not absorbed in the form of food, but supposed to spread through space, magic seems to us more strangely magic. Still, the underlying principle remains the same and agrees with our experience in the case of smell and heat. Instead of eating the strongest parts of a strong animal a person may wear them somewhere on his body. From this *amulet* the power quality will permeate the owner. Since there are many capacities which a rich man will wish to possess he may be forced to carry along a bundle of different power substances, one for each purpose—as he really does in West Africa. Contact is, of course, better than mere neighborhood. A few years ago they had the first national sweepstake in a country of Western Europe. A sailor won the big prize. When he came to the capital in order to get his money, the girls in the office crowded around the man and touched his body with their fingers. Apparently they felt that some of his luck-power might be conducted to themselves.

For reasons which I have mentioned above, considerable power may be contained in an object which, to European eyes, does not look conspicuous. This is generally true of those substances which are the main parts of so-called fetishes in West Africa. It is widely recognized at

---

[6] H. Junod, *The life of a South African tribe.* (2nd ed.) London: Macmillan, 1927, pp. 47 ff.

present that as a rule these objects are not idols or images of gods, but mana-batteries like our storage cells. Their preparation by special experts involves the same principle of causation by transmission. In a special hut, protected against disturbing influences, the prospective new fetich is put near an old powerful battery and thus gradually charged.[7] It is in line with such ideas that when wrongly treated even the best fetich may lose much of its power. If that happens it is recharged or sold at a lower rate.

Even "imitative" magic, at first one of the more surprising activities of primitive man, seems to follow from the same principles: naïve realism in an extreme form and causation by transmission. At the time when rain should fall certain Mexican Indians carry a baby around the fields. The child is known to contain the power of nearly inexhaustible wetness. Apparently this quality will spread and soon it will begin to rain. I hope I do not exaggerate if I say that most monographs on primitive peoples contain reports about analogous practices. Often imitative magic produces the characteristics of an event rather than of any object. We know of several tribes where lightning or thunder is imitated as representative of thunderstorms and heavy rains.

I am not overlooking the fact that definite formulae and chants are generally quite as essential for magical purposes as powerful objects and performances. What can mere language have to do with mana? The obvious answer is that for naïve perception language may contain at least as much mana as any objects; and certainly it spreads. Once more our lack of understanding is self-produced. We know about sound waves, we have learned that in language indifferent auditory phenomena are merely associated with meanings. Such knowledge makes us unfit to realize what language is for the unsophisticated mind: a stream of often forceful content that issues from the mouth of man, full of hatred in one case, of love in another, of despair in a third. How could primitive people come upon the theory that language consists of sounds to which the hearer adds a subjective interpretation? Whatever may be true functionally, from a phenomenological point of view even we must acknowledge that this is not a correct description of language, that for naïve apprehension meanings are *in* the words and sentences of common speech. Small wonder that the native's naïve realism remains consistent in this case.

May I take an example from one of Malinowski's books. When

---

[7] E. Pechüel-Loesche, *Volkskunde von Loango.* Stuttgart: Strecker, 1907, p. 366.

among the Trobriand people a woman expects a baby much has to be done for the child's health and beauty. One practice is this: Other women prepare a special skirt or coat for the mother. During their work definite formulae, sweet words about beauty, are spoken literally into the coat. Carefully folded, so that the wind cannot reach the inside and thus remove the charm, the cloth is carried to the mother who, with the coat, covers herself with the mana of those words.

In anthropological literature similar ideas are even applied to questions of human personality. Phenomenologically this seems a sound procedure. Some persons have a strikingly powerful appearance; and many people are conspicuous for their particular varieties of perceptible personality-mana. When we think of unusual people, perhaps for a moment only, of Mussolini, of Lloyd George, of Greta Garbo, there is before us, often with a visual image, a characteristic and distinctive quality of being or living in each case. We cannot define it, yet it is obvious enough; it has the earmarks of a von Ehrenfels quality, comparable with the Mozart-character of some music and the Brahms-quality of another.

Since even common people talk and act in their individual manner, in all of them there is *some* mana which gives them or, perhaps, *is* their particular kind of aliveness. At certain times, however, this power does not show so clearly; apparently it is absent. This would not be more surprising than that heat or a smell are here now and elsewhere later. Take the case of the man who is sleeping in his hut. Compared with what he is in daytime, he seems to be completely lacking in his distinctive personal essence. In the morning when he awakens it will be evident again. Where, then, has it been in the meantime? The man had a dream in which "he" was in another village. Thus we see where his personal power roamed while his body lay inert in the hut. When temporarily outside the body, that power will of course behave as human persons do. The dream tells us about its concrete activities. If these were of a criminal nature, punishment will seem to be fully justified. Lévy-Bruhl assumes that for native belief a man may be in two places at the same time, and that we can do no more than accept such an extraordinary contention. I hesitate to adopt this skeptical attitude so long as, in the manner just indicated, a more plausible interpretation is available.

Is this one more attempt to offer a standard solution for all anthropological enigmas? It is not meant to be. Criticizing another thesis, Lowie has once said, "that its very simplicity should militate against its acceptance." [8] I admit that the principles which I have tried to apply to primitive behavior are simple. But, then, only the very simplest forms of such behavior have been given an interpretation; and the discussion ends at a point where both problems and possible explanations begin to assume a higher degree of complexity. Hardly a word has been said about primitive religion, none about primitive art, again none about social life with all its institutions and ramifications. I am convinced that in these fields, too, psychology can be of more help to anthropology now than, say, thirty or even twenty years ago. But for such help other principles besides those of the present essay will have to be introduced. Even the problems which have been treated present certain aspects which can hardly be understood on such a narrow psychological basis. (Causation by transmission, for example, is doubtless an essential factor in primitive thinking.) But we know many primitive beliefs which, although somewhat similar to those discussed above, can nevertheless not be reduced to this principle. Lévy-Bruhl is right, I believe, in his assumption that typical cases of "participation" do not involve what we should call causation in any of its forms.

A more serious objection might be raised precisely on the ground that primitive society as such and its overwhelming influence on the individual have not been mentioned at all. No special form of magic, for instance, to which I have refered should, according to this criticism, be interpreted in terms of "general" psychology. Only in the group, as products of its creative faculty, can such practices ever arise; to the group the individual owes his magical beliefs; and as the nature of group life varies from one part of the world to another, the importance of magic and its special forms vary correspondingly.

This objection, it seems to me, is partly justified insofar as no attempt has really been made to explain any differences which, in such matters, are found between the various peoples of the globe. These differences are remarkable and of the greatest interest for anthropology. The reason why they have not been discussed is quite simple. One cannot do it without at once becoming involved in all the major disputes of present anthropology. On the other hand such a discussion was not strictly necessary. To some extent magic exists in practically every society. If my interpretation is right, at least some of its major premises are not peculiar to a few specific tribes, but are the common property of all mankind below a certain high level of sophistication. From this com-

---

[8] R. H. Lowie, *op. cit.*, p. 259.

mon stock, which general developmental psychology is entitled to study and to explain, different societies, with their different environments and histories, have in fact derived different varieties of actual practices. I do not believe that we can fully understand the origin of such varieties before we know on what ground magic in general grows. That this ground is the group as such, and that the individual is no more than an empty container for the products of group mentality, seems to me an unacceptable thesis. If the individual were intrinsically incapable of such attitudes as fear, respect, aversion, love, and joy, of such functions as perception, learning, and memory, no influences of the group, however strong, could ever produce in him these mental events. It is my contention that the same applies to the psychological sources of magic. What springs from these sources is codetermined by the particular tradition of the group. Much magic also applies to group relationships as such, but the group contains no ultimate source of magic which is not also found in the individual.

*Solomon E. Asch*

SWARTHMORE COLLEGE

# EFFECTS OF

# GROUP PRESSURE UPON

# THE MODIFICATION AND

# DISTORTION OF JUDGMENTS

We shall here describe in summary form the conception and first findings of a program of investigation into the conditions of independence and submission to group pressure. This program is based on a series of earlier studies conducted by the writer while a Fellow of the John Simon Guggenheim Memorial Foundation. The earlier experiments and the theoretical issues which prompted them are discussed in a forthcoming work by the writer [1] on social psychology.

Our immediate object was to study the social and personal conditions that induce individuals to resist or to yield to group pressures when the latter are perceived to be *contrary to fact*. The issues which this problem raises are of obvious consequence for society; it can be of decisive importance whether or not a group will, under certain conditions, submit to existing pressures. Equally direct are the consequences

Reprinted with permission from *Groups, Leadership and Men,* edited by Harold Guetzkow. Pittsburgh: Carnegie Press, 1951.

[1] S. E. Asch, *Social psychology.* New York: Prentice-Hall, 1952.—Ed.

for individuals and our understanding of them, since it is a decisive fact about a person whether he possesses the freedom to act independently, or whether he characteristically submits to group pressures.

The problem under investigation requires the direct observation of certain basic processes in the interaction between individuals, and between individuals and groups. To clarify these seems necessary if we are to make fundamental advances in the understanding of the formation and reorganization of attitudes, of the functioning of public opinion, and of the operation of propaganda. Today we do not possess an adequate theory of these central psychosocial processes. Empirical investigation has been predominantly controlled by general propositions concerning group influence which have as a rule been assumed but not tested. With few exceptions investigation has relied upon descriptive formulations concerning the operation of suggestion and prestige, the inadequacy of which is becoming increasingly obvious, and upon schematic applications of stimulus-response theory.

The bibliography lists articles representative of the current theoretical and empirical situation. Basic to the current approach has been the axiom that group pressures characteristically induce psychological changes *arbitrarily*, in far-reaching disregard of the material properties of the given conditions. This mode of thinking has almost exclusively stressed the slavish submission of individuals to group forces, has neglected to inquire into their possibilities for independence and for productive relations with the human environment, and has virtually denied the capacity of men under certain conditions to rise above group passion and prejudice. It was our aim to contribute to a clarification of these questions, important both for theory and for their human implications, by means of direct observation of the effects of groups upon the decisions and evaluations of individuals.

THE EXPERIMENT AND FIRST RESULTS

To this end we developed an experimental technique which has served as the basis for the present series of studies. We employed the procedure of placing an individual in a relation of radical conflict with all the other members of a group, of measuring its effect upon him in quantitative terms, and of describing its psychological consequences. A group of eight individuals was instructed to judge a series of simple, clearly structured perceptual relations—to match the length of a given line with one of three unequal lines. Each member of the group announced his judgments publicly. In the midst of this monotonous "test" one individual found himself suddenly contradicted by the entire group, and this contradiction was repeated again and again in the course of the experiment. The group in question had, with the exception of one member, previously met with the experimenter and received instructions to respond at certain points with wrong—and unanimous—judgments. The errors of the majority were large (ranging between ½ in. and 1¾ in.) and of an order not encountered under control conditions. The outstanding person—the critical subject—whom we had placed in the position of a *minority of one* in the midst of a *unanimous majority*— was the object of investigation. He faced, possibly for the first time in his life, a situation in which a group unanimously contradicted the evidence of his senses.

This procedure was the starting point of the investigation and the point of departure for the study of further problems. Its main features were the following: (1) The critical subject was submitted to two contradictory and irreconcilable forces—the evidence of his own experience of an utterly clear perceptual fact and the unanimous evidence of a group of equals. (2) Both forces were part of the immediate situation; the majority was concretely present, surrounding the subject physically. (3) The critical subject, who was requested together with all others to state his judgments publicly, was obliged to declare himself and to take a definite stand vis-à-vis the group. (4) The situation possessed a self-contained character. The critical subject could not avoid or evade the dilemma by reference to conditions external to the experimental situation. (It may be mentioned at this point that the forces generated by the given conditions acted so quickly upon the critical subjects that instances of suspicion were rare.)

The technique employed permitted a simple quantitative measure of the "majority effect" in terms of the frequency of errors in the direction of the distorted estimates of the majority. At the same time we were concerned from the start to obtain evidence of the ways in which the subjects perceived the group, to establish whether they became doubtful, whether they were tempted to join the majority. Most important, it was our object to establish the grounds of the subject's independence or yielding—whether, for example, the yielding subject was aware of the effect of the majority upon him, whether he abandoned his judgment deliberately or compulsively. To this end we constructed a comprehensive set of questions which served as the basis of an individual interview immediately following the experimental period. Toward the conclusion of the interview each subject was informed fully of the purpose of the experiment, of his role and of that of the majority. The reactions to the disclosure of the purpose of the experiment became in fact an integral part of the procedure. We may state here that the information derived from the interview became an indispensable source of evidence and insight into the psychological structure of the experimental situation, and in particular, of the nature of the individual differences. Also, it is not justified or advisable to allow the subject to leave without giving him a full explanation of the experimental conditions. The experimenter has a responsibility to the subject to clarify his doubts and to state the reasons for placing him in the experimental situation. When this is done most subjects react with interest and many

## TABLE 1

### LENGTHS OF STANDARD AND COMPARISON LINES

| Trials | Length of Standard Line (in inches) | Comparison Lines (in inches) | | | Correct Response | Group Response | Majority Error (in inches) |
|---|---|---|---|---|---|---|---|
| | | 1 | 2 | 3 | | | |
| 1 | 10 | 8¾ | 10 | 8 | 2 | 2 | — |
| 2 | 2 | 2 | 1 | 1½ | 1 | 1 | — |
| 3 | 3 | 3¾ | 4¼ | 3 | 3 | 1 * | +¾ |
| 4 | 5 | 5 | 4 | 6½ | 1 | 2 * | −1.0 |
| 5 | 4 | 3 | 5 | 4 | 3 | 3 | — |
| 6 | 3 | 3¾ | 4¼ | 3 | 3 | 2 * | +1¼ |
| 7 | 8 | 6¼ | 8 | 6¾ | 2 | 3 * | −1¼ |
| 8 | 5 | 5 | 4 | 6½ | 1 | 3 * | +1½ |
| 9 | 8 | 6¼ | 8 | 6¾ | 2 | 1 * | −1¾ |
| 10 | 10 | 8¾ | 10 | 8 | 2 | 2 | — |
| 11 | 2 | 2 | 1 | 1½ | 1 | 1 | — |
| 12 | 3 | 3¾ | 4¼ | 3 | 3 | 1 * | +¾ |
| 13 | 5 | 5 | 4 | 6½ | 1 | 2 * | −1.0 |
| 14 | 4 | 3 | 5 | 4 | 3 | 3 | — |
| 15 | 3 | 3¾ | 4¼ | 3 | 3 | 2 * | +1¼ |
| 16 | 8 | 6¼ | 8 | 6¾ | 2 | 3 * | −1¼ |
| 17 | 5 | 5 | 4 | 6½ | 1 | 3 * | +1½ |
| 18 | 8 | 6¼ | 8 | 6¾ | 2 | 1 * | −1¾ |

* Starred figures designate the erroneous estimates by the majority.

express gratification at having lived through a striking situation which has some bearing on wider human issues.

Both the members of the majority and the critical subjects were male college students. We shall report the results for a total of fifty critical subjects in this experiment. In Table 1 we summarize the successive comparison trials and the majority estimates.

The quantitative results are clear and unambiguous.

1. There was a marked movement toward the majority. One-third of all the estimates in the critical group were errors identical with or in the direction of the distorted estimates of the majority. The significance of this finding becomes clear in the light of the virtual absence of errors in control groups, the members of which recorded their estimates in writing. The relevant data of the critical and control groups are summarized in Table 2.

2. At the same time the effect of the majority was far from complete.

TABLE 2

DISTRIBUTION OF ERRORS IN EXPERIMENTAL AND
CONTROL GROUPS

| Number of Critical Errors | Critical Group * $(N = 50)$ | Control Group $(N = 37)$ |
|---|---|---|
| | F | F |
| 0 | 13 | 35 |
| 1 | 4 | 1 |
| 2 | 5 | 1 |
| 3 | 6 | |
| 4 | 3 | |
| 5 | 4 | |
| 6 | 1 | |
| 7 | 2 | |
| 8 | 5 | |
| 9 | 3 | |
| 10 | 3 | |
| 11 | 1 | |
| 12 | 0 | |
| Total | 50 | 37 |
| Mean | 3.84 | 0.08 |

* All errors in the critical group were in the direction of the majority estimates.

The preponderance of estimates in the critical group (68 per cent) was correct despite the pressure of the majority.

3. We found evidence of extreme individual differences. There were in the critical group subjects who remained independent without exception, and there were those who went nearly all the time with the majority. (The maximum possible number of errors was 12, while the actual range of errors was 0–11.) One-fourth of the critical subjects was completely independent; at the other extreme, one-third of the group displaced the estimates toward the majority in one-half or more of the trials.

The differences between the critical subjects in their reactions to the given conditions were equally striking. There were subjects who remained completely confident throughout. At the other extreme were those who became disoriented, doubt-ridden, and experienced a powerful impulse not to appear different from the majority.

For purposes of illustration we include a brief description of one independent and one yielding subject.

*Independent.* After a few trials he appeared puzzled, hesitant. He announced all disagreeing answers in the form of "Three, sir; two, sir"; not so with the unanimous answers. At trial 4 he answered immediately after the first member of the group, shook his head, blinked, and whispered to his neighbor: "Can't help it, that's one." His later answers came in a whispered voice, accompanied by a deprecating smile. At one point he grinned embarrassedly, and whispered explosively to his neighbor: "I always disagree—darn it!" During the questioning, this subject's constant refrain was: "I called them as I saw them, sir." He insisted that his estimates were right without, however, committing himself as to whether the others were wrong, remarking that "that's the way I see them and that's the way they see them." If he had to make a practical decision under similar circumstances, he declared, "I would follow my own view, though part of my reason would tell me that I might be wrong." Immediately following the experiment the majority engaged this subject in a brief discussion. When they pressed him to say whether the entire group was wrong and he alone right, he turned upon them defiantly, exclaiming: "You're *probably* right, but you may be wrong!" To the disclosure of the experiment this subject reacted with the statement that he felt "exultant and relieved," adding, "I do not deny that at times I had the feeling: 'to heck with it, I'll go along with the rest.' "

*Yielding.* This subject went with the majority in 11 out of 12 trials.

He appeared nervous and somewhat confused, but he did not attempt to evade discussion; on the contrary, he was helpful and tried to answer to the best of his ability. He opened the discussion with the statement: "If I'd been the first I probably would have responded differently"; this was his way of stating that he had adopted the majority estimates. The primary factor in his case was loss of confidence. He perceived the majority as a decided group, acting without hesitation: "If they had been doubtful I probably would have changed, but they answered with such confidence." Certain of his errors, he explained, were due to the doubtful nature of the comparisons; in such instances he went with the majority. When the object of the experiment was explained, the subject volunteered: "I suspected about the middle—but tried to push it out of my mind." It is of interest that his suspicion was not able to restore his confidence and diminish the power of the majority. Equally striking is his report that he assumed the experiment to involve an "illusion" to which the others, but not he, were subject. This assumption too did not help to free him; on the contrary, he acted as if his divergence from the majority was a sign of defect. The principal impression this subject produced was of one so caught up by immediate difficulties that he lost clear reasons for his actions, and could make no reasonable decisions.

A FIRST ANALYSIS OF INDIVIDUAL DIFFERENCES

On the basis of the interview data described earlier, we undertook to differentiate and describe the major forms of reaction to the experimental situation, which we shall now briefly summarize.

Among the *independent* subjects we distinguished the following main categories:

1. Independence based on *confidence* in one's perception and experience. The most striking characteristic of these subjects is the vigor with which they withstand the group opposition. Though they are sensitive to the group and experience the conflict, they show a resilience in coping with it, which is expressed in their continuing reliance on their perception and the effectiveness with which they shake off the oppressive group opposition.

2. Quite different are those subjects who are independent and *withdrawn*. These do not react in a spontaneously emotional way, but rather on the basis of explicit principles concerning the necessity of being an individual.

3. A third group of independent subjects manifest considerable ten-

sion and *doubt,* but adhere to their judgments on the basis of a felt necessity to deal adequately with the task.

The following were the main categories of reaction among the *yielding* subjects, or those who went with the majority during one-half or more of the trials.

*1. Distortion of perception under the stress of group pressure.* In this category belong a very few subjects who yield completely, but are not aware that their estimates have been displaced or distorted by the majority. These subjects report that they came to perceive the majority estimates as correct.

*2. Distortion of judgment.* Most submitting subjects belong to this category. The factor of greatest importance in this group is a decision the subjects reach that their perceptions are inaccurate, and that those of the majority are correct. These subjects suffer from primary doubt and lack of confidence; on this basis they feel a strong tendency to join the majority.

*3. Distortion of action.* The subjects in this group do not suffer a modification of perception nor do they conclude that they are wrong. They yield because of an overmastering need not to appear different from or inferior to others, because of an inability to tolerate the appearance of defectiveness in the eyes of the group. These subjects suppress their observations and voice the majority position with awareness of what they are doing.

The results are sufficient to establish that independence and yielding are not psychologically homogeneous, that submission to group pressure (and freedom from pressure) can be the result of different psychological conditions. It should also be noted that the categories described above, being based exclusively on the subjects' reactions to the experimental conditions, are descriptive, not presuming to explain why a given individual responded in one way rather than another. The further exploration of the basis for the individual differences is a separate task upon which we are now at work.

EXPERIMENTAL VARIATIONS

The results described are clearly a joint function of two broadly different sets of conditions. They are determined first by the specific external conditions, by the particular character of the relation between social evidence and one's own experience. Second, the presence of pronounced individual differences points to the important role of personal factors, of factors connected with the individual's character structure. We reasoned that there are group conditions which would produce independence in all subjects, and that there probably are group conditions which would induce intensified yielding in many, though not in all. Accordingly we followed the procedure of *experimental variation,* systematically altering the quality of social evidence by means of systematic variation of group conditions. Secondly, we deemed it reasonable to assume that behavior under the experimental social pressure is significantly related to certain basic, relatively permanent characteristics of the individual. The investigation has moved in both of these directions. Because the study of the character qualities which may be functionally connected with independence and yielding is still in progress, we shall limit the present account to a sketch of the representative experimental variations.

### The Effect of Non-unanimous Majorities

Evidence obtained from the basic experiment suggested that the condition of being exposed *alone* to the opposition of a "compact majority" may have played a decisive role in determining the course and strength of the effects observed. Accordingly we undertook to investigate in a series of successive variations the effects of *non-unanimous* majorities. The technical problem of altering the uniformity of a majority is, in terms of our procedure, relatively simple. In most instances we merely directed one or more members of the instructed group to deviate from the majority in prescribed ways. It is obvious that we cannot hope to compare the performance of the same individual in two situations on the assumption that they remain independent of one another. At best we can investigate the effect of an earlier upon a later experimental condition. The comparison of different experimental situations therefore requires the use of different but comparable groups of critical subjects. This is the procedure we have followed. In the variations to be described we have maintained the conditions of the basic experiment (e.g., the sex of the subjects, the size of the majority, the content of the task, and so on) save for the specific factor that was varied. The following were some of the variations we studied:

*1. The presence of a "true partner."* (a) In the midst of the majority were *two* naïve, critical subjects. The subjects were separated spatially, being seated in the fourth and eighth positions, respectively. Each therefore heard his judgment confirmed by one other person (provided the other person remained independent), one prior to, the other subsequently to announcing his own judgment. In addition, each experienced a break in the unanimity of the majority. There were six pairs of critical subjects. (b) In a further variation the "partner" to the critical subject was a member of the group who had been instructed to respond correctly throughout. This procedure permits the exact control of the partner's responses. The partner was always seated in the fourth position; he therefore announced his estimates in each case before the critical subject.

The results clearly demonstrate that a disturbance of the unanimity of the majority markedly increased the independence of the critical subjects. The frequency of pro-majority errors dropped to 10.4 per cent of the total number of estimates in variation (a), and to 5.5 per cent in variation (b). These results are to be compared with the frequency of yielding to the unanimous majorities in the basic experiment, which was 32 per cent of the total number of estimates. It is clear that the presence in the field of *one other* individual who responded correctly was sufficient to deplete the power of the majority, and in some cases to destroy it. This finding is all the more striking in the light of other variations which demonstrate the effect of even small minorities provided they are unanimous. Indeed, we have been able to show that a unanimous majority of three is, under the given conditions, far more effective than a majority of eight containing one dissenter. That critical subjects will under these conditions free themselves of a majority of seven and join forces with one other person in the minority is, we believe, a result significant for theory. It points to a fundamental psychological difference between the condition of being alone and having a minimum of human support. It further demonstrates that the effects obtained are not the result of a summation of influences proceeding from each member of the group; it is necessary to conceive the results as being relationally determined.

2. *Withdrawal of a "true partner."* What will be the effect of providing the critical subject with a partner who responds correctly and then withdrawing him? The critical subject started with a partner who responded correctly. The partner was a member of the majority who had been instructed to respond correctly and to "desert" to the majority in the middle of the experiment. This procedure permits the observation of the same subject in the course of transition from one condition to another. The withdrawal of the partner produced a powerful and unexpected result. We had assumed that the critical subject, having

gone through the experience of opposing the majority with a minimum of support, would maintain his independence when alone. Contrary to this expectation, we found that the experience of having had and then lost a partner restored the majority effect to its full force, the proportion of errors rising to 28.5 per cent of all judgments, in contrast to the preceding level of 5.5 per cent. Further experimentation is needed to establish whether the critical subjects were responding to the sheer fact of being alone, or to the fact that the partner abandoned them.

*3. Late arrival of a "true partner."* The critical subject started as a minority of one in the midst of a unanimous majority. Toward the conclusion of the experiment one member of the majority "broke" away and began announcing correct estimates. This procedure, which reverses the order of conditions of the preceding experiment, permits the observation of the transition from being alone to being a member of a pair against a majority. It is obvious that those critical subjects who were independent when alone would continue to be so when joined by another partner. The variation is therefore of significance primarily for those subjects who yielded during the first phase of the experiment. The appearance of the late partner exerts a freeing effect, reducing the level to 8.7 per cent. Those who had previously yielded also became markedly more independent, but not completely so, continuing to yield more than previously independent subjects. The reports of the subjects do not cast much light on the factors responsible for the result. It is our impression that having once committed himself to yielding, the individual finds it difficult and painful to change his direction. To do so is tantamount to a public admission that he has not acted rightly. He therefore follows the precarious course he has already chosen in order to maintain an outward semblance of consistency and conviction.

*4. The presence of a "compromise partner."* The majority was consistently extremist, always matching the standard with the most unequal line. One instructed subject (who, as in the other variations, preceded the critical subject) also responded incorrectly, but his estimates were always intermediate between the truth and the majority position. The critical subject therefore faced an extremist majority whose unanimity was broken by one more moderately erring person. Under these conditions the frequency of errors was reduced but not significantly. However, the lack of unanimity determined in a strikingly consistent way the *direction* of the errors. The preponderance of the errors, 75.7 per cent of the total, was moderate, whereas in a parallel experiment in which the majority was unanimously extremist (i.e., with the "compromise" partner excluded), the incidence of moderate errors was reduced to 42 per cent of the total. As might be expected, in a unanimously moderate majority, the errors of the critical subjects were without exception moderate.

## The Role of Majority Size

To gain further understanding of the majority effect, we varied the size of the majority in several different variations. The majorities, which were in each case unanimous, consisted of 16, 8, 4, 3, and 2 persons, respectively. In addition, we studied the limiting case in which the critical subject was opposed by one instructed subject. Table 3 contains the means and the range of errors under each condition.

### TABLE 3

ERRORS OF CRITICAL SUBJECTS WITH UNANIMOUS MAJORITIES OF DIFFERENT SIZE

| Size of majority | Control | 1 | 2 | 3 | 4 | 8 | 16 |
|---|---|---|---|---|---|---|---|
| N | 37 | 10 | 15 | 10 | 10 | 50 | 12 |
| Mean number of errors | 0.08 | 0.33 | 1.53 | 4.0 | 4.20 | 3.84 | 3.75 |
| Range of errors | 0–2 | 0–1 | 0–5 | 1–12 | 0–11 | 0–11 | 0–10 |

With the opposition reduced to one, the majority effect all but disappeared. When the opposition proceeded from a group of two, it produced a measurable though small distortion, the errors being 12.8 per cent of the total number of estimates. The effect appeared in full force with a majority of three. Larger majorities of four, eight, and sixteen did not produce effects greater than a majority of three.

The effect of a majority is often silent, revealing little of its operation to the subject, and often hiding it from the experimenter. To examine the range of effects it is capable of inducing, decisive variations of conditions are necessary. An indication of one effect is furnished by the following variation, in which the conditions of the basic experiment were simply reversed. Here the majority, consisting of a group of sixteen, was naïve; in the midst of it we placed a single individual who responded wrongly according to instructions. Under these conditions the members of the naïve majority reacted to the lone dissenter with amusement and disdain. Contagious laughter spread through the group at the droll minority of one. Of significance is the fact that the members lack awareness that they draw their strength from the majority, and that their reactions would change radically if they faced the dissenter individually. In fact, the attitude of derision in the majority turns to seriousness and increased respect as soon as the minority is increased to three. These observations demonstrate the role of social support as a source of power and stability, in contrast to the preceding investigations which stressed the effects of withdrawal of social support, or to be more exact, the effects of social opposition. Both aspects must be explicitly considered in a unified formulation of the effects of group conditions on the formation and change of judgments.

### The Role of the Stimulus Situation

It is obviously not possible to divorce the quality and course of the group forces which act upon the individual from the specific stimulus conditions. Of necessity the structure of the situation molds the group forces and determines their direction as well as their strength. Indeed, this was the reason that we took pains in the investigations described above to center the issue between the individual and the group around an elementary and fundamental matter of fact. And there can be no doubt that the resulting reactions were directly a function of the contradiction between the objectively grasped relations and the majority position.

These general considerations are sufficient to establish the need of varying the stimulus conditions and of observing their effect on the resulting group forces. We are at present conducting a series of investigations in which certain aspects of the stimulus situation are systematically altered.

One of the dimensions we are examining is the magnitude of discrepancies above the threshold. Our technique permits an easy variation of this factor, since we can increase or decrease at will the deviation of the majority from the given objective conditions. Hitherto we have studied the effect of a relatively moderate range of discrepancies. Within the limits of our procedure we find that different magnitudes of discrepancy produce approximately the same amount of yielding. However, the quality of yielding alters: as the majority becomes more extreme, there occurs a significant increase in the frequency of "compromise" errors. Further experiments are planned in which the discrepancies in question will be extremely large and small.

We have also varied systematically the structural clarity of the task, including in separate variations judgments based on mental standards. In agreement with other investigators, we find that the majority effect grows stronger as the situation diminishes in clarity. Concurrently, however, the disturbance of the subjects and the conflict quality of the situation decrease markedly. We consider it of significance that the majority achieves its most pronounced effect when it acts most painlessly.

SUMMARY

We have investigated the effects upon individuals of majority opinions when the latter were seen to be in a direction contrary to fact. By means of a simple technique we produced a radical divergence between a majority and a minority, and observed the ways in which individuals coped with the resulting difficulty. Despite the stress of the given conditions, a substantial proportion of individuals retained their independence throughout. At the same time a substantial minority yielded, modifying their judgments in accordance with the majority. Independence and yielding are a joint function of the following major factors: (1) The character of the stimulus situation. Variations in structural clarity have a decisive effect: with diminishing clarity of the stimulus conditions the majority effect increases. (2) The character of the group forces. Individuals are highly sensitive to the structural qualities of group opposition. In particular, we demonstrated the great importance of the factor of unanimity. Also, the majority effect is a function of the size of group opposition. (3) The character of the individual. There were wide, and indeed, striking differences among individuals within the same experimental situation. The hypothesis was proposed that these are functionally dependent on relatively enduring character differences, in particular those pertaining to the person's social relations.

REFERENCES

1. Asch, S. E. Studies in the principles of judgments and attitudes: II. Determination of judgments by group and by ego-standards. *J. soc. Psychol.*, 1940, 12, 433–465.
2. Asch, S. E. The doctrine of suggestion, prestige and imitation in social psychology. *Psychol. Rev.*, 1948, 55, 250–276.
3. Asch, S. E., Block, H., and Hertzman, M. Studies in the principles

of judgments and attitudes: I. Two basic principles of judgment. *J. Psychol.,* 1938, 5, 219–251.

4. Coffin, E. E. Some conditions of suggestion and suggestibility: A study of certain attitudinal and situational factors influencing the process of suggestion. *Psychol. Monogr.,* 1941, 53, No. 4.

5. Lewis, H. B. Studies in the principles of judgments and attitudes: IV. The operation of prestige suggestion. *J. soc. Psychol.,* 1941, 14, 229–256.

6. Lorge, I. Prestige, suggestion, and attitudes. *J. soc. Psychol.,* 1936, 7, 386–402.

7. Miller, N. E., and Dollard, J. *Social learning and imitation.* New Haven: Yale University Press, 1941.

8. Moore, H. T. The comparative influence of majority and expert opinion. *Amer. J. Psychol.,* 1921, 32, 16–20.

9. Sherif, M. A study of some social factors in perception. *Arch. Psychol.,* 1935, No. 187.

10. Thorndike, E. L. *The psychology of wants, interests, and attitudes.* New York: Appleton-Century, 1935.

*Solomon E. Asch*

SWARTHMORE COLLEGE

# FORMING IMPRESSIONS

# OF PERSONALITY

We look at a person and immediately a certain impression of his character forms itself in us. A glance, a few spoken words are sufficient to tell us a story about a highly complex matter. We know that such impressions form with remarkable rapidity and with great ease.[1] Subsequent observation may enrich or upset our first view, but we can no more prevent its rapid growth than we can avoid perceiving a given visual object or hearing a melody. We also know that this process, though often imperfect, is also at times extraordinarily sensitive.

This remarkable capacity we possess to understand something of the character of another person, to form a conception of him as a human being, as a center of life and striving, with particular characteristics forming a distinct individuality, is a precondition of social life. In what manner are these impressions established? Are there lawful principles regulating their formation?

One particular problem commands our attention. Each person confronts us with a large number of diverse characteristics. This man is

---

Reprinted with permission from the *Journal of Abnormal and Social Psychology,* Vol. 41, No. 3, July, 1946.

[1] The present investigation was begun in 1943 when the writer was a Fellow of the John Simon Guggenheim Memorial Foundation.

courageous, intelligent, with a ready sense of humor, quick in his movements, but he is also serious, energetic, patient under stress, not to mention his politeness and punctuality. These characteristics and many others enter into the formation of our view. Yet our impression is from the start unified; it is the impression of *one* person. We ask: How do the several characteristics function together to produce an impression of one person? What principles regulate this process?

We have mentioned earlier that the impression of a person grows quickly and easily. Yet our minds falter when we face the far simpler task of mastering a series of disconnected numbers or words. We have apparently no need to commit to memory by repeated drill the various characteristics we observe in a person, nor do some of his traits exert an observable retroactive inhibition upon our grasp of the others. Indeed, they seem to support each other. And it is quite hard to forget our view of a person once it has formed. Similarly, we do not easily confuse the half of one person with the half of another. It should be of interest to the psychologist that the far more complex task of grasping the nature of a person is so much less difficult.

There are a number of theoretical possibilities for describing the process of forming an impression, of which the major ones are the following:

1. A trait is realized in its particular quality. The next trait is similarly realized, etc. Each trait produces its particular impression. The total impression of the person is the sum of the several independent impressions. If a person possesses traits a, b, c, d, e, then the impression of him may be expressed as:

I. Impression $= a + b + c + d + e$

Few if any psychologists would at the present time apply this formulation strictly. It would, however, be an error to deny its importance for the present problem. That it controls in considerable degree many of the procedures for arriving at a scientific, objective view of a person (e.g., by means of questionnaires, rating scales) is evident. But more pertinent to our present discussion is the modified form in which Proposition I is applied to the actual forming of an impression. Some psychologists assume, in addition to the factors of Proposition I, the operation of a "general impression." The latter is conceived as an affective force possessing a plus or minus direction which shifts the evaluation of the several traits in its direction. We may represent this process as follows:

I*a*. Impression =

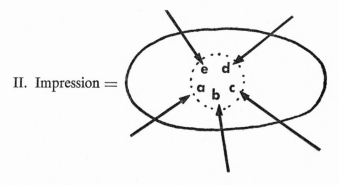

$$a + b + c + d + e + G$$

To the sum of the traits there is now added another factor, the general impression.

2. The second view asserts that we form an impression of the entire person. We see a person as consisting not of these and those independent traits (or of the sum of mutually modified traits), but we try to get at the root of the personality. This would involve that the traits are perceived in relation to each other, in their proper place within the given personality. We may express the final impression as

II. Impression =

It may appear that psychologists generally hold to some form of the latter formulation. The frequent reference to the unity of the person, or to his "integration," implying that these qualities are also present in the impression, point in this direction. The generality of these expressions is, however, not suitable to exact treatment. Terms such as unity of the person, while pointing to a problem, do not solve it. If we wish to become clear about the unity in persons, or in the impression of persons, we must ask in what sense there is such unity, and in what manner we come to observe it. Secondly, these terms are often applied interchangeably to Propositions II and I*a*. It is therefore important to state at this point a distinction between them.

For Proposition II, the general impression is not a factor added to the particular traits, but rather the perception of a particular form of relation between the traits, a conception which is wholly missing in I*a*. Further, Proposition I*a* conceives the process in terms of an imposed affective shift in the evaluation of separate traits, whereas Proposition II deals in the first instance with processes between the traits each of which has a cognitive content.

Perhaps the central difference between the two propositions becomes clearest when the accuracy of the impression becomes an issue. It is implicit in Proposition II that the process it describes is for the subject a necessary one if he is to focus on a person with maximum clarity. On the other hand, Proposition Ia permits a radically different interpretation. It has been asserted that the general impression "colors" the particular characteristics, the effect being to *blur* the clarity with which the latter are perceived. In consequence the conclusion is drawn that the general impression is a source of error which should be supplanted by the attitude of judging each trait in isolation, as described in Proposition I. This is the doctrine of the "halo effect" (9).

With the latter remarks, which we introduced only for purposes of illustration, we have passed beyond the scope of the present report. It must be made clear that we shall here deal with certain processes involved in the forming of an impression, a problem logically distinct from the actual relation of traits within a person. To be sure, the manner in which an impression is formed contains, as we shall see, definite assumptions concerning the structure of personal traits. The validity of such assumptions must, however, be established in independent investigation.

The issues we shall consider have been largely neglected in investigation. Perhaps the main reason has been a one-sided stress on the subjectivity of personal judgments. The preoccupation with emotional factors and distortions of judgment has had two main consequences for the course investigation has taken. First, it has induced a certain lack of perspective which has diverted interest from the study of those processes which do not involve subjective distortions as the most decisive factor. Secondly, there has been a tendency to neglect the fact that emotions too have a cognitive side, that something must be perceived and discriminated in order that it may be loved or hated. On the other hand, the approach of the more careful studies in this region has centered mainly on questions of validity in the final product of judgment. Neither of the main approaches has dealt explicitly with the process of forming an impression. Yet no argument should be needed to support the statement that our view of a person necessarily involves a certain orientation to, and ordering of, objectively given, observable characteristics. It is this aspect of the problem that we propose to study.

The plan followed in the experiments to be reported was to read to the subject a number of discrete characteristics, said to belong to a person, with the instruction to describe the impression he formed. The subjects were all college students, most of whom were women.[2] They were mostly beginners in psychology. Though they expressed genuine interest in the tasks, the subjects were not aware of the nature of the problem until it was explained to them. We illustrate our procedure with one concrete instance. The following list of terms was read: *energetic—assured—talkative—cold—ironical—inquisitive—persuasive*. The reading of the list was preceded by the following instructions:

> I shall read to you a number of characteristics that belong to a particular person. Please listen to them carefully and try to form an impression of the kind of person described. You will later be asked to give a brief characterization of the person in just a few sentences. I will read the list slowly and will repeat it once.

The list was read with an interval of approximately five seconds between the terms. When the first reading was completed, the experimenter said, "I will now read the list again," and proceeded to do so. We reproduce below a few typical sketches written by subjects after they heard read the list of terms:

> He seems to be the kind of person who would make a great impression upon others at a first meeting. However as time went by, his acquaintances would easily come to see through the mask. Underneath would be revealed his arrogance and selfishness.

> He is the type of person you meet all too often: sure of himself, talks too much, always trying to bring you around to his way of thinking, and with not much feeling for the other fellow.

> He impresses people as being more capable than he really is. He is popular and never ill at ease. Easily becomes the center of attraction at any gathering. He is likely to be a jack-of-all-trades. Although his interests are varied, he is not necessarily well-versed in any of them. He possesses a sense of humor. His presence stimulates enthusiasm and very often he does arrive at a position of importance.

---

[2] The writer wishes to express his gratitude to the following colleagues for their help in the performance of these experiments in their classes: Drs. B. F. Riess, L. Welch, V. J. McGill, and A. Goldenson of Hunter College; Drs. M. Blum and A. Mintz of the College of the City of New York; Dr. Lois Adams, Mr. Michael Newman, and Mr. Herbert Newman of Brooklyn College.

Possibly he does not have any deep feeling. He would tend to be an opportunist. Likely to succeed in things he intends to do. He has perhaps married a wife who would help him in his purpose. He tends to be skeptical.

The following preliminary points are to be noted:

1. When a task of this kind is given, a normal adult is capable of responding to the instruction by forming a unified impression. Though he hears a sequence of discrete terms, his resulting impression is not discrete. In some manner he shapes the separate qualities into a single, consistent view. All subjects in the following experiments, of whom there were over 1,000, fulfilled the task in the manner described. No one proceeded by reproducing the given list of terms, as one would in a rote memory experiment; nor did any of the subjects reply merely with synonyms of the given terms.

2. The characteristics seem to reach out beyond the merely given terms of the description. Starting from the bare terms, the final account is completed and rounded. Reference is made to characters and situations which are apparently not directly mentioned in the list, but which are inferred from it.

3. The accounts of the subjects diverge from each other in important respects. This will not be surprising in view of the variable content of the terms employed, which permits a considerable freedom in interpretation and weighting.

In the experiments to be reported the subjects were given a group of traits on the basis of which they formed an impression. In view of the fact that we possess no principles in this region to help in their systematic construction, it was necessary to invent groupings of traits. In this we were guided by an informal sense of what traits were consistent with each other.

The procedure here employed is clearly different from the everyday situation in which we follow the concrete actions of an actual person. We have chosen to work with weak, incipient impressions, based on abbreviated descriptions of personal qualities. Nevertheless, this procedure has some merit for purposes of investigation, especially in observing the change of impressions, and is, we hope to show, relevant to more natural judgment.

More detailed features of the procedure will be described subsequently in connection with the actual experiments. We shall now inquire into some of the factors that determine the content and alteration of such impressions.

## I. CENTRAL AND PERIPHERAL CHARACTERISTICS

### VARIATION OF A CENTRAL QUALITY

Observation suggests that not all qualities have the same weight in establishing the view of a person. Some are felt to be basic, others secondary. In the following experiments we sought for a demonstration of this process in the course of the formation of an impression.

Experiment 1

Two groups, A and B, heard read a list of character qualities, identical save for one term. The list follows:

A. intelligent—skillful—industrious—*warm*—determined—practical—
    cautious
B. intelligent—skillful—industrious—*cold*—determined—practical—
    cautious

Group A heard the person described as "warm"; Group B, as "cold."

*Technique.* The instructions were as described above. Following the reading, each subject wrote a brief sketch.

The sketches furnish concrete evidence of the impressions formed. Their exact analysis involves, however, serious technical difficulties. It seemed, therefore, desirable to add a somewhat simpler procedure for the determination of the content of the impression and for the purpose of group comparisons. To this end we constructed a check list consisting of pairs of traits, mostly opposites. From each pair of terms in this list, which the reader will find reproduced in Table 1, the subject was instructed to select the one that was most in accordance with the view he had formed. Terms were included which were quite different from those appearing in the basic list, but which could be related to them. Of necessity we were guided in the selection of terms for the check list (as well as for the experimental lists) by an informal sense of what was fitting or relevant. Some of the terms were taken from written sketches of subjects in preliminary experiments. In the examination of results we shall rely upon the written sketches for evidence of the actual character of the impressions, and we shall supplement these with the quantitative results from the check list.

There were 90 subjects in Group A (comprising four separate classroom groups), 76 subjects in Group B (comprising four separate classroom groups).

## TABLE 1

### CHECK LIST I

| | |
|---|---|
| 1. generous—ungenerous | 10. ruthless—humane |
| 2. shrewd—wise | 11. good-looking—unattractive |
| 3. unhappy—happy | 12. persistent—unstable |
| 4. irritable—good-natured | 13. frivolous—serious |
| 5. humorous—humorless | 14. restrained—talkative |
| 6. sociable—unsociable | 15. self-centered—altruistic |
| 7. popular—unpopular | 16. imaginative—hard-headed |
| 8. unreliable—reliable | 17. strong—weak |
| 9. important—insignificant | 18. dishonest—honest |

*Results.* Are the impressions of Groups A and B identical, with the exception that one has the added quality of "warm," the other of "cold"? This is one possible outcome. Another possibility is that the differentiating quality imparts a general plus or minus direction to the resulting impression. We shall see that neither of these formulations accurately describes the results.

We note first that the characteristic "warm-cold" produces striking and consistent differences of impression. In general, the A-impressions are far more positive than the B-impressions. We cite a few representative examples:

*Series A ("warm")*

A person who believes certain things to be right, wants others to see his point, would be sincere in an argument, and would like to see his point won.

A scientist performing experiments and persevering after many setbacks. He is driven by the desire to accomplish something that would be of benefit.

*Series B ("cold")*

A very ambitious and talented person who would not let anyone or anything stand in the way of achieving his goal. Wants his own way, he is determined not to give in, no matter what happens.

A rather snobbish person who feels that his success and intelligence set him apart from the run-of-the-mill individual. Calculating and unsympathetic.

This trend is fully confirmed in the check-list choices. In Table 2 we report the frequency (in terms of percentages) with which each term in the check list was selected. For the sake of brevity of presentation we state the results for the positive term in each pair; the reader may determine the percentage of choices for the other term in each pair by subtracting the given figure from 100. To illustrate, under Condition A of the present experiment, 91 per cent of the subjects chose the designation "generous"; the remaining 9 per cent selected the designation "ungenerous." Occasionally, a subject would not state a choice for a particular pair. Therefore, the number of cases on which the figures are based is not always identical; however, the fluctuations were minor, with the exception of the category "good-looking—unattractive," which a larger proportion of subjects failed to answer.

## TABLE 2

### CHOICE OF FITTING QUALITIES (PERCENTAGES)

| | Experiment 1 | | Experiment 2 | | | Experiment 3 | |
| --- | --- | --- | --- | --- | --- | --- | --- |
| | "Warm" $N = 90$ | "Cold" $N = 76$ | Total $N = 56$ | "Warm" $N = 23$ | "Cold" $N = 33$ | "Polite" $N = 20$ | "Blunt" $N = 26$ |
| 1. generous | 91 | 8 | 55 | 87 | 33 | 56 | 58 |
| 2. wise | 65 | 25 | 49 | 73 | 33 | 30 | 50 |
| 3. happy | 90 | 34 | 71 | 91 | 58 | 75 | 65 |
| 4. good-natured | 94 | 17 | 69 | 91 | 55 | 87 | 56 |
| 5. humorous | 77 | 13 | 36 | 76 | 12 | 71 | 48 |
| 6. sociable | 91 | 38 | 71 | 91 | 55 | 83 | 68 |
| 7. popular | 84 | 28 | 57 | 83 | 39 | 94 | 56 |
| 8. reliable | 94 | 99 | 96 | 96 | 97 | 95 | 100 |
| 9. important | 88 | 99 | 88 | 87 | 88 | 94 | 96 |
| 10. humane | 86 | 31 | 64 | 91 | 45 | 59 | 77 |
| 11. good-looking | 77 | 69 | 58 | 71 | 53 | 93 | 79 |
| 12. persistent | 100 | 97 | 98 | 96 | 100 | 100 | 100 |
| 13. serious | 100 | 99 | 96 | 91 | 100 | 100 | 100 |
| 14. restrained | 77 | 89 | 82 | 67 | 94 | 82 | 77 |
| 15. altruistic | 69 | 18 | 44 | 68 | 27 | 29 | 46 |
| 16. imaginative | 51 | 19 | 24 | 45 | 9 | 33 | 31 |
| 17. strong | 98 | 95 | 95 | 94 | 96 | 100 | 100 |
| 18. honest | 98 | 94 | 95 | 100 | 92 | 87 | 100 |

We find:

1. There are extreme reversals between Groups A and B in the choice of fitting characteristics. Certain qualities are preponderantly assigned to the "warm" person, while the opposing qualities are equally prominent in the "cold" person. This holds for the qualities of (1) generosity, (2) shrewdness, (3) happiness, (4) irritability, (5) humor, (6) sociability, (7) popularity, (10) ruthlessness, (15) self-centeredness, (16) imaginativeness.

2. There is another group of qualities which is *not* affected by the transition from "warm" to "cold," or only slightly affected. These are: (8) reliability, (9) importance, (11) physical attractiveness, (12) persistence, (13) seriousness, (14) restraint, (17) strength, (18) honesty.

These results show that a change in one character quality has produced a widespread change in the entire impression. Further, the written sketches show that the terms "warm-cold" did not simply add a new quality, but to some extent transformed the other characteristics. With this point we shall deal more explicitly in the experiments to follow.

That such transformations take place is also a matter of everyday experience. If a man is intelligent, this has an effect on the way in which we perceive his playfulness, happiness, friendliness. At the same time, this extensive change does not function indiscriminately. The "warm" person is not seen more favorably in all respects. There is a range of qualities, among them a number that are basic, which are not touched by the distinction between "warm" and "cold." Both remain equally honest, strong, serious, reliable, etc.

The latter result is of interest with reference to one possible interpretation of the findings. It might be supposed that the category "warm-cold" aroused a "mental set" or established a halo tending toward a consistently plus or minus evaluation. We observe here that this trend did not work in an indiscriminate manner, but was decisively limited at certain points. If we assume that the process of mutual influence took place in terms of the actual character of the qualities in question, it is not surprising that some will, by virtue of their content, remain unchanged.[3]

The following will show that the subjects generally felt the qualities "warm-cold" to be of primary importance. We asked the subjects in certain of the groups to rank the terms of Lists A and B in order of their importance for determining their impression. Table 3, containing the distribution of rankings of "warm-cold," shows that these qualities ranked comparatively high. At the same time a considerable number of subjects relegated "cold" to the lowest position. That the rankings are not higher is due to the fact that the lists contained other central traits.

These data, as well as the ranking of the other traits not here reproduced, point to the following conclusions:

---

[3] This by no means excludes the possibility that the nuances of strength, honesty, etc., do change in relation to "warm-cold."

1. The given characteristics do not all have the same weight for the subject. He assigns to some a higher importance than to others.

2. The weight of a given characteristic varies—within limits—from subject to subject.

TABLE 3

RANKINGS OF "WARM" AND "COLD": EXPERIMENT 1

| Rank | "Warm" | | "Cold" | |
|------|--------|------------|--------|------------|
| | N | Percentage | N | Percentage |
| 1 | 6 | 14 | 12 | 27 |
| 2 | 15 | 35 | 8 | 21 |
| 3 | 4 | 10 | 1 | 2 |
| 4 | 4 | 10 | 2 | 5 |
| 5 | 4 | 10 | 3 | 7 |
| 6 | 3 | 7 | 2 | 5 |
| 7 | 6 | 14 | 13 | 33 |
| | 42 | 100 | 41 | 100 |

Certain limitations of the check-list procedure need to be considered: (1) The subject's reactions are forced into an appearance of discreteness which they do not actually possess, as the written sketches show; (2) the check list requires the subject to choose between extreme characteristics, which he might prefer to avoid; (3) the quantitative data describe group trends; they do not represent adequately the form of the individual impression. Generally the individual responses exhibit much stronger trends in a consistently positive or negative direction. For these reasons we employ the check-list results primarily for the purpose of comparing group trends under different conditions. For this purpose the procedure is quite adequate.

OMISSION OF A CENTRAL QUALITY

That the category "warm-cold" is significant for the total impression may be demonstrated also by omitting it from the series. This we do in the following experiment.

Experiment 2

The procedure was identical with that of experiment 1, except that the terms "warm" and "cold" were omitted from the list read to the subject (intelligent—skillful—industrious—determined—practical—

cautious). Also, the check list was identical with that of experiment 1, save that "warm-cold" was added as the last pair. There were three groups, consisting of a total of 56 subjects.

Under these conditions the selection of fitting characteristics shows a significant change. The distribution of choices for the total group (see Table 2, column labeled "Total") now falls between the "warm" and "cold" variations of experiment 1. It appears that a more neutral impression has formed.

The total group results are, however, largely a statistical artifact. An examination of the check-list choices of the subjects quickly revealed strong and consistent individual differences. They tended to be consistently positive or negative in their evaluations. It will be recalled that the terms "warm-cold" were added to the check list. This permitted us to subdivide the total group according to whether they judged the described person on the check list as "warm" or "cold." Of the entire group, 23 subjects (or 41 per cent) fell into the "warm" category. Our next step was to study the distribution of choices in the two subgroups. The results are clear: the two subgroups diverge consistently in the direction of the "warm" and the "cold" groups, respectively, of experiment 1. (See Table 2.) This is especially the case with the two "warm" series, which are virtually identical.

It is of interest that the omission of a term from the experimental list did not function entirely as an omission. Instead, the subjects inferred the corresponding quality in either the positive or negative direction. While not entirely conclusive, the results suggest that a full impression of a person cannot remain indifferent to a category as fundamental as the one in question, and that a trend is set up to include it in the impression on the basis of the given data. In later experiments too we have found a strong trend to reach out toward evaluations which were not contained in the original description.

VARIATION OF A PERIPHERAL QUALITY

Would a change of *any* character quality produce an effect as strong as that observed above? "Warm" and "cold" seem to be of special importance for our conception of a person. This was, in fact, the reason for selecting them for study. If there are central qualities, upon which the content of other qualities depends, and dependent qualities which are secondarily determined, it should be possible to distinguish them objectively. On this assumption the addition or omission of peripheral qualities should have smaller effects than those observed in experiment 1. We turn to this question in the following experiment.

Experiment 3

The following lists were read, each to a different group:

A. intelligent—skillful—industrious—*polite*—determined—practical—
   cautious
B. intelligent—skillful—industrious—*blunt*—determined—practical—
   cautious

The A group contained 20, the B group 26 subjects.

TABLE 4

RANKINGS OF "POLITE" AND "BLUNT": EXPERIMENT 3

|  | A: "Polite" | | B: "Blunt" | |
| --- | --- | --- | --- | --- |
| Rank | N | Percentage | N | Percentage |
| 1 | 0 | 0 | 0 | 0 |
| 2 | 0 | 0 | 4 | 15 |
| 3 | 0 | 0 | 3 | 12 |
| 4 | 2 | 10 | 5 | 19 |
| 5 | 3 | 16 | 6 | 23 |
| 6 | 4 | 21 | 1 | 4 |
| 7 | 10 | 53 | 7 | 27 |
|  | 19 | 100 | 26 | 100 |

The changes introduced into the selection of fitting characteristics in the transition from "polite" to "blunt" were far weaker than those found in experiment 1 (see Table 2). There is further evidence that the subjects themselves regarded these characteristics as relatively peripheral, especially the characteristic "polite." If we may take the rankings as an index, then we may conclude that a change in a peripheral trait produces a weaker effect on the total impression than does a change in a central trait. (Though the changes produced are weaker than those of experiment 1, they are nevertheless substantial. Possibly this is a consequence of the thinness of the impression, which responds easily to slight changes.)

TRANSFORMATION FROM A CENTRAL TO A PERIPHERAL QUALITY

The preceding experiments have demonstrated a process of discrimination between central and peripheral qualities. We ask: Are certain qualities constantly central? Or is their functional value, too, dependent on the other characteristics?

### Experiment 4

We selected for observation the quality "warm," which was demonstrated to exert a powerful effect on the total impression (experiments 1 and 2). The effect of the term was studied in the following two series:

A. obedient—weak—shallow—*warm*—unambitious—vain
B. vain—shrewd—unscrupulous—*warm*—shallow—envious

Immediately "warm" drops as a significant characteristic in relation to the others, as the distribution of rankings appearing in Table 5 shows. (Compare Table 3 of experiment 1.)

### TABLE 5

RANKINGS OF "WARM" AND "COLD": EXPERIMENT 4

| | "Warm" | | | | "Cold" | |
| | Series A | | Series B | | Series C | |
| Rank | N | Percentage | N | Percentage | N | Percentage |
|---|---|---|---|---|---|---|
| 1 | 1 | 4 | 0 | 0 | 1 | 5 |
| 2 | 0 | 0 | 0 | 0 | 0 | 0 |
| 3 | 2 | 9 | 1 | 5 | 3 | 15 |
| 4 | 6 | 27 | 4 | 19 | 2 | 10 |
| 5 | 7 | 30 | 4 | 19 | 1 | 5 |
| 6 | 7 | 30 | 12 | 57 | 2 | 10 |
| 7 | — | — | — | — | 11 | 55 |
| | 23 | 100 | 21 | 100 | 20 | 100 |

More enlightening are the subjects' comments. In Series A the quality "warm" is now seen as wholly dependent, dominated by others far more decisive.

I think the warmth within this person is a warmth emanating from a follower to a leader.

The term "warm" strikes one as being a dog-like affection rather than a bright friendliness. It is passive and without strength.

His submissiveness may lead people to think he is kind and warm.

A more extreme transformation is observed in Series B. In most instances the warmth of this person is felt to lack sincerity, as appears in the following protocols:

I assumed the person to appear warm rather than really to be warm.

He was warm only when it worked in with his scheme to get others over to his side. His warmth is not sincere.

A similar change was also observed in the content of "cold" in a further variation. The subject heard List B of experiment 1 followed by Series C below, the task being to state whether the term "cold" had the same meaning in both lists.

C. intelligent—skillful—sincere—*cold*—conscientious—helpful—modest

All subjects reported a difference. The quality "cold" became peripheral for all in Series C. The following are representative comments:

The coldness of 1 (experiment 1) borders on ruthlessness; 2 analyses coldly to differentiate between right and wrong.

1 is cold inwardly and outwardly, while 2 is cold only superficially.

1: cold means lack of sympathy and understanding; 2: cold means somewhat formal in manner.

Coldness was the foremost characteristic of 1. In 2 it seemed not very important, a quality that would disappear after you came to know him.

That "cold" was transformed in the present series into a peripheral quality is also confirmed by the rankings reported in Table 5.

We conclude that a quality, central in one person, may undergo a change of content in another person, and become subsidiary. When central, the quality has a different content and weight than when it is subsidiary.

Here we observe directly a process of grouping in the course of which the content of a trait changes in relation to its surroundings. Secondly, we observe that the functional value of a trait, too—whether, for example, it becomes central or not—is a consequence of its relation to the set of surrounding traits. At the same time we are able to see more clearly the distinction between central and peripheral traits. It is inadequate to say that a central trait is more important, contributes more quantitatively to, or is more highly correlated with, the final impression than a peripheral trait. The latter formulations are true, but they fail to consider the qualitative process of mutual determination between traits, namely, that a central trait determines the content and the functional place of peripheral traits within the entire impression. In Series A, for example, the quality "warm" does not control the meaning of "weak," but is controlled by it.

The evidence may seem to support the conclusion that the same quality which is central in one impression becomes peripheral in another. Such an interpretation would, however, contain an ambiguity. While we may speak of relativity in the functional value of a trait within a person, in a deeper sense we have here the opposite of relativity. For the sense of "warm" (or "cold") of experiment 1 has not suffered a change of evaluation under the present conditions. Quite the contrary; the terms in question change precisely because the subject does not see the possibility of finding in this person the same warmth he values so highly when he does meet it (correspondingly for coldness).

Experiment 5

The preceding experiments have shown that the characteristics forming the basis of an impression do not contribute each a fixed, independent meaning, but that their content is itself partly a function of the environment of the other characteristics, of their mutual relations. We propose now to investigate more directly the manner in which the content of a given characteristic may undergo change.

Lists A and B were read to two separate groups (including 38 and 41 subjects, respectively). The first three terms of the two lists are opposites; the final two terms are identical.

A. kind—wise—honest—*calm—strong*
B. cruel—shrewd—unscrupulous—*calm—strong*

The instructions were to write down synonyms for the given terms. The instructions read: "Suppose you had to describe this person in the same manner, but without using the terms you heard, what other terms would you use?" We are concerned with the synonyms given to the two final terms.

In Table 6 we list those synonyms of "calm" which occurred with different frequencies in the two groups. It will be seen that terms appear in one group which are not at all to be found in the other; further, some terms appear with considerably different frequencies under the two conditions. These do not, however, include the total group of synonyms; many scattered terms occurred equally in both groups.

### TABLE 6

#### SYNONYMS OF "CALM": EXPERIMENT 5

|  | "Kind" Series | "Cruel" Series |
|---|---|---|
| serene | 18 | 3 |
| cold, frigid, icy, cool, calculating, shrewd, nervy, scheming, conscienceless | 0 | 20 |
| soothing, peaceful, gentle, tolerant, good-natured, mild-mannered | 11 | 0 |
| poised, reserved, restful, unexcitable, unshakable | 18 | 7 |
| deliberate, silent, unperturbed, masterful, impassive, collected, confident, relaxed, emotionless, steady, impassive, composed | 11 | 26 |

We may conclude that the quality "calm" did not, at least in some cases, function as an independent, fixed trait, but that its content was determined by its relation to the other terms. As a consequence, the quality "calm" was not the same under the two experimental conditions. In Series A it possessed an aspect of gentleness, while a grimmer side became prominent in Series B.[4]

Essentially the same may be said of the final term, "strong." Again, some synonyms appear exclusively in one or the other groups, and in the expected directions. Among these are:

Series A: fearless—helpful—just—forceful—courageous—reliable
Series B: ruthless—overbearing—overpowering—hard—inflexible—unbending—dominant

---

[4] In an earlier investigation the writer (2) has dealt with basically the same question though in a very different context. It was there shown that certain phenomena of judgment, which appeared to be due to changes of evaluation, were produced by a shift in the frame of reference.

The data of Table 6 provide evidence of a tendency in the described direction, but its strength is probably underestimated. We have already mentioned that certain synonyms appeared frequently in both series. But it is not to be concluded that they therefore carried the same meaning. Doubtless the same terms were at times applied in the two groups with different meanings, precisely because the subjects were under the control of the factor being investigated. To mention one example: the term "quiet" often occurred as a synonym of "calm" in both groups, but the subjects may have intended a different meaning in the two cases. For this reason Table 6 may not reveal the full extent of the change introduced by the factor of embedding.

The preceding experiments permit the following conclusions:

1. There is a process of discrimination between central and peripheral traits. All traits do not have the same rank and value in the final impression. The change of a central trait may completely alter the impression, while the change of a peripheral trait has a far weaker effect (experiments 1, 2, and 3).

2. Both the cognitive content of a trait and its functional value are determined in relation to its surroundings (experiment 4).

3. Some traits determine both the content and the function of other traits. The former we call central, the latter peripheral (experiment 4).

II. THE FACTOR OF DIRECTION

If impressions of the kind here investigated are a summation of the effects of the separate characteristics, then an identical set of characteristics should produce a constant result. Is it possible to alter the impression without changing the particular characteristic? We investigate this question below.

Experiment 6

The following series are read, each to a different group:

A. intelligent—industrious—impulsive—critical—stubborn—envious
B. envious—stubborn—critical—impulsive—industrious—intelligent

There were 34 subjects in Group A, 24 in Group B.

The two series are identical with regard to their members, differing only in the order of succession of the latter. More particularly, Series A opens with qualities of high merit (intelligent—industrious), proceeds to qualities that permit of a better or poorer evaluation (impulsive—

critical—stubborn), and closes with a dubious quality (envious). This order is reversed in Series B.

A considerable difference develops between the two groups taken as a whole. The impression produced by A is predominantly that of an able person who possesses certain shortcomings which do not, however, overshadow his merits. On the other hand, B impresses the majority as a "problem," whose abilities are hampered by his serious difficulties. Further, some of the qualities (e.g., impulsiveness, criticalness) are interpreted in a positive way under Condition A, while they take on, under Condition B, a negative color. This trend is not observed in all subjects, but it is found in the majority. A few illustrative extracts follow:

*Series A*

A person who knows what he wants and goes after it. He is impatient at people who are less gifted, and ambitious with those who stand in his way.

Is a forceful person, has his own convictions and is usually right about things. Is self-centered and desires his own way.

The person is intelligent and fortunately he puts his intelligence to work. That he is stubborn and impulsive may be due to the fact that he knows what he is saying and what he means and will not therefore give in easily to someone else's idea which he disagrees with.

*Series B*

This person's good qualities such as industry and intelligence are bound to be restricted by jealousy and stubbornness. The person is emotional. He is unsuccessful because he is weak and allows his bad points to cover up his good ones.

This individual is probably maladjusted because he is envious and impulsive.

In order to observe more directly the transition in question, the writer proceeded as follows. A new group ($N = 24$) heard Series B, wrote the free sketch, and immediately thereafter wrote the sketch in response to Series A. They were also asked to comment on the relation between the two impressions. Under these conditions, with the transition occurring in the same subjects, 14 out of 24 claimed that their impression suffered a change, while the remaining 10 subjects reported no change. Some of the latter asserted that they had waited until the entire series was read before deciding upon their impression. The following are a few comments of the changing group:

You read the list in a different order and thereby caused a different type of person to come to mind. This one is smarter, more likeable, a go-getter, lively, headstrong, and with a will of his own; he goes after what he wants.

The first individual seems to show his envy and criticism more than the second one.

This man does not seem so bad as the first one. Somehow, he seems more intelligent, with his critical attitude helping that characteristic of intelligence, and he seems to be industrious, perhaps because he is envious and wants to get ahead.

The check-list data appearing in Table 7 furnish quantitative support for the conclusions drawn from the written sketches.

## TABLE 7

### CHOICE OF FITTING QUALITIES (PERCENTAGES)

|  | Experiment 6 | | Experiment 7 | |
|---|---|---|---|---|
|  | Intelligent → Envious (N = 34) | Envious → Intelligent (N = 24) | Intelligent → Evasive (N = 46) | Evasive → Intelligent (N = 53) |
| 1. generous | 24 | 10 | 42 | 23 |
| 2. wise | 18 | 17 | 35 | 19 |
| 3. happy | 32 | 5 | 51 | 49 |
| 4. good-natured | 18 | 0 | 54 | 37 |
| 5. humorous | 52 | 21 | 53 | 29 |
| 6. sociable | 56 | 27 | 50 | 48 |
| 7. popular | 35 | 14 | 44 | 39 |
| 8. reliable | 84 | 91 | 96 | 94 |
| 9. important | 85 | 90 | 77 | 89 |
| 10. humane | 36 | 21 | 49 | 46 |
| 11. good-looking | 74 | 35 | 59 | 53 |
| 12. persistent | 82 | 87 | 94 | 100 |
| 13. serious | 97 | 100 | 44 | 100 |
| 14. restrained | 64 | 9 | 91 | 91 |
| 15. altruistic | 6 | 5 | 32 | 25 |
| 16. imaginative | 26 | 14 | 37 | 16 |
| 17. strong | 94 | 73 | 74 | 96 |
| 18. honest | 80 | 79 | 66 | 81 |

Under the given conditions the terms, the elements of the description, are identical, but the resulting impressions frequently are not the same. Further, the relations of the terms to one another have not been disturbed, as they may have been in experiments 1 and 2, with the addition and omission of parts. How can we understand the resulting difference?

The accounts of the subjects suggest that the first terms set up in most subjects a *direction* which then exerts a continuous effect on the latter terms. When the subject hears the first term, a broad, uncrystallized but directed impression is born. The next characteristic comes not as a separate item, but is related to the established direction. Quickly the view formed acquires a certain stability, so that later characteristics are fitted—if conditions permit [5]—to the given direction.

Here we observe a factor of primacy guiding the development of an impression. This factor is not, however, to be understood in the sense of Ebbinghaus, but rather in a structural sense. It is not the sheer temporal position of the item which is important as much as the functional relation of its content to the content of the items following it.[6]

TABLE 8

RANKING OF "ENVIOUS": EXPERIMENT 6

| Rank | Intelligent → Envious | | Envious → Intelligent | |
|---|---|---|---|---|
| | N | Percentage | N | Percentage |
| 1 | 5 | 15 | 7 | 29 |
| 2 | 4 | 11 | 4 | 17 |
| 3 | 5 | 15 | 5 | 21 |
| 4 | 3 | 9 | 2 | 8 |
| 5 | 4 | 11 | 2 | 8 |
| 6 | 13 | 39 | 4 | 17 |
| | 34 | 100 | 24 | 100 |

[5] For an instance in which the given conditions may destroy the established direction, see experiment 8 below.

[6] In accordance with this interpretation the effect of primacy should be abolished—or reversed—if it does not stand in a fitting relation to the succeeding qualities, or if a certain quality stands out as central despite its position. The latter was clearly the case for the quality "warm-cold" in experiment 1 (see Table 1) which, though occupying a middle position, ranked comparatively high.

The distinction between the two senses of primacy could be studied experimentally by comparing the recall of an identical series of character qualities in

Some further evidence with regard to this point is provided by the data with regard to ranking. We reproduce in Table 8 the rankings of the characteristic "envious" under the two conditions.

Experiment 7

It seemed desirable to repeat the preceding experiment with a new series. As before, we reversed the succession of terms. Unlike the preceding series, there is no gradual change in the merit of the given characteristics, but rather the abrupt introduction at the end (or at the beginning) of a highly dubious trait. The series were:

A. intelligent—skillful—industrious—determined—practical—cautious—
evasive
B. evasive—cautious—practical—determined—industrious—skillful—
intelligent

While the results are, for reasons to be described, less clear than in the experiment preceding, there is still a definite tendency for A to produce a more favorable impression with greater frequency. We report below the more extreme protocols in each series.

*Series A*
He seems to be a man of very excellent character, though it is not unusual for one person to have all of those good qualities.

A scientist in an applied field, who does not like to discuss his work before it is completed. Retiring and careful—but brilliant. Works alone, does not like to be annoyed with questions. A very dynamic man.

A normal, intelligent person, who sounds as if he would be a good citizen, and of value to all who know him.

He seems to have at least two traits which are not consistent with the rest of his personality. Being *cautious* and *evasive* contradicts his positive qualities. Altogether, he is a most unattractive person—the two above-mentioned traits overbalancing the others.

*Series B*
This is a man who has had to work for everything he wanted—therefore he is evasive, cautious and practical. He is naturally intelligent, but his struggles have made him hard.

---

two groups, one of which reads them as a discrete list of terms, the other as a set of characteristics describing a person.

He is out for himself, is very capable but tends to use his skill for his own benefit.

He is so determined to succeed that he relies on any means, making use of his cunning and evasive powers.

Questioning disclosed that, under the given conditions, the quality "evasive" produced unusual difficulty. Most subjects in both groups felt a contradiction between it and the series as a whole. In response to the question, "Were there any characteristics that did not fit with the others?" 11 out of 27 in Group A mentioned "evasive" while it was mentioned by 11 out of a total of 30 in Group B.

It is of interest to observe how this crucial term was dealt with by individual subjects. Some in Group A felt unable to reconcile it with the view they had formed; consequently they relegated it to a subsidiary position and, in the most extreme cases, completely excluded it. Others reported the opposite effect: the final term completely undid their impression and forced a new view. The following comments are illustrative:

*Series A*

I put this characteristic in the background and said it may be a dependent characteristic of the person, which does not dominate his personality, and does not influence his actions to a large extent.

I excluded it because the other characteristics which fitted together so well were so much more predominant. In my first impression it was left out completely.

It changed my entire idea of the person—changing his attitude toward others, the type of position he'd be likely to hold, the amount of happiness he'd have—and it gave a certain amount of change of character (even for traits not mentioned), and a tendency to think of the person as somewhat sneaky or sly.

Similar reactions occur in Group B, but with changed frequencies.

The importance of the order of impressions of a person in daily experience is a matter of general observation and is perhaps related to the process under investigation. It may be the basis for the importance attached to first impressions. It is a matter of general experience that we may have a "wrong slant" on a person, because certain characteristics first observed are given a central position when they are actually subsidiary, or vice versa.

Experiment 8

We studied the factor of direction in yet another way. Series A of experiment 6 was divided in two parts and presented to a new group as a description of two persons. The new series were:

A. intelligent—industrious—impulsive
B. critical—stubborn—envious

*Procedure.* (1) Series A was read to this group (Group 1), followed by the written sketch and the check list. (2) The subjects were instructed that they would hear a new group of terms describing a second person. Series B was read and the usual information was obtained. (3) Upon completion of the second task the subjects were informed that the two lists described a single person. They were instructed to form an impression corresponding to the entire list of terms. Certain questions were subsequently asked concerning the last step, which will be described below. A control group (Group 2) responded only to the entire list of six terms (as in Series A of experiment 6), and answered some of the final questions.

We are concerned mainly to see how Group 1 dealt with the final task, the establishing of an impression based on the two smaller series. That Lists A and B were widely different will be clear in the check-list results of Table 9.

Most subjects of Group 1 expressed astonishment at the final information (of Step 3) and showed some reluctance to proceed. In response to the question, "Did you experience difficulty in forming an impression on the basis of the six terms," the majority of Group 1 (32 out of 52) replied in the affirmative. The reasons given were highly uniform: the two sets of traits seemed entirely contradictory.

I had seen the two sets of characteristics as opposing each other. It was hard to envision all these contradictory traits in one person.

The person seemed to be a mass of contradictions.

He seemed a dual personality. There are two directions in this person.

On the other hand, only a minority in Group 2 (9 out of 24) report any difficulty. Further, the reasons given by the latter are entirely different from those of Group 1. These subjects speak in very general terms, as:

These characteristics are possessed by everyone in some degree or other. The terms do not give an inclusive picture.

Only two subjects in Group 2 mentioned contradiction between traits as a source of difficulty.

## TABLE 9

CHOICE OF FITTING QUALITIES: EXPERIMENT 8 (PERCENTAGES)

|  | Intelligent—Industrious—Impulsive (N = 52) | Critical—Stubborn—Envious (N = 52) |
|---|---|---|
| 1. generous | 87 | 6 |
| 2. wise | 48 | 3 |
| 3. happy | 84 | 0 |
| 4. good-natured | 74 | 3 |
| 5. humorous | 87 | 12 |
| 6. sociable | 89 | 24 |
| 7. popular | 94 | 9 |
| 8. reliable | 85 | 47 |
| 9. important | 90 | 24 |
| 10. humane | 87 | 19 |
| 11. good-looking | 81 | 36 |
| 12. persistent | 85 | 67 |
| 13. serious | 87 | 83 |
| 14. restrained | 16 | 37 |
| 15. altruistic | 66 | 0 |
| 16. imaginative | 65 | 15 |
| 17. strong | 94 | 50 |
| 18. honest | 100 | 58 |

The formation of the complete impression proceeds differently in the two groups. Series A and B are at first referred, in Group 1, to entirely different persons. Each is completed in its direction, and the fact that they come successively seems to enhance the contrast between them. It is therefore difficult for them to enter the new impression. Some subjects are unable to reconcile the two directions completely; in consequence their divergence becomes the paramount fact, as the following protocols illustrate:

The directions reacted on each other and were modified, so that the pull in each direction is now less strong. This gives a Jekyll and Hyde appearance to this person.

I applied A to the business half of the man—as he appeared and acted during working hours. B I referred to the man's social life.

The independent development of A and B is on the other hand prevented in Group 2, where they function from the start as parts of one description.[7]

This conclusion is in general confirmed by the following observation. To the question: "Did you proceed by combining the two earlier impressions or by forming a new impression?" the following responses are obtained: 33 of 52 subjects answer that they formed a new impression, different from either A or B; 12 subjects speak of combining the two impressions, while 7 subjects assert that they resorted to both procedures. The following are typical responses in the first subgroup:

I couldn't combine the personalities of A and B. I formed an entirely new impression.

I can conceive of the two sets of characteristics in one person, but I cannot conceive of my impressions of them as belonging to one person.

As I have set down the impressions, one is exactly the opposite of the other. But I can fit the six characteristics to one person.

That the terms of Series A and B often suffered considerable change when they were viewed as part of one series becomes evident in the replies to another question. The subjects were asked, "Did the terms of the series A and B retain for you their first meaning or did they change?" Most subjects describe a change in one or more of the traits, of which the following are representative:

In A *impulsive* grew out of imaginativeness; now it has more the quality of hastiness.

*Industriousness* becomes more self-centered.

*Critical* is now not a derisive but rather a constructive activity.

*Stubborn* had an entirely personal meaning; now it refers to being set in one's ideas.

The tenor of most replies is well represented by the following comment:

---

[7] The procedure of "successive impressions" here employed might be extended to the study of the effect of early upon later impressions. For example, the impression resulting from the sequence (A) + (B) might be compared with the reverse sequence (B) + (A), and each of these with the sequence (A + B) or (B + A).

When the two came together, a modification occurred as well as a limiting boundary to the qualities to which each was referred.

III. STRONGLY SIMPLIFIED IMPRESSIONS

To a marked degree the impressions here examined possess a strongly unified character. At the same time they lack the nuances and discriminations that a full-fledged understanding of another person provides. Therefore they can be easily dominated by a single direction. We propose now to observe in a more direct and extreme manner the formation of a global impression.

Experiment 9

We select from the series of experiment 1 three terms, *intelligent—skillful—warm,* all referring to strong positive characteristics. These form the basis of judgment. The results appear in the first column of figures in Table 10.

TABLE 10

CHOICE OF FITTING QUALITIES: EXPERIMENT 9 (PERCENTAGES)

| | Intelligent—Skillful—Warm (N = 34) | Warm (N = 22) | Cold (N = 33) |
|---|---|---|---|
| 1. generous | 100 | 100 | 12 |
| 2. wise | 97 | 95 | 11 |
| 3. happy | 100 | 100 | 10 |
| 4. good-natured | 100 | 100 | 8 |
| 5. humorous | 100 | 100 | 12 |
| 6. sociable | 100 | 100 | 9 |
| 7. popular | 100 | 100 | 6 |
| 8. reliable | 100 | 100 | 87 |
| 9. important | 84 | 68 | 54 |
| 10. humane | 97 | 100 | 17 |
| 11. good-looking | 72 | 95 | 57 |
| 12. persistent | 100 | 78 | 97 |
| 13. serious | 100 | 68 | 97 |
| 14. restrained | 66 | 41 | 97 |
| 15. altruistic | 97 | 91 | 3 |
| 16. imaginative | 82 | 95 | 9 |
| 17. strong | 97 | 74 | 87 |
| 18. honest | 100 | 100 | 81 |

There develops a one-directed impression, far stronger than any observed in the preceding experiments. The written sketches, too, are unanimously enthusiastic. The impression also develops effortlessly.

Negative characteristics hardly intrude. That this fails to happen raises a problem. Many negative qualities could quite understandably be living together with those given. But the subjects do not as a rule complete them in this direction. This, indeed, they seem to avoid.

### Experiment 9a

The next step was to observe an impression based on a single trait. There are two groups; one group is instructed to select from the check list those characteristics which belong to a "warm" person, the second group those belonging to a "cold" person. The results appear in the last two columns of Table 10.

In order to show more clearly the range of qualities affected by the given terms, we constructed a second check list (Check List II) to which the subjects were to respond in the manner already described. The results are reported in Table 11.

A remarkably wide range of qualities is embraced in the dimension "warm-cold." It has reference to temperamental characteristics (e.g.,

## TABLE 11

CHECK LIST II: CHOICE OF FITTING QUALITIES:
EXPERIMENT 9a (PERCENTAGES)

|  | Warm (N = 22) | Cold (N = 33) |  | Warm (N = 22) | Cold (N = 33) |
|---|---|---|---|---|---|
| 1. emotional | 100 | 12 | unemotional | 0 | 88 |
| 2. practical | 40 | 73 | theoretical | 60 | 27 |
| 3. optimistic | 95 | 17 | pessimistic | 5 | 83 |
| 4. informal | 95 | 0 | formal | 5 | 100 |
| 5. cheerful | 100 | 18 | sad | 0 | 82 |
| 6. short | 91 | 8 | tall | 9 | 92 |
| 7. modest | 86 | 9 | proud | 14 | 91 |
| 8. imaginative | 95 | 28 | unimaginative | 5 | 72 |
| 9. thin | 15 | 93 | stout | 85 | 7 |
| 10. intelligent | 81 | 96 | unintelligent | 19 | 4 |
| 11. brave | 91 | 74 | cowardly | 9 | 26 |
| 12. pale | 15 | 97 | ruddy | 85 | 3 |

optimism, humor, happiness), to basic relations to the group (e.g., generosity, sociability, popularity), to strength of character (e.g., persistence, honesty). It even includes a reference to physical characteristics, evident in the virtually unanimous characterizations of the warm person as short, stout, and ruddy, and in the opposed characterizations of the cold person.

The differences between "warm" and "cold" are now even more considerable than those observed in experiment 1. No qualities remain untouched. But even under these extreme conditions the characterizations do not become indiscriminately positive or negative. "Warm" stands for very positive qualities, but it also carries the sense of a certain easy-goingness, of a lack of restraint and persistence, qualities which are eminently present in "cold." A simplified impression is not to be simply identified with a failure to make distinctions or qualifications. Rather, what we find is that in a global view the distinctions are drawn bluntly.

The consistent tendency for the distribution of choices to be less extreme in experiment 1 requires the revision of an earlier formulation. We have said that central qualities determine the content and functional value of peripheral qualities. It can now be seen that the central characteristics, while imposing their direction upon the total impression, were themselves affected by the surrounding characteristics.

Upon the conclusion of the experiments, the subjects were asked to state the reason for their choice of one predominant direction in their characterizations. All agreed that they felt such a tendency. Some cannot explain it, saying, in the words of one subject: "I do not know the reason; only that this is the way it 'hit' me at the moment"; or: "I did not consciously mean to choose the positive traits." Most subjects, however, are explicit in stating that the given traits seemed to require completion in one direction. The following statements are representative:

These qualities initiate other qualities. A man who is warm would be friendly, consequently happy. If he is intelligent, he would be honest.

The given characteristics, though very general, were good characteristics. Therefore other good characteristics seemed to belong. When, for example, I think of a person as warm, I mean that he couldn't be ugly.

This was the tenor of most statements. A few show factors at work of a somewhat different kind, of interest to the student of personality, as:

I naturally picked the best trait because I *hoped* the person would be that way.

I went in the positive direction because *I* would like to be all those things.

It is of interest for the theory of our problem that there are terms which simultaneously contain implications for wide regions of the person. Many terms denoting personal characteristics show the same property. They do not observe a strict division of labor, each pointing neatly to one specific characteristic; rather, each sweeps over a wide area and affects it in a definite manner.[8]

Some would say that this is a semantic problem. To do so would be, however, to beg the question by disposing of the psychological process that gives rise to the semantic problem. What requires explanation is how a term, and a highly "subjective" one at that, refers so consistently to so wide a region of personal qualities. It seems similarly unfruitful to call these judgments stereotypes. The meaning of stereotype is itself badly in need of psychological clarification. Indeed, in the light of our observations, a stereotype appears (in a first approximation) to be a central quality belonging to an extremely simplified impression.

We propose that there is, under the given conditions, a tendency to grasp the characteristics in their most outspoken, most unqualified sense, and on that basis to complete the impression. The subject aims at a clear view; he therefore takes the given terms in their most complete sense. (What is said here with regard to the present experiment seems to apply also to the preceding experiments. In each case the subject's impression is a blunt, definite characterization. It lacks depth but not definiteness. Even when the view is of a mediocre character, it is outspokenly so.) The comments of the subjects are in agreement with the present interpretation.

---

[8] On the basis of the last findings an objection might be advanced against our earlier account of the distinction between central and peripheral traits. If, as has just been shown, "warm" refers to such a wide range of qualities, then the force of the demonstration (see experiment 1) that it exerts a great effect on the final impression seems to be endangered. Is it to be wondered at that this quality, which is single only in a linguistic sense, but psychologically plural, should be so effective? And should not the distinction be drawn rather between qualities which contain many other qualities and qualities—such as "politeness"—that are much more specific in range?

The objection presupposes that a quantitatively larger number of qualities will exert a greater effect than a smaller number. But this assumption is precisely what needs to be explained. Why does not the more inclusive term provide a greater number of occasions for being affected by other terms? What the assertion fails to face is that there is a particular direction of forces.

IV. SIMILARITY AND DIFFERENCE OF IMPRESSIONS

The preceding discussion has definite consequences for the perception of identity and difference between the characteristics of different persons. Of these the most significant for theory is the proposition that a given trait in two different persons may not be the same trait, and contrariwise, that two different traits may be functionally identical in two different persons. We turn now to an investigation of some conditions which determine similarity and difference between personal qualities.

Experiment 10

I. The group has before it Sets 1, 2, 3, and 4 with instructions to state (1) which of the other three sets most resembles Set 1, and (2) which most resembles Set 2.

| Set 1 | Set 2 | Set 3 | Set 4 |
|-------|-------|-------|-------|
| quick | quick | slow | slow |
| skillful | clumsy | skillful | clumsy |
| helpful | helpful | helpful | helpful |

One quality—"helpful"—remains constant in all sets. The other two qualities appear in their positive form in Set 1, and are changed to their opposites singly and together in the three other sets.

A remarkable uniformity appears in the findings, reported in Table 12.

TABLE 12

RESEMBLANCE OF SETS: EXPERIMENT 10

| Set | Set 1 Resembles | | Set 2 Resembles | |
|-----|-----|-----|-----|-----|
| | N | Percentage | N | Percentage |
| 1 | 0 | 0 | 7 | 9 |
| 2 | 10 | 13 | 0 | 0 |
| 3 | 68 | 87 | 5 | 6 |
| 4 | 0 | 0 | 66 | 85 |
| | 78 | 100 | 78 | 100 |

Set 1 is equated with Set 3 in 87 per cent of the cases, while its similarity to Set 2 is reported in only 13 per cent of the cases. Similarly, Set 2 is asserted to resemble Set 4 in 85 per cent of the cases, while the resemblance to Set 1 drops to 9 per cent.

The choice of similar sets cannot in this case be determined merely on the basis of the number of "identical elements," for on this criterion Sets 2 and 3 are equally similar to 1, while Sets 1 and 4 are equally similar to 2. What factors may be said to determine the decisions with regard to similarity and difference?

We come somewhat closer to an answer in the replies to the following question: "Which characteristics in the other sets resemble most closely (a) 'quick' of Set 1? (b) 'quick' of Set 2? (c) 'helpful' of Set 1? (d) 'helpful' of Set 2?" The results appear in Table 13.

## TABLE 13

### RESEMBLANCE OF QUALITIES: EXPERIMENT 10

| "Quick" of Set 1 Resembles | N | Percentage | "Quick" of Set 2 Resembles | N | Percentage |
|---|---|---|---|---|---|
| "quick" of set 2 | 11 | 22 | "quick" of set 1 | 10 | 24 |
| "helpful" of set 2 | 1 | 2 | "slow" of set 4 | 21 | 51 |
| "slow" of set 3 | 16 | 32 | "clumsy" of set 4 | 7 | 17 |
| "skillful" of set 3 | 21 | 42 | "slow" of set 3 | 2 | 5 |
| "helpful" of set 3 | 1 | 2 | "helpful" of set 3 | 1 | 3 |
| | 50 | 100 | | 41 | 100 |

| "Helpful" of Set 1 Resembles | N | Percentage | "Helpful" of Set 2 Resembles | N | Percentage |
|---|---|---|---|---|---|
| "helpful" of set 2 | 7 | 15 | "helpful" of set 1 | 5 | 11 |
| "helpful" of set 4 | 2 | 4 | "quick" of set 1 | 2 | 4 |
| "helpful" of set 3 | 33 | 68 | "slow" of set 4 | 2 | 4 |
| "skillful" of set 3 | 6 | 13 | "helpful" of set 4 | 30 | 65 |
| | | | "clumsy" of set 4 | 4 | 9 |
| | | | "slow" of set 3 | 3 | 7 |
| | 48 | 100 | | 46 | 100 |

We see that qualities which, abstractly taken, are identical, are infrequently equated, while qualities which are abstractly opposed are equated with greater frequency. For example, the quality "quick" of Sets 1 and 2 is matched in only 22 and 24 per cent of the cases, respectively, while "quick" of Set 1 is, in 32 per cent of the cases, matched with "slow" of Set 3, and "quick" of Set 2 with "slow" of Set 4 in 51 per cent of the cases.[9]

At this point the reports of the subjects become very helpful. They were requested at the conclusion to state in writing whether the quality "quick" in Sets 1 and 2 was identical or different, together with their reasons, and similarly to compare the quality "slow" in Sets 3 and 4. The written accounts permit of certain conclusions, which are stated below.

*The content of the quality changes with a change in its environment.* The protocols below, which are typical, will show that the "quicks" of Sets 1 and 2 are phenomenally different, and similarly for the "slows" of Sets 3 and 4.

The quickness of 1 is one of assurance, of smoothness of movement; that of 2 is a forced quickness, in an effort to be helpful.

1 is fast in a smooth, easy-flowing way; the other (2) is quick in a bustling way—the kind that rushes up immediately at your request and tips over the lamps.

3 takes his time in a deliberate way; 4 would like to work quickly, but cannot—there is something painful in his slowness.

3 is slow in a methodical, sure way, aiming toward perfection; in 4 it implies a certain heaviness, torpor.

*The dynamic sources of the quality are relationally determined.* In the protocols we observe a process of mutual determination between traits. They are grasped as not simply contiguous to one another but in dynamic relation, in which one is determined by, or springs from, the other.

1 is quick because he is skillful; 2 is clumsy because he is so fast.

Great skill gave rise to the speed of 1, whereas 2 is clumsy because he does everything so quickly.

---

[9] In a forthcoming publication the writer will deal with theoretically similar issues in the context of a problem in social psychology. This will be the report of an investigation of changes in the content of identical social assertions when they function as part of different frames of reference. [S. E. Asch, *Social psychology*. New York: Prentice-Hall, 1952. Chap. 15.—Ed.]

The quality slow is, in person 3, something deliberately cultivated, in order to attain a higher order of skill.

In 3 slowness indicates care, pride in work well done. Slowness in 4 indicates sluggishness, poor motor coördination, some physical retardation.

Speed and skill are not connected as are speed and clumsiness. Without exception, "quick" is perceived to spring from skill (skillful → quick); but the vector in Set 2 is reversed, "clumsy" becoming a consequence of speed (clumsy ← quick). While Sets 1 and 3 are identical with regard to the vectors, Set 2 is not equivalent to 4, the slowness and clumsiness of 4 being sensed as part of a single process, such as sluggishness and general retardation (slow ⇆ clumsy).

*Dynamic consequences are grasped in the interaction of qualities.* "Quick" and "skillful" (as well as "slow" and "skillful") are felt as coöperating, whereas "quick" and "clumsy" cancel one another.

2 drops everything fast. He is fast but accomplishes nothing. The clumsy man might be better off if he were slow.

The second person is futile; he is quick to come to your aid and also quick to get in your way and under your hair.

1 can afford to be quick; 2 would be far better off if he took things more slowly.[10]

In the light of these comments, which are representative, we are able to formulate the prevailing direction of the relations within the sets.

In Sets 1 and 3 the prevailing structure may be represented as:

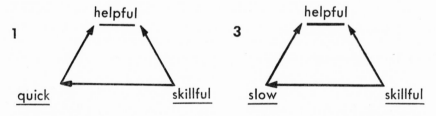

"Quick-slow" derive their concrete character from the quality "skillful"; these in turn stand in a relation of harmony to "helpful," in the sense that they form a proper basis for it and make it possible.

---

10 Parallel experiments in which the last term of the sets was changed to "not helpful" gave results essentially identical with the above.

In Sets 2 and 4 the characteristic structures are as follows:

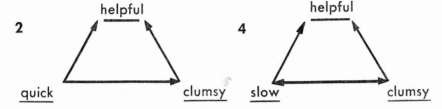

But now these stand in a relation of inherent contradiction to the quality "helpful," the fulfillment of which they negate.

Our results contain a proportion of cases (see Tables 12 and 13) that are contrary to the described general trend. These do equate the characteristic of 1 and 2 and of 3 and 4. They require explanation. It is especially important to decide whether the disagreements are capricious or whether they have an understandable basis. As a rule we find in these cases that the given quality is viewed in a narrower, more limited way. For example, these subjects view "quick" of Sets 1 and 2 in terms of sheer tempo, deliberately excluding for the moment considerations of fitness. The following protocols are illustrative:

These persons' reactions to stimuli are both quick, even though the results of their actions are in opposite directions.

They are both quick, but they differ in the success of their actions.

The two terms are basically the same, for both would execute their tasks with their individual maximum speed.

II. The reader will readily think of other sets of characteristics involving similar processes. In view of the fact that such analyses have not been previously reported, we select for brief description a few additional examples.

The task was to state whether the term "aggressive" was alike or different in Sets 1 and 2, and 3 and 4, respectively. This example will be of particular interest to psychologists, in view of current discussions of aggressiveness.

| Set 1 | Set 2 | Set 3 | Set 4 |
|-------|-------|-------|-------|
| active | lazy | weak | strong |
| helpful | unhelpful | sensitive | self-centered |
| *aggressive* | *aggressive* | *aggressive* | *aggressive* |

Nineteen out of 20 subjects judge the term to be different in Sets 1 and 2; 17 out of 20 judge it to be different in Sets 3 and 4. Some representative reports follow:

The aggressiveness of 1 is friendly, open, and forceful; 2 will be aggressive when something offends him.

The aggressiveness of 1 is an expression of confidence in his abilities, of his strength of will and mind; in 2 it is a defensive measure to cover sensitivity.

3 will be aggressive to try to hide his weakness. The aggressiveness of 4 is a natural result of his strength and self-centeredness.

4 is aggressive because he has needs to be satisfied and wishes nothing to stand in his way; 3 has the aggressiveness of self-pity and indecision.

In nearly all cases the sources of aggression and its objects are sensed to be different. In consequence, the form it takes and its very psychological content become different in the series compared.

Substantially the same results are observed in another group in the comparison of "unaggressive" in Sets 1 and 2 below.

| Set 1 | Set 2 |
|-------|-------|
| active | weak |
| helpful | sensitive |
| *unaggressive* | *unaggressive* |

Twenty-eight out of 30 subjects call "unaggressive" different in the two series. Some of their reasons follow:

Unaggressive in 1 might mean that he does not push or force his way into things. In the second case it may mean meekness or fear of people.

1 does not care to be aggressive; 2 lacks the stamina for it.

2 does not fight back at the world nor try to rise above his weaknesses.

The word "aggressive" must have the same connotations in both cases; otherwise why not use different terms to express different things?

III. The second and third terms in Sets 1 and 2 below were compared, respectively.

| Set 1 | Set 2 |
|---|---|
| intelligent | impulsive |
| *critical* | *critical* |
| *stubborn* | *stubborn* |

All subjects in a group of 31 judged the term "critical" to be different in the two sets; while 19 (or 61 per cent) judged "stubborn" as different. A few of the remarks follow:

*Critical:*
1 is critical because he is intelligent; 2 because he is impulsive.

The intelligent individual is critical in a constructive manner; the impulsive one probably hurls criticism unthinkingly.

The intelligent person may be critical in a completely impersonal way; 2 may be critical of people, their actions, their dress, etc.

*Stubborn:*
The stubbornness of an intelligent person is more likely to be based on reason and it can be affected by reasoning.

The intelligent person might be stubborn about important things, things that mean something to him, that he knows something about; whereas an impulsive person might be stubborn just to be contrary.

An intelligent person may be stubborn because he has a reason for it and thinks it's the best thing to do, while an impulsive person may be stubborn because at the moment he *feels* like it.

Some representative statements defending the identity of "stubborn" in the two series follow:

Stubbornness to me is the same in any language. Of course, an intelligent person may have a better reason for being stubborn than an impulsive one, but that does not necessarily change the degree of stubbornness.

Both refuse to admit to anything that does not coincide with their opinion.

In my opinion there is only one kind of stubbornness—an unswerving desire either to do or not to do a certain thing.

IV. In the following series the second and third terms were to be compared:

|     | Set 1 | Set 2 |
| --- | --- | --- |
|     | warm | cold |
|     | *witty* | *witty* |
|     | *persuasive* | *persuasive* |

Twenty-seven of 30 subjects judged "persuasive" as different; all judged "witty" to be different. A few of the comments follow:

*Witty:*
1 laughs with the audience; 2 is either laughing at or trying to make others laugh at some one. 2 is satirical, not humorous.

1 has a jolly and happy-go-lucky wit. 2 will use wit as one uses a bow and arrow—with precision. He will have a target which will not be missed.

The wit of the warm person touches the heart. The cold person's wit is touched with irony.

*Persuasive:*
1 is persuasive in trying to help others; 2 in trying to help himself.

2 may persuade through fear.

2 would be detached in his arguments; 1 would appeal more to the inner emotional being of others.

V.  The term "gay" was compared in the following series:

|     | Set 1 | Set 2 |
| --- | --- | --- |
|     | *gay* | *gay* |
|     | intelligent | stupid |
|     | industrious | lazy |

Twenty-seven of 30 subjects call "gay" different. Some representative reasons follow:

They may both be equally gay, but the former is different. The stupid person can be gay over serious, sad matters, while the intelligent person is gay with reason.

The first person's gaiety comes from fullness of life; 2 is gay because he knows no better.

1 knows when to be gay and when not to be.

The gaiety of 1 is active and energetic; the gaiety of 2 is passive.

The intelligent person is gay in an intelligent way.

They are the same—gaiety has no relation to intelligence and industriousness.

The foregoing observations describe a process of relational determination of character qualities. A given quality derives its full concrete content from its place within the system formed by the relations of the qualities. Some qualities are seen as a dynamic outgrowth of determining qualities. Qualities are seen to stand in a relation of harmony or contradiction to others within the system. These processes set requirements for the comparison of impressions. Identical qualities in different structures may cease to be identical: the vectors out of which they grow may alter, with the consequence that their very content undergoes radical change. In the extreme case, the same quality in two persons will have different, even opposed, meanings, while two opposed qualities will have the same function within their respective structures.

DISCUSSION

The investigations here reported have their starting point in one problem and converge on one basic conclusion. In different ways the observations have demonstrated that forming an impression is an organized process; that characteristics are perceived in their dynamic relations; that central qualities are discovered, leading to the distinction between them and peripheral qualities; that relations of harmony and contradiction are observed. To know a person is to have a grasp of a particular structure.

Before proceeding it may be helpful to note two preliminary points. First: For the sake of convenience of expression we speak in this discussion of forming an impression of a person, though our observations are restricted entirely to impressions based on descriptive materials. We do not intend to imply that observations of actual persons would not involve other processes which we have failed to find under the present conditions; we are certain that they would (see pp. 282 ff.). But we see no reason to doubt that the basic features we were able to observe are also present in the judgment of actual persons. Secondly: We have not dealt in this investigation with the role of individual differences, of which the most obvious would be the effect of the subject's own personal qualities on the nature of his impression. Though the issue of individual differences is unquestionably important, it seemed desirable to turn first to those processes which hold generally, despite individual differences. A proper study of individual differences can best be pursued when a minimum theoretical clarification has been reached.

Let us briefly reformulate the main points in the procedure of our subjects:

1. There is an attempt to form an impression of the *entire* person. The subject can see the person only as a unit; [11] he cannot form an impression of one-half or of one-quarter of the person. This is the case even when the factual basis is meager; the impression then strives to become complete, reaching out toward other compatible qualities. The subject seeks to reach the core of the person *through* the trait or traits.

2. As soon as two or more traits are understood to belong to one person, they cease to exist as isolated traits, and come into immediate dynamic interaction.[12] The subject perceives not this *and* that quality, but the two entering into a particular relation. There takes place a process of organization in the course of which the traits order themselves into a structure. It may be said that the traits lead an intensely social life, striving to join each other in a closely organized system. The representation in us of the character of another person possesses in a striking sense certain of the qualities of a system.

3. In the course of this process some characteristics are discovered to be central. The whole system of relations determines which will become central. These set the direction for the further view of the person and for the concretization of the dependent traits. As a rule the several traits do not have equal weight. And it is not until we have found the center that we experience the assurance of having come near to an understanding of the person.

4. The single trait possesses the property of a part in a whole. A change in a single trait may alter not that aspect alone, but many others —at times all. As soon as we isolate a trait we not only lose the distinctive organization of the person; the trait itself becomes abstract.

---

[11] To be sure, we do often react to people in a more narrow manner, as when we have dealings with the ticket collector or bank teller. It cannot, however, be said that in such instances we are primarily oriented to the other as a person. The moment our special attitude would give way to a genuine interest in the other, the point stated above would fully apply.

[12] We cannot say on the basis of our observations whether exceptions to this statement occur, e.g., whether some traits may be seen as accidental, having no relation to the rest of the person. It seems more likely that even insignificant traits are seen as part of the person.

The trait develops its full content and weight only when it finds its place within the whole impression.

5. Each trait is a trait of the entire person. It refers to a characteristic form of action or attitude which belongs to the person as a whole. In this sense we may speak of traits as possessing the properties of Ehrenfels qualities. Traits are not to be considered as referring to different regions of the personality, on the analogy of geographical regions which border on another.

6. Each trait functions as a *representative* of the person. We do not experience anonymous traits, the particular organization of which constitutes the identity of the person. Rather the entire person speaks through each of his qualities, though not with the same clearness.

7. In the process of mutual interaction the concrete character of each trait is developed in accordance with the dynamic requirements set for it by its environment. There is involved an understanding of necessary consequences following from certain given characteristics for others. The envy of a proud man is, for example, seen to have a different basis from the envy of a modest man.

8. On this basis consistencies and contradictions are discovered. Certain qualities are seen to coöperate; others to negate each other. But we are not content simply to note inconsistencies or to let them sit where they are. The contradiction is puzzling, and prompts us to look more deeply. Disturbing factors arouse a trend to maintain the unity of the impression, to search for the most sensible way in which the characteristics could exist together,[13] or to decide that we have not found the key to the person. We feel that proper understanding would eliminate, not the presence of inner tensions and inconsistencies, but of sheer contradiction. (It may be relevant to point out that the very sense of one trait being in contradiction to others would not arise if we were not oriented to the entire person. Without the assumption of a unitary person there would be just different traits.)

9. It follows that the content and functional value of a trait change with the given context. This statement expresses for our problem a principle formulated in Gestalt theory with regard to the identity of parts in different structures (8, 10). A trait central in one person may be seen as secondary in another. Or a quality which is now referred to

---

[13] Indeed, the perception of such contradiction, or of the failure of a trait to fit to the others, may be of fundamental importance for gaining a proper view. It may point to a critical region in the person, in which things are not as they should be.

the person may in another case be referred to outer conditions. (In the extreme case a quality may be neglected, because it does not touch what is important in the person.)

We conclude that the formation and change of impressions consist of specific processes of organization. Further, it seems probable that these processes are not specific to impressions of persons alone. It is a task for future investigation to determine whether processes of this order are at work in other important regions of psychology, such as in forming the view of a group, or of the relations between one person and another.

It may be of interest to relate the assumptions underlying the naïve procedure of our subjects to certain customary formulations. (1) It should now be clear that the subjects express certain definite assumptions concerning the structure of a personality. The gaining of an impression is for them not a process of fixing each trait in isolation and noting its meaning. If they proceeded in this way the traits would remain abstract, lacking just the content and function which make them living traits. In effect our subjects are in glaring disagreement with the elementaristic thesis which assumes independent traits (or traits connected only in a statistical sense) of constant content. (2) At the same time the procedure of our subjects departs from another customary formulation. It is equally far from the observed facts to describe the process as the forming of a homogeneous, undifferentiated "general impression." The unity perceived by the observer contains groupings the parts of which are in more intimate connection with each other than they are with parts of other groupings.[14] Discrimination of different aspects of the person and distinctions of a functional order are essential parts of the process. We may even distinguish different degrees of unity in persons. Increasing clearness in understanding another depends on the increased articulation of these distinctions. But in the process these continue to have the properties of parts in a single structure.

If we may for the purpose of discussion assume that the naïve procedure is based on a sound conception of the structure of personality, it would by no means follow that it is therefore free from misconceptions and distortions. But in that case the nature of errors in judgment

---

[14] If we may assume that the situation in the observed person corresponds to this view, an important conclusion follows for method, namely, that we can study characteristics of persons without an exhaustive knowledge of the entire person.

would have to be understood in a particular way. It would be necessary
to derive the errors from characteristics of the organizational processes
in judgment. The present investigation is not without some hints for
this problem. It points to the danger of forcing the subject to judge
artificially isolated traits—a procedure almost universally followed in
rating studies—and to the necessity of providing optimal conditions for
judging the place and weight of a characteristic within the person (unless of course the judgment of isolated traits is required by the particular problem). Under such conditions we might discover an improvement in the quality of judgment and in agreement between judges. At
the same time this investigation contains some suggestions for the study
of errors in factors such as oversimplification leading to "too good" an
impression, viewing a trait outside its context or in an inappropriate
context.

Returning to the main theoretical conceptions described earlier (see
pp. 238–240) it is necessary to mention a variant of Proposition I,
which we have failed so far to consider and in relation to which we
will be able to state more precisely a central feature of Proposition II.
It would be a possible hypothesis that in the course of forming an impression each trait interacts with one or more of the others, and that
the total impression is the summation of these effects. The impression
would accordingly be derived from the separate interaction of the components, which might be represented as follows:

$$I b. \text{ Impression} = \begin{array}{c} a \rightleftarrows b \\ a \rightleftarrows c \\ a \rightleftarrows d \\ a \rightleftarrows e \\ b \rightleftarrows c \\ \text{etc.} \end{array} \quad \text{or} \quad a + b + c + d + e$$

It is important to note that this formulation is in a fundamental regard different from Proposition II. The latter proposition asserts that
each trait is seen to stand in a particular relation to the others as part
of a complete view. The entire view possesses the formal properties of
a structure, the form of which cannot be derived from the summation
of the individual relations.[15] In the same manner that the content of

---

[15] For a basic treatment of the concept of structure the reader is referred to
M. Wertheimer (10).

each of a pair of traits can be determined fully only by reference to their mutual relation, so the content of each relation can be determined fully only with reference to the structure of relations of which it is a part. This we may illustrate with the example of a geometrical figure such as a pyramid, each part of which (e.g., the vertex) implicitly refers to the entire figure. We would propose that this is the basis for the discovery of central and peripheral traits and for assertions such as that a given person is "integrated," "restricted," etc.

On the other hand, the notion of structure is denied in all propositions of the form I, including I*b*. In the latter, an assumption is made concerning the interaction of qualities, which has the effect of altering the character of the *elements*. Once we have taken account of this change, we have in the final formulation again a sum of (now changed) elements:

I*b*.  Impression $= \bar{a} + \bar{b} + \bar{c} + \bar{d} + \bar{e}$

In still another regard there is a difference between Propositions II and I*b*. This has to do with the nature of the interaction between the traits. In terms of Proposition II the character of interaction is determined by the particular qualities that enter into the relation (e.g., "warm-witty" or "cold-witty"). It is doubtful, however, whether a theory which refuses to admit relational processes in the formation of a whole impression would admit the same relational processes in the interaction of one trait with another.

In view of the fact that Proposition I*b* has not, as far as we know, been explicitly formulated with reference to the present problem, it becomes necessary to do so here, and especially to state the process of interaction in such a manner as to be consistent with it. This we might do best by applying certain current conceptions. We could speak of traits as "conditioned verbal reactions," each of which possesses a particular "strength" and range of generalization. Interaction between traits would accordingly be assimilated to the schema of differential conditioning to single stimuli and to stimuli in combination, perhaps after the manner of the recent treatment of "stimulus configurations" by Hull (4, 5).[16]

---

[16] Proceeding in the same manner, it would be possible to restate some of our observations in terms such as the following: (1) the distinction between central and peripheral traits would be referred to a difference between conditioned reactions of greater and lesser strengths; (2) the change from a central to a peripheral trait could be explained by the displacement of a response by other, stronger responses; (3) the factor of direction might be dealt with in terms of changes in the temporal appearance of stimuli; (4) strongly unified impressions could be

How consistent would this interpretation be with the observations we have reported? It seems to us that there are grave difficulties in the way of such an interpretation. Insofar as the terms of conditioning are at all intelligible with reference to our problem, the process of interaction can be understood only as a quantitative increase or diminution in a response. This is not, however, the essential characteristic of interaction as we have observed it, which consists in a change of content and function. The gaiety of an intelligent man is not more or less than the gaiety of a stupid man; it is different in quality. Further, the conditioning account seems to contain no principle that would make clear the particular direction interaction takes.

Here we may mention a more general point. We have referred earlier to the comparative ease with which complex situations in another person are perceived. If traits were perceived separately, we would expect to encounter the same difficulties in forming a view of a person that we meet in learning a list of unrelated words. That we are able to encompass the entire person in one sweep seems to be due to the structured character of the impression.[17] In terms of an interaction theory of component elements, the difficulty in surveying a person should be even greater than in the formulation of Proposition I, since the former must deal with the elements of the latter plus a large number of added factors.

In order to retain a necessary distinction between the process of forming an impression and the actual organization of traits in a person, we have spoken as if nothing were known of the latter. While we cannot deal with the latter problem, one investigation is of particular relevance to the present discussion. We refer to the famous investigation of Hartshorne and May (3), who studied in a variety of situations the tendencies in groups of children to act honestly in such widely varied matters as copying, returning of money, correcting one's schoolwork, etc. The relations between the actions of children in the different situations were studied by means of statistical correlations. These were generally low. On the basis of these results the important conclusion was drawn that qualities such as honesty are not consistent characteristics

an expression of highly generalized reactions; etc. Such formulations would, however, fail to deal adequately with the central feature of our findings, namely, changes in the quality of traits and the organized form of the impression.

[17] It should not, however, be concluded that our views of persons are crystal clear. In fact, they lack the precision with which we grasp a mathematical theorem. We rarely feel that we have exhausted our understanding of another person. This has partly to do with the fact that the person is in constant change.

of the child but specific habits acquired in particular situations, that "neither deceit, nor its opposite, honesty, are unified character traits, but rather specific functions of life situations." Having accepted this conclusion, equally fundamental consequences were drawn for character education of children.

Abstracting from the many things that might be said about this work, we point out only that its conclusion is not proven because of the failure to consider the structural character of personality traits. As G. W. Allport (1, pp. 250 ff.) has pointed out, we may not assume that a particular act, say the clandestine change by a pupil of an answer on a school test, has the same psychological meaning in all cases.[18] Once this point is realized, its consequences for the thesis of Hartshorne and May become quite threatening. Let us consider a few of the possibilities in the situation, which would be classified as follows by Hartshorne and May:

*Honest:*
1. The child wants to alter his answer on a test but fears he will be caught.
2. He does not change because he is indifferent to the grade.

*Dishonest:*
1. The child changes his answer because he is devoted to his teacher and anxious not to lose her regard.
2. He cannot restrain the impulse to change the wrong answer into the answer he now knows to be correct.

Psychologically, none of these acts are correctly classified. Further, two of these are classified in precisely the wrong way. The child who wishes to cheat but is afraid does not belong in the honest category, while the child who cannot bear to leave the wrong answer uncorrected does not necessarily deserve to be called dishonest. We do not intend to say that the psychological significance of the reactions was as a rule misinterpreted; for the sake of illustration we have chosen admittedly extreme examples. But the failure to consider the psychological content introduces a serious doubt concerning the conclusions reached by Hartshorne and May.

A far richer field for the observation of the processes here considered would be the impressions formed of actual people. Concrete experience with persons possesses a substantial quality and produces a host of ef-

---

[18] See also discussion by D. W. MacKinnon (7, pp. 26 ff.).

fects which have no room for growth in the ephemeral impressions of this investigation. The fact that we are ourselves changed by living people, that we observe them in movement and growth, introduces factors and forces of a new order. In comparison with these, momentary impressions based on descriptions, or even the full view of the person at a given moment, are only partial aspects of a broader process.

In such investigation some of the problems we have considered would reappear and might gain a larger application. Other problems, which were of necessity excluded from the present investigation, could be clarified in such an approach. We mention one which is of particular importance. It was a constant feature of our procedure to provide the subject with the traits of a person; but in actual observation the discovery of the traits in a person is a vital part of the process of establishing an impression. Since observation gives us only concrete acts and qualities, the application of a trait to a person becomes itself a problem. Is characterization by a trait, for example, a statistical generalization from a number of instances? Or is it the consequence of discovering a quality within the setting of the entire impression, which may therefore be reached in a single instance? In the latter case, repeated observation would provide not simply additional instances for a statistical conclusion, but rather a check on the genuineness of the earlier observation, as well as a clarification of its limiting conditions. Proceeding in this manner, it should be possible to decide whether the discovery of a trait itself involves processes of a structural nature. Only direct investigation based on the observation of persons can furnish answers to these questions.

In still another regard did our investigation limit the range of observation. In the views formed of living persons past experience plays a great role. The impression itself has a history and continuity as it extends over considerable periods of time, while factors of motivation become important in determining its stability and resistance to change.

Even within the limits of the present study factors of past experience were highly important. When the subject formed a view on the basis of the given description, he as a rule referred to a contemporary, at no time to characters that may have lived in the past; he located the person in this country, never in other countries. Further, experiments we have not here reported showed unmistakably that an identical series of traits produced distinct impressions depending on whether we identified the person as a man or woman, as a child or adult. Distinctions of this order clearly depend on a definite kind of knowledge obtained in the past. Indeed, the very possibility of grasping the meaning of a trait presupposes that it had been observed and understood.

That experience enters in these instances as a necessary factor seems clear, but the statement would be misleading if we did not add that the possibility of such experience itself presupposes a capacity to observe and realize the qualities and dynamic relations here described. The assertion that the properties of the impression depend on past experience can only mean that these were once directly perceived. In this connection we may refer to certain observations of Köhler (6, pp. 234 ff.) concerning our understanding of feelings in others which we have not observed in ourselves, or in the absence of relevant previous experiences. In his comprehensive discussion of the question, G. W. Allport (1, pp. 533 ff.) has equally stressed the importance of direct perception of a given structure in others, of our capacity for perceiving in others dynamic tendencies.

Nor do we consider it adequate to assert that in the present investigation our subjects were merely reproducing past observations of qualities and of the ways in which they modify each other. When the subject selected a certain trait as central (or when he deposed a once central trait to a minor role within a new context) it is by no means clear that he was guided by specific, acquired rules prescribing which traits will be central in each of a great number of constellations. It seems more in accordance with the evidence to suppose that the system of the traits itself points to a necessary center. And as we have mentioned earlier, the interaction between two traits already presupposes that we have discovered—whether in the past or in the present—the forces that work between them. Given the quality "quick" we cannot unequivocally infer the quality "skillful"; [19] but given "quick-skillful" we try to see how one grows out of the other. We then discover a certain constancy in the relation between them, which is not that of a constant habitual connection.

While an appeal to past experience cannot supplant the direct grasping of qualities and processes, the role of past experience is undoubtedly great where impressions of actual people extending over a long period are concerned. Here the important question for theory is whether the factors of past experience involve dynamic processes of the same order that we find at work in the momentary impression, or whether

---

[19] That it is at times difficult to infer qualities on the basis of central traits is due to such factors as the lability of the person, the degree to which the actions of a person are directed by a single center, as well as situational forces.

these are predominantly of the nature of associative bonds. It seems to us a useful hypothesis that when we relate a person's past to his present we are again relying essentially on the comprehension of dynamic processes.

REFERENCES

1. Allport, G. W. *Personality: a psychological interpretation.* New York: Holt, 1937.
2. Asch, S. E. Studies in the principles of judgments and attitudes: II. Determination of judgments by group and by ego standards. *J. soc. Psychol.,* 1940, 12, 433–465.
3. Hartshorne, H., and May, M. A. *Studies in deceit.* New York: Macmillan, 1928; Hartshorne, H., May, M. A., and Maller, J. B. *Studies in service and self-control.* New York: Macmillan, 1929; Hartshorne, H., May, M. A., and Shuttleworth, F. K. *Studies in the organization of character.* New York: Macmillan, 1930. The three constitute *Studies in the nature of character* by the Character Education Inquiry, Teachers College, Columbia University, in coöperation with the Institute of Social and Religious Research.
4. Hull, C. L. *Principles of behavior.* New York: Appleton-Century, 1943.
5. Hull, C. L. The discrimination of stimulus configurations and the hypothesis of afferent neural interaction. *Psychol. Rev.,* 1945, 52, 133–142.
6. Köhler, W. *Gestalt psychology.* New York: Liveright, 1929.
7. MacKinnon, D. W. The structure of personality. In J. McV. Hunt (Ed.), *Personality and the behavior disorders,* Vol. I. New York: Ronald Press, 1944.
8. Ternus, J. Experimentelle Untersuchungen über phänomenale Identität. *Psych. Forsch.,* 1926, 7, 81–136.
9. Thorndike, E. L. A constant error in psychological rating. *J. appl. Psychol.,* 1920, 4, 25–29.
10. Wertheimer, M. *Productive thinking.* New York: Harper, 1945.

# Mary Henle

GRADUATE FACULTY, NEW SCHOOL FOR SOCIAL RESEARCH

# ON FIELD FORCES

## INTRODUCTION

Although a number of authors have called attention to field forces, the concept has found no place in motivational theory. It is the purpose of the present paper to describe a method of demonstrating field forces and to indicate their importance for a psychology of motivation.

The term "field forces" is here used to refer to motivational forces arising from parts of the psychological field other than the individual. Since the concept has not found general acceptance, I shall start with a brief discussion of it and with examples of the operation of field forces.

Köhler (10) has pointed to the necessity for distinguishing between the locus and the reference of experiences. While all experiences presuppose physiological processes in the *organism,* they need not all refer to the *self;* their reference may be to the perceived environment. As Asch remarks in a discussion of this distinction (2, p. 292): "All experiences are, to be sure, mine, but only a small fraction of them refer to me; I am right to locate my toothache in my body and to locate my country outside it."

Wertheimer (12) and Asch have applied this same distinction to problems of motivation. Motives, like other psychological processes, presuppose physiological events in the individual's nervous system;

Reprinted with permission from the *Journal of Psychology,* Vol. 43, Second half, April, 1957. Copyright by The Journal Press.

their locus is thus the organism. But they *may* refer to parts of the psychological field other than the ego; forces may arise from the experienced requirements of a situation, of persons and events outside the self. For the sake of convenience, the latter forces will be designated field forces, while the term ego forces will be applied to those motivational forces arising in the person.[1]

Field forces seem to be important in the initiation of behavior whenever we feel that there are situations which call for action, as contrasted with those in which *we* need to act. For example, the response to the request from a stranger, "Got a match, bud?" is one in which the person acts to meet the requirements of a perceived situation rather than those of an existing ego need. Or we right an object which is about to fall. Again, we say that a person or a scene compels our attention, that a man needs help, that an activity attracts us. We think of a person as caught in the web of circumstances.

In all these cases the forces that initiate action seem to arise mainly from the perceived circumstances. It must be understood, however, that where field forces are operating (as also, of course, in the case of ego forces) both personal and environmental conditions are involved in the determination of behavior. Where forces arise from the demands of a situation, these demands must be perceived by the individual, and his resources must be brought into play in their service. A situation may cry out for action, but if this cry falls on deaf ears, or on the sensitive ears of a person incapable of acting, there will be no action (cf. 7). Illustrations of the ways in which demands of the field must be related to those of the self to be effective will be given below.

Thus the operation of field forces, as of ego forces, presupposes not only a role of the experienced situation in the determination of behavior, but also a role of the person (forces from the ego as well as the non-ego in the person, as also his abilities, attitudes, and resources). But the important point is that the role of each is different in the two cases. This difference is of considerable interest for theory. Where ego forces

---

[1] Actually both terms are misnomers. The ego is, of course, part of the psychological field. Thus the name "field forces" is an abbreviation for the expression "forces arising in the psychological field exclusive of those arising in the person." Again, it cannot be assumed that all motivational forces arising in the person are ego forces in any precise sense; much of our motivation stems from parts of the person which are not ego. Since, however, even these forces require the coöperation of the ego for their expression, and since their reference is to the person, the term "ego forces" will be extended to include them. Perhaps more accurate terms would be "field-referent forces" and "ego-referent forces."

are primary, the role of the environment is to provide incentive objects and means and barriers to the satisfaction of the person's needs. In instances in which field forces initiate action, if we are to believe our phenomenal experience, it is not mainly the ego that uses its surroundings; it seems, rather, to lend itself to them.

Although phenomenal experience argues eloquently for a role for field forces in the initiation of behavior, there have been a number of reasons for its neglect:

1. First, it must be admitted that this experience is ambiguous. For example, social and objective interest, interest in the people, things, and events in the world around us, seems to offer some of the most convincing evidence that forces may arise from parts of the psychological field outside ourselves. But such facts have been handled by the assumption of a gregarious need, a curiosity drive, a need for understanding, and the like. Such an assumption presupposes, of course, that the forces in question refer to the person. Again, a heroic act of self-sacrifice to rescue another may be saved for the hedonistic principle by the supposition of the prospect of reward in heaven; or else masochistic or other unconscious tendencies may be held responsible.[2]

While other difficulties with this kind of solution will be mentioned below, it may be stated here that it does no more than to push the problem to a different level. As has been pointed out elsewhere (8), even if all motivational forces are viewed as referring to the individual, it is still important to distinguish between those ego forces in the service of a situation and those in the service of the individual (cf. also 2, p. 318).

2. A second reason for the neglect of field forces is that special relations quickly become established between the individual and the incentive object or activity. Take a case in which we may assume that an object or activity attracts the individual: the object quickly becomes transformed through the person's occupation with it (8). For example, a scientist undertakes a particular line of work because he sees that certain issues remain unsettled; let us suppose that he has no other stake, conscious or unconscious, in the problem. Soon it becomes *his* problem: criticism of the work may become criticism of him, etc. So it is

---

[2] Of course, instances of behavior which appear to go against the interests of the ego are not, in themselves, evidence that field forces have initiated the behavior. In the present example, there may indeed be neurotic reasons for the sacrifice, or some other need of the ego may be stronger than self-preservation. It cannot be established in advance, without intimate knowledge of the circumstances, that any particular act is predominantly in the service of the ego or predominantly in the service of the situation.

when we form sentiments. A system comes to be established including the needs both of the individual and of the object. The relations between field forces and ego forces will be discussed more specifically below. The point of present interest is that the fact that such relations are quickly established obscures the question of the source of the action.

3. Perhaps the most compelling reason for the neglect of field forces is that it has not been possible in research to separate them from ego forces. It is scarcely possible to set up in the laboratory situations whose demands are so compelling that the person is caught up in them regardless of his own needs. In the typical experiment on motivation a need or intention is aroused in the subject to perform some activity. The activity or the experimental situation may have particular demands of its own, demands which would produce certain effects. But these cannot be separated from the consequences of the need which had to be aroused to get the individual to participate in the experimental activity in the first place. Not only does the *task* need to be done (a field force); the *individual* needs to do it (an ego force). With the interrupted task technique, for example, the subject both perceives the interrupted activity —perceives that the demands of the task have not been met—and is himself interrupted. Heretofore it has not been possible experimentally to separate these two kinds of demands. Of the two kinds of forces operating in such a situation, ego forces alone have received adequate attention, in accordance with current theory. The requirements of the task have been overlooked. (The importance of the perceived demands of a task for its resumption has been suggested elsewhere; cf. 8.)

THE OBSERVER TECHNIQUE

Before a strong case can be made out for the importance of field forces for motivational theory, it seems necessary to be able to demonstrate them. To this end it is necessary to separate the two kinds of motivation —field forces and ego forces. For this purpose the "observer technique" has been devised.

In the "observer experiment" one individual—we will call him the observer (O)—merely watches a subject performing a series of tasks, but is not himself permitted to participate. The performing S is known little or not at all to O, so that the latter has no personal interest in S's successes and failures. If, now, some of the tasks are interrupted, then in the case of O there will be operating essentially no forces deriving from his own needs to complete the tasks, only forces deriving from the perceived incompleteness of the activities (or the perceived lack of satisfaction of S's need)—that is to say, only field forces. If these latter are important in the determination of behavior, then O should show such effects of interruption as the superiority of incomplete tasks in recall (13) or increased attractiveness of the interrupted activities (4). On the other hand, if it is the unsatisfied (ego) need which is responsible for these effects, incomplete tasks should be treated no differently from completed ones by O.

Experiments performed under the conditions described have shown that Os do recall incomplete tasks (i.e., tasks which S has had to leave unfinished) better than completed ones (3). Furthermore, when offered a choice among tasks similar to those which they have just seen S performing, they choose tasks like those on which S has been interrupted significantly more often than chance; the attractiveness of the interrupted tasks has been enhanced for the Os. Some force must exist which favors the interrupted tasks in the case of the Os. The forces responsible must arise from O's cognitive grasp of the experimental situation. Since his own needs are not primarily involved—since he is not interrupted nor allowed to complete tasks, and since he himself runs no risk of failure—ego-referent forces cannot be mainly responsible for the obtained differences between interrupted and completed tasks. The results speak, rather, for the operation of field forces.

It might, of course, be argued that seeing S fail in an activity may play into an O's own deep-seated feelings of insecurity, and that his choice of the interrupted task represents an effort to cope with the aroused anxiety. While the experimental situation minimizes such a possibility,[3] it cannot be eliminated in all cases. But even in such cases it must be remembered that the forces responsible for the effect include field-referent forces arising from the perceived failure, which coöperate with tendencies in O himself. Again, it might be held that O identifies with the (unknown) S, and that his ego needs are thus vicariously involved. This seems to me to be begging the question. We hardly seem to have gained in understanding by subsuming the observer effect under the little-understood processes of identification and empathy. On the contrary, the observer technique seems to offer the possibility of someday investigating these very processes.

---

[3] Since the experiments are concerned with the effects of interruption, not of failure, cases of obvious failure are eliminated from the tabulated results.

RELATIONS OF FIELD FORCES AND EGO FORCES

Since the experimental isolation of field forces has been stressed, it must now be repeated that, except under the most artificial experimental conditions, field-referent forces operate always in conjunction with ego forces. Although the specific relations between the two kinds of forces require investigation, we may begin to describe some of the ways in which they operate in relation to each other.

1. Certain essential demands of the person must be met before there can be any real turning outward of interest. In other words, a certain level of satisfaction of ego needs is necessary before the individual can respond to field forces. An impressive illustration is found in Sir Ernest Shackleton's account of his effort to reach the South Pole (quoted by Leeper, 11, p. 26):

During the last weeks of the journey outwards, and the long march back, we really thought of little but food. The glory of the great mountains that towered high on either side, the majesty of the enormous glacier up which we traveled so painfully, did not appeal to our emotions to any great extent. . . .

Practically the whole imaginative life of semistarved men may thus be preoccupied with thoughts and fantasies about food and eating; and there is no reason to think that the situation is different in the case of the emotionally starved.

In this same connection an observation of Asch's is pertinent (2, p. 304): "In a developed individual the presence of a coherent ego is a necessary condition of action; the carrying out of complex actions requires a knowledge of and a reference to the self."

2. Under usual conditions there seems to be a genuine coöperation between field forces and ego forces, the one reinforcing the other. Take, for example, the question of ethnic prejudices. A good deal of recent investigation has looked for personality correlates of such prejudices, displaced hostility for example; in other words it has looked to ego forces for an explanation. On the other hand, we may not forget that a stereotype or image of the minority group exists in the culture. If the group really possessed the characteristics attributed to it, one could not help disliking its members. And similarly, if a person unthinkingly accepts this cultural image, he cannot help disliking the group. In other words, forces making for the prejudice may arise from the cultural image of the minority group as well as from tendencies in the prejudiced

individual's personality; we must consider field forces as well as ego forces.

For the sake of argument let us grant both positions. Suppose, now, that we have established in a given case that displaced aggression is responsible for the prejudice. It will still be true that the individual finds some particular target for his hostility rather than some other one; he hates the minority group instead of kicking his dog. Thus forces arising out of the properties of the cultural image coöperate with his own tendency. Or we may find that a person unthinkingly accepts the cultural image of the minority group, which image is then the principal source of the forces responsible for the prejudice. But it is still worth investigating whether he may not find something in the image to hate in particular—so that forces in himself coöperate with those arising from the (here wrongly) perceived object.

Indeed, so close is the coöperation between field forces and ego forces that it is perhaps more accurate to speak of two aspects of all motivation rather than of two kinds of forces.

3. Again, conflicts may arise between the demands of the ego and those of the field.[4] Conflicts between pleasure and duty may be (but need not be) of this kind.[5]

4. A special case in which field forces and ego forces are in opposition is that in which the one blinds the person to the requirements of the other, so that no conflict is experienced. For example, an individual may be so involved in a personal problem that he cannot attend properly to his work, or he misses an appointment, or he may be immune to other demands of the field. Or else one may be so caught in an activity that legitimate ego needs may be neglected. For example, we read until too late, not because we want to continue reading, but because we cannot put the book down. In a very important sense, it is the book that holds us, not we who hold the book.[6]

---

[4] Of course conflicts also exist between various personal forces as well as between simultaneously active field forces.

[5] It is important not to confuse the present problem with a moral one, although the considerations discussed here have application to questions of ethics (9, 12). To distinguish between the needs of the person and the requirements of the situation does not imply that the former are selfish. Not everything in the interests of the person is egotistical. The concept of field forces carries no implication that these should take precedence over ego forces. The opposite is equally often the case. And there are instances in which the needs of the person are the most important objective requirements of the field (cf. 2, p. 312 f.).

[6] In this example, it will be noted, forces from the field blind the reader to certain personal needs, but require the coöperation of others. Thus the absorbing book must be absorbing to *him*.

FIELD FORCES IN A THEORY OF MOTIVATION

If we incorporate the concept of field force into a theory of motivation, several problems seem to be simplified, and others appear in a different perspective. The enormous diversity of adult human motivation has presented difficulties to need or instinct theories as well as to S-R accounts (cf. 1). Likewise Allport's solution of functional autonomy of motives (1) has not escaped criticism, and different interpretations of the evidence Allport adduces in support of this doctrine have been suggested (2, pp. 343 ff.). The concept of field force offers another solution to this problem. It proposes to deal with the tremendous variety of human motivation in terms of properties of force in the perceived objects and events outside the self. It seems difficult to account for our specifically appropriate response to the request "Got a match?" in terms of a gregarious propensity or a need for affiliation or nurturance alone. But if this request itself is perceived as eliciting forces which coöperate with tendencies in the individual, the difficulties seem to disappear.

This example suggests another, closely related question whose solution is facilitated by the assumption of field forces: the question of how specific or how inclusive a segment of activity to employ in our concept of needs. Are we to invoke a need for offering matches to account for the corresponding action? It was seen above that a gregarious need does not account for the specificity of the behavior. But if we regard needs as specific enough to account for each act, we have lost the advantages of a need theory in bringing order to the diversity of behavior. Again the concept of field forces offers a third possibility which seems to avoid the difficulties of the other two. Specificity is introduced if perceived objects and events of the environment possess the attributes of force; and we can retain a concept of need inclusive enough to organize the data of behavior.

In the study of field forces we are investigating forces arising from the cognitive appreciation of the situation confronting the individual. This is one aspect of a much larger problem, that of the cognitive side of motives and emotions in general. Motives and emotions are not purely irrational; they have their cognitive aspect as well. This problem has been raised by Wertheimer and carried farther by Asch; elsewhere it has been fairly generally neglected. Nevertheless I believe this point is implicit in every theory of motivation and affect. It is implicit in every theory that takes for granted a certain appropriateness of the emotion to the situation in which it arises; it is silently contained in every view that speaks of pathology where this appropriateness is lacking.[7]

This general problem of the cognitive aspect of motives and emotions has been neglected for precisely the same reason that our particular problem of field forces has been neglected: it has been impossible to separate the affective aspect of the experience from the cognitive. At the same time that the individual perceives the situation confronting him, something is happening to him. It may be that we are now in possession of a conceptual tool and a method which will permit investigation of this larger problem.

Finally, the concept of field forces suggests a new view of certain problems in the phenomenology of motivation—an area of problems that seems to have got lost in the interest in unconscious motivation. I mentioned earlier that common experience is ambiguous as evidence for the initiation of action from the field. It must now be added that there is a further ambiguity. At times we incorrectly refer the source of action or experience to the experienced situation or to the self. The concept of projection in part describes cases of the first kind; for example, self-rejection may be translated into rejection by another. Conversely, an experience may erroneously be referred to the self; to use a parallel example, rejection by an important person may be translated in part into rejection by the self. The facts described as introjection and identification are relevant in this connection. In dealings with others we may erroneously take or assign credit or blame. How are we to understand these instances? If they are simply errors in locating the source of motivational forces—if the reference of our phenomenal experience to ourselves or to the perceived surroundings is not to be relied on—it might be argued that much of the case for field forces collapses.

Actually, these are probably limiting cases, and are probably not simply errors in the reference of an experience. We need to know more of the psychological processes involved before the bearing of these instances on the present problem will become clear. Meanwhile, it seems safe to say that both field forces and ego forces are operating in

[7] Cf. Anna Freud (5, p. 42): "We expect children normally to react to these particular occurrences with these specific affects. But, contrary to expectation, observation may show us a very different picture. For example, a child may exhibit indifference when we should have looked for disappointment, exuberant high spirits instead of mortification, excessive tenderness instead of jealousy. In all these cases something has happened to disturb the normal process. . . ."

all these cases and that, in ways that still have to be understood, their interaction results in errors of emphasis.

In the case of projection, except in the most extreme instances, we are probably never dealing simply with an incorrect view of the sources of forces. There may be, rather, an oversensitization, because of a problem in the individual, to something that actually exists in the other. We do not project at random.[8] (The incorrect emphasis on the field forces in these instances remains, of course, to be explained. If an ego need can blind us to the requirements of the field, there is no reason why one cannot blind us to other forces in the person.)

The case of erroneous reference to the self is at present more difficult to understand. Two directions of thinking suggest themselves. First, while a force originating outside the self may be referred to the self, its outside reference may also be present. If the rejection by the other is translated into self-rejection, this need not obscure the original rejection. It seems plausible, then, that intervening cognitive processes may account in part for the new reference of the experience. The rejection by the other may lead to a search for and emphasis upon the deficiencies of the self. Or it may play into existing feelings of self-rejection.

Perhaps a more significant, but more obscure, point in the same connection concerns the nature of relations. The other person represents, fulfills, brings out, reflects, or in some way "fits" part of the individual. The other is not simply an outer figure, but an inner figure as well (one who corresponds more or less closely to the outer one or to aspects of the outer one) if he is to stand in these relations to the self. Thus it seems likely, in our example (though the processes involved are by no means clear), that rejection by the other *is* rejection by the self. The same issue is seen more clearly in cases involving projection: we may refuse to have anything to do with a person who appeals to, supports or in some way represents a part of ourselves that we will have nothing to do with. Here rejection of the (suitable) other is rejection of part of the self; again ego forces and field forces are at work.

The same kinds of considerations seem to apply even more obviously to the example of the wrong assignment of credit or blame. In joint undertakings responsibility probably never lies only in the self or only in the (objective) other.

---

[8] Cf. Freud (6, p. 236): "We begin to see that we describe the behavior of both jealous and persecuted paranoiacs very inadequately by saying that they project outwards onto others what they do not wish to recognize in themselves.

"Certainly they do this; but they do not project it into the sky, so to speak, where there is nothing of the sort already. . . ." (Cf. also 5, p. 130.)

We have been dealing in these examples with one aspect of the problem of how we experience our own motivation—viz., the reference of forces to the person or the field. With this as a starting point, other aspects of this problem may become clear. For example, A and B have a falling out. A considers B responsible, while B thinks that an outsider, C, made the trouble between them. Each may then structure the relevant facts of the case about his own view of the reference of the difficulty, so that the two may come out with entirely different versions.

SUMMARY

It has been suggested that it is time to revise current ego-centered theories of motivation to give a place to field forces, those motivational forces arising from the experienced requirements of situations and persons outside the self. A method of demonstrating field forces, the observer technique, has been described, and some of the relations between field forces and ego forces have been indicated. The place of the concept of field force in a theory of motivation was discussed. The assumption offers a new solution to the problem of the diversity and specificity of human motivation. In addition, it provides one approach to the neglected problem of the cognitive side of motivation and emotions. Finally, certain problems of the phenomenology of motivation were discussed in the light of the concept of field force.

REFERENCES

1. Allport, G. W. *Personality*. New York: Holt, 1937.
2. Asch, S. E. *Social psychology*. New York: Prentice-Hall, 1952.
3. Baltimore, G., *et al.* Some cognitive aspects of a motivational field. Unpublished research, New School for Social Research, 1953.
4. Cartwright, D. The effect of interruption, completion, and failure upon the attractiveness of activities. *J. exp. Psychol.*, 1942, 31, 1–16.
5. Freud, A. *The ego and the mechanisms of defense*. London: Hogarth Press and the Institute of Psycho-Analysis, 1937.
6. Freud, S. Certain neurotic mechanisms in jealousy, paranoia and homosexuality. In *Collected papers*. London: Hogarth Press and the Institute of Psycho-Analysis, 1924, Vol. II, pp. 232–243.
7. Henle, M. On activity in the goal region. *Psychol. Rev.*, 1956, 63, 299–302.
8. Henle, M., and Aull, G. Factors decisive for resumption of interrupted activities: the question reopened. *Psychol. Rev.*, 1953, 60, 81–88.
9. Köhler, W. *The place of value in a world of facts*. New York: Liveright, 1938.

10. Köhler, W. *Gestalt psychology.* (Rev. ed.) New York: Liveright, 1947.
11. Leeper, R. *Psychology of personality.* Eugene: University of Oregon Press, 1947.
12. Wertheimer, M. Some problems in the theory of ethics. *Soc. Res.,* 1935, 2, 353–367. [See pp. 29–41 of the present book.]
13. Zeigarnik, B. Das Behalten erledigter und unerledigter Handlungen. *Psychol. Forsch.,* 1927, 9, 1–85.

# PART V

# PSYCHOLOGY OF

# EXPRESSION AND ART

*Rudolf Arnheim*

SARAH LAWRENCE COLLEGE

# THE GESTALT THEORY

# OF EXPRESSION

What is the exact location and range of the territory covered by the term
"expression"? Thus far, no generally accepted definition exists. In order
to make clear what is meant by expression in the present paper, it is
therefore necessary to indicate (1) the kind of perceptual stimulus
which involves the phenomenon in question, and (2) the kind of
mental process to which its existence is due. This delimitation of our
subject will show that the range of perceptual objects which carry expression according to Gestalt theory is unusually large and that expression is defined as the product of perceptual properties which various
other schools of thought consider nonexistent or unimportant.

(1) In present-day usage, the term "expression" refers primarily
to behavioral manifestations of the human personality. The appearance
and activities of the human body may be said to be expressive. The
shape and proportions of the face or the hands, the tensions and the
rhythm of muscular action, gait, gestures, and other movements serve
as objects of observation. In addition, expression is now commonly
understood to reach beyond the observed person's body. The "projective techniques" exploit characteristic effects upon, and reactions to,
the environment. The way a person dresses, keeps his room, handles the

Reprinted with permission from the *Psychological Review*, Vol. 56, No. 3,
May, 1949.

language, the pen, the brush; the colors, flowers, occupations he prefers; the meaning he attributes to pictures, tunes, or inkblots; the story he imposes on puppets; his interpretation of a dramatic part—these and innumerable other manifestations can be called "expressive" in that they permit conclusions about the personality or the temporary state of mind of the individual. Gestalt psychologists extend the range of expressive phenomena beyond this limit. For reasons which will be discussed, they consider it indispensable to speak also of the expression conveyed by inanimate objects, such as mountains, clouds, sirens, machines.

(2) Once the carrier of expression is determined, the kind of mental process must be indicated which is charged with producing the phenomenon. It is the contention of Gestalt psychology that the various experiences commonly classified under "perception of expression" are caused by a number of psychological processes, which ought to be distinguished from each other for the purpose of theoretical analysis. Some of these experiences are partly or wholly based upon empirically acquired knowledge. The mere inspection of many half-smoked cigarettes in an ashtray would suggest no connection with nervous tension to a visitor from a planet inhabited by nonsmokers. The letters EVVIVA GUERRA and EVVIVA DON PIO scribbled all over the walls of an Italian village will reveal the mentality of the natives only to someone who happens to know that these words pay homage to a champion cyclist and the village priest. For the purpose of the present paper, the use of past experience for the interpretation of perceptual observations will be excluded from the field of expression and referred to the psychology of learning. We shall be concerned only with instances in which, according to Gestalt psychology, sensory data contain a core of expression that is perceptually self-evident. The way a person keeps his lips tightly closed or raises his voice or strokes a child's head or walks hesitatingly is said to contain factors whose meaning can be understood directly through mere inspection. Instances of such direct expression are not limited to the appearance and behavior of the subject's own body. They are also found in such "projective" material as the stirring red of a woman's favorite dress or the "emotional" character of the music she prefers. In addition, inanimate objects are said to convey direct expression. The aggressive stroke of lightning or the soothing rhythm of rain impress the observer by perceptual qualities which according to Gestalt psychology must be distinguished theoretically from the effect of what he knows about the nature of these happenings. It is

assumed, however, that practically every concrete experience combines factors of both kinds.

*Procedures and findings.* What is expression, and what enables the observer to experience it? By means of which perceptual factors and in what way do stimulus configurations evoke such experiences in the onlooker? During the last twenty-five years or so, numerous experimental investigations have been devoted to the phenomena of expression, but hardly any of them have tried to answer our questions. Limited as they were to the connection between how a person behaves and what happens in him psychologically, they centered upon the certainly important problem: To what extent are observers, untrained or trained, gifted or average, capable of getting valid information about a person's temporary state of mind or his more permanent psychical constitution from an inspection of his face, voice, gait, handwriting, etc.?

This is true for the various matching experiments, which are conveniently summarized by Woodworth (24, pp. 242–256) and by Allport and Vernon (1, pp. 3–20). Similarly, in the field of the projective techniques psychologists have looked for correlations between personality traits and reactions to environmental stimuli. Almost invariably, these stimuli contain factors of the kind which concern the present paper. However, thus far, little explicit discussion has been devoted to the question why and how the given percepts provoke the observed reactions. There is evidence that the whole structure of a face rather than the sum of its parts determines expression (2). But which structural features make for what expression and why? In the Rorschach test, the typical reactions to color are probably based on expression. But why are emotional attitudes related to color rather than shape? Ernest G. Schachtel has done pioneer work in this field, pointing out, for instance, that responses to colors and to affect-experiences are both characterized by passive receptivity (19). On the whole, however, questions of this kind have been answered thus far by summary and scantily supported theoretical assertions.

A few remarks are in order on the investigations which have tested the accomplishments of observers. A glance at the results reveals a curious contrast. One group of experimenters reports essentially negative findings. Another, consisting mainly of Gestalt psychologists, asserts that observers judge portraits, handwritings, and similar material with a measure of success that clearly surpasses chance. Pessimistic generalizations have been drawn from the studies of the first type. The subject of expression is sometimes treated with the buoyant unkindness that distinguished the early behavioristic statements on introspection. This attitude has not encouraged research.

The main reason for the conflicting results can be found in differences of approach. The investigators of the first type asked: How validly can the bodily expression of the average person or of a random member of a particular group of people be interpreted? In other words, they focused on the important practical question of the extent to which expression can be relied upon in everyday life. On the other hand, the Gestalt psychologists preferred the common scientific procedure of purifying as carefully as possible the phenomenon under investigation. They searched for the most favorable condition of observation. A major part of their efforts was spent in selecting and preparing sets of specimens which promised to demonstrate expression clearly and strongly (2, p. 8).

Some of the factors which may account for the often disappointing results obtained in experiments with random material are the following. (a) Everyday observation suggests that the structural patterns of character, temperament, mood, are not equally clear-cut in all people. While some individuals are pronouncedly depressed or lighthearted, strong or weak, harmonious or disharmonious, warm or cold, others strike us as indefinite, lukewarm, fluid. Whatever the exact nature of such indefiniteness, one would expect the corresponding faces, gestures, handwritings to be equally vague in form and therefore in expression. When one examines material of this kind, one notices in some cases that the decisive structural features are not sharply defined. In other cases, factors which are clear-cut in themselves add up to something that shows neither harmony nor conflict but a lack of unity or relatedness, which renders the whole meaningless, inexpressive. Many telling examples can be found among the composite faces made up by the summation of unrelated parts for experimental purposes. If observers can cope with such material at all, they do so presumably by guessing what these artifacts are meant to mean rather than by having the experience of live expression. (b) The presence of a portrait photographer's camera tends to paralyze a person's expression, and he becomes self-conscious, inhibited, and often strikes an unnatural pose. (c) Candid shots are momentary phases isolated from a temporal process and a spatial context. Sometimes they are highly expressive and representative of the whole from which they are taken. Frequently they are not. Furthermore the angle from which a shot is made, the effect of lighting on shape, the rendering of brightness and color values, as well as modifications through retouching, are factors which make it impossible to accept a random photograph as a valid likeness. (d) If for purposes of matching experiments a number of samples is combined at random, accidental similarities of expression may occur, which will make distinction difficult, even though every specimen may be clear-cut in itself. Further reasons for the lack of consistent results are discussed by Wolff (23, p. 7).[1]

The conclusion seems to be that the recognition of expression has been proven to be reliable and valid under optimal conditions. For the average face, voice, gesture, handwriting, etc., the results are likely to be less positive. However, in order to establish this fact trustworthily, the additional obstacles created by unsuitable experimental conditions will have to be reduced.

*Associationist theories.* What enables observers to judge expression? The traditional theory, handed down to our generation without much questioning, is based on associationism. In his essay on vision Berkeley (4, § 65) discusses the way in which one sees shame or anger in the looks of a man.

Those passions are themselves invisible: they are nevertheless let in by the eye along with colours and alterations of countenance, which are the immediate object of vision, and which signify them for no other reason than barely because they have been observed to accompany them: without which experience, we should no more have taken blushing for a sign of shame, than of gladness.

Darwin, in his book on the expression of emotions, devoted a few pages to the same problem (7, pp. 356–359). He considered the recognition of expression to be either instinctive or learned. "Children, no doubt, would soon learn the movements of expression in their elders in the same manner as animals learn those of man," namely, "through their associating harsh or kind treatment with our actions."

Moreover, when a child cries or laughs, he knows in a general manner what he is doing and what he feels; so that a very small exertion of reason would

---

[1] Since there is no reason to expect that every photograph will reproduce essential features of expression, it would be interesting to know by which criterion the photographs for the Szondi test (18) have been selected. If an integral feature of the test consists in establishing the reactions of people to the personalities of homosexuals, sadistic murderers, etc., two questions arise. (1) Is there a complete correlation between these pathological manifestations and certain clear-cut personality structures? (2) Are the latter suitably expressed in the photographs? These problems are avoided if the test is meant simply to investigate people's responses to a given set of portraits, whatever their origin.

tell him what crying or laughing meant in others. But the question is, do our children acquire their knowledge of expression solely by experience through the power of association and reason? As most of the movements of expression must have been gradually acquired, afterwards becoming instinctive, there seems to be some degree of *a priori* probability that their recognition would likewise have become instinctive.

In Darwin's view, the relationship between expressive bodily behavior and the corresponding psychical attitude was merely causal. Expressive gestures were either remnants of originally serviceable habits or due to "direct action of the nervous system." He saw no inner kinship between a particular pattern of muscular behavior and the correlated state of mind.

A variation of the associationist theory contends that judgments of expression are based on stereotypes. In this view, interpretation does not rely on what belongs together according to our spontaneous insight or repeated observation but on conventions, which we have adopted ready-made from our social group. We have been told that aquiline noses indicate courage and that protruding lips betray sensuality. The promoters of the theory generally imply that such judgments are wrong, as though information not based on first-hand experience could never be trusted. Actually, the danger does not lie in the social origin of the information. What counts is that people have a tendency to acquire simply structured concepts on the basis of insufficient evidence, which may have been gathered first-hand or second-hand, and to preserve these concepts unchanged in the face of contrary facts. While this may make for many one-sided or entirely wrong evaluations of individuals and groups of people, the existence of stereotypes does not explain the origin of physiognomic judgments. If these judgments stem from tradition, what is the tradition's source? Are they right or wrong? Even though often misapplied, traditional interpretations of physique and behavior may still be based on sound observation. In fact, perhaps they are so hardy because they are so true.

*Empathy.* The theory of empathy holds an intermediate position between the traditional and a more modern approach. This theory is often formulated as a mere extension of the association theory, designed to take care of the expression of inanimate objects. When I look at the columns of a temple, I know from past experience the kind of mechanical pressure and counterpressure that occurs in the column. Equally from past experience I know how I should feel myself if I were in the place of the column and if those physical forces acted upon and within my own body. I project my feelings into the column and by such animation endow it with expression. Lipps, who developed the theory, stated that empathy is based on association (16, p. 434). It is true, he also says, that the kind of association in question connects "two things belonging together, or being combined by necessity, the one being immediately given in and with the other." But he seems to have conceived of this inner necessity as a merely causal connection, because immediately after the statement just quoted he denies explicitly that the relationship between the bodily expression of anger and the angry person's psychical experience could be described as an "association of similarity, identity, correspondence" (p. 435). Like Darwin, Lipps saw no intrinsic kinship between perceptual appearance and the physical and psychological forces "behind" it. However, he did see a structural similarity between physical and psychological forces in other respects. After discussing the mechanical forces whose existence in an inanimate object is inferred by the observer through past experience, Lipps writes the following remarkable passage:

And to (the knowledge of these mechanical forces) is furthermore attached the representation of possible internal ways of behavior of my own, which do not lead to the same result but are of the same character. In other words, there is attached the representation of possible kinds of my own activity, which in an analogous fashion, involves forces, impulses, or tendencies, freely at work or inhibited, a yielding to external effect, overcoming of resistance, the arising and resolving of tensions among impulses, etc. Those forces and effects of forces appear in the light of my own ways of behavior, my own kinds of activity, impulses, and tendencies and their ways of realization (16, p. 439).

Thus Lipps anticipated the Gestalt principle of isomorphism for the relationship between the physical forces in the observed object and the psychical dynamics in the observer; and in a subsequent section of the same paper he applies the "association of similarity of character" even to the relationship between the perceived rhythm of musical tones and the rhythm of other psychical processes that occur in the listener. Which means that in the case of at least one structural characteristic, namely rhythm, Lipps realized a possible inner similarity of perceptual patterns and the expressive meaning they convey to the observer.

*The Gestalt approach.* The Gestalt theory of expression admits that correspondences between physical and psychical behavior can be discovered on the basis of mere statistical correlation but maintains that repeated association is neither the only nor the common means of arriving at an understanding of expression. Gestalt psychologists hold that expressive behavior reveals its meaning directly in perception. The approach is based on the principle of isomorphism, according to which processes which take place in different media may be nevertheless similar in their structural organization. Applied to body and mind, this means that if the forces which determine bodily behavior are structurally similar to those which characterize the corresponding mental states, it may become understandable why psychical meaning can be read off directly from a person's appearance and conduct.

It is not the aim of this paper to prove the validity of the Gestalt hypothesis.[2] We shall limit ourselves to pointing out some of its implications. Only brief presentations of the theory are available so far. However, Köhler's (12, pp. 216–247) and Koffka's (10, pp. 654–661) remarks about the subject are explicit enough to indicate that isomorphism on only two levels, namely the psychical processes which occur in the observed person and the corresponding behavioral activity, would be insufficient to explain direct understanding of expression through perception. In the following an attempt will be made to list a number of psychological and physical levels, in the observed person and in the observer, at which isomorphic structures must exist in order to make the Gestalt explanation possible.

Let us suppose that a person A performs a "gentle" gesture, which is experienced as such by an observer B. On the basis of psychophysical parallelism in its Gestalt version it would be assumed that the tenderness of A's feeling (Table 1, level I) corresponds to a hypothetical process in A's nervous system (level II) and that the two processes, the psychical and the physiological, are isomorphic, that is to say, similar in structure.

The neural process will direct the muscular forces which produce the gesture of A's arm and hand (level III). Again it must be assumed that the particular dynamic pattern of mechanical action and inhibi-

---

[2] For that purpose, observations of infants are relevant. Even in his day, Darwin was puzzled by the fact that young children seemed directly to understand a smile or grief "at much too early an age to have learnt anything by experience" (7, p. 358). According to Bühler (6, p. 377), "the baby of three or four months reacts positively to the angry as well as to the kind voice and look; the five-to-seven-months-old baby reflects the assumed expression and also begins to cry at the scolding voice and threatening gesture" on the basis of "direct sensory influence." Further evidence will have to come from detailed demonstrations of structural similarities. (Cf. pp. 319–321.)

tion in A's muscles corresponds structurally to the configuration of physiological and psychical forces at the levels II and I. The muscular action will be accompanied with a kinesthetic experience (level IV), which again must be isomorphic with the other levels. The kinesthetic experience need not always take place and is not strictly indispensable. However, the structural kinship of the experienced gentleness of his gesture and the equally experienced gentleness of his mood will make A feel that his gesture is a fitting manifestation of his state of mind.

## TABLE 1

### ISOMORPHIC LEVELS

| A. Observed person | |
|---|---|
| I. State of mind | Psychological |
| II. Neural correlate of I | Electrochemical |
| III. Muscular forces | Mechanical |
| IV. Kinesthetic correlate of III | Psychological |
| V. Shape and movement of body | Geometrical |
| B. Observer | |
| VI. Retinal projection of V | Geometrical |
| VII. Cortical projection of VI | Electrochemical |
| VIII. Perceptual correlate of VII | Psychological |

Finally, the muscular forces of level III will cause A's arm and hand to move in a, say, parabolic curve (level V); and again the geometric formation of this curve would have to be isomorphic with the structure of the processes at the previous levels. An elementary geometrical example may illustrate the meaning of this statement. Geometrically, a circle is the result of just one structural condition. It is the locus of all points that are equally distant from one center. A parabola satisfies two such conditions. It is the locus of all points that have equal distance from one point and one straight line. The parabola may be called a compromise between two structural demands. Either structural condition yields to the other.[3] Is there any possible connection between these geometrical characteristics of the parabola and the particular configuration of physical forces to which we attribute gentleness? One may point to the kind of physical process that produces parabolic pat-

---

[3] One can express this also in terms of projective geometry by saying that the parabola as a conic section is intermediate between the horizontal section, namely the circle, and the vertical section, the straight-edged triangle.

terns. In ballistics, for instance, the parabolic curve of a trajectory is the result of a "compromise" between the direction of the original impulse and the gravitational attraction. The two forces "yield" to each other.[4]

At this point the description must shift from the observed person A to the observer B. B's eyes receive an image (level VI) of the gesture performed by A's arm and hand. Why should this image produce in B the impression that he is observing a gentle gesture? It may be true that the geometrical pattern of the gesture as well as the configuration of muscular forces which has created this pattern can both be characterized structurally as containing compromise, flexibility, yielding. But this fact in itself is not sufficient to explain the direct experience which B is said to receive by his perceptual observation. It becomes clear at this point that the Gestalt theory of expression is faced not only with the problem of showing how psychical processes can be inferred from bodily behavior, but that the primary task consists in making plausible the fact that the perception of shape, movement, etc., may convey to the observer the direct experience of an expression which is structurally similar to the organization of the observed stimulus pattern.

A's gesture is projected on the retinae of B's eyes [5] and, by way of the retinal images, on the visual cortex of B's cerebrum (level VII). Correspondingly, B perceives A's gesture (level VIII). Is there a pos-

---

[4] One of the principles on which the analysis of handwritings is based indicates that the script pattern reflects dynamic features of the writer's motor behavior, which in turn is produced by a characteristic configuration of muscular forces. The same isomorphism of muscular behavior and resulting visible trace has found applications in the technique of drawing. Langfeld (15, p. 129) quotes Bowie (5, pp. 35 and 77–79) concerning the principle of "living movement" (*Sei Do*) in Japanese painting: "A distinguishing feature in Japanese painting is the strength of the brush stroke, technically called *fude no chikara* or *fude no ikioi*. When representing an object suggesting strength, such, for instance, as rocky cliff, the beak or talons of a bird, the tiger's claws, or the limbs and branches of a tree, the moment the brush is applied the sentiment of strength must be invoked and felt throughout the artist's system and imparted through his arm and hand to the brush, and so transmitted into the object painted."

[5] At this stage a number of factors may interfere with the adequate projection of decisive characteristics of body A on the receptor organ of B. In our specific example it will depend, for instance, on the angle of projection, whether or not the perspective retinal image will preserve the essential structural features of the parabolic movement or transform it into a stimulus trace of unclear or clearly different structure. (In photographs and motion pictures such factors influence the kind of expression obtained from the reproduction of physical objects.) Similar factors will influence the veracity of other perceptual qualities which carry expression.

sible similarity of the geometrical structure of the stimulus configuration and the structure of the expression which it conveys to the observer? We may go back to our mathematical analysis of the circle and the parabola. Simple experiments confirm what artists know from experience, namely that a circular curve looks "harder," less flexible, than a parabolic one. In comparison with the circle the parabola looks more gentle. One could try to explain this finding by assuming that the observer knows, through past experience, the geometrical characteristics of such patterns or the nature of the physical forces which frequently produce them. This would take us back to the associationist theory. Along Gestalt lines another explanation suggests itself.

The projection of the perceptual stimulus on the visual cortex can be assumed to create a configuration of electrochemical forces in the cerebral field. The well-known Gestalt experiments in perception suggest that retinal stimulations are subjected to organizational processes when they reach the cortical level. As a result of these processes the elements of visual patterns are perceived as being grouped according to Wertheimer's rules. Furthermore, any visual pattern appears as an organized whole, in which some predominant elements determine the over-all shape and the directions of the main axes, while others have subordinate functions. For the same reasons, modifications of objective shape and size are perceived under certain conditions.

It will be observed that all these experimental findings focus upon the effects of the strains and stresses which organize the cortical field. Is there any reason to assume that only the *effects* of these dynamic processes, namely the groupings, the hierarchies of structural functions, and the modifications of shape and size, are reflected in perceptual experience? Why should not the strains and stresses of the cortical forces themselves also have their psychological counterpart? It seems plausible that they represent the physiological equivalent of what is experienced as expression.

Such a theory would make expression an integral part of the elementary processes of perception. *Expression, then, could be defined as the psychological counterpart of the dynamic processes which result in the organization of perceptual stimuli.* While concrete verification is obviously far away, the basic assumption has gained in concreteness since Köhler and Wallach (14) have explained phenomena of perceptual size, shape, and location through the action of electrochemical forces. The future will show whether the theory can be extended to covering the phenomena of expression.

It is possible now to return to the question of how the perception of shape, movement, etc., may convey to an observer the direct experience of an expression which is structurally similar to the organization of the observed stimulus pattern. We referred previously to the constellations of physical forces which will induce an object to pursue a parabolic path. The physicist may be able to tell whether the example from ballistics is invertible. Will a parabolic pattern, such as the one projected on the cortical field, under certain conditions set off a configuration of forces which contains the structural factors of "compromise" or "yielding"? If so, isomorphism of the cortical forces and those described as levels I-V could be established.

This brings the description of isomorphic levels to an end. If the presentation is correct, the Gestalt-theoretical thesis would imply that an observer will adequately gauge another person's state of mind by inspection of that person's bodily appearance if the psychical situation of the observed person and the perceptual experience of the observer are structurally similar by means of a number of intermediate isomorphic levels.

*Expression as a perceptual quality.* The definition which was given above suggests that expression is an integral part of the elementary perceptual process. This should not come as a surprise. Perception is a mere instrument for the registration of color, shape, sound, etc., only as long as it is considered in isolation from the organism of which it is a part. In its proper biological context, perception appears as the means by which the organism obtains information about the friendly, hostile, or otherwise relevant environmental forces to which it must react. These forces reveal themselves most directly by what is described here as expression.

There is psychological evidence to bear out this contention. In fact, the observations on primitives and children cited by Werner (21, pp. 67–82) and Köhler (13) indicate that "physiognomic qualities," as Werner calls them, are even more directly perceived than the "geometric-technical" qualities of size, shape, or movement. Expression seems to be the primary content of perception. To register a fire as merely a set of hues and shapes in motion rather than to experience primarily the exciting violence of the flames presupposes a very specific, rare, and artificial attitude. Even though the practical importance of, and hence the alertness to, expression has decreased in our culture, it cannot be maintained that a basic change has taken place in this respect. Darwin (7, pp. 359–360) noted that people sometimes observe and describe facial expression without being able to indicate the features of form, size, direction, etc., which carry it. In experimental work, one notices that even with the object directly in front of their eyes, subjects find it a hard and uncomfortable task to take note of the formal pattern. They constantly fall back upon the expressive characteristics, which they describe freely and naturally. Everyday experience shows that people may clearly recall the expression of persons or objects without being able to indicate color or shape. Asch observes: "Long before one has realized that the color of the scene has changed, one may feel that the character of the scene has undergone change" (3, p. 85). Finally, there is the fact that the artist's, writer's, musician's approach to their subject is principally guided by expression.[6]

*Generalized theory.* Thus far, the phenomenon of expression has been discussed essentially in its best-known aspect, namely, as a physical manifestation of psychical processes. However, some of the foregoing considerations implied that expression is a more universal phenomenon. Expression does not only exist when there is a mind "behind" it, a puppeteer that pulls the strings. Expression is not limited to living organisms, which possess consciousness. A flame, a tumbling leaf, the wailing of a siren, a willow tree, a steep rock, a Louis XV chair, the cracks in a wall, the warmth of a glazed teapot, a hedgehog's thorny back, the colors of a sunset, a flowing fountain, lightning and thunder, the jerky movements of a bent piece of wire—they all convey expression through the various senses. The importance of this fact has been concealed by the popular hypothesis that in such cases human expression is merely transferred to objects. If, however, expression is an inherent characteristic of perceptual factors, it becomes unlikely that nonhuman expression should be nothing but an anthropomorphism, a "pathetic fallacy." Rather will human expression have to be considered a special case of a more general phenomenon. The comparison of an object's expression with a human state of mind is a secondary process (cf. p. 315). A weeping willow does not look sad because it looks like a sad person. It is more adequate to state that since the shape, direction, and flexibility of willow branches convey the expression of passive hanging, a comparison with the structurally similar psychophysical pattern of sadness in humans may impose itself secondarily.

Expression is sometimes described as "perceiving with imagination." In doing so Gottshalk (9) explains that "something is perceived as if it

---

[6] This has led to the erroneous notion that all perception of expression is aesthetic.

were actually present in the object of perception, although literally it is only suggested and not actually there. Music is not literally sad or gay or gentle; only sentient creatures or creatures with feeling, such as human beings, could be that." If our language possessed more words which could refer to kinds of expression as such, instead of naming them after emotional states in which they find an important application, it would become apparent that the phenomenon in question is "actually present in the object of perception" and not merely associated with it by imagination.

Even with regard to human behavior, the connection of expression with a corresponding state of mind is not as compelling and indispensable as is sometimes taken for granted. Köhler (12, pp. 260–264) has pointed out that people normally deal with and react to the expressive physical behavior in itself rather than being conscious of the psychical experiences reflected by such behavior. We perceive the slow, listless, "droopy" movements of one person as against the brisk, straight, vigorous movements of another, but do not necessarily go beyond the meaning of such appearance by thinking explicitly of the psychical weariness or alertness behind it. Weariness and alertness are already contained in the physical behavior itself; they are not distinguished in any essential way from the weariness of slowly floating tar or the energetic ringing of the telephone bell.

This broader conception has practical consequences. It suggests, for instance, that the phenomenon of expression does not belong primarily under the heading of the emotions or personality, where it is commonly treated. It is true that the great contributions which the study of expression has in store for these fields of psychology are thus far almost untapped. However, the experience of the last decades shows that little progress is made unless the nature of expression itself is clarified first.[7]

*Secondary effects.* Strictly speaking, the phenomenon of expression is limited to the levels V–VIII of Table 1. That is, the term "expression," as used in this paper, refers to an experience which takes place when a sensory stimulus affects the visual cortex of an observer's brain. The processes which may have given rise to the stimulus as well as those

---

[7] Once this is done, it will be possible and necessary to approach the further problem of the influences which the total personality exerts upon the observation of expression. To Vincent van Gogh, cypress trees conveyed an expression which they do not have for many other people. Cf. Koffka (10, p. 600).

which the cortical stimulation provokes in other brain centers are supplementary.

Once perceptual stimulation has taken place, a number of secondary happenings may follow. (1) The observer B may deduce from the expression of B's bodily behavior that particular psychical processes are going on in A's mind; that is, through the perception of level V the observer gains knowledge about level I. The observation of a gentle gesture leads to the conclusion: B is in a gentle mood. This conclusion may be based on an isomorphic similarity between the observed behavior and a state of mind known or imaginable to the observer. In other cases, the conclusion may rely on past experience. Yawning, for instance, conveys the direct expression of sudden expansion; but the connection between yawning and fatigue or boredom is discovered by learning. The same seems to be true for the spasmodic outbursts of sound which we call laughter and which in themselves are so far from suggesting mirth that they remain permanently incomprehensible to the chimpanzee, who otherwise "at once correctly interprets the slightest change of human expression, whether menacing or friendly" (11, p. 307). It is important to realize that an expression may be correctly perceived and described, yet the inferences derived from it may be wrong. If, in an experiment, 80 per cent of the observers agree on an "erroneous" attribution, it is not sufficient to dismiss the result as an instance of failure. The high amount of agreement represents a psychological fact in its own right. The reliability of the observers' responses to a perceptual stimulus is a problem quite different from the validity of such responses, i.e., the question whether the observers' diagnosis is "true."

(2) The observed expression may bring about the corresponding state of mind in B. In perceiving A's gentle behavior, the observer himself may experience a feeling of tenderness. (Lipps speaks of "sympathetic empathy" as distinguished from "simple empathy" [16, p. 417].) (3) The observed expression may provoke the corresponding kinesthetic experience, e.g., a feeling of relaxed softness. The effects described under (2) and (3) may be instances of a kind of "resonance" based on isomorphism. Just as a sound calls forth a vibration of similar frequency in a string, various levels of psychological experience, such as the visual, the kinesthetic, the emotional seem to elicit in each other sensations of similar structure. (4) The perceived expression may remind B of other observations in which a similar expression played a role. Thus past experience is considered here not as the basis for the

apperception of expression; instead, the direct observation of expression becomes the basis for comparison with similar observations in the past.

*The role of past experience.* While there is no evidence to support the hypothesis that the central phenomenon of expression is based on learning, it is worth noting that in most cases the interpretation of the perceived expression is influenced by what is known about the person or object in question and about the context in which it appears. Mere inspection will produce little more than over-all impressions of the forces at work, strong and clear-cut as such an experience may be. Increasing knowledge will lead to more differentiated interpretations, which will take the particular context into account. (As an example, one may think of the expression conveyed by the behavior of an animal whose habits one does not know and the changes that occur with closer acquaintance.) Knowledge does not interfere with expression itself, it merely modifies its interpretation, except for cases in which knowledge changes the appearance of the carrier of expression, that is, the perceptual pattern itself. For instance, a line figure may change its perceptual structure and therefore its expression if it is suddenly seen as a human figure. A lifted eyebrow is seen as tense because it is perceived as a deviation from a known normal position. The expression of Mongolian eyes or Negro lips is influenced, for a white observer, by the fact that he conceives them as deviations from the normal face of his own race.

In Gestalt terms, past experience, knowledge, learning, memory are considered as factors of the temporal context in which a given phenomenon appears. Like the spatial context, on which Gestaltists have concentrated their attention during the early development of the theory, the temporal context influences the way a phenomenon is perceived. An object looks big or small depending on whether it is seen, spatially, in the company of smaller or larger objects. The same is true for the temporal context. The buildings of a middle-sized town look tall to a farmer, small to a New Yorker, and correspondingly their expression differs for the two observers. Mozart's music may appear serene and cheerful to a modern listener, who perceives it in the temporal context of twentieth-century music, whereas it conveyed the expression of violent passion and desperate suffering to his contemporaries against the background of the music they knew. Such examples do not demonstrate that there is no intrinsic connection between perceptual patterns and the expression they convey but simply that experiences must not be evaluated in isolation from their spatial and temporal whole-context.

Knowledge often merges with directly perceived expression into a more complex experience. When we observe the gentle curve of a coachman's whip while being aware at the same time of the aggressive use of the object, the resulting experience clearly contains an element of contradiction. Such contradictions are exploited by artists; compare, in motion pictures, the uncanny effect of the murderer who moves softly and speaks with a velvety voice.

Finally, the perceptual experience of expression can be influenced by the kind of training which in artistic and musical instruction is known as making students "see" and "hear." By opening people's eyes and ears to what is directly perceivable, they can be made to scan the given sensory pattern more adequately and thus to receive a fuller experience of its expression. A neglected or misled capacity for responding perceptually can be revived or corrected.

*The role of kinesthesia.* Frequently people feel that another person, whom they are observing, behaves physically the way they themselves have behaved before. They get this impression even though at that time they probably did not watch themselves in the mirror. It may be that they compare their own state of mind as they remember it from the former occasion with the expression conveyed by the bodily behavior of the other person and/or with the state of mind reflected in that behavior. Probably the kinesthetic perception of one's own muscular behavior plays an important part in such situations. If muscular behavior and kinesthetic experience are isomorphic, it becomes explainable why at times one is so keenly aware of one's own facial expression, posture, gestures. One may feel, for instance: Right now, I look just like my father! The most convincing example is furnished by actors and dancers, whose bodily performance is created essentially through kinesthetic control. And yet their gestures are understandable to the audience visually. This suggests that there is a valid correspondence between bodily behavior and the related kinesthetic perception. The problem of what enables an infant to imitate an observer who smiles or shows the tip of his tongue belongs in the same category. Of particular interest is the fact that the blind express their feelings—even though imperfectly—in spite of their inability to observe expression in others visually. The blind also understand certain gestures on the basis of their own kinesthetic experiences.

The blind man, like the person who sees, is aware of the gestures he makes when under the influence of various emotions. He shrugs his shoulders and raises his arms to express his disdain and amazement. The same gestures recognized by him in a statue will evoke within him the same sentiments (20, p. 320).

Isomorphism would seem to account also for the fact that it often suffices to assume a particular posture (levels III and IV) in order to enter into a corresponding state of mind (level I). Bending the head and folding the hands is more than an accidentally chosen posture of praying, which derives its meaning merely from tradition. The kinesthetic sensation which accompanies this posture is structurally akin to the psychical attitude called devotion. "Bowing" to a superior power's will is a mental condition so directly related to the corresponding bodily gesture that its common linguistic description uses the physical to describe the psychological. Rituals not only express what people feel but also help them to feel the way the situation requires. By straightening our backbones we produce a muscular sensation which is akin to the attitude of pride, and thus introduce into our state of mind a noticeable element of bold self-sufficiency.[8]

Even the "practical" motor activities are accompanied more or less strongly by structurally corresponding states of mind. For instance, hitting or breaking things normally seems to evoke the emotional overtone of attack. To assert merely that this is so because people are aggressive would be an evasion of the problem. But if the dynamic character of the kinesthetic sensation which accompanies hitting and breaking resembles the emotional dynamics of attack, then the one may be expected to evoke the other—by "resonance" (cf. p. 315). (This kinship makes it possible for aggressiveness, wherever it exists, to express itself through such motor acts.) Probably this parallelism holds true for all motor activity. Muscular behavior such as grasping, yielding, lifting, straightening, smoothing, loosening, bending, running, stopping seems to produce mental resonance effects constantly. (In consequence, language uses all of them metaphorically to describe states of mind.) The psychosomatic phenomena of pathological "organ-speech" ("I cannot stomach this!") may be considered the most dramatic examples of a universal interdependence. The range and the importance of the phenomenon are not acknowledged as long as one studies expression only in motor activities that are not, or not any more, serviceable. It

---

[8] James's theory of emotion is based on a sound psychological observation. It fails where it identifies the kinesthetic sensation with the total emotional experience instead of describing it as a component which reinforces and sometimes provokes emotion because of the structural similarity of the two.

seems safe to assert that all motor acts are expressive, even though in different degrees, and that they all carry the experience of corresponding higher mental processes, if ever so faintly. Therefore, it is inadequate to describe expressive movements as mere atavisms, the way Darwin did. They are physical acts which take place because of their inner correspondence with the state of mind of the person who performs them. To use one of Darwin's examples: a person who coughs in embarrassment is not simply the victim of a meaningless association between a state of mind and a physical reaction, which was or can be serviceable under similar circumstances. Rather does he produce a reaction which he experiences to be meaningfully related to his state of mind. The bodily accompaniment completes the mental reaction. Together they form an act of total psychophysical behavior. The human organism always functions as a whole, physically and psychically.

This view permits an application to the theory of art. It highlights the intimate connection of artistic and "practical" behavior. The dancer, for instance, does not have to endow movements with a symbolic meaning for artistic purposes, but uses in an artistically organized way the unity of psychical and physical reaction which is characteristic for human functioning in general.

In a broader sense, it is the direct expressiveness of all perceptual qualities which allows the artist to convey the effects of the most universal and abstract psychophysical forces through the presentation of individual, concrete objects and happenings. While painting a pine tree, he can rely on the expression of towering and spreading which this tree conveys whenever it is seen by a human eye, and thus can span in his work the whole range of existence, from its most general principles to the tangible manifestations of these principles in individual objects.

*An illustration.* It has been pointed out in the beginning that experimenters have been concerned mostly with the question whether and to what extent observers can judge a person's state of mind from his physical appearance. In consequence, the psychological literature contains few analyses of perceptual patterns with regard to the expression they convey. As an example of the kind of material which is badly needed in this field, Efron's study on the gestures of two ethnical groups (8) may be cited. He describes the behavior of Eastern Jews and Southern Italians in New York City by analyzing the range, speed, plane, coordination, and shape of their movements. A comparison of these findings with the mentalities of the two groups would probably produce excellent illustrations of what is meant by the structural similarity of psychical and physical behavior. Among the experimental investigations, Lundholm's early study (17) may be mentioned. He asked eight laymen in art to draw lines, each of which was to express the affective tone of an adjective given verbally. It was found, for instance, that only straight lines, broken by angles, were used to represent such adjectives as exciting, furious, hard, powerful, while only curves were used for sad, quiet, lazy, merry. Upward direction of lines expressed strength, energy, force; downward direction, weakness, lack of energy, relaxation, depression, etc. Recently Willmann (22) had thirty-two musicians compose short themes, meant to illustrate four abstract designs. Some agreement among the composers was found concerning the tempo, meter, melodic line, and amount of consonance, chosen to render the characteristics of the drawings. Subsequently the designs and compositions were used for matching experiments.

Because of the scarcity of pertinent material, it may be permissible to mention here an experiment which is too limited in the number of cases and too subjective in its method of recording and evaluating the data to afford a proof of the thesis we are discussing. It is presented merely as an example of the kind of research which promises fruitful results.[9] Five members of the student dance group of Sarah Lawrence College were asked individually to give improvisations of the following three subjects: sadness, strength, night. Rough descriptions of the dance patterns which resulted were jotted down by the experimenter and later classified according to a number of categories. Table 2 presents the findings in an abbreviated form. The numerical agreement is high but obviously carries little weight. As a point of method, it may only be mentioned that instances of disagreement cannot be taken simply to indicate that there was no reliable correspondence between task and performance. Sometimes, the task allows more than one valid interpretation. For instance, "strength" expresses itself equally well in fast and in slow movement. "Night" is less directly related to one particular dynamic pattern than "sadness" or "strength."

Most tempting is the comparison between the movement patterns and the corresponding psychical processes. Such comparison cannot be carried through with exactness at this time mainly because psychology has not yet provided a method of describing the dynamics of

---

[9] The data were collected and tabulated by Miss Jane Binney, a student at Sarah Lawrence College.

## TABLE 2

ANALYSIS OF DANCE MOVEMENTS IMPROVISED BY FIVE SUBJECTS

|  | Sadness | Strength | Night |
|---|---|---|---|
| *Speed:* | 5: slow | 2: slow<br>1: very fast<br>1: medium<br>1: decrescendo | 5: slow |
| *Range:* | 5: small, enclosed | 5: large, sweeping | 3: small<br>2: large |
| *Shape:* | 3: round<br>2: angular | 5: very straight | 5: round |
| *Tension:* | 4: little tension<br>1: inconsistent | 5: much tension | 4: little tension<br>1: decrescendo |
| *Direction:* | 5: indefinite, chang-<br>ing, wavering | 5: precise, sharp,<br>mostly forward | 3: indefinite, chang-<br>ing<br>2: mostly downward |
| *Center:* | 5: passive, pulled<br>downward | 5: active, cen-<br>tered in body | 3: passive<br>2: from active to<br>passive |

states of mind in a way which would be more exact scientifically than the descriptions offered by novelists or everyday language. Nevertheless, it can be seen from our example that the dynamic patterns of expressive behavior permit relatively concrete and exact descriptions in terms of speed, range, shape, etc. Even the crudely simplified characterizations given in the table seem to suggest that the motor traits through which the dancers interpreted sadness reflect the slow, languishing pace of the psychological processes, the indefiniteness of aim, the withdrawal from the environment, the passivity—all of which distinguish sadness psychologically. The fact that expressive behavior is so much more readily accessible to concrete scientific description than the corresponding psychical processes deserves attention. It suggests that in the future the study of behavior may well become the method of choice, when psychologists undertake the task of reducing emotions and other psychical processes to configurations of basic forces. Already the analysis of handwriting has led to a number of categories (pressure, size, direction, proportion, etc.) which invite a search for the corresponding psychological concepts.

Our example will also show why it is fruitless to dismiss the phenomena of expression as "mere stereotypes." If it can be demonstrated that the dynamics of psychical and physical processes are structurally interrelated and that this interrelation is perceptually evident, the question of whether and to what extent the performance and its interpretations are based on social conventions loses importance.

REFERENCES

1. Allport, G. W., and Vernon, P. E. *Studies in expressive movement.* New York: Macmillan, 1933.
2. Arnheim, R. Experimentell-psychologische Untersuchungen zum Ausdrucksproblem. *Psychol. Forsch.,* 1928, 11, 2–132.
3. Asch, S. E. Max Wertheimer's contribution to modern psychology. *Soc. Res.,* 1946, 13, 81–102.
4. Berkeley, G. *An essay toward a new theory of vision.* New York: Dutton, 1934.
5. Bowie, H. P. *On the laws of Japanese painting.* San Francisco: Elder, 1911.
6. Bühler, C. The social behavior of children. In C. Murchison (Ed.), *A handbook of child psychology.* Worcester, Mass.: Clark University Press, 1933. Pp. 374–416.
7. Darwin, C. *The expression of the emotions in man and animals.* New York: Appleton, 1896.
8. Efron, D. *Gesture and environment.* New York: King's Crown, 1941.
9. Gottshalk, D. W. *Art and the social order.* Chicago: University of Chicago Press, 1947.
10. Koffka, K. *Principles of Gestalt psychology.* New York: Harcourt, Brace, 1935.
11. Köhler, W. *The mentality of apes.* New York: Harcourt, Brace, 1925.
12. Köhler, W. *Gestalt psychology.* New York: Liveright, 1929.
13. Köhler, W. Psychological remarks on some questions of anthropology. *Amer. J. Psychol.,* 1937, 50, 271–288. [See pp. 203–221 of the present book.]
14. Köhler, W., and Wallach, H. Figural after-effects: An investigation of visual processes. *Proc. Amer. phil. Soc.,* 1944, 88, 269–357.
15. Langfeld, H. S. *The aesthetic attitude.* New York: Harcourt, Brace, 1920.
16. Lipps, T. Aesthetische Einfühlung. *Z. Psychol.,* 1900, 22, 415–450.
17. Lundholm, H. The affective tone of lines. *Psychol. Rev.,* 1921, 28, 43–60.
18. Rapaport, D. The Szondi test. *Bull. Menninger Clin.,* 1941, 5, 33–39.
19. Schachtel, E. G. On color and affect. *Psychiat.,* 1943, 6, 393–409.
20. Villey, P. *The world of the blind.* London: Duckworth, 1930.
21. Werner, H. *Comparative psychology of mental development.* New York: Harper, 1940.

22. Willmann, R. R. An experimental investigation of the creative process in music. *Psychol. Monogr.,* 1944, 57, No. 261.
23. Wolff, W. *The expression of personality.* New York: Harper, 1943.
24. Woodworth, R. S. *Experimental psychology.* New York: Holt, 1938.

*Solomon E. Asch*

SWARTHMORE COLLEGE

# THE METAPHOR:

# A PSYCHOLOGICAL

# INQUIRY

## AN OBSERVATION

When we turn to the study of cognition of persons,[1] it is natural to ask about the differences between things and persons as psychological stimuli. We do this in order to state more sharply the problems peculiar to interpersonal cognition. Proceeding in this way, one soon reaches a conclusion of importance. The study of person cognition is, in good part, the study of the ways in which we observe and take into account

Reprinted from *Person Perception and Interpersonal Behavior,* edited by Renato Tagiuri and Luigi Petrullo, with the permission of the publishers, Stanford University Press. Copyright 1958 by the Board of Trustees of Leland Stanford Junior University.

[Additional data are to be found in the following source: Solomon E. Asch. On the use of metaphor in the description of persons. In H. Werner (Ed.), *On expressive language*. Worcester, Mass.: Clark University Press, 1955.—Ed.]

[1] The writer wishes to thank Dr. Helen Peak and Dr. A. Irving Hallowell for their thoughtful criticisms of this paper at the Symposium on Person Perception.

This study was done with the help of a grant from the Ford Foundation.

perceptions, intentions, thoughts, and passions of others. These phenomena we find in persons, not as a rule in things.

This is a sound and fruitful starting point. But as soon as we agree to this, another question obtrudes itself. Persons and things are also similar in many respects; there is much they share in common. At this point, we might be tempted to conclude that those features present in things and in persons may well be reserved for a general psychology of cognition; we would thus free ourselves to concentrate on the problems specific to this area. This would be a sensible conclusion if it did not obscure a range of questions that may be fundamental. It is possible that the similarities between persons and things are of definite concern to the cognition of persons.

This discussion takes its start from the following observation of our language: when we describe the workings of emotions, ideas, or trends of character, we almost invariably employ terms that also denote properties and processes observable in the world of nature. Terms such as *warm, hard, straight* refer to properties of things and of persons. We say that a man thinks straight; that he faces a hard decision; that his feelings have cooled. We call persons deep and shallow, bright and dull, colorful and colorless, rigid and elastic. Indeed, for the description of persons we draw upon the entire range of sensory modalities.

This dual function is not restricted to property terms, or adjectives. Action names or verbs also possess this dual function. We hunger and thirst for knowledge; we carry thoughts in our minds; our hopes are kindled and shattered. We find the same dual function in noun terms; so, we speak of a flash of wit, of winds of doctrine, and climates of opinion. "Depth" psychology is today nearly a technical term.

Finally, the language of social experience and action reveals the same characteristic. We are joined to people with ties and bonds; classes are high and low; groups exert pressure, maintain distance from other groups, and possess atmosphere.

There is apparently no aspect of nature that does not serve to express psychological realities. Light and darkness express the conditions of knowledge and ignorance, while the action of rivers and storms and the change of the seasons are the images in which we describe the vicissitudes of life and the data of inner experience. Conversely, there are, it seems, hardly any psychological terms *sui generis,* denoting psychological operations exclusively. (Whether there are any terms with an exclusively psychological reference is a question of interest that we have not investigated.) Our language has not established a distinct vocabulary pertaining exclusively to psychological phenomena. To be sure, we possess many terms that have become specialized in a psychological direction (e.g., hope, jealousy, wrath). However, their etymology reveals that they once had a clear physical reference.

This way of speaking has, for most of us, every mark of being literal. *Hard* describes a person as directly as a rock. Indeed, as a rule, we are not aware of the double function of terms; they develop their concrete meaning in each context in apparent independence of the meaning they have in other contexts. Further, when we do become aware of the duality, it strikes us, members of the same language community, as singularly appropriate. It makes considerable sense to speak of a *spotless* character, or of *black* treason. This is the language we employ spontaneously to describe the life of feelings and ideas.

These observations bear a curious relation to a long-standing concern of psychologists. We have disciplined ourselves to an attitude of distrust toward what we call anthropomorphism. Yet here we find, apparently, the reverse tendency developed to the fullest extent. Every man employs the language of naïve physics when he is talking about psychological matters, including his private experiences.

What is the nexus that unites under the same term, such as *straight,* a property of surfaces, paths, movements, and of certain operations of thinking or trends of character? We propose to explore the grounds of this phenomenon and to examine its relevance to human thinking.

A QUESTION

What was said so far leads to the following empirical question: does the characteristic under discussion belong to human languages generally, or is it restricted to those from which the present observations started? The question is a twofold one: (a) Do historically independent languages employ the same morphemes to designate physical and psychological properties? (b) If so, do languages belonging to different families also agree in the detailed couplings they make?

The questions prompted the investigation now to be described. We drew up a list of adjectives which, in English, have the double function mentioned above, in order to establish whether there are morphemes in other historically unrelated languages that refer to the same sets of physical and psychological properties. Included among the terms were the following: warm, cold, hot; right, left; dull, bright, pale, shining; straight, twisted, crooked; sweet, bitter; colorful, colorless, white, black (and some other color terms); rough, smooth, slippery; dry, wet; clear, cloudy; deep, shallow; high, low; broad, rounded, sharp; hard, soft.

Our purpose required the examination of languages belonging to different families and, as far as possible, separated in time and space. Among the languages selected were: (a) *Old Testament Hebrew,* belonging to the Semitic branch of the Semito-Hamitic family, and dating back to approximately 1,000 B.C.; (b) *Homeric Greek,* a member of the Indo-European family dating back to approximately 800 B.C.; (c) *Chinese,* a member of the Sino-Tibetan family (the examples for Chinese were either colloquial or literary; it was often not possible to distinguish between them); (d) *Thai,* a member of the Sino-Tibetan family; (e) *Malayalam,* a member of the Dravidian family, spoken in southwestern India; (f) *Hausa,* a member of the Sudanese family, spoken in Western Africa by approximately thirteen million people; (g) *Burmese,* also a member of the Sino-Tibetan family.

The informants were either scholars or native speakers. The informant was given the English term and asked to state the morpheme which, in the given language, described the same or most similar physical property. (Where possible, the morpheme was transcribed phonemically; if a phonemic analysis was not available, phonetic transcriptions were used.) He was then invited to give a few instances of phrases or sentences in which the morpheme referred to physical properties; these were transcribed, and the literal translation into English of each morpheme was obtained, followed by the English equivalent of the entire expression. This first step had the purpose of establishing the distribution of the term in physical contexts, and of permitting us to decide whether it corresponded to the English equivalent. Thereupon, the informant was asked whether the same morpheme referred also to psychological properties. If it did, he illustrated the usage with phrases or sentences; these were first translated literally and then idiomatically.[2]

Our first finding is that all the languages here examined contain terms that simultaneously describe both physical and psychological qualities.

To what extent is there agreement among languages in the pairing of physical and psychological properties? For illustration we have selected the results obtained for the terms *sweet, bitter, sour;* these appear below.

Each of these languages possesses some morphemes that refer to the

[2] I wish to acknowledge the indispensable aid of Dr. Joseph R. Applegate in obtaining data from informants and in the work of transliteration.

*Sweet*

| | |
|---|---|
| Hebrew: | sweet to the soul (said of pleasant words) (Prov. 16:24) |
| Greek: | sweet laughter, voice (etymologically linked with the verb of "please") |
| Chinese: | a sweet smile (colloquial); sweet, honeyed words = specious words |
| Thai: | to be sweet is to faint; to be bitter is medicine = beware of people with whom you have relations |
| Hausa: | I don't feel sweetness = I don't feel well |
| Burmese: | face sweet = pleasant-faced; voice sweet = pleasant voice; speech sweet = pleasant speech |

*Bitter*

| | |
|---|---|
| Hebrew: | I will complain in the bitterness of my soul (Job 7:11) |
| Greek: | bitter pain, bitter tears |
| Chinese: | bitter fate = hard lot in life (literary and colloquial) |
| Thai: | as in English |
| Hausa: | bitterness of character = an unpleasant disposition; he felt (or perceived) the bitterness of this talk = he was very upset by this talk |
| Burmese: | to speak bitterly = to speak in an unfriendly manner |

*Sour*

| | |
|---|---|
| Hebrew: | for my heart was soured (Psalms 73:21) |
| Chinese: | sour man = a misanthrope; sour heart = sick at heart, grieved |
| Burmese: | I am very sour toward that person = I detest that person |

same paired properties as those found in the other languages. In this respect, there is impressive agreement. The usages recorded above will not offer difficulty to an English-speaking person.

The following question may be raised concerning the significance of the data here presented. Perhaps the terms *sweet, bitter, sour* merely designate generally positive and negative qualities on the psychological side. If so, they would point only grossly to their intended meanings, and would fail to represent more differentiated characteristics. Closer study does not sustain this conclusion. *Sweet* does not stand for just any positive psychological quality; it is not employed, for example, to describe courage or honesty. It seems appropriate to conclude that it describes, in the main, those psychological characteristics that we may call soothing. Similarly, *bitter* and *sour* are not synonymous with any negative quality. Our records do not contain reference to bitter or sour fear.[3]

---

[3] Related evidence in the same direction will be found in S. E. Asch (3).

There are also divergences in the data. (*a*) We often found that a morpheme of a given language denotes only a physical quality. The reasons for this restriction of meaning we have not had the opportunity to study; we can, therefore, offer only some partial conjectures. A language lacking an extended psychological vocabulary will often not name qualities of persons that are common currency in other languages. If, for example, the category of intelligence is not of outstanding importance, we will not find terms such as *penetrating* or *bright* to qualify it. There may also be a failure to employ a given morpheme in the psychological direction because another term already meets this need. In such cases it would be of value to identify the other morpheme, and to establish whether it too has a dual reference. Unfortunately we did not realize the import of this question until late in the investigation. (*b*) A given term may, in each language, develop a somewhat different range of meanings. The data above offer only limited evidence for this statement (e.g., the reference to sweet as specious, in the Chinese). The evidence, as a whole, contains other such instances. For example, *sharp lips* in the Chinese and Hausa stands for fluency or glibness. In these cases, it is not difficult to discern that the several meanings are by no means heterogeneous; they are specializations of a more general property in which they all share. It is noteworthy that some terms, such as *straight* and *crooked,* develop a remarkably uniform psychological meaning, in contrast with others, such as *hot* and *cold.*[4] (*c*) In some instances, by no means the most frequent, we cannot readily deduce or fully understand after the fact the psychological sense of a term. In Thai, for example, *spoiled heart* is to be sad, while *heart spoiled* is to be discouraged. In these cases, we can only anticipate the most general direction. A fuller understanding would perhaps require a familiarity with the syntactical properties of the language.

We have not found instances that could be called contradictory. The data permit us rather to speak of agreement and absence of agreement. It is indeed hard at this point to specify strictly what a contradictory finding would be. It might seem that directly opposed usages in two languages would be an instance of contradiction; for example, if the term designating physical straightness referred also to dishonesty. No investigator would be content, however, to leave the matter at this point. He would attempt to discover whether there was a relation between these meanings evident to the speakers of the language. If no

---

[4] *Ibid.*

such relation could be found, the issue would be left in doubt. If, however, the connection between the terms was clarified, the contradiction would at the same time dissolve. Clarification, in this context, stands for a connection that is understandable both to the speaker and to the inquirer.

The present data are incomplete in one important respect. Since we confined ourselves to a limited number of languages and to a limited set of terms, we lack systematic information about the degree of agreement among languages, or about the consistency among languages with respect to particular terms. We cannot therefore account systematically for the presence and absence of agreement between one language and another, or for consistency in respect to any one term, or for the far more extended incidence of double-function terms in some languages than in others. Far more detailed investigations would be necessary for this purpose. This limitation is a barrier to a complete theory of the phenomena in question, but it does not, we would propose, throw doubt on the positive findings we have reported. We conclude that there is no inevitable agreement, but the agreement that occurs is lawful and substantial.

THE CONCEPTUAL BASIS OF DUAL TERMS

The substantial agreement we have found among languages establishes that the dual function here examined is not a fortuitous product. From the linguistic evidence alone, even if it were more complete, we could not, of course conclude about the responsible operations. For this purpose we need a psychological analysis. In what follows, we will attempt to see how the agreements for which we found evidence might arise.

An explanation of the data requires an answer to two questions, one general and the other special. We need, first, to clarify the fact that there are terms denoting both physical and psychological properties. In addition, we have to account for the particular joining of given physical and psychological properties by an identical term.

That we describe psychological happenings in terms that have also a physical reference should not raise a thorny issue.[5] We come to know about persons by observation of their actions; this is the source of our knowledge about the motives and thought of other persons. We have

---

[5] It should be clear from the context that the terms "physical" and "psychological" refer in this discussion throughout to phenomenal data. Both are part of the phenomenal field. This discussion deals with the relations between experienced physical and psychological data, not with the objective mind-body problem.

no access to their experiences except through observation of what they do, of their posture and of the expressions furnished by the changing appearances of the face and the tone of voice. The observer and observed are distinct systems between whom there is no psychological continuity; our knowledge of others is mediated by the physical energies that leave them and reach us.[6] It is therefore by no means surprising that the terms descriptive of experience are so often "physicalistic."

The second and main task is to account for the specific joining of a given physical and psychological experience. We need to understand how a term such as *warm* or *hard* comes to designate certain particular properties of human action.

We see two main directions that an interpretation of dual terms may take. One possibility is that we experience certain events in persons and things as similar in some fundamental respects, and therefore describe them with the same term. If so, the terms of dual reference name similarities that we observe to be intrinsic. The significant alternative is one in terms of association by contiguity. Dual terms may be the consequence of stable associative connections established between dissimilar physical and psychological conditions that regularly share some stimulus properties.

Both alternatives, which are obviously not mutually exclusive, rely on past experience but in ways that are fundamentally different. The thesis of intrinsic similarity requires that a present datum, say the observation that a person is *soft,* make contact with the trace of earlier experiences pertaining to softness in things. This step is necessary if the identical term is to refer to both settings by similarity. However, the contact between the present experience and the aftereffect of the earlier experiences, or the grasp of their resemblance, is not itself learned, being the direct result of perceived similarity. In contrast, the associative interpretation excludes the relation of similarity, relying instead on a specific association at a given point of time between two heterogeneous stimuli that need bear no resemblance to each other.

According to the contiguity interpretation, a psychological event is designated by a physical term when the property corresponding to the latter is one component of it. Thus we say that a person *reddened* to indicate that he was embarrassed, or that he *paled* when we want to convey that he was frightened.

Although language often designates an entire situation by naming a part of it, it is doubtful whether this operation accounts for dual

---

[6] For a fuller discussion of this point see S. E. Asch (2, Chap. 5).

terms completely or even in greater part. It is often not possible to find the particular physical component in the psychological setting; the use of the term *colorful* in relation to persons might serve as an example. Further, the contiguity interpretation cannot account for the absence of complete agreement among languages. These, as well as some other reasons that might be mentioned, limit the value of this interpretation.

Any attempt at an interpretation in terms of stimulus similarity meets at the outset the difficulty, mentioned earlier, that we often cannot find in the psychological and physical settings the stimulus conditions that they presumably share. At this point it becomes necessary to examine more carefully the content of the terms in question.

What are we trying to say when we call a thing, say the surface of a table, *hard?* We mean that it resists change when pushed or pressed, that it supports other things placed upon it without changing its own form. Hardness is resistance to change imposed by external forces; it describes a mode of interaction. Correspondingly, what is soft takes on the form of things acting upon it, as does the tablecloth that follows the contours of a surface. What now is the sense of *hard* when it refers to a person? It describes an interaction that is formally similar. We see a man refusing the appeal of another. This interaction we experience as a force proceeding from one person, having as its aim the production of a change in the other, which, however, fails to *move* him, or which produces *resistance.* The hardness of a table and of a person concerns events radically different in content and complexity, but the schema of interaction is experienced as dynamically similar, having to do with the application of force and of resulting action in line with or contrary to it. What holds in the preceding instance applies to the other terms in the same category. *Warm,* aside from thermal qualities, stands for bringing closer, or for drawing into a union, while *cold* excludes or isolates. *Colorful* designates not only the possession of color but also the presence of diversity capable of eliciting interest.[7]

The conclusion we draw, and one we consider essential to a solution of the present problem, is that the terms under discussion refer not alone to unique sensory qualities, but to functional properties or modes of interaction. They do not denote exclusively the "raw materials" of experience; they are also the names of *concepts.* A sensationalistic psychology, whose hold upon us has not completely relaxed, obscures this point and hinders us from seeing that *straightness, depth, sharpness* en-

---

[7] I am indebted to Dr. Fritz Heider for an illuminating discussion of this point.

compass far more than those selected aspects that lend themselves to psychophysical investigation. We need to guard against the unwitting assumption that these data are as narrow as their current technical meanings; as a rule they include important dynamic and physiognomic properties that are as yet less accessible to exact investigation.

The concepts in question have little in common with abstract logical operations. They are not generalizations of what is common to an array of different instances. Rather they are concrete cognitive operations in terms of which we naïvely comprehend events and similarities between them.

The conclusion we have reached is that when we describe psychological events in the same terms we employ for the description of the forces of nature—of fire, sea, wind—we are referring to functional properties they share. We see natural events as conductors of the same fundamental forces that we find in the human sphere. Therefore we speak spontaneously of *seeing* a point, of *shedding light on* or *illuminating* a problem, of *penetrating to the heart of* a matter. The dual terms of this study derive from this source, being shorthand names for functional relations and forces.

We have sketched a first approach to the experienced relation between physical and psychological events. It is helpful in raising a number of questions that can be studied empirically. It should, for example, be possible to investigate, in a relatively straightforward way, the development in children of the usages here described, and their role in the mastery of language. This inquiry also suggests a point of departure for thinking about the general problem of metaphor. It is, perhaps, not too much to hope that the study of these questions could contribute to our knowledge of cognitive functions and to a lessening of the gap that has, too long, continued between psychology and the humanities.

**REFERENCES**

1. Aristotle. *De Poetica.*
2. Asch, S. E. *Social psychology.* New York: Prentice-Hall, 1952.
3. Asch, S. E. On the use of metaphor in the description of persons. In H. Werner (Ed.), *On expressive language.* Worcester, Mass.: Clark University Press, 1955.
4. Hornbostel, E. M. The unity of the senses. *Psyche,* 1927, 1–7.
5. Klages, L. *Vom Wesen des Bewusstseins.* Leipzig: J. A. Barth, 1921.
6. Köhler, W. *Gestalt psychology.* New York: Liveright, 1929.
7. Vico, G. B. *The new science.* Translated from 3d Ed. (1744) by T. G. Bergin and M. H. Fisch. Ithaca: Cornell University Press, 1948.

*Rudolf Arnheim*

SARAH LAWRENCE COLLEGE

# EMOTION AND FEELING

# IN PSYCHOLOGY

# AND ART

In many of the more recent writings on art, words like "emotion" and "feeling" have been made to work overtime. The burden of describing the content and function of artistic activity has been carried by them to a considerable degree. Clive Bell asserts that "the starting-point for all systems of aesthetics must be the personal experience of a peculiar emotion," which he calls "the aesthetic emotion" (4, pp. 6, 7). Elsewhere we read that art expresses emotion and requires emotion and that beauty is an emotional element. There are also emotional aspects of design as well as cosmic emotions; and poetic language is said to express "feeling or emotion presented as the qualitative character of imaginal content" (20, p. 145). When the meaning of such terms is taken for granted, even the kind of sensitive description of which aestheticians have given us many will not serve to clarify the nature of artistic activity as compared to other activities of the human mind. The implied definitions are either so broad that the statements lose concrete sense, or so narrow that they make art look like an outlet for highstrung ladies.

If the dissatisfied reader turns to the psychology of emotion he dis-

Reprinted with permission from *Confinia Psychiatrica,* Vol. 1, No. 2, 1958.

covers that writers from Descartes to Claparède (21, p. 124) have prefaced their expositions of the subject with the assertion that it makes for the most deficient and confused chapter in the whole field. A few decades ago textbook writers were at a loss as to what to say about emotion (21, p. 18). This situation still prevails in academic psychology, which has limited itself to some irritated discussion of whether emotion is to signify everything or nothing and, for the rest, has concentrated on the interesting physiological aspects of the phenomenon. At the same time clinical psychology, less inhibited by scruples about theory, has set off a veritable inflation, comparable to that in aesthetics. Professionals and laymen speak of "emotional adjustment" and "emotional deprivation," "emotional conflict" and "emotional immaturity," "uncanny emotions" and "emotional disorders." The term "covers" almost everything not strictly perceptual or intellectual—wishes, attitudes, judgments, reactions, intuitions, opinions, disturbances. The present paper will suggest that an appropriate trimming of the term "emotion" might discipline the thinking of the clinicians, relieve the bad conscience of the theorists, and reopen to scientific research neglected central areas of psychology. In the second part of the paper, an examination of some of the psychological problems that are hidden in aesthetics by a catch-all jargon will illustrate questions still to be answered for psychology in general.

*Emotion as a category per se.* Most psychologists seem to agree with the layman that there are "emotions," i.e., that among the genera of mental state there is one called "emotion," which is made up of various species. There is no agreement on the number and names of these species. Some authors present lists of "primary emotions," from which an indefinite number of secondary ones is to be derived. Others have sample collections of "emotions." Woodworth (26, p. 410) groups "feelings and emotions" under the following keynotes: pleasure, displeasure, mirth, excitement, calm, expectancy, doubt, surprise, desire, aversion, anger. Leeper (17, p. 16) selects "fear, anger, feelings of guilt, feelings of grief, affection, pride in the doing of good work, enjoyment of beautiful music, and enjoyment of companionship." Here again one notices that the only common denominator is a negative one: "purely" motivational processes, such as instincts, and "purely" perceptual and intellectual ones are excluded. Everything else is stored in the large receptacle for used and discarded matter, labeled "emotion." And there it rests.

The term "emotion," however, suggests a positive meaning; etymologically it refers to agitation, physical, at first, and also mental, later on. In fact, at an elementary level of psychological theorizing the term is reserved for states of high-pitched agitation, such as rage and panic. Hence the view that emotion is disruptive by definition. Once theorists look beyond the more patent aspects of the phenomenon, they discover that the spectacular extreme states are nothing but high degrees of the excitation inherent in all mental activity. This point has been made so clearly by several writers that one wonders why it has not yet become a common property of psychological thinking. McDougall (18, p. 148) used the swatting of a fly as an example to show that an initially almost neutral activity can work up to a clearly "emotional" state with no other change but in the degree of excitement. Similarly Meyer (19) and Duffy (6, 7, 8, 9) pointed out that emotion is not an additional mode of experience but a component of all experience. Duffy proposed to drop the old term entirely and to speak instead of the degree of excitation, that is, the extent of activation or arousal. To her, this dimension of intensity is one of the two "cross-sectional concepts" that apply to all behavior, the other being a motivational and cognitive one, "goal direction (incl. responses to relationships)." Compare here also Masserman's recent energetic statement (22, pp. 40 ff.).

Apparently this more adequate view is hard to accept, even for psychologists who endorse it in principle. Koffka, for instance (15, p. 401), cites McDougall with approval, insists that emotion must not be treated as a thing, describes it as a dynamic characteristic applying to "certain psychophysical processes," and continues a few lines later to use the term "emotions" in the plural. Schlosberg (24), in presenting what he calls the "activation theory of emotion," speaks at times as though he recognized intensity as the dimension of human behavior corresponding to what is commonly called "emotion" ("activation would seem to be a very good name for what emotion does to us") but proceeds to point out "one obvious failing" of his theory: "It deals only with the intensive dimension and takes no account of differentiation among the various emotions."

*Emotions as motives or cognitions.* Authors who assume that "emotions" represent a specific category of mental state run into instructive difficulties. Leeper (17), after rejecting disruptiveness and disorganization as differentiating traits of emotion, presents a criterion of his own. He describes emotions as a subclass of motive, distinguished from the more elementary "bodily drives or physiological motives such as hunger, thirst, toothache, and craving for salt" by their complexity. When animals become "more complex in their receptor equipment, motor equipment, and capacity for learning," they develop fear based on past experience, interest in the offspring not dependent on physiological impulses, an urge to explore, etc. This is the kind of motive Leeper calls "the emotions." His terminology accomplishes the feat of denying the emotional quality to hunger and toothache and of identifying emotions by means of properties that by no stretch of the term can be described as specifically emotional, namely, the cognitive and motivational capacities for learning, understanding, foresight, interest, curiosity.

Attempts to describe emotions as a subclass of cognition do not seem to fare better. According to Broad (5), an emotion is a cognition that has an emotional quality. "To be fearing a snake . . . is to be cognising something—correctly or incorrectly—as a snake, and for that cognition to be toned with fearfulness." It will be noticed that in the example the cognitive aspect of the reaction is limited to the identification of the snake rather than including, as it surely must, the recognition of its fearsomeness. Once this correction is made, nothing seems to remain of the "emotional quality" but the sheer, unspecific excitement, which accompanies the (cognitive) realization of danger and the (conative) desire to escape. More in general, the reader of Broad's paper finds that the characteristics attributed by the author to the "emotions" (motived and unmotived, misplaced, appropriate and inappropriate, etc.) do not apply to the emotional but to the cognitive aspects of the reactions in question. Therefore it seems hardly justified to call these reactions "emotions." On the other hand, calling them "cognitions" leaves the description clearly incomplete.

*A label that stops research.* Academic psychology is driven to call certain mental states "emotions" because it is accustomed to distributing all psychological phenomena into the three compartments of cognition, motivation, and emotion instead of realizing that every mental state has cognitive, motivational, and emotional components, and cannot be defined properly by any one of the three. In the cases of cognition and motivation the pigeonholing procedure has had grave consequences for research. Only processes which—without obvious distortion of their nature—can be described as pure percepts, pure acts of thinking or learning, pure motives, etc., are being given more than cursory attention by scientific psychologists. One can strip hunger of its cognitive and emotional aspects and classify it as a motive, and a glance at a blue triangle may not be seriously falsified by being called a perception. But the more relevant psychological phenomena resist such treatment. Hope or pride, for instance, do not fit into either box: they inseparably combine certain views of people and situations with certain needs. They are neither motives nor percepts, and therefore scientific psychologists do not deal with them. They can speak about sex but have little to say about love because love is no instinct. Hate, ambition, honesty, grief, trust, happiness, courage, shame, admiration, modesty —things like these have always been considered the characteristic stirrings of the human mind; but their study has found no place in scientific psychology. It is left to philosophers who still consider the analysis of the mind as their business; to clinicians, who are forced by practical necessity to deal with the essentials; and to common-sense talk inside and outside of textbooks and lectures. Much of such discussion does not meet scientific standards; but it is also true that scientific standards will have to fit the essential tasks of psychology if we wish to develop a discipline that, by the standards of the great poets and thinkers and by those of the common man, deserves to be called a science of the human mind.

Academic psychologists have not simply overlooked the existence of the salient features of the mind. Since they could not fit them into the two main boxes, "motivation" and "cognition," they put them in the third and called them "emotions." The trouble with this third category has been that, whereas there are enough mental states that can be trimmed to look like pure motives or pure perceptions, the excitement of emotion is dominant only in rare extremes and even then is nothing but an unspecific by-product of what the person perceives, knows, understands, and desires. Hence the embarrassed searching for something to talk about in the chapter on the emotions, and the attempts to equip them with cognitive and conative features in order to give them body, variety, function. Once such essentially perceptual experiences as pleasure and pain, and such complex states as sadness and joy, had been filed under "emotion" there was no stopping, so that by now we have the above-cited lists of "emotions," which read like the inventory of a storage vault.

We are not dealing here with a matter of mere terminology nor even with one of conceptual tidiness alone. By pigeonholing the essential objects of true psychological interest, academic psychologists have removed them from the grasp of research. No better treatment than disorderly enumeration can be given them as long as they remain labeled as "emotions" because the emotional component offers no understanding of the processes that cause the excitement. The history of medicine offers useful analogies. In the olden days people fell sick with "the fever." What we recognize now as a symptom was then considered the nature of the illness. Not before the causal processes of infection, etc., became the center of interest was it possible to understand the diseases and to distinguish them adequately from each other. Nowadays people have "emotional difficulties." But when, for instance, a college student cannot use his intelligence and his interest, this does not happen because he is "emotionally upset," but he is emotionally upset because such conative factors as thwarted wishes and such cognitive ones as his particular perception of himself and the world around him interfere with his work. And when a person "reacts emotionally" he does not replace reason with emotion but replaces one set of motives and percepts with another, less appropriate one, for instance, by viewing a controversy as a matter of personal attack. As long as the psychologist thinks and acts as a clinician the crude labeling by symptom may matter little. For the psychologist as an academic scientist, however, it has the effect of putting the phenomenon on a sidetrack and thus removing it from the work on motivation and cognition, by which alone it can profit and to which, in turn, it gives its *raison d'être*. Something is wrong if the theorist and experimentalist wait for the clinician to figure out, under the pressure of his practical obligations, what "anxiety" is. We must not blame the clinician if our more relevant concepts give off a sickroom smell; he has done more than his share.

Perhaps the academic psychologist will defend himself by saying that scientific virtue requires him to limit himself to simpler problems until he is ready to deal with the complex ones. But it is one thing to proceed with caution and another not to envisage the goal. By hiding the central processes under the cloak of emotion we help make ourselves blind to the true object of our science. Recent attempts to put the milled-out vitamins back in the bread are thus far conceived as studies of the mutual influence of "motives" and "percepts." It remains to be seen whether this promising development will lead to the exploration of mental states that cannot be reduced either to motives or to percepts but are compounds of motivational, cognitive, and emotional factors from the outset.

*Models of the past.* The historian will have to tell us who contributed what to this development. Surely it would seem unjust to blame the great masters of the seventeenth century for it. It is misleading, although technically correct, for instance, to state that "Descartes specified six primary emotions" (27, p. 27). In *Les Passions de l'Ame,* Descartes divided the functions of the soul into active and passive ones (actions and passions). Passions are affections of the soul, caused either by the soul itself or by the body. Those caused by the body are subjectively attributed either to outer objects (seeing the light of a torch) or to the body (feeling hunger or pain), or they seem to be produced by the soul itself. These latter, the sentiments of wonder, love, hatred, desire, joy, and sadness, plus their derivations, are named passions in the more restricted sense. Of them Descartes says that they may be called perceptions in that they are passive, or *sentiments* in that the soul receives them in the same way as the objects of the outer senses, or, "even better, one may call them emotions of the soul, not only because this name may be given to all changes that come about in the soul . . . but particularly because among all the kinds of activity the soul can have there are none that agitate and shake it so strongly as do these passions" (article 28). "Emotions," then, means "agitations," and the term is used to describe one attribute of the mental reactions Descartes continues to call "passions" throughout his treatise. In fact, the first and foremost of them, namely wonder, is said to be devoid of emotion because it does not regard good and evil but is merely the surprised attention given to rare objects (articles 70, 71).

Spinoza also keeps the emotional aspect of human reactions in its proper subordinate place. Where Descartes speaks of passions the *Ethics* uses the term *affectus,* meaning on the one hand affections of the body by which the power of action in the body is increased or diminished, aided or restrained, and on the other hand the conscious awareness (*ideae*) of these affections (book III, def. 3). The basic affection is conscious desire (*cupiditas*) which is experienced as pleasure (*laetitia*) when it is furthered and as displeasure (*tristitia*) when it is hampered in its striving for greater perfection (book III, prop. 57). From these primary affections derive the others, all of which are defined in cognitive and motivational terms, for instance, love as pleasure—that is, unhampered stirring—concomitant with the awareness of an external cause (book III, prop. 13). Primitive though such a definition may be, it invites and permits further investigation, as distinguished from our present conception of love as a kind of nondescript quiver.

*Feeling.* In the field of aesthetics, the generation of Bell (4) and Fry (11) preferred to speak of "emotions" whereas writers such as Prall and Langer rely heavily on the word "feeling." Prall (20, p. 147) defines aesthetic experience as "the full felt response to what is directly given," and to Langer (16, p. 40) "art is the creation of forms symbolic of human feeling." Psychologists speak of feelings as well as of emotions but the distinction between the two terms is admittedly unclear. "Emotion" tends to describe agitation or to designate a state of mind by the agitation it involves. "Feeling" centers about cognitive reactions that seem to defy further decomposition. Aveling, for instance (21, p. 49), restricts the term "feeling" to pleasure-unpleasure because they "seem to be irreducible to any other conscious experience whereas all other 'feelings' can be reduced either to cognitive or to conative processes." McDougall also appears unwilling to treat "pleasant and unpleasant feelings" as compounds of percepts and strivings. He concedes to them the status of one of the "three distinguishable but inseparable aspects of all mental activity"—knowing, striving, and feeling—(18, p. 146) whereas emotion is considered nothing but the degree of excitement found in any such activity. To Claparède "feelings are useful in our conduct while emotions serve no purpose" (21, p. 126). He lists as feelings not only such percepts as pain but also such "intellectual feelings" as surprise, curiosity, doubt, that is, the emotionally toned reactions to intellectual or perceptual insight, as well as James's "feelings of relations" (14, I, p. 245), those seemingly nonintellectual and nonperceptual cognitions to which reference will be made later. Here again psychology hardly can be said to offer much clarification to the theorist of art.

*A conceptual framework.* The foregoing discussion will have shown that the misuse of the terms "emotion" and "feeling" is only a local consequence of a more general defect of psychological reasoning, namely, the habit of defining any mental act by one of its components. To remedy this situation, a first step has already been suggested: for all but the most elementary purposes a mental process must be described as a compound of phenomena that come under several basic concepts. It seems necessary to go further, however, and to think of these concepts as being subordinated rather than coördinated and as mutually inclusive rather than exclusive. What such a conceptual framework might look like can be indicated here only in the crudest tentative fashion.

The most inclusive concept is that of perception. It holds the entire inventory of things and happenings of which a person is aware, either consciously or unconsciously. We distinguish here, first of all, percepts of the outer physical world (a horse, my hands, a thunderstorm) from percepts of the inner physical world (a sweet taste, a tightening muscle, a pain in the neck). In its current usage the term "perception" is limited to these two groups of experiences. But among the percepts of the inner physical world there should also be included those that are not due to the stimulation of sensory organs outside of the brain; we may call them informally "intracerebral percepts" (thoughts, desires, memories, imagery) as distinguished from the "extracerebral percepts," which are "sensed." A thought is no less directly perceived than a table. Perception, then, is the top level of the psychological hierarchy.

At a second level, various categories of percepts can be distinguished from each other. There is, to repeat, the basic distinction between extracerebral and intracerebral percepts, plus the frequent interaction of both (a listener thinks about what he is hearing; a painter organizes an image of shapes and colors into a meaningful pattern). Images may be extracerebral or intracerebral, that is, sensed or imagined, and are distinguished from the abstract concepts of reasoning. Reasoning is distinguished from intuitive thinking ("feeling").

At a third level there are various attributes of percepts. We need to mention only two, which are shared by all percepts, regardless of category. First, all percepts possess directed tension. This attribute is sensed, for instance, in the upward striving of a poplar tree, the rising or falling of a musical scale, a cat's rubbing his fur against the leg of his master, the impingements of colors, sounds, smells, or touch upon the self, or the expansion of one's breathing chest; it is also perceived intracerebrally when the self "sends out" its capacities of seeing, hearing, touching for the sensory exploration of the outer and the inner world, or when we yearn for a loved person or press a train of thought towards its goal. This omnipresent quality of directed tension is commonly called "expression" when it is found in sensory percepts. In intracerebral percepts it is known as "motivation."

All directed tension has an intensity—which is the second universal attribute of mental processes to be mentioned here. The impact of a colored light, a noise, the ocean surf, or the sting of an injection needle may be perceived as being strong or weak, and, similarly, goal-directed strivings vary in intensity. When applied to intracerebral percepts the level of intensity can be described as "emotion."

The conceptual framework that has been sketched here implies that "emotions" and "feelings" are not independent entities but rather terms referring to properties that are better defined by other psychological concepts. This approach will now be applied to problems concealed by the two words in the field of the arts.

Among the reasons why the words "emotion" and "feeling" are frequently chosen to describe the artistic processes are the following three:

1. Art is said to be made and sought because it gives pleasure; and pleasure is described as "an emotion."

2. The particular aspects of reality caught and reproduced by the work of art are said to be accessible neither to sensory perception nor to the intellect but instead to a third cognitive capacity, called "feeling."

3. The aspects of reality inherent in the work of art are not only received as factual information but arouse states of mind that are called "emotions" or "feelings."

*1. Pleasure—an unspecific criterion.* Words such as "pleasure," "delight," "enjoyment" abound in the writings on art; Santayana, for instance, defines beauty as "pleasure regarded as the quality of a thing" (23, p. 49). Nevertheless, not much needs to be said about the hedonistic theory.

Since little is gained by describing a mental phenomenon as "emotion," that is, by its mere intensity, we ask instead: What kind of percept is "pleasure"? We find it to be a sensory percept of the inner physical world, a state of well-being, experienced in the body. Typically the sensation is connected with some directed tension, such as a drive of the self toward the pleasure-giving object, or a tonic expansion of the self, or a positively experienced let-up of pressure. In such a description nothing can be found that leads to a distinction between pleasure derived from art and pleasure derived from any other source, for instance, food. The erroneous impression that there is a specific "aesthetic pleasure" is due to the fact that a given component of a mental state receives, from the total state, modifications that are easily attributed to the nature of the component itself. If the pleasure derived from a piece of sculpture "feels" different than that derived from food, the difference is due to the context, since everything that can be cited to characterize it is a part of the difference between looking at sculpture and tasting food. Pleasure as such is no more specific than the purr of a cat.

Pleasure always indicates that the given situation conforms to some need of the organism—a need for stimulation or distension. But this attribute of pleasure is, again, not distinctive. Therefore, the hedonistic definition, according to which art is what produces pleasure, conveys nothing but the trivial fact that art satisfies some kind of need; it provides a pseudo-answer, which tends to dry up curiosity. Scores of studies in so-called experimental aesthetics have missed their more relevant data by being based on the question: "Do you like it?" rather than: "What do you perceive?"

If we wish to go further, we must move beyond pleasure itself and ask with what kinds of state pleasure is associated in the particular case of art. Answers can be drawn from the whole range of percepts, those of the outer as well as those of the inner world, sensory and nonsensory. The harmony of a color scheme or a musical chord may give pleasure; so may the well-balanced, integrated, and clearly directed movements experienced by a dancer through the muscle tensions in his body. Memory joins sensory perception when a pleasurable correspondence is discovered between the configuration of forces observed in a pattern of shapes and colors and that inherent in a significant life situation.

These are not attributes but causes of pleasure. By examining the conditions that produce pleasure, art can be distinguished from other sources of satisfaction. It also becomes possible to make inferences about the nature of the specific needs served by art. Such an approach invites research rather than leading it into a dead end.

*2. "Feeling" as perception and unconscious judgment.* There is common agreement on the fact that art presents sensory patterns, images, and thoughts not for their own sake but as mere forms, capable of transmitting something else. The final content of the work of art is usually described as "emotions" or "feelings." Thus, Roger Fry calls the work of art "an expression of emotions regarded as ends in themselves" (11, p. 29). In the older writers, assertions of this kind refer mostly to internal states such as fear, joy, sadness, whereas the more recent ones have broadened the offering. According to Prall, the feelings conveyed by the artist "may range from the hard look of iron machines or polished brass railings to delicate shallows of light among grass stems, from feelings of the lightest gaiety to feelings of fate and doom" (20, p. 160).

Art, then, deals with the kind of mental state that—as I showed earlier—psychology has failed to investigate. Psychologists have been satisfied with attaching labels. Accordingly, when they experimented with "expression," that is, with the manifestations of such mental states in perceivable patterns (a human face, a piece of music) they did not investigate these manifestations either. They concentrated on finding out what qualities of sadness, or calmness, or passion observers were willing to attribute to the object and to what extent this was done "correctly." But they rarely asked what particular audible or visible features of the object determined the reactions of the observers. The question of how observers accomplished their feats was not made a part of the study but taken care of by some untested assumption. The traditional belief, for example, that in such experiments observers rely on associations established in the past, makes it unnecessary to study the nature of either the mental or the behavioral phenomena involved. Correlations among unknowns will suffice. Aestheticians have hardly done better, except that their answer to the question: How do people do it? tends to be: By feeling! rather than: By association. They prefer to attribute the accomplishments of the artist and his public to a cognitive faculty *sui generis,* neither perceptual nor intellectual.

Suppose now we wished to find out why people see pride in the Napoleonic stance of an actor or a marble figure; and suppose we were unwilling to gloss over the problem by simply relying on the assumption that observers know from past experience how proud people carry themselves. In examining the stimulus we would notice a head raised above the plane of human interaction, eyes closed or looking upward, a body stretched to its greatest height, a chest ostentatiously presented, hands withholding acceptance and coöperation by hiding between the buttons of the waistcoat or in the trouser pockets. These features would not suggest any kinship with pride as long as pride were nothing but an unknown "emotion." But if we tried to do our psychological duty by studying a proud person's state of mind, even the most primitive examination would show that such a person perceived in the outer world creatures so inferior to his own excellence that they could only be dominated, not dealt with as equals. We would find him striving to tower over them and to impress his superiority upon them. We might also notice "emotion," that is, the degree of tension or excitement involved, but it would tell us nothing specific. Rather would the places and directions of the vectors observed in the outer physical world (the image of the Napoleonic figure) be discovered to have an isomorphic affinity with the vectors operating in the "intracerebral percepts" of proud rising, withdrawing, displaying, etc. The obstructive split between outer dynamics and inner dynamics, caused by the separation of "perception" from "motivation," would be overcome.

Once we examine concretely what people do when they apprehend expression, it becomes apparent that the instrument they use is perception, not some other mysterious cognitive faculty. Perception not of the static aspects of shape, size, hue, or pitch, which can be measured with some yardstick, but of the directed tensions conveyed by these same stimuli. Which particular properties of visible and audible patterns contain the dynamic features has been shown elsewhere (2, 3). Decisive for the present discussion is that they are as immediately perceptual as are dimensions, quantities, or locations. It is owing to a traditional preference for static conceptions that Western theorizing has tended to exclude the dynamic aspects from perception and to assign them either to a kind of internally generated projection or to the special, negatively defined faculty of "feeling" (1).

The fuller way of perceiving, which stresses directed tensions, is a prerequisite for, but not a monopoly of, the aesthetic attitude. Once it is understood that the capacity to apprehend artistic expression grows out of unrestricted everyday observation, an artificial distinction will break down, and research in the general psychology of perception will cross-fertilize with that in the field of art.

Our assertion that it is uneconomical and misleading to assume the existence of "feeling" has been derived so far from a discussion of the relatively simplest processes, namely, the passive apprehension of perceptual patterns, both sensory and nonsensory. But art involves more than perceiving the dynamic quality of, say, rapid attack in the swoop of a seagull or the argument of a trial lawyer. It requires, for instance, an ability to judge the correctness of a compositional structure in the visual arts or music as to balance, unity, rhythm. In such tasks the intellect, which can apply conceptual rules such as those of proportion, plays only a minor part. Rather is the judgment of right and wrong performed by mere looking and listening, often without any awareness of the criteria that determine it. It takes a stubborn effort—successful only in the good teacher or critic—to make some such criteria explicit. But again we should be most reluctant to attribute these "intuitive" judgments to a cognitive faculty *sui generis*. What guides the artist or connoisseur turns out to be the same tensions that we have recognized as the very basis of perception. In a successful composition the forces that make up the pattern are in balance; but, if the work is incomplete or unsuccessful, pushes and pulls within the pattern indicate not only that something is wrong but also where correction should apply and in what directions it should proceed. Here again, artistic "feeling," to the extent to which it is an intuitive response to the given structure, is nothing but ordinary perception. It is a capacity not different in principle from that displayed by a tightrope walker or even of a dog who balances a stick in his mouth.

One step further, and we remember that art goes beyond the perceivable pattern. Artistic expression has always a semantic function; the painted and carved images stand for referents, and so do the shapes of music and the events and thoughts described by the poet. Therefore, art requires the judging of meaning, relevance, and truth, and again the task is accomplished largely by the mysterious capacity of "feeling." Is the artist's presentation relevant for, or true to, the kind of thing for which it stands? Does the particular sunflower that models for the artist or is seen on his canvas by the beholder look the way sunflowers look— to them? Does it conform to their conceptions of the nature of flowers in general? Does its dynamic pattern of, say, graceful heaviness capture a way of behavior worth capturing? These judgments are not simply perceptual, although ultimately they refer to percepts. They are based on the observer's entire life experience and involve his convictions, values, biases, memories, preferences. They presuppose translations of intellectual conclusions into perceptual images, and vice versa; and at the moment at which they take place they necessarily require a lightning-fast comparison of the given individual object with this complex precipitate of thought and vision.

Here again "feeling" is defined merely by exclusion. It describes a cognitive capacity that is neither mere perceiving nor based on conscious logical operations of the intellect. Here, too, no guiding criteria may be observable. How does the human mind perform such feats?

In searching for the answer, the student of art discovers one of the most astonishing gaps in the program of modern psychology. If we remember to how large an extent all human activity, from the driving of a car and the adding up of digits to the dealing with other people and the solution of creative problems in art and science, is done "intuitively" or "mechanically," that is, without conscious awareness of the processes that determine the action, it is hard to understand why psychologists limit their interest in this basic aspect of our functioning to the special case of the Freudian repression. The mere fact that so many of our judgments of right and wrong are made before we know why we make them should be sufficient to alert the profession. William James estimated that "a good third of our psychic life consists in these rapid premonitory perspective views of schemes of thought not yet articulate" (14, I, p. 253).

Judging by the accomplishments of these unconscious performances, we must conclude that mental capacities of the highest order are at work: reasoning, selecting, comparing, problem solving by restructuring, etc. But are these processes the same as their counterparts, known from conscious experience? And if so, do they function the same way? What should be made of the ample anecdotal evidence according to which scientific and artistic thinking of the highest caliber can solve, under the protective cover of the unconscious, problems whose solutions the conscious mind vainly struggled to find? (12, 13). Is perhaps unconscious creation less subject to the sets or other constraints that hamper conscious invention? Psychoanalysis has given illustrations of what distinguishes conscious from unconscious reasoning but it has also uncovered certain striking similarities. For instance, the dream mechanisms of condensation, fusion, displacement of function, and symbolism (10, chap. 6) closely resemble typical, and often conscious, operations of the artist.

Unless concrete research suggests that the processes here involved are fundamentally different from those operating in conscious experience there is no reason to imitate Molière's doctoral candidate, who explained the sleep-inducing effect of opium by a *virtus dormitiva*.

*3. The aesthetic "experience."* Up to this point, art has been discussed as though it were nothing but a transmitter of information about visible objects or audible events, subject matter, and the significant patterns of forces that are inherent in such material. But art not only acknowledges the presence of, say, agitation in a piece of music or bewildered wavering in the thoughts of Hamlet; it makes the artist and his public "feel" these dynamic states as personal "experiences." Tolstoy defined art as "a human activity consisting in this that one man consciously, by means of certain external signs, hands on to others feelings he has lived through, and that others are infected by these feelings and also experience them" (25, p. 123). What is the nature of such experiences?

In the aesthetic discussions of this question the use of the word "feeling" has made for a curious pseudo-problem. The notion was introduced by the theory of empathy, according to which architecture or music owed its expressiveness to past experiences of the observer, projected by him upon suitable objects. When the theory was abandoned by all those who realized that properties of the percepts themselves are responsible for the bulk of expression, the terminology remained and with it the problem of how a lifeless object could manifest "feelings" if they were not cast upon it by some "pathetic fallacy." According to Langer, who entitled her recent book on aesthetics *Form and Feeling,* "The solution of the difficulty lies . . . in the recognition that what art expresses is *not* actual feeling, but ideas of feeling" (16, p. 59). This formulation hides the problem by the word "expresses"; for either Langer's "ideas" are received, the way ideas usually are, as intellectual information, in which case the main difference between an artistic and a purely informative statement is neglected by the formulation; or the ideas are "felt," that is, are "feelings," in which case the dilemma remains what it was.

Once the terminological camouflage is removed, it appears that three different states—or perhaps three degrees of one state—must be distinguished in the phenomenon under discussion.

(a) At a first level, the difference between the mere apprehension of information and the fuller artistic "experience" is identical with that between the static and the dynamic properties of percepts. A piece of music can be played or listened to in a way that conveys nothing but an assembly of pitches and durations. The resulting sounds are "dead" because by lacking dynamics they lack the main structural quality of life; and they are no concern of anybody because only by exhibiting patterns of forces that it shares with the human mind can music build a connection between two media that otherwise are alien to each other: the extracerebral world of pure sounds and the intracerebral one of human striving. Similarly as long as Hamlet's monologues are only understood but not perceived as a zigzag course of motivational vectors they remain in the domain of the psychologist or historian. So far, then, there is nothing in aesthetic "experience" that was not discussed in the preceding section as a property of ordinary perception.

(b) Dynamic features will enliven not only the percepts of the outer physical world, such as music, statues, or buildings, but also those of the inner world, notably the kinesthetic sensations of the actor and the dancer. As a carrier of expressive patterns the performer's body is a perceptual object, just as removed from the self of the perceiver as a painting he may be looking at; and he directs and controls his instrument according to kinesthetic pushes and pulls just as the painter uses visual dynamics to judge his composition on the canvas. In a similar fashion the actor or dancer perceives and controls the dynamics of the "intracerebral percepts" that are part of his performance, the reckless striving of the tyrant, the panicky speculations of the fugitive, or the passive yielding of the lover. Such a technique, which takes advantage of the full perceptual experience, is clearly distinguished from the cold display of appropriate gestures on the stage.

These examples show that the various functions of a person's body or mind can serve him as vehicles for expressive dynamic patterns. The technique of the performer helps to illustrate what happens when the experience of looking at a painting or listening to music goes beyond the perception of directed tensions in the visible and audible object: while watching one of Picasso's "blue" figures the beholder may find that the bending under pressure, so compellingly perceived in the painting, invades his own attitude of body and mind through a kind of resonance. Yet just as the actor's perception of what is going on within himself can leave him in the position of the detached observer and director, so the personal participation in the dynamics found in the painting or music does not necessarily entwine the beholder's or listener's self.

(c) The difference between "feeling" the part of Romeo and deluding oneself into "being" Romeo has been amply discussed by the practicians and the theorists of the stage. But the use of a loose terminology makes it hard to distinguish psychologically between cases in which the self acts as a detached perceiver of a dynamic state and others in which the self is the very center of such a state. The difference between feeling fear within oneself and being afraid is illustrated perhaps by the well-known effect of adrenalin injections. Yet the fact that a theatergoer may tremble with Romeo and nevertheless enjoy the show at the same time has been considered a troublesome contradiction.

What happens when the self does become the center of the dynamic state it perceives? Do we have to assume that a still broader range of the mind than that envisaged under (b) is seized by the perceived pattern? Or is the process more in the nature of a contact established with the affected regions? There is no answer as long as the lack of research keeps the discussion at a crudely amateurish level.

The familiar notion of "aesthetic distance" rejects the involvement of the self as discussed here under (c) and recommends an attitude compatible with either (a) or (b). But when Tolstoy speaks of the "feelings" by which the reader or listener is "infected" he means states of the self. So, presumably, does Langfeld when he asserts that both phylogenetically and ontogenetically "we can trace in the development of aesthetic appreciation a gradual diminution of the emotional response" (21, p. 350).

The range of responses to perceived dynamic patterns is a problem not limited to matters of art. In general psychology it connects with the study of a variety of phenomena, such as pity, sympathy, self-control, self-estrangement, persona, spontaneity, or affectation. Here are tasks that will be noticed and approached when "emotions" and "feelings" will have ceased to obstruct the view.

SUMMARY

Many fundamental psychological processes have been filed away under the heading "emotion" and thereby removed from the necessary and fruitful contact with research on motivation and perception. "Emotion" is not a kind of mental activity but merely the amount of excitation accompanying any mental activity at all. The psychology of art is used as an example to show that the vague term "emotion" hides from sight a number of basic problems, such as those of aesthetic pleasure, perceived expression, intuitive judgment, and the resonance effect of dynamic states.

REFERENCES

1. Arnheim, R. The Gestalt theory of expression. *Psychol. Rev.,* 1949, 56, 156–171. [See pp. 301–323 of the present book.]
2. Arnheim, R. Perceptual and aesthetic aspects of the movement response. *J. Pers.,* 1951, 19, 265–281.
3. Arnheim, R. *Art and visual perception.* Berkeley and Los Angeles: University of California Press, 1957.
4. Bell, C. *Art.* London: Chatto and Windus, 1931.
5. Broad, C. D. Emotion and sentiment. *J. Aesthet. Art Crit.,* 1954, 13, 203–214.
6. Duffy, Elizabeth. Emotion: an example of the need for reorientation in psychology. *Psychol. Rev.,* 1934, 41, 184–198.
7. Duffy, Elizabeth. The conceptual categories of psychology: a suggestion for revision. *Psychol. Rev.,* 1941, 48, 177–203.
8. Duffy, Elizabeth. An explanation of "emotional" phenomena without the use of the concept "emotion." *J. gen. Psychol.,* 1941, 25, 283–293.
9. Duffy, Elizabeth. Leeper's "motivational theory of emotion." *Psychol. Rev.,* 1948, 55, 324–335.
10. Freud, S. *The interpretation of dreams.* New York: Macmillan, 1927.
11. Fry, R. *Vision and design.* London: Chatto and Windus, 1929.
12. Ghiselin, B. (Ed.) *The creative process.* Berkeley and Los Angeles: University of California Press, 1952.
13. Hadamard, J. S. *An essay on the psychology of invention in the mathematical field.* Princeton: Princeton University Press, 1945.

14. James, W. *The principles of psychology.* New York: Dover, 1950.
15. Koffka, K. *Principles of Gestalt psychology.* New York: Harcourt, Brace, 1935.
16. Langer, Susanne K. *Feeling and form.* New York: Scribner, 1953.
17. Leeper, R. W. A motivational theory of emotion to replace "emotion as disorganized response." *Psychol. Rev.,* 1948, 55, 5–21.
18. McDougall, W. *The energies of men.* New York: Scribner, 1933.
19. Meyer, M. F. That whale among the fishes—the theory of emotions. *Psychol. Rev.,* 1933, 40, 292–300.
20. Prall, D. W. *Aesthetic analysis.* New York: Crowell, 1936.
21. Reymert, M. L. (Ed.) *Feelings and emotions: the Wittenberg Symposium.* Worcester, Mass.: Clark University Press, 1928.
22. Reymert, M. L. (Ed.) *Feelings and emotions: the Mooseheart Symposium.* New York: McGraw-Hill, 1950.
23. Santayana, G. *The sense of beauty.* New York: Scribner, 1896.
24. Schlosberg, H. Three dimensions of emotion. *Psychol. Rev.,* 1954, 61, 81–88.
25. Tolstoy, L. *What is art? and Essays on art.* New York: Oxford University Press, 1942.
26. Woodworth, R. S. *Psychology.* (4th ed.) New York: Holt, 1940.
27. Young, P. T. *Emotion in man and animal.* New York: Wiley, 1943.